PREFACE

*Many SOULS have contributed to this bc
contributed to my LIFE, many SOULS de
sacrifice, for their time and for their contributions. We are never alone,
we think that we are, but we are led, we are guided, we are supported,
we are directed, yes sometimes we are even pushed; if that is what is
necessary for us to grasp the opportunity or to learn the lesson which is
presented to us.*

*I feel very humble, for without the input from ALL those about me, all
those in my Peer- Group, yes even those who have brought to me the
hard lessons of rejection!, it would not have been possible for me to be
here today, in this lifetime, writing this book.*

*A huge thank you therefore to ALL those on the Earth-Plane who have
enriched my life; I ask for your indulgence and your forgiveness for any
unhappiness which I have brought into your lives, both this one and the
many previous encounters. I hope and pray that we BOTH have learnt
and progressed from the relationships and will continue to do so.
I wish to include here my family, friends, acquaintances, colleagues,
girlfriends, lovers, wives, children, and in particular those who are
identified in this book. I hope that you will be sympathetic to my reasons
for recording our experiences, and will not feel too offended by me
making this Public knowledge. All the names have been changed to
protect your anonymity, unless you choose otherwise.
A particular big thank you to the Heavenly Father for this opportunity
and the trust given to me, to my Guides and to High Spirit, for their
unceasing, tireless efforts, and to those Souls who have gone before
and have chosen to return to help me.(i.e.Ted, Emma, Gertie, Alice,
Albert etc.)*

♦ *The purpose of this Book is to help Others to follow, for them to
hopefully gain the Understanding, and so to bring LOVE, Compassion
and Understanding into their own Lives and into the Lives of
everyone they meet and every LIFE-FORM they have contact with.*
♦ *The purpose of this Book is to help YOU to progress towards the
LIGHT, so that we ALL have a future on this planet, Earth.
That future is to built upon mutual respect, caring, sharing and
understanding of the roles that we all play, so that the lessons can
be learned in peace and harmony, if at all possible.*
♦ *The purpose of this Book is to help to prepare a platform of
Understanding, to prepare the World for the coming of the new
MESSIAH.*

- *The purpose of this Book is to raise Funds, so as to support the work of the new CHURCH of GOD on EARTH, and to publicise its existence.*
- *The purpose of this Book is to provide guidance, teaching and assistance to any who wish to promote LOVE, to find their SOUL within, to help to save the planet for future Generations, to help to bring about Heaven on Earth.*
- *The purpose of this Book is to help to correct the beliefs of many associated with the man-made Religions throughout the World.*

I am not saying that much of what is done in the name of GOD is incorrect. ANY action or belief which supports GOD and which teaches LOVE, Harmony, Peace, Compassion, Sharing, Caring, and Tolerance to Others is to be praised and to be supported.
Let no One be BIGOTED. Let no One believe that 'they' are greater than another. Let no One cause suffering to Others and try to hide behind a religious banner.

see Web Site: www.cogoe.org.uk for further information.

JOHN OLIVER NEWARK 25.09.2,000

Published by BADGER INVESTMENTS
              PO BOX 119
              BICESTER DO
              OX26 4WD
              UK

Printed by   www. lighteningsource. com

First Edition   May 2003   ISBN 0-9542060-1-0

INDEX

Appendices

INTRODUCTION

1.00 This book has been written at the instigation of High Spirit who work tirelessly on behalf of the One Supreme Power (GOD) to bring enlightenment, peace, love and harmony to every life-form in our World and also to those life-forms who exist throughout the Universe.

1.01 The purpose for the Book is to help to prepare those who are willing to listen, in readiness for the new Millennium. It is necessary for the World to change, so that all life-forms have the opportunity to survive. Without a significant movement towards Light, Love and Goodness there can be no doubt that the Human Race as we know it today, will not survive.

1.02 The question is, if you were GOD, what would you do to change peoples attitudes, the way in which they relate to each other and also to the rest of the Nature's creation ?
Evil continues to take an upper-hand; week-after-week and month-after-month we learn of Genocide, Slavery, Poverty, Greed, Wars and Atrocities, we learn of Rain Forest devastation, we learn of Genetically Modified Foods, we learn of Aids and Ozone holes in the Atmosphere, 150,000 Abortions in 1997 in the UK. alone. Mankind is destroying the balance of Nature.

1.03 The difficulty is the free-Will which has been granted to Mankind. Let no-one doubt that what has been given can also be removed. GOD has used Floods, Plagues, the forces of Nature, to control Mankind and to enable Man to start again viz. Noah, Atlantis. GOD has sent Jesus, Buddha, Mohammed, and other prophets to tell us how to act, how to treat our neighbours and indeed to warn us that unless we change our actions that the wrath of GOD will descend. Alas, nothing so far has had a lasting effect.

1.04 Into this situation a new measure is to be introduced. The Human Race is to be brought to a new level of Spiritual Awareness, so that all can receive heightened communication with Spirit and with GOD. It is hoped and believed that if Humans understand the 'raison d'etre' for all their actions, then there is the greater hope that correct choices will be made. Guidance can be given and ALL can then move towards the Light and Love of GOD.

1.05 The World is to be prepared for the coming of the new Messiah.
KEYPOINTS INT1 :
(a) Question every Meeting, every Event, every Action, it all has a purpose, there is no such thing as pure coincidence.
(b) Define EVIL or SIN as any occurrence or thought which is against LOVE.
(c) GOD cannot be <u>blamed</u> for any of the disasters which have befallen Mankind, we live in balance with Nature and our Environment. When Mankind destroys or changes that balance, we invite and create a reaction.

1.06 The name of this book, the timing of this book, the name of the new Church and the words within this book have all been supplied by High Spirit and transcribed by me and by other Mediums. In the same way the Bible was written; humans were instrumental in recording their observations and writing down the words of Jesus. Jesus was perhaps the greatest Spiritual Medium who has ever walked the Earth-Plane. He was a human Being, with a wonderful ancient Spirit, who chose to sacrifice himself, so that the Human Race could learn and be made aware of the Love of GOD, the survival of the Spirit, and the manner in which we should love and behave to each other.

1.07 Jesus was a man who was declared by High Spirit as a Son of GOD, he was given the Holy Ghost (Holy Spirit, Solar Force, Christ Spirit, etc) and a significant sector of his Spirit was that of GOD. <u>YOU too can also aspire to become a Son or Daughter of God,</u> by giving your life to GOD, by carrying out his works and by achieving the necessary awareness so that you the mind-Being, can be at-one with your Soul and can communicate with High Spirit. We all have in the Spirit, a part of GOD, some, have more than others.
KEYPOINT INT2
Jesus was a Man. Jesus became a Son of GOD through his choices and actions. You can also follow in his footsteps. High Spirit can choose to appoint you as a Son or Daughter of GOD, should this be appropriate for you.

1.08 Many will consider the Book of Truth and Knowledge as fiction, their minds will dismiss some or all of what is given. However, their Spirits will remember and when they return again to the Earth-Plane, as they must eventually, then their learning and receptivity will be that more advanced, which will enable their Souls to progress along the chosen Pathway. If they individually learn but one **KEYPOINT** then this Book will have been worthwhile.
(All that I personally add is that I have lived the life, heard the words, experienced the Events, suffered the pain, cried the tears. The Book represents my life and my interpretation of those experiences.

So, you can still say: what a fool!, he is deluded. I think not............
I thought and felt like you may now feel, until I had lived the life and
the incredible Experiences, which have steadily and slowly changed my
Perspective, my Attitudes and my Beliefs. All I can ask is that you
'read-on' with an open Mind and ponder on what is said before you
reach a final conclusion.)

1.09 For those of you who do believe; and for those of you who wish to
embrace, and explore, and find out for themselves about their Destinies;
then I hope that this Book will cause you to question every Meeting,
every Event and every Action which you take, and that which happens
to you. I hope that you will choose to search for your Spiritual
Awareness, that you will choose to respect every creation of Nature and
GOD, that you will choose to treat every person as you yourself would
wish to be treated.

1.10 And if you have the abilities, the time and the opportunity, then I
ask that you spread the word to Others and join or participate in the
local activities of a Spiritual Group. It is important that your objective is
not only to progress your own personal Awareness; but also to help
Others and so to lighten the total Environment and so to participate in
the ultimate goal of achievement of Heaven on Earth.
KEYPOINT INT3
HEAVEN will be achieved on the Earth-Plane, when a
critical number of Souls are enlightened. At this Time
the future of this Planet will be assured, and the Human
Race will have earned the right to remain here. At the
present time the Human Race is on trial and the Planet
is only loaned to us.

1.11 I reiterate, at risk is the survival of everything we know of in our
present World. What I ask is the point of accumulating wealth and
building a World based on the misery and suffering of Others, for that
World to be destroyed by Others, or by Nature, or by GOD.

1.12 I have used only forenames in order to protect those who do not
wish to be identified. I have also changed all of those forenames in
order to avoid the threatened litigation by some. I also wish to protect
those People who are still alive and do not wish to have publicity. I
apologise to anyone who may feel offended by my words, this was
never my intention.

1.13 I appreciate that many People are set in their ways, are devoted to
their own beliefs and are committed to existing Churches. I would only
ask them to read my words, and then to consider in their own Hearts
what is correct...

There are many books and many Religions, not all are incorrect, there are many good People about, there are many correct Concepts, and much can be learned from the Ancients and from our Ancestors.

However, what is completely wrong is Mankind's intolerance and Mankind's bigotry to Others. What is completely wrong is the sinful way in which religious Zealots practice hypocrisy and believe that their way is exclusive, to the exclusion of Others Beliefs.
What is unacceptable is that UNLESS Mankind changes its ATTITUDES and BEHAVIOUR, then ALL will fail ...
THERE IS NO CHOICE, WE HAVE TO CHANGE.

1.14 We, all, can choose to PRAY to the one GOD, or to JESUS, or through your own PROPHET to the one GOD. We, All, can choose to walk in the footsteps of Jesus.

1.15 The New Testament was written some 2,000 years ago in a language intended to be understood by Peoples living at that Time. Many passages of the complete Bible require considerable interpretation and cannot be taken literally. Nothing stands still, if it does it dies, it becomes a relic to be mis-interpreted and to be misunderstood. There are many good and wonderful words written in the Bible, many apply today, however some Religious Groups interpret the words to suit their own understanding. There are however, some basic premises which can be made...These concern :

✓ Existence of an All-powerful GOD
✓ Existence of Prophets who seek to tell God's message and to correct Mankind's Errors.
✓ GOD's wrath happens and Mankind suffers.
✓ Man's Evil ways bring retribution.
✓ Mankind has a choice, free-will is allowed.
✓ There is a good and loving way ahead.
✓ Spirits, Souls, Ghosts, Angels, do exist.
✓ There is a Life after Death.
✓ There is a Heaven, a Hell and many other Planes of Existence.
✓ We are part of Nature, if we disturb the balance, Nature will react to correct this.
✓ We return through many lifetimes to learn the lessons necessary. This is NOT a one-off. Reincarnation is an essential feature of our existence.
✓ We exist amongst a Peer-Group of some 40-50 Souls, the roles change from lifetime to lifetime so that we can have the opportunity of learning about ALL the aspects of LOVE.

- ✓ We create, through our actions, our own environment and our own Karma, our own future level of experience, be that happiness or suffering
- ✓ We are not alone in the Universe, there are many other more intelligent Species.
- ✓ We are all Energy, we all Inter-react.
- ✓ What you do as an Individual affects those around you. It is all CAUSE and EFFECT.
- ✓ You pre-chose this lifetime's Experiences before you were born. You chose your parents. You chose the lessons for your Soul to learn. If now you do not choose wisely you will have wasted this lifetime and a repetition will become necessary, not only for you but also for those of your Peer-Group who need to be involved. You become locked into a 'Cycle of Repetition'.
- ✓ Nothing happens by coincidence.
- ✓ Thoughts are as powerful as Actions - Beware !

Author's comments:
*These sentiments are but a few from the many **KEYPOINTS** which are listed throughout the Text. I make no apology for any repetition, as the Keypoints are drawn from the life Experience whenever this has occurred.*
A complete list of Spiritual Beliefs can be found in Appendix III of this Book; or visit the 'CHURCH OF GOD ON EARTH' web-site at:

< *www.cogoe.org.uk* >

CHAPTER 1. THE EARLY YEARS

1.00 I was born on 5th June 1944 and named Dennis Brian Newark. (hereafter known as JOHN). The family name was chosen for me as I discovered in 1998, as the name NEW...ARK, I sincerely hope, that subsequent events do not mean that the new Ark will become necessary. You will read elsewhere that one of my previous lives was as NOAH and prior to that as ABEL. I have no wish to impress or to 'blow my own trumpet', but merely through birthright of Spirit, I find myself on Earth again at this point in the Earth's History.

1.01 I grew up as the youngest child in a family of four; my parents were working/middle class, my father (Ted) born 10.10.07 being employed as a Superintendent supervising the unloading of ships at London Docks. He worked for Lord Vesty and was dependent for most of his life on a non-contributory Pension Scheme, which eventually, after 40 years produced only a pittance, but it was effective in locking him to that Company for fear of losing it. The only real opportunity for a better job came after World War 2, when Ted was offered a good position elsewhere, accepted this and then was stopped by Vesty/War Regulations from moving his job...so much for labour mobility in those days!.

1.02 Born in Brixton, London, England, he worked in a variety of minor clerical roles, before joining a large Meat and Food Business, and subsequently being relocated to manage a refrigerated Food Storage/Distribution Depot in Sutton Coldfield, Nottinghamshire, during the second World War. He liked the job, but his heart was in London and the family relocated at the first opportunity to Tooting Bec in South London in 1956, when I was twelve years of age. Dad (Ted) then worked shifts at the OXO depot on the South Side of the River Thames, near to Tooley Street. The work was never easy, with the Company being hog-tied by the militant docker Trade Unionists, who eventually destroyed the Dock trade in London. Every shift seemed to be a face-off between Management and Unions, as to payment for the job, dirt money, weather money, piece-rate, rate for the job, who was in the team, job and finish etc. etc.

1.03 Ted never enjoyed his retirement; he left his job on the Docks when 65 years old and then immediately commenced a series of security-type jobs, to provide the necessary income for the quality of life which he and mum sought. He died when 71 years of age, on the last evening of a holiday in Menorca, Spain, having fully retired for only 3 months. It took my brother and me, six weeks and a potential personal cost of £1,200 to recover Ted's body back from Spain to the UK.

Not the ideal place to die, with no Morgue facilities, and a requirement to be buried within 48 hours! Eventually, a special lead-lined coffin was flown-in, and the body was returned some four weeks later to the UK. Mum and dad had been on a coach trip around the Island that day and had seen the pauper's graves, where dad might have ended up if we had not repatriated him. Ted had lived through at least 3 heart attacks and 2 varicose-vein operations, he smoked to the end, enjoyed playing bridge(cards), socialising, gambling and drinking. A popular man, useless with cars, but he loved his garden and was moderately successful with DIY.

1.04 My mother, (Leonora born 15.10.14) grew up in Norfolk, Tivetshall, close by Gorleston, on the East Coast of the UK.; a family of five with two elder brothers. She does not recall a close, loving or happy childhood. Her own mother, Emma, died when she was six, and her father – a failed ex-Farmer turned milkman, re-married. The step-mother and the haughty, spoilt, young girl Leonora, did not meld together, and Leonora left home as soon as she could. More children were born and it fell to Leonora to leave school, against her wishes, to look after the other step-children. Her full brothers: Roland and Geoffrey were apprenticed as Electrician and Engineer, but there was insufficient money to pay fully for Leonora to be apprenticed as a Retail Assistant, so she had to pay her own way. The take-home pay was six pence per week. However, it was not all doom and gloom, there were better times, like the open-air life, camping and swimming in the North Sea. Eventually, when 15 years old, she planned to emigrate to South Africa, where most of her mother's family lived in Cape-Town, and they even sent to her the voyage-ticket. Alas, her father prevented her from leaving. I only learned in 2001 that Leonora was in fact born in Argentina, where her grandfather was an engineer when the railways were being built.

1.05 As a child I can remember the Daily Newspapers being sent from South Africa every week (to try to persuade the family to emigrate there). Because of the friction at home, Leonora moved to live with her mother's sister Aunt Ada, and then finally moved away alone, to live on Guernsey (in the Channel Isles) for two years, before returning to live in Northampton as an Insurance Clerk. That is where Ted and Leonora met, leading to the birth of Edward 10.05.43 and John 05.06.44 (author). Mum has fond memories of her time in Guernsey; it must have been quite daunting to go abroad for the first time, alone, not knowing anyone, and begin a new life.

1.06 I think my parents were happy, but you never can be certain what people hide. Money was always tight. In many ways children copy the role model of their parents. Ted had been married previously and paid dearly for his error. Ted and Leonora were married, when I was 7 years of age. Prior to that time, I had no knowledge that my father had been married before, paid maintenance money, and that Edward and I were true bastards! The revelation of this previous marriage only came to light from the certificate when he was dead. It was simply the fact that divorce was not acceptable in those days unless both parties agreed.

Ted did not wish Leonora to work, but she still managed some work to help provide extra income. They also both helped out with Charity work, and ran whist-drives for the Boy Scouts.

1.07 As children, up to 1956, we had no television, no telephone, no car, few carpets, an outside toilet, and perhaps one week's holiday away each year.....But for all the apparent absence of modern equipment, I still remember my childhood with happiness. Tunnelling in the local sand Quarry, playing football, cricket, rugby, hiding in the undergrowth, snow sledging, cub-Scouts and of course all that fruit-picking from the huge garden which Ted maintained.

In those days mum made jam and toffee and bottled fruit to help with the bills, she also worked part-time at the local Hospital, but Ted objected to this. When we moved to London, Edward and I joined the Boy-Scouts and subsequent Senior and Rover Scouts, both obtaining our Queen's Award.

I enjoyed the camping; hiking; Scout Band; annual Gang-Show; Bob-a-Job; jumble sales, church parades. Not to forget the Church of England youth Club, which organised weekly dances, indoor games and pilgrimages. By hiking and staying-over in Youth Hostels, we visited cathedrals throughout southern England. All of these activities were fitted-in after school homework, which on average took 2 hours per day. Saturdays were school Sports or spent working for pocket-money. I did the usual paper-round, leaflet round, model-making plastic kits for retail shop displays, perhaps thirty a week; cleaning silver-plate, and soon progressed to upholstery repairs and furniture removals at a local Shop.

1.08 Before we moved to London, Tony was a local friend, he was my age, lived close-by and we played together...see Appendix II. One Soul, Past Lives.

It grieves me to think that none of my children ever enjoyed the life experience of Scouts or Youth Clubs...their lives have followed a different route, but I cannot but help feel that they may have missed-out.

How can computer games substitute for group activities? I always remember the County Scouting Activities as brilliant; inter-Group competitions and outward-bound type activities, sometimes all night. Hiking around Switzerland and camping on the Matterhorn at 13,000 feet (from Zermatt)

KEYPOINT TEY1
Children need interaction with others, in order to learn the skills of Communication. It cannot be sensible or desirable for children to spend too much time alone or on computer Games many of which only to instil into them violence as a norm.

1.09 Edward, my brother and I, were always rivals. It started from day one, he was the eldest, the quicker of wit, the least shy and as far as I was concerned, the favourite son. We shared the same double-bed up to the age of 8 years, it was always a battle to keep enough bed-clothes to stay warm. A race to eat enough food at each meal and it was impossible to find a local girl he had not 'known and contaminated', from my viewpoint. I blushed so easily and was so shy, he had a clear run. When I stayed at school, at age sixteen years, to complete 'A' level G.C.E's, Edward was already at work in the London Metropolitan Police, earning a reasonable wage (loads of overtime) with a good lodging allowance. The money allowed holidays with my parents, and a good quality of life.

1.10 Five years later when I began my first job, following a degree at Sheffield University, my work took me to Bristol. Thereafter I never lived close enough to my parents to see them on a regular basis and money was always tight. The rivalry with Edward was ever present in my mind for their affection. We just didn't seem to have a warm, close, relationship. Friendly, yes, but not the type where I felt that I could talk about personal problems or feelings.

KEYPOINT TEY2
Parents need to make a conscious effort, to try to ensure that jealousy, rivalry, or personal preferences do not cause any of their children to feel neglected, unloved or second best.

1.11 A closeness developed with Leonora, following Ted's death and my own personal relationship problems, which caused me to need a shoulder-to-cry-on. Perhaps it was a sub-conscious rejection by Leonora, for she almost died when I was born, perhaps I was too jealous of the attention they seemed to me to give to Edward, or perhaps it was me hiding my emotions, which caused me to create a distance. I still do not know the real reasons. My father now in Spirit tells me that he always loved-me, but that his behaviour had been conditioned by his own father, Albert. Edward was always the demanding, vociferous child, so he got most of the attention.

12

1.12 I regret as a child, being excluded from the lounge, as it was impossible for me to complete my homework with the TV on (we got one in 1956), so hour after hour, I needed to sit alone to study ... this must have conditioned me to feeling 'alone and rejected'.

I resented the fact that mum and dad were not prepared to turn the TV off for even a short while, so that I could sit and work in the same room as them.

I passed the eleven-plus Exam and went to Southwell Minister Grammar School, Notts. When dad decided to move to London, I was asked if I wished to board at the school, but the excitement of a move to London and the wish to be with my parents, caused me to choose to go with them. We moved in February, when the local London, Tooting Bec Grammar School was full, so I took a place at Wandsworth Grammar School, about to convert to Comprehensive School. For some reason, my parents wished Edward and me to go to the same school! Wandsworth was a complete waste of one year of my education, as I sat and repeated the lessons which I had previously covered at Southwell School. To me the ethos of the Comprehensive School is wrong, why place pupils who wish to work, in the same Environment as those who only seek to disrupt and detract from Education?

1.13 Edward, my elder brother, failed the eleven-plus exam, whilst we lived in Mansfield, Notts. where I was born. He went to the local secondary modern School until the family moved to Tooting in London, where Sidney, one of Ted's brothers owned a property. We occupied the first floor of the Victorian house. Edward had one advantage I didn't, he knew precisely from the age of 13 that he wished to join the Police force, even against the advice of his School Careers Master; and it has taken me 54 years to find a role for this lifetime. When in the Police, Edward passed the Civil Service Exams with flying colours, and rapidly progressed through the ranks to Detective Inspector in the Metropolitan Force, and Fraud Squad...

But for being stitched-up by a colleague, over the disappearance of a hand-revolver, which had been used in evidence at a trial (following the award of the George Medal for bravery!) Edward would probably have ended up as a Chief Constable. As such, he was demoted back to uniform-rank from Detective Inspector, and back to the level of Inspector. He subsequently needed to work his way back up to Superintendent before being compulsorily retired after 33 years of service. Edward married Polly when 21 years of age, they have two children Timothy and Evelyn.

1.14 Edward was always a ladies man, (I suppose eventually I became one too!) but there to my knowledge, has been only one major blip to the relationship with Polly, when their youngsters were still small. Subsequently, Edward suffered an accident whilst on a narrow canal boat holiday with his family, and then developed leukaemia, which has blighted his life ever since. His feet slipped into the canal while mooring a narrow boat, and in trying to save his fall he broke his wrist on the side of the boat.

The eight hour wait for treatment at the John Radcliffe Hospital in Oxford, when soaking wet and in extreme pain, I believe was the trigger for the leukaemia. Mind you Edward always was 'accident-prone', a feature which his son Timothy seems to follow! In many ways, it seems to me that the relationship has survived over the years through the care, which Polly has needed to, and has always willingly bestowed upon Edward.

KEYPOINTS TEY3

(a) 'Like Father Like Son' is very much true in some aspects of our metabolism. It is as if you are caught in a 'circle of Life'. Be aware of any recurring features in your Family history, and make a deliberate effort to avoid this repetition……..see appendix IV on how to develop your Spiritual Awareness.

(b) Dis-ease may be caused by accident, stress or illness, which seems to trigger a susceptibility to infection. I am certain that much can be learnt from analysis of the Earthly events prior to any major dis-ease arising. The Spiritual causes for dis-ease are highlighted later in the text.

1.15 My up-bringing was strictly normal, influenced by the experience of a nominally Christian family; my contact with the Church of England was through Sunday school, Scouting and Youth Club. My parents were not regular church-goers. My father Ted had been compelled as an 'altar-boy' to go to church two or three times daily. His experiences caused him to lose respect for all he knew, except for the Reverend Pilkington, who progressed from Holy Trinity Church, Tooting, London, to St. Paul's Cathedral in London. My mother was also forced to attend church, as her aunt Ada was very religious, and so she rebelled against going as soon as she could.

1.16 I was baptised as a baby, and chose to be confirmed when 14 years of age. Reverend Pilkington took the Confirmation Classes. Issues such as 'the Trinity' and belief in GOD were discussed but never adequately explained. It was enough to keep an open mind and to accept that an understanding would be reached later in life. I believed in a GOD, an ultimate Power…I wished my children to be brought up as Christian and all my four children were baptised.

I also believed in being good, working hard, playing hard, and living by values. But I have learned, that unless your values are challenged, you tend to live in your own comfort-zone and allow the world to pass you by.

1.17 I was pretty naive as a child; my sexuality was not awakened until I met my first girl-friend when I was sixteen. Prior to that age, my only experience was of kissing and masturbation.
Edward, my brother, had jumped on me one day! And, as boys' camping together, we used to play and fool around. The initiation ceremony for your first scout-Camp was to be stripped naked and daubed with boot-polish; I could always run fast enough to escape, but Edward was not so fortunate! I was also chased by a male curate, who wished to kiss me when I was 11 years old. (even the Church of England!)
I always remember how at the tender age of 16, I took a girl from the Church Youth Club to the Planetarium in London, and got the hardest erection I can remember. Fortunately I carried a mackintosh in front of me, it didn't occur to me to relieve myself, it was something I did not do regularly. The erection lasted for four hours - can you imagine hiding this projection all that time. There was no relationship, so all this was pretty new to me. I was fairly anti to all the local girls; one had hurt me through rejection, and Edward knew the rest.

1.18 It wasn't until I met DOREEN at an inter-school sixth-form Dance, that I learned all about sex and physical desire. We met when I was 17 and we married when I left University at the age of 21 years...During that period we loved and explored each other's bodies and in some ways were lucky that Doreen did not become pregnant. The one area that was completely ignored in my education was relationships and feelings, and how to handle personal problems. You are taught where the bits are, but you are not told about 'climaxes' and how 'to make love' or to satisfy your partner. Dad gave a sex-book to Edward to read and then to pass-on to me. We never spoke together.
KEYPOINT TEY4
Formal Education needs to include discussion about relationships and feelings. The teaching of mechanics alone is not enough.

1.19 Doreen lived in Fulham, London, with her parents and brother. When we met she was a nervous wreck. The father George, was having a relationship with a neighbour, Sybil, whose husband had died, so he left and escaped the chaos of the home every night. The mother Dot, was looking after her own mother, who was partially sighted, in the home and was a tyrant. Her presence, I believe, led to the parent's divorce.

There were only two bedrooms and Dot was neither very worldly nor practical. I used to cycle the five miles from Tooting to Fulham, with my underwear soaked with sperm, night after night, but my parents never said anything to me. In fact, they were very supportive of the friendship.

When I obtained a place at Sheffield University, Doreen obtained a place at St. Gabriel's Teacher Training College in South London, and my parents offered her the spare bedroom in their flat in Tooting.

I secretly modified the connecting door between our bedrooms, which had previously been sealed-up, so that we could sleep together when I was home. Initially I returned once per month, mainly hitch-hiking down the M1, I even thumbed a lift in a Rolls-Royce ! This then progressed to my returning fortnightly, and then weekly.

1.20 In the second year I travelled by motorbike - a Matchless 250cc Sports, with drop handlebars, definitely too small and somewhat under-powered for my size and weight, but it did a remarkable job. I grew a beard and moustache to protect my face, and would arrive black with mud and splattered with flies. My appreciation of the goodness and humanity of people was heightened by me breaking down at 00.15am (midnight) with a horrendous grating noise from the primary-chain case. I was passing through the city of Newark, Notts. and pulled into a petrol Station just as it closed. In response to my request for direction to a garage, the van-driver ahead of me said "follow me" and led me several miles to his home. As his unsuspecting wife gave me soup, the husband turned a new tab-washer on his workshop lathe, I refitted the motorcycle primary chain and sprocket and off I went at 03.00am.

My faith in human nature restored by those wonderful people; I only regret that I could never find the house again to say thank you properly !

1.21 The difference between School and University was amazing, it was like walking out of a door and suddenly becoming an adult. I was not ready for University. I had not been taught at school how to learn. I was fed-up with books and Examinations.

Ted had said to me that I should get a job at 18 years old and that he would not pay for me to go to University. It was a friendly enough conversation, but I resolved to see whether I could obtain a scholarship to pay for my University.

1.22 I was fortunate, and through a Daily Telegraph advertisement, managed to obtain a scholarship from the then Steel Company of Wales, Steel Division, Port Talbot, South Wales. The Interview and Selection process was complex and demanding, spread over several weekends.

It did my self-confidence a great deal of good to be thrust into Group Discussion Sessions with Observers. Then Math's tests, English tests, Interviews, Psychology tests etc.

1.23 I needed University like a hole in the head, having passed four 'A' level G.C.E's. I was ready for a break and change of scene, but instead found myself at Sheffield University, on a general Engineering course, plus Chemical Engineering and Fuel Technology. The first year was 40 hours of lectures per week, plus Saturday morning practicals or Engineering Drawing, which then needed completion. When you consider that some Art students had no more than 6 hours of lectures per week, I began to question my choice ! I never managed to obtain a place in a Hall of Residence, so it was a case of finding local 'digs' as best one could. I consider I was very fortunate in my choice of land-ladies.

The course fees were paid and I received £350 per month from the Steel Company and a further £50 per annum from the Education Authority. The first year this paid for the deposit on a motorbike, the second year I purchased an Engagement Ring for Doreen.

1.24 Doreen worked Saturdays at the Truman's Shoe Shop in Putney, South London. Her manager started taking her out, he had a car and an income, so I felt pretty inferior in comparison. I think that it was the fear of losing Doreen which prompted me to propose marriage. She accepted and we became engaged. We agreed to wait until I completed University and had an income. In the event the date was planned - I had no job and we had no-where to live. All was sorted two weeks before the wedding, we still had little money and just about enough for the deposit on a Flat, we found a Flat to rent in Bristol in two hours, and then bought a double-bed, bed-room Suite, cooker, and twenty square yards of red linoleum, etc. all from the one Department store on hire-purchase!.
I had assumed, incorrectly, that the Steel Company of Wales would wish me to work for them when I completed my course, but alas, both the Training Manager, and the Recruitment Manager had died in the time I was at Sheffield; and SCOW 'Steel Company of Wales' did not want me.

1.25 I suppose in their eyes I failed at University, no excuses, but 8 weeks before my exams at the end of the first year, I dispatched my University notes in a trunk from Sheffield to London by British Rail, they did not arrive until 3 months later. Not very helpful when they were needed for exam revision. I passed 12 of the 13 one-and-a-half-hour exams, the one I dipped was Applied Math's, which I had an 'A' level for. Nevertheless, it was said that unless you passed all of the Exams at the first sitting that I could not sit for an Honours degree.

I was too shy to challenge the ruling, in fact, not one discussion took place on the subject with anyone. At the Finals, I turned up and found that I could answer every 'honours question', but all of the 'Ordinary' questions were extremely difficult. I know now, that it was the wrong Degree for me, but without guidance, how was I to know ? I always felt that I should have studied medicine, but I had stopped Biology at the age of 13 and thought that it was then impossible for me to do medicine.

KEYPOINTS TEY5

a) Shyness is like a disease. If you are afraid or too timid to ask a question, How will you ever learn? I was too shy to go to school play rehearsals or to ask questions in Class, too shy to talk to girls. Shyness should be treated like an illness.

b) An extrovert brother, with a quicker mind, does not help!

c) A dominant parent can also prevent a child developing their own character.

1.26 During the first University summer vacation, I worked as a Ward Orderly in the Tooting Mental Hospital, in South London, on shifts. It was 1963, I had received no training, and my duties were to cook the Breakfasts and to wash-up. To assist with the patients and to help in any other way ... such as carrying the dead bodies to the Morgue.

I was locked into the senile Ward, as a lad of 19, it was a tragedy. Men who had good minds were alongside men who had lost their minds, some were kept alive on 'Complan'.(powdered milk protein) There were approx. 40 men in the Ward. My understanding was, that the people with good minds had no-one to look after them, so they had to have beds in the same Ward as those who had lost their minds. The Gym facilities were excellent, but the set-up was a tragedy, to place men with good Minds alongside gibbering Idiots, who were there to die, must equate to extreme inhumanity and torture.

KEYPOINT TEY6

There must be a better way found to care for our older folks. Civilisation must mean a shared responsibility. Society must change. It is not correct for an aged Relative to be capable of destroying a marriage; neither is it right to treat older Folk with inhumanity.

1.27 It was some days before I recognised two of my Aunts visiting one of the senile men in the Ward. I had not noticed the name, Newark, by the bed, it was my grandfather! Disowned by my own father, for he was thrown out of the house by Ted because he was so violent and unpleasant to his wife (Ted's mother, Alice, a lovely lady I never remember).

Ted always said of his own father that he never gave to him one thing in his whole life ... A Sergeant-Major, who expected everyone to live by the Army code, even though they were not in the Army. (he always slept with a gun under his pillow) Grandfather was 96 years old and partially senile, he died some months later. When I told him who I was, he thought thereafter that I was Ted his son.

KEYPOINT TEY7
Do unto others as you would have them do unto you. Grandfather gave nothing and created animosity. He therefore reaped what he had sowed.

1.28 Three near-misses come to mind, when I might had died. Whoever says you are not guided to safety ? I can relate to :
a) On a bicycle, deciding to cycle late at night in the pitch-dark between two approaching cyclists. At the last minute, I decided not to - the two approaching cyclists were the sidelights of an oncoming ten tonne HGV !
b) On a motorbike in dense fog, losing the road and missing a telegraph pole by an inch and ending up in a hedgerow.
c) On foot in a blizzard on the Moors, being completely blinded and wondering whether I would survive.

KEYPOINT TEY8
We all have a Guardian Angel who is there to help us at critical times, so that we make the right choices or decisions for our own survival. Without this, the programmed learning which this lifetime is all about, on many occasions would be cut short by misfortune. (ps. Not all systems are perfect, human choices can sometimes destroy the best laid plans. Consider however the people who are only alive because they miss a flight, do not feel well, have a dream about misfortune. etc)

1.29 Up to the age of 50 years, I had always been fascinated by the 'Unknown', but had never pursued any aspect, nor even taken the trouble to read or find out anything more. At University, when 19 years old, I witnessed the power of mind, and the power of Hypnosis over bodily pain (Psychology Dept.), when 8 inch needles were pushed through the demonstration assistant's arms, without her showing pain, at a Hypnosis lecture. Doreen had also bought me the book 'The Bloxham Tapes', on Regression Case History, written by Dr. Bloxham in South Wales, which proved to me that we did experience previous Lives. Friends had warned me off Seances, Ouija Boards and such-like. I had a natural repulsion to horror-movies or John Wheatley books, as these frightened me, and as such were not enjoyable. I had no recollection of any of my dreams ! So I can say that I believed in some supernatural powers, but had no personal experience which I could relate to.

1.30 There have been several articles, both on television and in national Newspapers in the 1990's, which must have caused people to question and challenge some of the traditional Church beliefs.

a)The first, concerns an article in the Sunday Times titled 'Coincidence'. This told the story of a Boat disaster, in which two survivors ate the cabin boy, who died first, in order that they might survive. The book was published and some 20 years later, the incident actually happened, to the exact detail of the names of the characters, their roles and the name of the boat.

b) The second incident was the subject of a TV documentary and article about a child in India, who at the age of 7 asked his parents to take him to a village some 30 miles away, to which he had never been before. When taken to the particular family he spoke of, he identified his wife and all the members of her/his family. The husband had been killed on the day the child was born! These articles are to the best of my re-collection.

KEYPOINT TEY9

There is evidence, if we look around us and have an open-Mind, that the Soul does continue beyond this single lifetime, and that many features of our lifetime are pre-planned many years before we experience them.

1.31 I remember the first time Doreen and I had intercourse, we went on our first holiday together to Cornwall by coach, we were 18 years old at the time. Having decided that we would have sex, Doreen went into the chemist's shop and bought some toothpaste. The second shop she bought Durex and then was so embarrassed, she flushed them, unused, down the toilet. I then bought a packet myself and we used them ... She was a virgin with hymen intact, so it took us several tries to enjoy the experience. We stayed in this delightful cottage near Tintagel - separate bedrooms each with a double bed. Every morning the landlady brought a tray of tea and biscuits to our rooms. Day one was OK, I took the tray for both rooms. Day two was OK, Doreen took the tray for both rooms. Day three was interesting - we got it wrong, the landlady knocked on the bedroom with no-one inside, so quick as a flash, Doreen opened our door and said "shush, he's still asleep, I've just popped in to say hallo". She took the tray and closed the door. I just laid there in mild amusement and wonderment. Style!

1.32 The marriage to Doreen lasted 19 years, it was a good solid marriage in many respects. Certainly for the initial 7 years, we were totally committed to each other and to building our home and family. Money was always tight and what we had was largely spent on DIY or household effects.

We lived for 2-3 years in flats around the Bristol area, whilst I worked for RTZ at Avonmouth. I worked in the Profit Improvement Dept. as a Fuel Technologist. I enjoyed the job, but the pay was poor and there was little scope for promotion (a policy change), so I decided to leave. Whilst at RTZ (Imperial Smelting Corp.) I was involved on many chemical processes including ISCEON manufacture and the smelting of Zinc and Lead. Isceon is one of the chemicals identified as responsible for the hole in the protective Ozone Layer, which prevents the risk of cancer from the sun's rays..

1.33 My second job was as Shift Controller with the South Eastern Gas Board at their East Greenwich works, London. As such, at the tender age of 24 years, I was nominally responsible on shift for up to 600 people, producing Towns gas and the control of gas Distribution to most of Southern London and the South West of England. We moved to live in Ruislip, Middlesex and I commuted by car each day across London.

The house I purchased belonged to Doreen's Grandmother, who had died and the mother had inherited the property. She wished to sell the property to divide the capital between her husband and children. The Grandmother had refused to allow Dot, her daughter, to use the property, so it had stood empty for 8 years. The food was still in the larder, no electricity, no water, no heating and the garden two feet high overgrown. So began my DIY phase, with no one to teach me, I learned the hard way from books and by doing it wrong. With no money available to pay others, I carried out the conveyancing myself, re-wired the house, re-plumbed, insulated, plastered, painted, decorated the whole house and fitted central heating. All of this work took time and money, but we were basically happy.

1.34 Ford - our first son had been born at home 06.05.69, followed by Brian on 24.09.71. Both babies were large, Ford was over 12lbs and broke the nappy he was weighed in. Brian was 9lbs 5oz....

The day Ford was born, I had the floorboards up and was fitting the microbore pressure central heating system. In hindsight, Doreen should really have had a Caesarean birth. I would strongly recommend any father to be present at his child's birth, as it is one of the most emotional and wonderful experiences of your life. Ford's head finally came through shaped like a 'cigar' with a full head of red hair, the Afterbirth was deteriorating and I burnt it with the bloody sheets etc. on a circular brick barbeque which I had built in the garden.

My most vivid memory is Doreen on her knees and thumping the bed saying "I want to die" over and over again. I picked Ford up to show him off to friends, and held him up above my head, at arms' length. He then proceeded to pee all over me!

Being the size he was, Ford was almost straight onto solid foods and he was essentially a happy child. Dot, Doreen's mother was very good and agreed to commute from Hammersmith to baby-sit, so that Doreen could return to work a few days a week. Doreen was a pretty good Primary School teacher, whose special ability was music.

1.35 We led a pretty active social life with the usual round of parties, many at our house and many fancy-dress. My philosophy was simply that I was happily married for 51 weeks a year, but wished to have one week when I was 'FREE'. This being the parties.

But for all that, nothing ever transpired for me at that time beyond the occasional embrace. That was until we were influenced by Barbara and Fred, who were heavily into wife-swapping ... They lived a completely 'modern' lifestyle, in which there was no restriction on sexual relationships. Indeed, they claimed that their marriage survived on third-party experiences and they were stimulated by discussing what they had done.

Doreen and Barbara were best friends, so I suppose it was only a matter of time before we became involved, particularly as we used to travel as a foursome for weekends away. Fred and Barbara were very shrewd business people and made a lot of money very quickly with Computers, Nursing and Courier Businesses. Their lifestyle reflected this with a number of cars and properties that followed. Both were certainly 'ac/dc' and happy to be in group-sex and voyeurism. Their particular lifestyle lasted until Barbara decided to have a baby and wished it to have an American nationality, so she went to the USA and while she was there, Fred moved in with one of his mistresses.

1.36 Doreen was never fully happy with the arrangement, so it was stopped, but the friendship remained. I certainly enjoyed my freedom and wished it to continue. I believed that a man can separate sex from love, so as far as I was concerned, it was merely an experience and my marriage was safe.

I remember having sex and 'coming' four times within 24 hours and being red-raw, because Barbara had shaved and her pubic-hair was growing back like a hedgehog ! On another occasion, I was led into this bedroom fitted with four or five mattresses and nothing else except a table lamp - no sheets or blankets .

C'est la vie ! I always thought I should have been a Mormon with more than one wife (see Appendix II. One Soul, Past Lives.)

Thereafter, I suppose that over the years there were a number of relationships, none as far as I was concerned ever affected the marriage...Doreen and I had a good relationship, a beautiful home, two lovely children and an excellent social life.

1.37 I justified my extra-marital behaviour, on the basis that it stimulated my marital relationship, gave me the excitement I sought, and did not interfere with the marriage. I felt that I had missed-out on the interchange of relationships, which normally takes place as a teenager and in your twenties, before you tie the knot. My advice to any youngster would certainly be: Don't even consider marriage until you reach the late twenties; the difficulty being that you change as you grow, your attitudes, your interests and your outlook.............

You are indeed fortunate if your partner changes with you, for you could well grow apart. I now know that the human cycle is seven years; during seven years every cell of your body is replaced; this can also affect your character and your relationships. In particular the one with your partner viz. seven year itch! There are many truths contained in so called 'old wives tales'

KEYPOINTS TEY10
a) Your attitudes, your interests, are likely to change every seven years. This is particularly true in your early years.
b) It is essential to defer significant relationship decisions until a later 'Age of Maturity' has been reached.

1.38 My work at East Greenwich Gas Works demanded shifts, and long hours travelling each way. When I was home, it was DIY, car maintenance and entertaining. We had a good life, nice friends and the boys were happy and doing well at school. I still feel somewhat guilty that I did not allow more time for my family, in particular my boys. I became interested in mini-Rugby for my boys, they seemed to enjoy the game and Doreen and I gradually became more and more involved, until I ended up in charge of the section - with 160 boys registered aged between 5 and 12 years. I had twenty Rugby Coaches, Secretary, Social Chairman, Senior Coach, Fixture Secretary etc. So away all week and away all weekend, was not a good recipe for a successful marriage !

I had moved jobs from Greenwich to Watford Reformer Plant as Shift Engineer. (I was very proud of holding the record for 'restart' after a power failure, 20 minutes from power failure to self-generation of electricity and restart of Naphtha Reformer to manufacture Towns Gas. Then, alas, exploitation of North Sea Gas, around 1970, and collapse of the Manufacturing Towns Gas Industry.

KEYPOINT TEY11
You need to work-at, and to devote time, energy, and communication, to all those aspects of your life which you value. Do not take anything, or anyone for granted. Balance is necessary in all aspects of your life.

1.39 I moved to the J. Lyons Group as Process Manager, in charge of four shifts processing soluble coffee. All the chemical Engineering Processes, and then to Materials Manager, Packing Manager and Production Planning Manager, which included Purchasing. As Packing Manager, I was responsible for 300 employees on three shifts ... a selection of 27 Nationalities with only one white lady.

So I was educated in Trade Unionism, multi-nationals, legalities, and every other aspect of manufacturing and personnel including Recruitment, Training, Hygiene, Discipline etc. together with all aspects of Business operations. During this period I studied at night school for membership of the Institute of Works Managers (later Institute of Management) and became a Chartered Engineer.

My time at Lyons was testing, but enjoyable. Unfortunately, the Business in total was going through a dire time, the Directors had borrowed some £600 millions for Business Acquisitions, but they borrowed in dollars - bought badly, and seemingly did not have the nous to sort the business problems. Exchange rates went adverse and Lyons was purchased by Allied Breweries. I joined the Profit Improvement Unit as a Management Consultant. This involved living from a suitcase, away from home in hotels, for one year out of two.

1.40 Whilst all this was happening, we had relocated from Ruislip to Penn, Buckinghamshire and then to Ledborough Lane, Beaconsfield, Bucks. A detached four bed house, built in 1906 with a large garden. I renovated the house and all seemed well. A good lifestyle and family situation. Monies were tight, but we could see better times ahead. So what went wrong? I was not happy with my consultant Job situation, so I found another job as Site/Factory Manager with Spillers Foods in their Bermondsey Depot, East London. This was my ideal Job situation, but in order to commute reasonably, it meant leaving home by 06.45am and returning at 8.00pm. On reflection, I must have been a pretty absent husband and father! The house needed complete renovation, which I proceeded to do over the following four years.

1.41 The Selling Agents held an Auction in the property, just prior to my completion date for the conveyancing. They sold the paintings, lined curtains, carpets etc. I bid for the lovely red wilton fitted carpet, but there were Dealers present, so all that I ended up with were a few curtains. When we moved in I found two wall safes and eventually the keys. One safe contained £85 and the other 1905 maundy money (which I still have). I kept both and felt that justice had been done, for the property had stood empty for some time, been inherited by the present seller who had refused to adjust the sale price following my survey, which showed that the water-tank in the loft was about to collapse.

1.42 Inside the maundy money case, was a silver-cake paper-horseshoe. I am told, by Spirit, that this belonged to Ted - my father, who had known the lady who used to live in the Property. Ted chose to stay with Leonora... Like father like son?
Who would have guessed that we shared the same house and that I would purchase the very house which my father used to visit. Doreen and I bought the house in 1975 for £35,000.
KEYPOINTS TEY12
a) There is no such thing as coincidence. Everything happens for a reason, to cause us to reflect, or to choose, or to learn.
b) History is repeated until or unless we make the right choices.

1.43 The Site employed 135 people across two Factories, the Bakery, which produced 400 tonnes of Winalot and Spillers Shapes dog biscuits 5 days/week and the Soya/Bread Improver Factory and Test Bakery. I took over control of the Site and Dog Biscuit Factory from my boss, who had been promoted over the three Factories in the Division. The other two Factories were located in the Liverpool area; I reasoned that provided the London Factory was the lowest cost producer, with the best labour relations, the fact also that we were close to the Market in the South, would guarantee our survival. This philosophy held good for four years, but then I could not have foreseen Ken Livingston and his low-fare policy and the left-wing political LCC who wished to impose a HGV ban/restriction on vehicles entering the Greater London area.

My Site also suffered from road access difficulty, being positioned east of Tower Bridge in the London borough of Southwark. Southwark at that time in 1985 was only 4% private industry, with 60% of the Rate income being used to service the existing loan debt. Not a healthy situation ... Neither was the 45% Rate-rise that year to pay for the cheap Public Transport Policy....!

1.44 Very good to have cheap fares to take people to their non-existent manufacturing jobs. I tried my best, but the inevitable happened, Spillers now owned by Dalgety, decided to pull-out of London.
The Chamber of Commerce tried with the Politicians to no avail. There were Public Meetings with Politicians to protest, every Factory worker had an individual leaflet to attend, but not one bothered. They were more interested in the short-term redundancy payment !

1.45 A tragedy in many respects, I had made a 50 year service presentation six months earlier to a Chargehand, just before he retired. Nineteen members of his family had worked at the Site; his Company Pension was £8.50 pa. The Stock Control Manager, who also controlled a Budget of £2.5 million for the Council; was not the most effective person. When I took over the Site, the computer Stock figure did not agree with the physical Stock count. Upon investigation, I found that £35,000 of dog biscuits had been supplied to major Supermarkets, Tesco, Sainsbury, Waitrose. etc. and never invoiced.

The money was fully recovered. No-one from Spillers ever said thank - you! The labour force was around 35% black or coloured people. When the Site closed, there were over 1,000 employees remaining, throughout Liverpool, Glasgow, Wisbech, London and Cockermouth, I was told that there were very few non-whites left throughout the UK. Black, or coloured job applicants, were simply rejected at Supervisor level. One of the Factory employees trapped and sold 3,500 pigeons to local Indian and Chinese Restaurants. The Accountant hid £30,000 of budget savings, because he did not believe we could be so efficient. I also found a flour Silo with a stock of sixteen tonnes of Flour, which had not moved for 8 years. Need I go on?

1.46 A year earlier in 1984, I was told that my Factory was to close, but that I could not tell anyone, not even my managers. The same week Edward - my brother, was told that he had leukaemia, there was no treatment, and he had less than six months to live. Doreen - my wife, also told me that she did not love me and was leaving me with our children (Ford and Brian). What a week ! I think I was shell-shocked, almost every aspect of my life was suddenly collapsing around me. My pride and joy, my Factory (an illusion, my experience told me later that people do not work for you, but you kid yourself that loyalty, service and working relationships actually mean something to the individuals concerned. Whereas, in reality it is the money which the majority work for) was to go. My brother was in trouble ... fortunately I was able to help as I did not believe there was no treatment and eventually Edward opted for experimental treatment at Charing Cross Hospital in London.

1.47 Doreen packed her bags and left. I had had no idea that she was having an affair with the male half of the classical violin/piano Duo she performed with.
I had been pleased that she had found another interest outside of her work and the family. I suppose to counter my Rugby interest, which took so much of my time, it made me feel less guilty.

For some seven years, she had been involved with helping out with the other ladies, then, I know not why, she suddenly stopped the involvement and I then felt the pressure for less involvement myself. I had progressed from observer to coach, then Social Chairman and on to Chairman of the Mini-Section. My own two boys were active playing members of successful teams. Doreen phoned that same night and said that felt she had made a terrible mistake and asked if she could return.

It was 03.45am - I agreed that she could return, but it was as if a light switch had been turned off. I no longer loved her and for all my philandering, what remnant of feelings or affection I had left, had now vanished. What was I to do ? My mind was set, but we had a family, a home, appearances to keep up.

I also decided that there was no way I wished to leave the home until Brian, my younger son had moved to Grammar School, and I had somewhere else to move to.

1.48 It took me a year, during which time I found a job in Yatton, near Bristol, still with Spillers Foods as a Factory Manager, Buyer and Development Manager for Caperns. Spillers agreed for me to sell my house in Beaconsfield and I bought two - one for myself in Weston-Super-Mare as a holiday home and one for Doreen and the boys in Penn, Buckinghamshire, so that the boys could continue with their schooling and Doreen with her job. The die was cast! I never intended for Doreen to share the Weston-Super-Mare home with me, but by the time of the move, I had formed a relationship with Elsa - my secretary in London. I could not stand for Doreen even to touch me, so I took to sleeping in the spare bedroom. It was a distressing time for the children and for Doreen too, who wished to re-kindle the relationship.

She attacked me one night with a saucepan when I got home at 2.00am, I needed to physically throw her off me! All was to no avail. With no feeling of love from me, there was little point to us continuing together. I did not seek a divorce; in my eyes, I felt we could have continued to be married, but to live apart, with me returning at the Weekends. I reasoned then that the family unit could then continue together. All was well in this respect until Doreen learnt from my children that I had been joined in Weston-Super-Mare by Elsa and her children, some three months later.

KEYPOINTS TEY13

a) My own experience of RELATE is that they do an excellent job. A full and frank discussion of each other's viewpoints can often lead to a reconciliation.
b) Professional counselling should be tried whenever a permanent relationship breaks-down, and before barriers are built and hardened positions are taken. Poor communication is often the major problem between Couples.

c) Couples should try every means to resolve issues and finances between themselves, BEFORE legal Intermediaries are brought-in.

d) A relationship cannot survive without love, there is little point in staying together solely for the sake of the children. The children will sense the animosity and it will affect their own characters and their future relationships. Better to seek a new relationship where love can flourish again.

##

CHAPTER 2. ELSA, a new Family

2.00 When I met Elsa, she was a single parent with two children - Joan 5 years of age and Daniel 2 years old. Elsa was West Indian from Grenada, with four brothers and three sisters, she had never been married and Joan was 'coloured' and Daniel 'black'. She jokingly said that she always wished to have one white, one coloured and one black! I liked her children and her family.

2.01 It is amazing sometimes how situations develop. When I joined the Dog-Biscuit Factory in East London, as Site Manager, there was already a West Indian secretary who I could not work with. She left after a few weeks and I advertised for a replacement. Appointments were made, but few actually turned-up for the Interview, or when they did they never came back. The Factory was some 100 yards down a narrow road, at Dock Head in Bermondsey, off Tooley Street. I eventually found that any female approaching by foot needed to walk the gauntlet of the 'cat-calls' and remarks from the East-End lorry drivers! Finally I short-listed two ladies. The one, white and attractive to me; an ex-school teacher looking for a new career. The other black, but an experienced secretary, who I did not fancy. I took the black girl, Elsa, as I felt my marriage could have been vulnerable if I taken the white lady. So you see, I did try on occasions to avoid temptation, not that it did me much good, as history was destined to prove.

2.02 The relationship with Elsa took time to develop. I suppose she acted as a 'buffer' between me and the Factory personnel and managers. She took my side and supported my actions in running the Site, which were not always popular. The Factory and Site was to say at the very least, neglected, disorganised, wasteful, filthy and inefficient. Into this situation I must have seemed like a purgative. It was fun, the staff were by and large friendly and co-operative and I enjoyed the challenge. Every aspect of the operation needed improvement and better control, which suited my background, my training and my experience. One of the first challenges was to raise the hygiene standards to Supermarket acceptability; this involved initially the exclusion of all the pigeons from the Manufacturing, Warehouse and Despatch Areas, the problem being the insect life from their 'droppings' infecting the flour and biscuit. Then there were the cats, which similarly fouled everywhere. Then there was the inside of the Plant and Equipment and Silos; almost everything needed internal fumigation to remove years of accumulation of filth and 'millions' of flour-weevils.

2.03 I also liked the environment, and the freedom from being totally in charge and able outside of the Factory to explore London, and of course to be closer to my brother and parents. Eventually, I got to meet Elsa's family and children, it was a culture shock, and took several years for me to stop feeling self-conscious when out and about with her. I was not used to mixing with Blacks socially, and certainly not being the only White amongst hundreds. I used to joke and say that "I could never live in South Africa or Northern Ireland". As Elsa was a black, of Catholic faith; and I was a white, of Church of England faith. She had had a difficult upbringing, in that her parents lived separate lives under one roof and she was an un-married mother. Her father had broken her jaw and thrown her out of the home; when he learned that she was pregnant. A 'one-night-stand'. Then, on the second occasion, a relationship which went wrong. The philosophy I suppose was different amongst the Blacks whom I knew; they did not seem to worry too much about marriage before children...

2.04 The family all did extremely well in their outlook, play and work situations. Baker, electrician, computer programmer, social worker, secretary etc. the mother was a hospital cook; three brothers and one sister were Karate Internationals and U.K. Champions. I had helped Elsa with her property purchase in Woolwich, East London, which was the area around which her family lived.

2.05 When Doreen heard about Elsa, through my children, she commenced divorce proceedings.

2.06 Doreen worked hard as a school teacher. I paid maintenance (as my father had done!) and tried my best to see as much of the children, Ford and Brian, as I could. It is difficult trying to be a father when you live 120 miles away; a round of 'visits' and Pubs and Restaurants to try to have a normal relationship, but nowhere you can really go to relax and call home. Doreen was okay, Elsa tried her best, but I am certain that my boys found it hard work. I carried the guilt for over twelve years. Every relationship problem, every difficulty the boys had, you place at your own door. I regret also not being there for them, not sharing their teen years, not seeing them grow up. I left when Ford was fourteen and Brian twelve years; significant years in each of their many previous lives ... see later.
When the break finally came, I wept bitterly. I cried so much that I could not drive the car. I went back to mum (Leonora), to recover that day; our relationship became closer, the barriers were lowered and we could talk for perhaps the first time.

KEYPOINT ENF1
You cannot walk away from your responsibilities, but if you acknowledge and accept that the Soul has chosen the life ahead, then you are not totally responsible for your actions. You should pray to GOD and ask for forgiveness. You should ask for forgiveness from your child's soul. You should do whatever you can to mitigate and ease the situation. YOU SHOULD THEN MOVE-ON. DO NOT CARRY THE GUILT, IT DOES NO-ONE ANY GOOD.

2.07 My brother Edward, helped to break down the racist attitude of my mother. Remember, her family lived in South Africa and mother seemed to me to have a typical 'better than them' opinion. One Christmas, I found myself with nowhere to go. For a peculiar set of circumstances, my family were all committed and I decided that all I could do was to turn up with Elsa on my mother's doorstep and she could choose. Me plus Elsa, or, no me ! The ice melted and a 'distant' relationship was established between the two of them.

2.08 I worked for four years in Bermondsey, a happy time before the Company hit falling profits and decided to close the operation. I was fortunate to relocate with Spillers to the West Country, as Factory, Development Manager and Buyer, for a pet-food Factory near Bristol. The breakdown of the relationship with Doreen was irretrievable in my mind, so the relocation provided the opportunity I needed to 'split' the family.

2.09 Elsa sold her house and moved down to join me in Weston-Super-Mare. I do not recall asking her to join me, but neither did I say "no". We were enjoying a reasonable physical relationship and I am not someone who wishes to live alone. It made sense for the children to relocate during the summer break and for Joan to move to Bristol Grammar School. The family fitted in well locally, Elsa made friends through contacts at the local Primary School and started up her own business - a quality retail shop for baby and children's clothes we called 'First Choice'.

2.10 Initially, all went quite well. The Factory business kept me quite busy, I drove on average 1,000 miles per week and set about improving the efficiency and cost productivity of the operation. When my 'Spillers' work was complete, I then needed to analyse VAT returns, wages and deal with invoices for 'First Choice'. Some work serving in the shop, some DIY on the house, some Rugby; a busy lifestyle!

2.11 There were obvious cost-reduction changes necessary to the Factory, such as to arrange for the postman to deliver the post and the milkman to deliver the milk!

One of the Process workers was also a van driver, who carried out these tasks and also collected two packers each day from their homes. When asked what job I wished him to do, I replied 'as a Process worker'. He responded that he was a Van Driver and wished to be made redundant. The man left and over the following months, his wife who worked in the Factory canteen, told of his new job with Welsh Television; working shift hours for filming, more money and perks such as complimentary Opera tickets. The man committed suicide as soon as his Bank loan monies ran out.

A lovely wife, with two teenage children. I felt responsible in some way, I even felt that I was blamed by some of the work-force ... my baptism of fire!

2.12 Daniel, Elsa's son, woke at 03.00 on Saturday morning doubled up in pain, he had had conjunctivitis twice. I took him direct to the local hospital, where he was admitted and put on a drip. He was four years old. By 14.00 he was released and sent home. He seemed to be all right for a week, then at 03.00hrs.on Saturday the following week, he was again doubled up in agony. I called the doctor(having been criticised the previous week!), he asked me to take Daniel straight to Hospital, where he was admitted and put on another drip. By 14.00 on the Saturday, the hospital wished to release him. I refused to take him home, and insisted upon a second opinion from another doctor, and further tests to establish what was wrong. The Hospital agreed to keep him in, and we collected him on the Sunday afternoon. Blood samples had been taken for analysis, and instructions were given for us to go with Daniel to the Royal Children's Hospital in Bristol on the Monday morning for the results of the tests.

2.13 No hint of any problem had previously been given, but Daniel was admitted that day and immediately commenced leukaemia treatment; radiography and chemotherapy. He was a fantastic patient and coped extremely well with his injections, hair loss and the restriction on his freedom. He became quite a celebrity with his extrovert, inquisitive personality, and cheerful approach. Quite amazing really how he would choose a vein to be injected in and then assist with the dilation. He would scurry around the Ward with his mobile drip feed, almost as if it didn't exist!

Time has shown him to be fortunate and he continues to be so. As far as I know the children around him in the hospital Ward, have all died and he has survived. At that time the survival rate was around 40% for 5 plus years.

In particular, we were helped by the Charity Group CLIC, (Cancer and Leukaemia in Childhood Trust) who provided free accommodation for parents to stay over adjacent to the Hospital, whilst their child was treated; and also a stress release, 'crisis' holiday flat in Devon.

I cannot praise enough the work which this Charity does.

2.14 I think that at one stage, I might have qualified for the most frequent Hospital Visitor Award ... Daniel's leukaemia was followed by Edward's leukaemia, my brother. Ted my father was a frequent in-patient, what with varicose vein operations and a series of Heart attacks. Then several Company employees needed visiting and so on. At least I was grateful that my own health was okay !

2.15 Elsa became pregnant. It was not intended, but she suffered badly from period pains and the doctor put her on the contraceptive pill to try to regulate the situation and reduce her pain. In switching types of pill, to avoid the headache side effects, she became pregnant. She was sick every day, so what with Daniel ill and needing to be taken from Weston-Super-Mare to Bristol for treatment, some thirty miles each way, and Elsa not well, help was necessary with the Shop. Whatever income was generated was insufficient to cover wages and fixed overheads. Coupled with poor stock- control, the shop quickly became a financial liability and a time, paperwork, and stress drag. During this period Joan, Elsa's daughter was probably feeling neglected and was demanding more attention from her mother.

2.16 At this time in my life my aspirations were purely materialistic and human. To build a new life for myself with Elsa and her family, to be successful in my work situation, to earn enough to support myself, my new family, to pay maintenance for my two boys, to still see my boys, to see my parents.
My life was extremely busy as it had always been, not one minute of idle inactivity; no time to relax or to think, simply non-stop, continuous activity. My mind never stilled, I always worked, in the Factory, in the home, in transit. Sleep was my only respite. There was always something that needed doing, and never enough time.
My philosophy of 'work hard and play hard' still applied, only now there was 120 miles between me and my boys, between me and my parents, and some 180 miles to Elsa's family in East London. And of course there was now the Shop and Elsa handicapped through pregnancy and Daniel's illness. I suppose that I was lucky to have the mentality, which coped with stress, and a new company car to dash around in.

2.17 Returning late one Sunday night in the darkness and rain, I was stopped by the Police when driving from the M4 Motorway onto the M5 at 120 mph (according to my speedometer). The Officer said that I was driving between 92 and 99 miles per hour, I argued against until I suddenly realised the nonsense of my action! I was summonsed at 99 mph. and fortunately escaped with my licence.

2.18 Helen was born on 29/7/86 in Weston, and Edwin followed on 9/4/88. I wished to call Edwin, Richard Edwin. but on announcing my choice at the Rugby Club, it immediately met with cries of laughter. I could not allow the child to be called 'dick-head', so I compromised on Edwin Richard.
Both children were born pure white, which was a shock to Elsa; but they changed colour to a golden brown after three weeks.

2.19 Within two years, we had moved again from Weston-Super-Mare to Bloxham - near Banbury, in Oxfordshire, as the business I was involved with, was sold and I had lost my job. I was the only one to go. It seemed a silly move to me, as trials and negotiations were well advanced to increase Turnover by 50% and the new Purchaser did not wish to use my knowledge at all for a friendly and controlled hand-over.

2.20 Edwin was born in Horton Hospital, Banbury. A disastrous sequence of events began, which could have been terminal for Edwin. He was born around 03.00, with the cord around his neck and a huge cyst in the Elsa's vagina, preventing the birth ... neither not known about until the final stages of labour, and no doctor or mid-wife on duty or available until the twelfth hour!

2.21 I believe the birth destroyed Elsa's interest in sex. She may well have a physical problem. Our relationship had been suffering for some years previously. Joan, Elsa's coloured daughter had become very selfish and perhaps jealous of her mother's relationship to me and Elsa needed to spend time as well with the other children. The result was that Joan would isolate herself from the family and live her own life as if we weren't there. Night after night, Elsa found it necessary to spend hours talking with Joan, to my exclusion. She always put the children before me and it seemed to me that she wished it that way. She insisted that the new baby should remain in the bedroom for eight months, which was ridiculous and restrictive in my eyes.
On three separate occasions, I deliberately waited to see how long it would be before she was interested in sex, three months passed by on each occasion.

2.22 Elsa told neighbours and friends, who told me, that she would much rather prefer to live on her own, and had no interest in being married.

2.23 The wedding almost did not happen - the Registrar said that unless she came within five minutes, she would be too late; we had all waited twenty-five minutes before Elsa appeared. On an earlier occasion, I had decided to leave a function without her, as she refused to leave; when she eventually returned, I was just leaving the car park.

Perhaps one should take more notice of these situations. We married because Elsa became pregnant and I felt that it was the right thing to do!

KEYPOINT ENL2

Do not marry for the wrong reasons. It is better to face the situation without the legalities getting in the way. If true love is not there, back-off and seek love elsewhere.

2.24 I found solace, sex and love with Mary for two years. Mary never demanded anything of me and we had many good times together. I was reluctant to leave my children, so the arrangement was ideal in many ways. Then one day Mary's neighbour's wife left him and she told me that she had fancied him for ten years and he was now available. I was devastated and lost two stones in weight through distress and unhappiness at losing Mary. Everyone around me thought that it was stress with my job which caused the problem, but I knew differently. It took me a year to forget about Mary and to move on. It might have been different if we had communicated better about our future plans and needs. Mary said that she could have tossed a coin to decide who to keep a relationship with; but he was free and I was not !

KEYPOINT ENL3

Time waits for no man. If you value someone, talk with them and let them know your feelings and your intentions!

2.26 I have two lovely children from the marriage to Elsa, but perhaps this was the marriage which should not have happened. As the Soul chooses the parents, my children would perhaps have been born to me in another relationship. Looking back years later this was a hard time and a hard experience.

- The job was not right for me;
- the relationship to Elsa was not happy;
- our physical sex was not good;
- the daughter's jealousy and relationship to me was a problem;
- the step-son's leukaemia was a tragedy;
- the shop was a financial and time drag,
- the race barrier needed to be handled with my family, and work situation...All for Learning?

KEYPOINTS ENL4

a) Recognise the difficulties in relationships and situations before you commit to a permanent arrangement.
b) Little events will happen to warn you and to try to prevent you from making profound mistakes. White Eagle, the Spirit Guide, calls these 'tugs', they are easily missed if you are not alert.

(here-after begins a new life-cycle which was to completely change my understanding of life and all that was significant to me)

##

CHAPTER 3. CONSTANCE(CONNIE) The Messenger

3.01 CONNIE applied for a job in Financial Services, to the office where my applications were processed, and where all my client files were kept. I was asked by my manager to interview her, and then subsequently, to look after her during her training period. (she lived close-by to me) She was a qualified hairdresser seeking a new challenge in her life; I agreed to use her initially for telephone work, and she accompanied me on a number of appointments before she finally decided to become a Sales Consultant. This was never my wish as my requirement was for a Sales Assistant, but my manager insisted that she become fully trained in her own right. A nice concept, but a financial disaster for Connie, who stopped her hairdressing completely, and then spent six months with no income and rising debts, whilst she trained and eventually qualified to sell financial products.
Unfortunately, even when trained to sell, when you are commission based; unless you do secure business you still receive no income.

3.02 When not earning money, Connie was fully involved in local events; such as Treasurer of the local Labour Party and Secretary of the local amateur Acting Society. This was on top of acting and singing herself, hairdressing and looking after her family, inclusive of a handicapped daughter - Jill. Connie also became involved with fund-raising for the local CLIC Charity.(The Cancer and Leukaemia Childhood Trust which helped us previously with Elsa's son)
The demands on her time were such, that her husband insisted on a meal out together one evening per week, simply for them to be able to spend some time together.
His objective in life was to emigrate to France, to renovate a derelict property which they owned some 100 kilometres south of Mont St. Michel in Brittany, Northern France.

3.03 The very concept of taking Connie to a remote area seemed to me personally, to be completely apposite to what she needed and was seeking from her life. He worked long hours as a sound Engineer and seemed to me to be running away from life and its responsibilities. Their property in Chipping Norton was run down through lack of care and basic maintenance, the excuse being that we were intending to emigrate. The same consideration applied to every aspect of their life and the state of their basic living equipment.

3.04 It took six months before Connie agreed to have sex with me; in fact I had decided to give up on any possibility of an affair, when she finally succumbed to my advances. I had just about been without sex for over a year, since Mary left me, and it seemed to me that I would never meet anyone else.

Connie was great in bed and we made love whenever we met; she was still having sex with her husband as well, so she was pretty active for a lady in her forties. We enjoyed our time together and the relationship blossomed. Elsa placed no demands on me and had told Connie, and the other neighbours that she would prefer to not be married.

(At this stage Connie worked for me, telephoning for financial appointments, as Elsa had chosen not to do this work)

I was reluctant to break the family unit in view of my previous experience with Doreen, so as long as my desires were satisfied I was happy to continue to support the family and live a double-life.

3.05 All was well until Christmas 1993 approached, and I ran out of excuses for not returning to my house in Bloxham late one night. There were two social Parties arranged with Connie, and I was determined to attend both of them. I decided to tell Elsa about the affair. I telephoned from Chipping Norton where Connie lived. Elsa gave me until midnight, some thirty minutes, to return home before she said she would put my clothes and my client files in the street. I returned for 12.03 and there were some of my clothes and confidential client files heaped on the kerb outside the house. I must have hurt her pride!

3.06 I could see no point in giving-up seeing Connie, as Elsa insisted I do; to simply co-exist in a love-less relationship. I knew that Connie's husband was hovering in the background, he had previously had suspicion of Connie having an affair, this had developed into a split and the husband had left the house to live alone in a flat in Bicester. I feared that if I did not act swiftly, then I would probably lose Connie.

(as I had already lost Mary)

KEYPOINT CM1

History does repeat itself unless you act to change the situation, or to learn the understanding. If you do not learn, the lessons will become more painful.

3.07 I decided to pack my belongings, files etc. when Elsa was out of the house and to move in with Connie. Elsa returned prematurely when I was packing; nevertheless, I moved-out to the dismay of the children who wrote me a very emotional pleading note asking for me to return, once again what should I do? Sacrifice my life for a veneer relationship with Elsa? Stay because of the children?

(I had wished to maintain the family Unit but my hand had been forced, I was forced to physically leave by Elsa and then subsequently she wished me to return, to walk-out on the loving relationship I had found.)

KEYPOINTS CM2

a) You must live your life to the full. Your children's Souls accepted the life knowing in advance the situations which were to develope.

b) This does not alleviate you from your responsibilities. You chose to have your children, you now are responsible for their up-bringing through to adult-hood; both Emotional, Educational, Physical, and in all other aspects of life.

3.08 I tried to make a family home for all of my children, and for them to feel welcome and comfortable. I had tried this previously with Elsa, her children, my children, and it had failed in my eyes. I had even organised a family holiday to Spain, eleven of us, with my brother's children as well. A twenty-four hour plus coach trip each way.

All that I wished to achieve were a few family meals together, but the girls had different ideas and wished to do their own thing.

Inevitably, with a new lady in your life, she needs to accept your children from previous relationships and you hers. If neither party complies or gives enough, your own personal relationship is stressed and the frequency of contact with the children is reduced.

KEYPOINTS CM3
a) It is essential for any new relationship to be successful, for both parties to accept each other's children as a part of the new unit.
b) A determined effort should be made by BOTH to overcome jealousy and to communicate over any problems.
c) Choices will need to be made if a wayward child is not to destroy a new relationship.

3.09 Connie had two children from a previous marriage. Jill and Roger. Jill had had a brain tumour almost from birth, and this had resulted in surgery at six months of age. She had lost part of her thyroid gland which had stopped her ability to grow, such that at the age of twenty-one she was only four feet ten inches tall with no prospect of further growth. Mature in other respects, she depended upon a shunt and tube from her brain to drain fluid from her head to her stomach. (when the family moved from Herts. to Oxon, the hospital records were lost by the NHS Hospitals, and the growth hormone treatment could not be restarted)

3.10 Because of her size, Jill had always been treated by the family as a child. Jill was originally expected to die within six months, but she survived; perhaps through the power of prayer, for Connie had tried every possible avenue for her survival.

It took Connie three years to teach Jill to walk and carry out basic tasks, the problem being that her retention of data was very short-term and her ability to 'imagine' and plan for herself was very small. The fact that I came to the household without this pre-knowledge meant that I treated Jill as a normal adult, and expected her to do a certain amount of work around the home. In time we also found a Charity who were prepared to support her employment.

This was called 'The Shaw Trust' who assessed Jill as 75 % capable of normal work, so they paid the Employer the 25 % shortfall on her output; we also identified a care-support home for her to be able to live an independent life. (close to where her boyfriend lived, and where her work was)

3.11 Then one day Jill was in trouble with fluid retention in her head. Surgery took place in the Radcliffe Infirmary, Oxford, England, and the Consultant confirmed the worst. The original tumour had re-grown, and was now so wrapped around her brain that it could not surgically be completely removed. He offered little hope of survival, but took tissue for testing. We prayed, the family prayed, we asked the Spiritualist Church members and individual Healers to pray.

Three days later the tissue results came through; Jill was okay, the Consultant could not believe the results, we were overjoyed. It causes you to think, to wonder, to question. What happened? Could Jill have really been cured by the power of prayer?

KEYPOINTS CM4

a) The power of prayer does work. Your prayers are always heard.

b) You must be very careful what you pray or wish for; as it may well happen. Often events happen in not quite the way in which we request, for our words are taken literally.
Consider: Is it your own selfish need that you are hoping to satisfy? Is it revenge you seek?

c) Remember, 'Do unto others as you wish unto yourselves'...there is a Law of Balance which applies. Do not bring hate or evil back onto yourself. GOD will deal with this need, GOD will effect a retribution.

d) It is necessary for YOU to LIVE your life, now. Your loved-one chose their life, however short. YOU chose this life, to come to terms with, to understand the emotions, for your Soul to learn to cope with this very situation.

e) Consider very carefully, is all this suffering to be wasted, so that the experience will need to be repeated. For ALL the players may have to return to this sequence of events because YOU would not learn, YOU were too stubborn, too hurt, too arrogant, too proud. Move on, learn, grasp the situation,

f) PRAY for healing for your loved-one and for yourself. Allow their Soul to progress, Allow your Soul to progress. Spread happiness and LOVE. Not all will be healed, you cannot change another's Karma, but you can and do influence your own.

3.12 I knew Connie was psychic, she read Tarot cards, she could hold objects and tell you something about their history. In meditation Circle she could tell you everyone else's experiences. At night, in her sleep, she would travel to a temple and help to comfort the Souls of children who had died during the previous daytime, and who were missing their parents.

I accompanied Connie to Spiritualist Church in Long Hanborough, Oxon, Witney; and also commenced one-to-one meditation sessions with a lady in Witney, but I must admit I felt or sensed nothing, and wondered if there was any real point to the exercise!

3.13 However, I needed to learn to relax. I was borderline for high blood-pressure and did not wish to take tablets for the rest of my life. I hoped that through meditation I could de-stress and be able to reduce my blood-pressure. But, I could never remember any dreams, I never experienced anything in 'meditation', I had no experience on which to base any assessment or evaluation of any 'occult' happening. All I had was curiosity, curiosity about ghosts, curiosity about GOD...Did Jesus ever exist?...where was Heaven?....How did hypnosis work?...What were the cold feelings in certain rooms?...Why do some people suffer so much?....why are some people successful and others not so?....what about the 'Bloxham tapes'....and regression into previous lives? ...coincidence, is there such a thing?....was there any purpose to our lives?

....So many questions and so few answers!

(I have always been seemingly incapable of doing nothing, to sit and fish by a river to me was a complete waste of time, likewise to sun-bathe on the beach, what a waste of time with so many other more interesting places to explore and people to meet. I did not enjoy reading because I had had to for work, for school and for University. Now work had caused me to lose pleasure from this activity. There was always a foot high of paper to read, it normally took me a week to read one Sunday news-paper. Then I used to drive upwards of 500-1,000 miles per week, 8 plus appointments per day. My boss always said I was a bad time manager but in-fact he was the bad time manager, my diary was full always, there was no time for him!)

3.14 I started to read spiritual books, to listen to meditation tapes and to accompany Connie to Spiritualist Church meetings. Then one evening, I had the shock of my life.!

I had been sitting quietly whilst the visiting medium, Mr Ron Moulding, had delivered his messages to almost everyone in the Hall....

'Does anyone, know anyone who has a wooden leg?...No-one spoke.
I said ' I have an uncle who has a false leg, I do not know if it is wood,
but he is not dead' 'It does not matter whether they have passed-over'
responded the Medium....'You do not believe do you?'....I protested ' I
would not say that, I am here to find out'.
The medium responded: ' I have someone who wishes to talk to you'...

3.15 ' Black is black, and white is white, I did not believe either and I was wrong'

It was a message from my father Ted, who died in 1978,...it was now
1996!!
The voice through the Medium then commenced to analyse my life, my
marriages, my work; he started by asking me not to feel guilty about not
spending enough time with my parents before he died...I had not told a
living person about that concern of mine. I was forced to the conclusion
that either the Medium could read my sub-conscious Mind; or there
really was 'a life after death' and not only that, but also a system for
communicating with Spirits in another world. I was reduced to tears and
cried profusely, to such an extent that the Medium moved-on to
someone else. Before he went he predicted two events to happen, both
did. One being the arrival of a solicitor's letter about divorce costs.!
(I checked later with my uncle Geoff in Norfolk, his false leg was made
of wood and covered with a skin)
KEYPOINTS CM5
**a) As with all abilities, some mediums and clairvoyants
are brilliant and some are not so capable. If you do not
like an individual's character or personality do not
give-up, try another.**
**b) No-one has to accept a word of what I write, all that
I can do is to relate my personal experiences. Hopefully
these will cause YOU to seek the answers, to make the
effort.**
**c) No-one else can do this for you, YOU need to make the
effort, to visit the Church, the Psychic, to read the
books, to pray, to observe Nature, to be aware of Events
and meetings and happenings around you.**
**d) Be aware of your PERSONAL FEELINGS about your
Being...Ask why?...Ask what does this mean?, Look for
repetitions in your life.**

3.16 Connie and I went on holiday to Crete that September, and I hired
a motor-scooter so that we could explore the Island and escape up into
the Mountains. We had a picnic in amongst the olive-Groves and made
love in amongst the trees...I had this desire to taste milk from Connie's
breasts, but this was never-to-be; she was not pregnant, in fact her
periods were becoming fewer and fewer, and I had had a vasectomy.

Suddenly Connie's breasts started to spray milk, she was lying on her back and without me touching them, they were like fountains.....a definite sign of the power of thought?.
KEYPOINTS CM6
a) Thoughts can be as powerful as Actions.
b) It is necessary always to be positive in our Thoughts. Your thoughts are known to GOD, your thoughts are also known to other Spirits, they certainly are to your own SOUL which can choose to take action to affect another Soul or Being.
c) How many times have you thought about someone, only to have them call you. The communication is MIND 'A' to SOUL 'A'..to SOUL 'B'..to MIND 'B' link which takes place. When two people achieve fully their Spiritual Awareness, they will be able to do this! Science calls this Telepathy.

3.17 On Connie's birthday we went out for a restaurant meal, together with my eldest son Ford who happened to be with us. The occasion went well until I went to the toilet! I returned to find Connie about to storm out of the restaurant, there had been no build-up, in my eyes, to any confrontation. I managed to patch over the differences, with Ford then threatening to walk out. He seemed to wish me to side with him and against Connie. I considered him to be completely out-of-order, especially on the special occasion of Connie's birthday. Eventually the two of them hugged; I will always remember Connie's words: ' I have never before felt so much hate in any person before.'
Little did I appreciate the significance of this Event, until many years later. I don't think that Ford ever forgave me for siding with Connie, and in many ways this episode was the beginning of a very difficult and isolated existence for him, when he withdrew from Society.
KEYPOINT CM7
The anger and hate arising from intense Emotions, is a key factor which shapes and changes our Attitudes. It is necessary to grasp the nettle, to confront and try to change and to modify the Understanding, before the rigidity of the Mind locks into our Attitudes the negative and powerful reactions of Hate, Revenge, Anger, Hostility, Pity, Animosity, Indifference.

3.18 I spent two years renovating Connie's house, she had decided to sell in order to give money to her husband and to payback his parents for the loan with which they had purchased the derelict house in Normandy, south of Rennes. We moved to a rented property in Banbury. Jill went into a care-residence house. Roger moved into a flat with a male friend; so we were alone together for the first time.
..........it was September 1997

3.19 Connie continued her mobile hairdressing Business and operated from a Salon two days a week. All seemed well until I went sailing with my brother and friends for one week, something I usually did each year. A few months later, Connie went on a hen party, a weekend boat cruise to Madrid, to say farewell to a colleague who was returning to Australia. Unbeknown to me, Connie formed a relationship with an Heavy Goods Vehicle driver.

Initially, she started to complain about my snoring, to the extent that I went for assessment at the local Hospital, sleep studies which pronounced me to be quite normal. Then she stated she did not wish to be cuddled in bed at night, when she was asleep, or to sleep with me. I rationalised this in view of her spiritual work, but it made me extremely unhappy.

3.20 She left two days after her fiftieth Birthday party, which I had secretly arranged for her. The whole family and friends; music from both brothers and parents; pub food; bed & breakfast...the works !

but to no avail...In retrospect, she must have planned her leaving and her future accommodation requirement some time before. I went to work one day and when I returned, she had left me a note on the kitchen table and no way of contacting her.

3.21 I tried unsuccessfully to meet with Connie, but I did not know where she was living and had no telephone number. It was some two weeks later before we spoke.

'I need my freedom!' 'You're too possessive!' 'Leave me some time to decide in my own mind whether I wish to return!'

'There is no-one else!' 'I need space on my own!'....I could not relate to any of these opinions, but decided that perhaps in a few weeks she would change her mind.

I knew where she worked, so I poured out my heart in writing, took and sent flowers and offered her 'the world', including marriage, a holiday in America and a new life running a Public House and Spiritual Centre. I considered that if only we could spend a few days together that all would be healed. It was not to be ...

3.22 The single-lady mutual support group in Chipping Norton was too effective. A band of single, divorced and separated who socialised and went clubbing almost every night of the week. A room, a house-share, or all seemed to be readily available. I soon learned about the regular clubbing to 04.00 hrs. and the progression of 'men friends'.

3.23 There followed a succession of Events within a two month time frame, which I would wish on no-one. My car broke down, my 750cc.motorbike broke down, the motorbike's keys jumped out of the ignition whilst on the M-40 (this is normally impossible). When I arrived at my destination, I could not switch off the engine.

I decided that I needed to disconnect the battery, which involved lifting the seat (key-locked) and in turn, removal of my travel bag. In repeating the cycle of events at the motorbike shop, so as to obtain the replacement key number, my travel bag was stolen. The bag contained my work diary, appointment schedule and my new reading glasses. The telephone failed, the toaster broke, the electric kettle broke and then the micro-wave failed. My motorbike was written-off, after being hit by a car which was leaving a Public-House as I tried to drive-by. The driver simply pulled-out in front of me. Most of my gear was torn and my lap-top computer was smashed. I started shaking two days later - it was as if everything was against me.

KEYPOINT CM8
You do bring onto yourself, your own 'good-fortune'. There is a time to change all connections and possessions associated with the Past, to enable you to more easily move forwards.

3.24 During May 1997, I packed up Constance's clothes and her personal items and cleared out her possessions, which she duly collected. I decided to sit-tight in the house in Banbury, to let the dust settle and to gather my thoughts. The following week, the eviction notice arrived, giving me one week to leave the premises.
I was horrified, this was just what I did not need. I protested, to no avail - the property owner had defaulted on the mortgage and the Coventry Building Society was seeking repossession. I had paid my rent, but the landlady had not paid the mortgage.
I fought the eviction in Court and threatened to expose the Coventry in the national press and so was granted two months in which to find alternate accommodation before the Bailiffs descended ... but where to live?

3.25 I turned to the Spiritualist Church for help, for counselling and for healing. I even sacrificed a day's rugby to attend an Awareness Development Circle. I was tearful, depressed and in need of help!
I could not sleep, I did not need sleep! At the circle I felt like 'a fish out of water', in the midst of many 'Mediums'. but several saw how distressed I was and gave me healing.
I would just burst out crying and sobbing at the slightest mention of Connie or my situation. I met later with one 'Medium' and it was suggested that I meet with three so as to obtain a clearer perspective of my situation. I have found all those people I have ever met with, to be warm and sympathetic and helpful.

3.26 I had been offered a free 'tarot reading' by a local lady - the 'Cotswold Soothsayer' at Constance's fiftieth party and decided to take up this option. Two key choices emerged :
a) I needed to walk away from the Past
b) If I truly left the Past behind then the Future could be successful in all aspects of love, finance and Spiritual progression.

KEYPOINTS CM9

a) There are some wonderful and kind people in the Spiritualist Church who can offer many words of comfort and sound advice to any who are distressed.

b) There are many Mediums who have genuine ability to read your Past, your Present and your Future. As with all walks of life, there are many around who have different levels of skill, ability and communication. Do not be deflected if your first experience is less than satisfactory, seek another.

(see tarot readings in appendix VII)

3.27 I decided that I needed to get out and about, and to meet new people. I had taken myself on Tour with High Wycombe Rugby Club, to Holland, for a break, and then down to my brother's home in Worthing where I spent an emotional night. It is good and sometimes necessary to cry and to release the Emotions. I also decided to learn Ball-room Dancing and Le-Jive. Le-Jive I found to be excellent fun and good to meet people. Here I met Jane, a Psychic, Masseuse and Nurse, we agreed to socialise and go-out together a few days later.

3.28 Following our evening together, the telephone woke me at 07.00hrs. It was Jane. 'I have been up since 04.00hrs. talking with my Spirit Guide, and have been asked to give you the following message'...........
'Unless you give up alcohol and caffeine you are going to have a heart-attack. You also need to masturbate every day to relieve your stress. Go at once to the Horton, Banbury Hospital, and obtain full information on how to deal with a heart attack.'...The message stopped me in my tracks.
I was drinking and living on next to no sleep. I was shaking slightly, but felt no symptoms. I went for a medical check-up and was pronounced A1. Jane did not wish to have any physical relationship with me, and we met only once again when I paid for a massage. I stopped all tea and coffee and alcohol for a week, and then resumed at a lower level.

3.29 It was some months later that Connie told me that she was 'the Messenger', her role was to awaken my awareness to Spirit and that was the sole reason for us coming together. She had completed her task and it was now time for her to move-on. We were never intended to fall in love.

She thanked me for our time together and said that I had helped build her confidence. From time to time in the future she would phone me to ask if I was all right, as she sensed that I was suffering.

3.30 In July 1977, now living in Aylesbury, I had seen an advert in the local paper for a Clairvoyant Fair at the local Football Club. I had fifteen minutes before needing to be with my young children so I popped into the Hall... There was only one of twelve tables free. The medium, Mr Garry Owen, said enough to me in two minutes for me to drive to Kettering, some eighty miles each way for a 'reading'....A complete stranger he said to me 'A lady whose name begins with 'C' has had a significant role to play in your life. She was 'the Messenger', to introduce you to Spiritual Awareness'. I was gob-smacked!

3.31 What did all this mean? Did Connie simply fulfil a pre-destined role and where did I fit in?

3.32 I had moved to Aylesbury to escape from Banbury, because I thought that Connie was moving there with her boyfriend, and I did not wish to see her and to hurt myself anymore. The 3-bedroom semi-detached house which I rented was ideal for me; the same cost as Banbury, but closer to London. It was also closer to another work-office at High Wycombe, and central for access to any of my four children. I decided to take in a lodger to help me with the costs of the house. Within the month I was joined by Arjun, a management Trainee at the local Rothman's Head Office in Aylesbury.

3.33 Connie phoned me one day out-of-the-blue, she had lost the baby she was expecting! (this was the first knowledge I had of her being pregnant), from the HGV Driver she had met on the Madrid run and subsequently. He had told her that he has another six children, by six different women, and was not prepared to commit to her, or to help her financially.
We met and talked, but she was too drunk and too distressed to be rational! ...
I had met her 'by chance' in a night-club in Evesham some weeks earlier, but she had refused to talk or to dance with me. I was alone and tried to avoid her but to no avail. Finally, in desperation, I walked onto the dance floor and held a pint of beer over her head, I hesitated to tip-it. She and others screamed; everyone stopped dancing; I simply lowered my arm and walked out of the Club...I often wished that I had emptied-it over her!

3.34 We talked occasionally on the telephone and met one day in September for a meal. My volvo car was up to 180,000 miles and the head-gasket was blown such that I needed to top-up with water every ten miles; even so I invited Connie back to my house in Aylesbury.

To my surprise she came and we had a super night together. The following day I ran her back by motor-bike to her car, which was still at the Italian restaurant in the Bartons. She said 'you were always the best in bed, and the motor-bike is fantastic'...thereafter, she refused any contact with me, just when I thought there might be a chance of a reconciliation. I gave her until 1st November to choose to return but she never did.

3.35 I rationalised and wondered whether it was:
- my personality being too dominant
- me being too possessive
- my snoring
- my occasional insensitive comments to her parents
- her need for freedom and independence
- her hormones changing
- her need to prove something, in achievement terms to herself
- her falling out of love and blaming me for her marriage break-up
- her job of the spiritual introduction was completed (in her eyes)
- her meeting the HGV driver and becoming pregnant?

...Or was it simply that she needed to move on.
Spirit messages subsequently have told me it was revenge, for I had left her in a previous lifetime some 250 years earlier,(karma)
...a decision in this lifetime which she has come to regret!
KEYPOINTS CM10
**a) What goes around comes around. There is no escape.
What you do unto others will return to you. (karma)
b) Give love to receive love. Give hate to suffer hate.
...even across different lifetimes a balance is struck.**

3.36 It finally took me seven months to switch-off from Connie. I had to do this to avoid hurting myself any more. I had lost two stones in weight, and I was not eating or sleeping properly. The one good feature was that the weight loss had cured my marginal high blood-pressure, so the potential need for tablets was removed....and, I was now curious to find out more about spiritual matters.
KEYPOINT CM11
Weight loss certainly reduces your Blood Pressure.

3.37 On 17th December 1997, I learned that:

- Connie was living with Mike who was 24 years younger than her.
- My mother, Leonora, had just recovered from a serious Operation.
- My brother had successfully completed his leukaemia Treatment.
- My eldest son, Ford, was contactable again, having fallen-out with me and Connie the previous year; he always considered Connie to be a witch, and anything Spiritual was concerned with the 'devil'.
........(viz. 3.17)

3.38 All was to improve, and I was finally able to walk away from Connie; but the wounds would take a lot longer to heal.

(many years later Spirit were to tell me that Connie's spiritual work with me was not completed. She was expected to teach me much more before leaving. The fact that she decided not to do this left them no choice but to move her on, to create a new life for her; and subsequently, to find a new Teacher for me!)

##

CHAPTER4. A NEW START?

4.00 I needed to meet people and to keep myself fully occupied. Life as a sales person is very lonely and I did not like much returning home to a solitary existence. In between being a Rugby Union Referee for the Oxon Society, handling mid-week, Saturday and Sunday games, I found time for Ball-room dancing lessons on Sunday evenings, jiving on Mondays or Thursdays and a singles' Disco on Fridays. Whenever possible my children would also come to stay at the weekends, so I would have food to buy, and to prepare for them.

KEYPOINTS ANS1

a) When ever it is necessary to forget someone, or an Event, it certainly helps to occupy your mind with other interests or activities. Keep a busy mind and do not brood.

b) It is sometimes necessary to TELL yourself to switch-off from that thought. Imagine that thought or event being 'washed away' by a sheet of water, or put that person behind your Door and bolt it firmly.

4.01 I met Anne at one of the Singles' Evenings, she was with a female friend and after the music finished at midnight, the two of them came home with me, some forty miles, and I cooked a Chinese meal at 02.00 hrs. This was just before I moved to Aylesbury and while I was still living in Banbury. She lived near High Wycombe, Anne was still bitter over the split with her husband some two years before, and I was able eventually to help and support her with the preparation of her divorce financial settlement. She had had a difficult childhood, being abused then, and now physically assulted by her husband when he got drunk. She had a minor stroke, breakdown, and needed six months in Hospital to recuperate. Whilst in Hospital the husband had 'disposed of ' her prize Afgan show-Dogs.

4.02 We got on reasonably well, but it was not a true love situation. We eventually tried 'Relate' to help to sort out the physical side of our relationship, so as to stop it floundering. Anne thought that I had a problem, but I knew that she was 'screwed-up' through the abuse and also had a serious female, medical problem, which finally needed surgery to resolve. The counselling certainly helped and eventually led to an improvement, but the chemistry between us was not strong enough to sustain the relationship. She considered that I drank too much and was afraid that I might hit her (I never did!). She also sought someone with more capital and with no children to worry about. She verbally tore me apart and broke-off the relationship just before a joint holiday to Turkey. However, we still decided to go on holiday together, because it was arranged and paid-for, but it was an unhappy time and Anne was ill with the problem which later needed surgery.

KEYPOINTS ANS2
a)Communication is the key to tackling any situation,
and to resolving differences.
b)A mediator, someone you both trust, even a complete
stranger, is an excellent way of highlighting
differences and sorting out possible solutions.
c)It is much easier to resolve a dispute when the
parties involved are still together, than when each has
hardened their views, separated, and then involved third
parties such as solicitors.

4.03 We stayed in Turkey in a Hotel near Bodrum; two strangers on
holiday together, to be honest I still wished to be with Constance; and
Anne I think anyone but me. She did not even wish to hold hands. On
the second day, a Saturday at 21.00hrs she was not feeling well and
decided to go to bed, she suggested I go out by myself, which I did. I
returned at 04.00hrs having met up with an English family. This episode
did not endear her to me! We went on trips every day, long coach trips
and repeated visits to carpet Factories! In particular we visited the ruined
City of Epheseus which was very memorable to me....little did I know
then what past lives and the future was to hold for me. Perhaps the key
feature of Epheseus is the Library, I was later to learn that in a previous
lifetime, I was responsible for collecting together some of the books and
scrolls which were stored in this library.
...see AppendixII.One Soul, Past Lives.

4.04 On the final day I decided to have a Turkish Bath massage and
there started a conversation with an interesting Lebanese lady called
'Raijah'. Raijah was an English Lecturer at the American University in
Lebanon, she was travelling alone and expressed interest in further
contact. I subsequently rang Lebanon and left messages to no avail.
Raijah is also the name of my spiritual Lion, my animal protector who
stands close-by. Also,
I have a Horse............. 'Bucephalus'
I have a Falcon............. 'Solum'
I have a Dog................ 'Peego'
All spiritual Beings from past lives who have chosen to remain with me,
'Peego' is from this lifetime and my time with Doreen. He is a male
Jacket-Russell Terrier, who was with us from six weeks of age for some
fifteen years.

4.05 Upon our return from Turkey, I returned to the singles' dances
alone, and at the second visit met Lorna. Lorna was a stunning blonde
who had been abandoned by her husband two years previously.(as was
Anne, both left for secretaries!) The husband had been a managing
director of a large company, and Lorna still tried to maintain that
lifestyle.

She had not yet come to terms with the fact that she had been rejected. Anne tried to re-kindle our relationship, but by this time I had met Lorna, and was not interested.

4.06 Lorna drove a red sports car and lived in a lovely house with her grown-up son and daughter in Chesham, Buckinghamshire, England. We had an enjoyable time together, mainly dances, weekends away, socialising and eating out. She objected to the fact that she needed to work and expected to be 'treated in the fashion she was used to'. In this climate we co-existed, and enjoyed each other's company, but it was questionable whether the relationship would develop any further.
 Lorna was anxious to keep me apart from her family as much as possible, neither was she keen to play 'mum' to my youngsters.

KEYPOINTS ANS3
a) A relationship cannot be complete, or successful, unless both parties give their full commitment. Neither can a new relationship succeed if either party cannot or will not walk away from previous relationships.
b) The PAST serves only to bring you to the Present.
c) You cannot retrieve the Past, whatever has happened is history, from which hopefully you have learnt your lessons so that it does not need to be repeated.
d) Where, How, When, With whom you make your future, is based upon Your CURRENT actions, thoughts and choices which you make now.

4.07 Lorna bought me two presents, which I remember well. A shaving-stick brush, and a casual jacket from Harrods Store, London, as a Christmas present in 1997.

4.08 I still attended spiritual Church during this period, but alone. On two occasions I was compared to an acorn, initially about to break-forth into a new oak-tree, and then some six months later as having established roots, a few inches high, and beginning to develop. An encouraging analogy when one considers the might of the fully grown Oak!

KEYPOINT ANS4
If you persist in your search for truth and understanding, you will receive these little 'Tugs' to encourage you.

4.09 Anne had had a powerful personal experience, but for some reason chose not to pursue her beliefs. Perhaps she blamed GOD for the loss of a close friend. I sensed that she was too bitter still with her personal experiences of life to want to associate with any higher ideals. I hope that she will reconsider at a future time.

4.10 Anne's new boyfriend was called Dennis, his birthday was the 5th June, he became known as 'little Dennis' in view of his height; I was called 'big Dennis'.
(same Christian name and birthday as me! There is no such thing as a coincidence!)
Anne had now become a good friend; someone to meet occasionally with and to talk to. She knew my children and my family and some of my friends. Anne was having a rough time. Medically, relationship-wise with her two sons, (one of whom disowned her when she initially gave her husband a second chance), her best female-friend's boyfriend had threatened her with a knife, she called the police. Little Dennis was two-timing her. She called me on Thursday, 26th in distress, and we met to talk on Friday, 27th March 1998.

4.11 I was driving from Aylesbury to Cheltenham on business, and then back to Helmdon near Banbury for an 20.00hrs appointment. Anne accompanied me in the car and we talked as I drove. Whilst in Cheltenham she went shopping, we met for lunch, and then we drove back to Banbury for my evening appointment. I dropped her at the cinema where she watched 'Titanic' and arranged to meet her at 22.30hrs in the Whateley Hall Hotel.

4.12 When I reached the Whately, the film had not yet ended so I went into the Hotel lobby for a drink. There was only one person sitting there, waiting alone. We struck up a polite conversation, I learned that she was separated, and in need of financial advice. I gave my business card, she gave her telephone number, and I agreed to call her the following week. Anne then re-joined us, the three of us talked, and then after fifteen minutes Anne and I left.
The Lady's name was HELANA.
KEYPOINT ANS4
Almost nothing happens by chance or by coincidence. Every situation is brought to you for your learning and for your choices to be made.

##

CHAPTER 5. HELANA's Role

5.00 I called Helana the following Wednesday, 1st April 1998, and we agreed to meet on the Friday at 19.00 hrs. I was not sure how the appointment would go, I had all of my financial paperwork to conduct a Financial Health Check, together with my lap-top for financial illustrations, but neither was to be needed. I had tried to meet later with Lorna, but she unusually was not available, visiting a friend and she wished to have a tête-à-tête without me. Equally so, she was not available the following day, nor evening, visiting her father alone. Lorna was neither available on Sunday, 5th or Monday 6th. It was to be the following Tuesday before Lorna wished to meet with me. Lorna had said to me that she was happy with our relationship as it was, and if I needed more, that I should find someone else as well.

5.01 On Friday, 3rd April 1998, the appointment with Helana progressed from work to dinner, drinks, and on to a night-club in Banbury. She then came home with me to Aylesbury. She was wearing a green, satin, mini-dress, was attractive and responsive. We slept together that night and she was subsequently not to leave my side until we had moved together to live in Ireland.

Helana was a Christian Spiritualist and regular attendee at the Banbury Spiritualist Church. A hairdresser and a psychic, like Connie; but additionally, she was able to write Spirit messages and to allow Spirit to talk through her when in Trance; or indeed when she was fully aware of the message. She was also able to communicate with her own and other Spirit Guides.

She had developed this ability through being isolated from human society for almost two years, through personal application; but most of all through the guidance and tutoring of her best-friend Judith.

(this isolation had occurred through her failed marital situation, combined with a lack of finance).

KEYPOINT HR1

Personal suffering, and the reaching an all-time low in your emotional life, almost seems to be a pre-requisite for the achievement of receptivity to the influence of GOD. It is a personal fact in my life that before a significant ATTITUDE change has occurred, I have been forced to that conclusion by personal hurt and distress. Such a shame that we cannot seemingly learn without suffering!

5.02 On the Saturday, 4th April, Helana invited me to accompany her to the village of Over Worton, some fifteen miles outside Banbury, Oxon. I drove towards the Village and parked the car for the final approach, we walked the final distance, perhaps some fifty yards. Suddenly, Helana was huddled by the kerb, sobbing profusely on the ground and unable to proceed any further. There followed the most incredible tale and one which was to change my life for ever.

5.03 Helana told of a existance in the 1700's when I was Richard Cookson, and she was Catherine; we secretly married and my father subsequently disinherited me from the Ledwell Estate. We visited the Church where we were married, and found the tomb-slabs where we were buried.
A summary of some of the lives which have been revealed to me, is to be found in the AppendixII. Past Lives, One Soul.
KEYPOINT HR2
There are alive today, people who can recall previous lifetime experiences. This surely must be definitive evidence of the survival of the Soul after physical death, and the existence of Reincarnation as the mechanism by which our Soul returns to the Earth-Plane, so that we can learn the lessons necessary for us to progress towards the True Light.

5.04 Helana accompanied me to the rugby union matches I was refereeing on the Saturday and the Sunday, and stayed over in Aylesbury. She acted as a Medium and convinced me that we were ' soul-mates' and it was our destiny to be together. We had been married in many lives previously, and Ford and Brian's spirits,(my children with Doreen my first wife) had been with us also in many other lifetimes....
Hour after hour, messages were brought to me from Jesus the Messiah, from Helana's Spirit Guide, from Mary the mother of Christ, from Joshua, from Jeroboam, and from many other Prophets.
I was told that I had one week in which to choose between a relationship with Helana or to continue my relationship with Lorna. It was not acceptable for me to continue to run the two relationships side-by-side, nor was it possible for me to have any longer in order to choose between the ladies.
KEYPOINTS HR3
a) Spirit always give us a choice. We may not like the choices, we may not choose wisely, but always we are given the option to walk away, to reject one option.
b) It is also important to emphasise that IF it is essential EVENTUALLY for us to follow a certain Pathway, that all that our personal choice will do is to postpone that Event. The situation will be returned to us, for us to choose again, perhaps next month, next year, or even in future lifetimes.

c) You travel through your many lifetimes with other
Souls, the role's will change from lifetime to lifetime,
repeating again and again until love and understanding
has been gained.
d) The Souls you travel with are known as your
Peer-Group, and can comprise some 40-50 in number.
e) Soul-mates are individual Souls with whom you are to
achieve perfect love. When this occurs, the Souls of the
two will be joined together in bonding forever as one.
f) You can achieve Soul-mates with more than one other
Soul. The bond can be made within an hour, that may be
the total extent of your physical time together, your
lives may then part and you would move on to new
relationships, BUT the BOND WILL ENDURE for all time and
will help to lighten the Aura of the Earth, and to bring
love to Others.
(...see the film 'The Titanic')

5.05 The nature of the messages, the sincerity, the different voices, the
authors, the way in which they were delivered, the passion of our
relationship, all these combined to convince me that our destinies were
to be together. I rationalised that these messages were either from
Aliens or from peoples from another World; but the significant feature
was that no harm was spoken, the talk was of helping Others, of love,
of making a difference to reduce Evil.
I knew that the relationship with Lorna was stagnating, so I decided to
meet with her and to break-off our relationship. I arranged to meet for a
meal and to tell her over-dinner the exceptional happenings since we last
met.

5.06 It was Tuesday, 7th April when we met, I had collected her from
her house on the Tuesday afternoon, she had just climbed out of the
bath when I called, we then made love, and afterwards I drove to our
favourite Italian Restaurant. During the meal I reviewed our relationship,
and then told her about the happenings since our previous meeting, and
the reasons for my subsequent decision to end our liaison. It was
difficult for me because I was very fond of Lorna; she was speechless
and simply asked me to take her home...
Helana was waiting for me when I returned, she started to move into my
house in Aylesbury on Good- Friday, 10th April.

5.07 Spirit messages were received every day, evening, and night; in
particular from Jesus and from High Spirit. We were told that monies
would be found for a move and that the Past was to be forgotten....
On 13th April, Jesus stated ' Do not allow anyone to come between
you; temptation will be there'. Also...
'I was only a man, you too can achieve what I achieved then, and even
more in the Future'.

KEYPOINTS HR4
a) Jesus is telling me that he was only a man. Not a GOD.
b) Jesus writes: ` The Soul is a complicated entity. All
living humans have Souls, these contain one part of the
Spirit of God which provides the life-force. In the case
of certain individuals, they are closer to GOD and so
their Souls contain a greater proportion of the GOD-
power (Christ Light etc.). In this way they are then
able to demonstrate greater powers of Healing, Love,
Compassion etc.
c) As Souls progress towards the one True Light, the
composition of their Souls are changed, so that they
acquire more and more of the GOD-light. This is
reflected in their Soul's total energy level and the
colour of their Aura.'

5.08 Over the subsequent few weeks, Helana settled into Aylesbury
with me and I introduced her progressively to my children, to my family
and to my friends...On 17th April we became engaged, and I then was
introduced to Judith, Helana's best friend, on 20th April.

5.09 On 11th May, I received a message from very High Spirit; this told
of a dramatic change which was to take place in my life.
My karma was to be changed.!   We needed to move from Aylesbury,
I would need to find a new job, we were to have children, possibly
twins; this was to be a new beginning and new Destiny for me. An
apology was given to me for the necessity to change my life so
completely...it was known that I had had a vasectomy, but this was not
to be a problem!!

KEYPOINTS HR5
a) There are seven levels of Spirituality, seven
progressive levels of attainment before the Soul can be
re-united with its perfect Spirit, and so achieve true
oneness with GOD in true love.
b) Heaven is positioned at level three; there are two
degrees of Hell below Heaven.
c) There is a hierarchy of High Spirit, above and beyond
level five, the level of human Spirit Guides, who
Monitor, Organise, Control and Direct all activities
on behalf of GOD...(compare this to the operation of any
Government.)
d) Karma can only be changed in exceptional
Circumstances.

5.10 My lifestyle did change dramatically. Every day, every evening and every night, Helana would receive messages from Spirit, both verbal and in writing; often in the middle of the night. I learned that between mid-night and 05.00hrs. is the ideal time for communication, when there is minimum interference from human activity.

KEYPOINTS HR6

a) **The Mind needs to be stilled, the human physical senses minimised, for us to become more receptive to Spirit.**

b) **Interference will occur from any Energy system in the vicinity......It is preferable to allow some two hours following the use of a Television or Washing Machine for interference to be minimised. Avoid the vicinity of Electrical Pylons or Generators.**

c) **Candles do attract Spirit,..both Light and Dark Spirits.**

d) **It is easier for Spirit to approach the Earth-Plane when Human activity is at a lower level, it should be appreciated that the Earth-Plane exists at a much lower vibrational level, and it is necessary for Higher Beings to 'descend' to our level for them to be able to easily communicate with us.**

(our brightest day has been described by Isaiah as a dark dismal place compared to the Realms in which Higher Spirit exist)

5.11 On Friday, 15th May 1999, in the afternoon, we attended the Roman Catholic funeral in London of Theresa, Elsa's mother. The Church was packed and the coffin was laid open for viewing during the Service. Helana stated that Theresa's Soul was present within her and singing throughout the Service. She took on the healing-stance of Jesus, who was also present. Afterwards, Elsa asked us to drive Helen, my daughter, to her school weekend Trip in Derbyshire. We eventually returned home at 05.00hrs.

KEYPOINTS HR7

a) **The Soul does not always need time for recovery from the experience of Death.**

b) **There exist hospitals in Heaven, where all the ailments and injuries from the Earth-Life are healed, but if the Soul is not too distressed then it may choose to remain on the Earth-Plane, to stay with its loved-ones, until a later, more appropriate time, for its to move to Heaven.**

c) **A problem can arise when the Soul does not accept that death of the Body has occurred, this often happens in cases of violent death, we then encounter the existence of Ghosts who choose to remain on the Earth-Plane, becoming progressively darker and darker, and may then need special help to be recovered. (see video Ghost)**

5.12 Helana told me of a repeating vision she had received, of a man standing at the top of a Tower; she could not quite see his face, but now she knew that it was me. Judith told of receiving the same vision.
KEYPOINT HR8
All visions or recurring dreams should be written down for later reflection. This is one of the ways that Spirit communicate with us, either to teach us about a past or present situation, but on many occasions, to fore-warn us of what is to happen if we pursue our present course.

5.13 On Saturday, 16th May, we visited Waddesdon Manor and the Five Arrows Hotel, met with Doreen and George her husband and Brian my son. Subsequently we attended a party in High Wycombe. Helana told me that we collected my Aura from the Hotel, left there when previously I visited there with Lorna; I gave Helana three daisies, as a chain which I had made on the hotel lawn; she pressed these into a book. Helana was very distressed at the Manor; crying and almost passing-out.
(It would seem that we have a past connection with the Rothschild family, possibly in France)

5.14 Later, Helana told of a vision of four children, one dark skinned, huddled together in the garden of Five Arrows Hotel, playing with daisy-chains, they are 5 -7 years of age, in white dresses with puffed sleeves. Subsequently, a message was received via Judith, that: Charmaine (called Sonja), Helen, Daisy-May, Charlotte, were all burned to death in a garden fire, in woods of the Waddesdon Manor in the 1600's Helana detected their Souls crying for help...
The daisy-chain represented the entwining of our Spirits forever.

5.15 We returned on 1st June and said prayers requesting help be given to the children, Jesus then came and led the children to Heaven, for them to be united with their families again...Helana asked of Jesus who was with us in the car, 'How is it possible for me to do this work?'
Jesus responded:
'Because you have the strongest mother's love of anyone alive in the World at this time'....It was necessary to wash thoroughly when we returned home; so as to clear ourselves of any Spirits from the Past.
KEYPOINTS HR9
a) There exist many lost Souls on the Earth-Plane in need of recovery. It is possible for a certain level of Light-Spirit to act to recover lost Souls.
b) Through prayer you can request the recovery by Angels of these lost Souls. Helana is able to do this work as she has the Holy Ghost within her Being.

c) The Holy Ghost is very unique and works for God. The Spirit of God may be present in many, but the Holy Ghost is only present in very few.
d) Washing, Bathing, Showering, Rain, all these activities with water serve to purify and 'wash-away' unwanted Souls.
Whenever you feel the un-wanton presence of darker Souls, the ritual of water purification is an excellent way to remove their influence.
e) Nature uses rain to purify the Earth. Any object, picture, photograph, left in the rain, or even sunlight, or a light source, will serve to lighten the Subject. (this is why Ireland is so wet, the rain is used to purge the Land of Evil)
e) Where-ever you go, who-ever you meet, their Souls or those in the vicinity may follow you and wish to influence your activities. If you return from a visit and sense an attitude change; it may well be appropriate to ask for protection and to wash away any unwanted Presence.

5.16 On Sunday,17th May, 1998, Spirit propose new names for both of us:

- Deirdre Alison is to be known as HELANA REBECCA
- Dennis Brian is to be RICHARD EDWARD,...this was subsequently changed to JOHN OLIVER

KEYPOINT   HR10
Names are important, both these choices of name were based upon achievements in previous Lives. ...'It is to be hoped in this lifetime that JOHN OLIVER will be able to achieve many of the virtues and gentle nature portrayed in previous lives using these names'

5.17 We are asked whether we prefer to have twins, or two single children by separate births. We choose two single children.

5.18 Albert, the spirit of the father of Catherine and Jack (now Helana and Phil) comes close with sadness, and is very heavy on Helana.
He seeks forgiveness from us for raping Catherine (Helana) and for causing all the unhappiness which he caused in the 1700's....On discussion between ourselves, we ask him to work for five years helping to heal and counsel rape victims; this we view as a reasonable penance to obtain our full forgiveness. Albert then departs with thanks. We are told that our own spiritual progress may be restricted until this 'event' is healed.

KEYPOINTS HR11
a) It may take many Centuries in order to heal and obtain
forgiveness from those you have caused to suffer. During
this period of time, the 'injuries' may continue and the
hate and evil may be perpetrated.
b) It will be necessary eventually to heal all of these
'sores' before complete Spiritual Awareness can be
attained.
c) Souls still retain their Emotional attachment and
Character between lifetimes, and as the Spirit never
forgets anything, grievances from the Past can rear
their head at any time, unless full Forgiveness has been
obtained.

5.19 We are requested to establish that Helana is not pregnant, and that
I, John, cannot make her pregnant.

5.20 I am told by Jesus that my spiritual Hearing is to progress; and that
I should learn to speak and read languages.

5.21 On Tuesday, 19th May, I travel on business to Sandy Lane,
Wiltshire, and we then visited Lacock Abbey.(Saxon Ancestry) .
Suddenly, Helana is frog-marched around the lake, almost at running
pace; she closes the perimeter gate and walks away, being told by Spirit
not to look back. Apparently, this was a very unhappy previous life for
Helana...through this visit we have both collected our Auras from the
Past....see AppendixII. One Soul, Past Lives.
The Business meeting complete, we are invited to stop for dinner and
then spend the whole evening talking spiritual matters; the introduction
to the couple came from a friend whose wife was a Client of mine,
before she died of cancer. The friend Godfrey has set himself the
mission of wishing to communicate with his deceased wife Susan, not
only to find-out that there is a 'Life-after-Death', but also to ask her
permission before he feels able to have another female relationship.
KEYPOINTS HR12
a) Where-ever we travel we leave an 'Aura-trail', very
much like a finger-print; but this Energy-Trail is part
of our Soul, and does influence the Environment we pass
over or through.
b) At times it may become necessary to recover our Aura-
Trail, for in this way the strength of our Soul is
increased. This recovery may well happen when we revisit
a location after many years.
c) The presence of the Aura-trail explains why we feel
comfortable when we return to certain locations.
d) It is not always desirable to collect our Aura-Trail,
for in so doing, we may remove the 'lightening'
influence from that location.

5.22 At the last minute I decide to return to Aylesbury by way of Hungerford and to use the A4 rather than the M4. We are asked by Spirit to park in the High Street. We are then asked to help the Spirits of some of the children; sixteen of whom who were murdered in Hungerford by a gunman who went berserk in 1987.

We are told that some of these children have still not accepted that they are dead. We join hands and say prayers.

The Spirits are collected by Angels and taken to Heaven. We sit and cry, in wonderment that we could have helped to recover these Souls.

KEYPOINTS   HR13

a) Many Spirits do not accept that their Earth life has ended. This can be a major problem for these Souls can end up wandering aimlessly about the Earth-Plane; they then become darker and darker losing what-ever enlightenment they have previously gained.

b) It all stems back to Freewill and Choice! We can choose to progress Spiritually, or to ignore the opportunity, to love or to hate, to move to Heaven or to remain on the Earth-Plane and to stagnate, to be born again or to need to be pushed.!

5.23 Helana is given a new Spirit Guide called Samuel. Samuel is Helana's fourth Guide.

 Judith in trance delivers a message to Helana: ' Samuel is honoured to be Helana's Guide, She is truly blessed. Helana must turn to Samuel only for true guidance; other Spirit who come to her are naughty! Helana must, must, must raise her Spirit more, She must question all messages given, she must think through every possibility.'

KEYPOINTS HR14

a) It is possible for 'naughty' Spirits to pretend to be your Guide and to bring you incorrect or mischievous messages.

b) It is preferable to be introduced to your Guide by a Mentor, you will come to recognise your Guide's messages by the words and expressions used. It is also very reassuring if a physical signal can also be agreed between you.

5.24 Lorna had bought me a new shaving-brush for a wet-shave. I kept the brush in the downstairs Cloakroom where I washed and shaved daily. On the morning of the 20th, to my amazement, there was a column of ants from the floor, up and across the sink, to the shaving-brush which was completely smothered. I dropped the brush into the waste-bin.

There were no ants anywhere else in the room and I never saw ants in the room again!

KEYPOINT HR15

Helana removing the influence of Lorna! Thoughts cause Actions!

5.25 Helana receives a message from Jesus encouraging her to spread the word about the Spirit World...'You will be guided what to say'... 'You are to relocate to Ireland; Judith is to join you there, but she will travel separately and she will live in a house close-by'.
We are also told that Judith has been my mother and Helana's sister in previous lives.
KEYPOINTS HR16
a) Spirit can and do introduce thoughts into your Mind.
b) Judith and Helana are members of my Peer-Group.

5.26 Helana confirms in Spirit writing that she is pregnant, the child is to be a daughter, and is to be named RACHAEL.

5.27 Jesus continues: 'History will repeat itself unless John obtains his Spiritual Awareness and the 'Chains of the Past are broken, true wealth is not in material possessions, but in Nature and in love...Your previous lives have been a cycle of wealth to non-wealth; you need to analyse carefully the causes and the effect, so that these can be changed. Understanding is necessary for you to be able to gain compassion, then you will be able to help Others.'
KEYPOINTS HR17
a) History does repeat itself until or unless we learn the lessons necessary for us to progress.
b) It is not unacceptable to have wealth or talents, but unless that wealth or those talents are shared and used for the betterment of Others, they will be taken away in this or subsequent lives.
c) The purpose for our lives is to achieve love, and for our Souls to learn the lessons and to gain the understanding. An appreciation of Beauty and Nature and the wonder of life is a good starting point for learning to understand and to begin to share your talents with Others.
d) When you have achieved your Spiritual Awareness, it is then possible to reach the understanding and to be able to break the cycle of History.

5.28 'Helana and your Spirit are entwined together now, for always, and for Eternity, whether you are physically together or not. The bond of love between you is so strong that it will enable you to heal others. Helana still grieves from the loss of a child in Biblical Times; now is the opportunity for you both to gather all your children together, and to see through the life of a child, from beginning to end, for both of you.'

5.29 Helana has a vision of an Eagle carved in granite, close to a pillar, on stony, hilly, rocky land, but it is flat near to the Eagle. We are told that we need to locate this.

5.30 On Friday, 22nd May...I take a semen sample to the Churchill Hospital in Oxford, for a re-test; if Helana was pregnant then it certainly would be miraculous and even more so if I could not have made her pregnant.!!...I am to keep this happening secret and not to seek publicity of any kind. This was in direct conflict to a previous message which asked me to make Church Leaders and Others aware of the special relationship between Helana and me.

(High Spirit have overridden the previous message from my Spirit Guide, as they wish to avoid any possibility of a repetition of the slaughter caused by King Herod in Biblical Times!)

KEYPOINTS HR18
a)A hierarchy exists in the world of Spirit.
b)It is be important to ensure that messages come from the highest level possible, particularly when they are of a profound nature.

5.31 The approach for appointments with representatives of the Catholic, Church of England and Elim Churches which I have made, are cancelled. Spirit have recommended that these meetings are delayed until my words are fully guided. That night Helana could not sleep. We have met with Judith and her Spirit is in need of love. Also the Spirits of the Hungerford children are coming to her, and we are asked to return to Hungerford.

5.32 Accordingly, on Saturday, 23rd May....we return to Hungerford and are asked to walk slowly through the town. We are asked to buy flowers and take coffee in one of the Hotels. The Spirits of the children come to us to say thank you. The flowers were a present from them; it was very moving and the tears rolled down my face.
In the afternoon we visited friends, Gerry and Pam near Didcot; and Jan in Chipping Norton, and then made our way to Hook Norton. I needed to visit some folks there. As I approached the house Helana suddenly stopped and would go no further. This was highly embarrassing and led to the loss of the friendship. In writing we learnt that their house was inhabited by a dark Spirit who was jealous and resentful of their presence.
He objected to the many alterations they were responsible for to the property. We offered to 'clear' the property for them but the wife said she was quite capable of sorting anything herself. They dismissed our actions as rude and the conversation as ridiculous. Jesus had promised to be with us, to protect us, whilst we did this work.

KEYPOINT HR19
Some people will never listen to you, they will not believe in Spirit or Ghosts or Apparitions. Their Minds are closed, and there is little you can say or do to influence them. When you meet these people, walk away and save your breath.

5.33 It is to be part of Helana's work to help recover these 'lost' Souls. We realised weeks later that she needed to face these situations; her own Spirit Guide, Samuel, was being somewhat over-protective; but by doing this she was not able to learn from the experience, or to carry-out the recovery work intended.

5.34 We plan to marry in October 1998, a Spiritualist church wedding. We decide to visit my friends Cor and Arien in Holland after the wedding. A honeymoon in Ireland, pre-wedding, and a holiday in France in 1999. 'The wedding-dress is to be green velvet and white flowers are to be purchased. 'Many will be invited, but many will not attend' We are told not to be concerned by this as the Church will be filled with Spirits.

5.35 I am told that Helana has the role to lead, guide and show the way forward to me. I must allow Helana to guide me. I MUST, MUST, MUST, learn to appreciate Beauty in all things.
Through hard work and application, obedience and compassion are the essential features which I need to find.
KEYPOINTS HR20
I am asked to:
a) Study the life of Jesus the Christ, and to allow him into my Heart.
b) Learn about People, Plants, Trees and the Animal Kingdom.
c) Learn to understand about all the Emotions: Grief, Pain, Sorrow, Love.
d) Listen to the words of songs, many have Spiritual significance…especially those of John Lennon. His Spirit comes regularly to Helana to help her.
e) Have complete faith and trust in Spiritual matters. …I do not need to study the Bible, as everything I need to know will be given by Spirit.

5.36 We are asked to arrange a short visit to Ireland; we will be guided as to where and when to go. We are told that :
'IRELAND is the heart of the World…if Ireland can be healed, the rest of the World will follow.
ENGLAND is the cleansing centre of the World.'

5.37 At this time Helana was pursuing her divorce settlement with Mervin, her ex-husband. They were divorced but there had never been any financial settlement and Helana was scratching an existence in one-room of the family home in Kings Sutton, Oxon. Her one and only real friend was Judith. The message is received from Spirit, that Helana is not to sell herself short; it is necessary spiritually for her to spell-out to Mervin the cost to her of all their years together.

She is to meet with solicitors prior to the Court case. Following the settlement, some monies are to be set-aside for her children.

KEYPOINT HR21

Spirit believe-in, and work towards achieving, Justice and Fairness in all matters.

5.38 On Bank Holiday Monday, 25th May,

a)I am asked by Spirit again, if I wish to continue with the gaining of my Spiritual Awareness, or, do I wish to walk away.

...I choose to continue.

b)Helana regressed in her sleep that night, back to Catherine, and also to a lifetime in Caernarfon Castle, in Wales; there is a need to heal the Past. Apparently, I was killed on my wedding-day to Helana. She thereafter locked herself away in the Castle...another unhappy lifetime!!

c)Jesus confirms: 'A move is necessary for you both to Northern Ireland, there is spiritual work for you to do there'.

d)We need to be able to move quickly, and a job-change will be necessary for me. Abel (Helana's son) and Edwin (my son) are to join us in Ireland. Ford will be a frequent visitor, Brian not so frequently. Helen (my daughter) has her own path to follow.

e)We wake up refreshed and are told that our Spirits have been taken during the night, for learning and relaxation .

5.39 Tuesday 26th May, is an odd Day:

a) I drive to London to see my mother. My deceased father Ted is sad, for Joyce my mother has stated that she has no wish to pursue any Medium contact with him. I tell her about the proposed move to Ireland and the possible change of job. She advises caution.

b) I return to Banbury for a work appointment and then visit Bloxham Spiritualist Church, for there is a circle development meeting which I have registered to join. Inside are twenty plus people in the Hall; we sit quietly after prayers and commence a guided meditation.

 Suddenly, I start coughing loudly and cannot stop, I make my apologies and have to leave the Hall.

Outside Judith is waiting for me; she wishes to question me about my relationship with Helana, who is having doubts about her lack of interest in the physical side of our relationship. Patience is advised for I am told that she has led a very sheltered life!

c) At 23.00 hrs. a message is received from Samuel, Helana's guide, Helana is in Trance:

'A new phase is to commence in your life together; your love and friendship will grow. Spirit are pleased with the progress you have made. Your Spirits have many lessons to learn from this and previous lives; you need to understand these lessons. Help will be given to you and there will be more regressions and visions. You are to re-live your past lives so that you can gain understanding. Your time together is to be precious for the World and its Peoples.

We are all God's children; Helana sends love to me and to many throughout the World. We are told that our Spirits work together whilst we sleep.'

KEYPOINTS HR22
a) For Spiritual progression to take place, it is necessary first to heal the Past.
b) Your Spirit Guides will not allow you to participate in spiritual work, if the spirits of those around to you are not in harmony.
c) The Spirits work whilst we sleep, or they may be taken for learning, relaxation or healing.

5.40 Helana lays-out three china birds on the table and three candles are lit. The mother bird is representative of herself; the other two are fledglings, one me John, the other is Philip; the candles represent each of us. I am asked to understand that there is no competition in this lifetime between Philip and me for Helana's love. Her love protects us both and our Spirits are entwined together.

5.41 Helana has been regressed to previous lives and so is aware of so much pain and suffering and sadness...
'She cannot forget about Philip, but his memory and Spirit have been dimmed for this lifetime...The conscious mind of Helana is yours John, the Spirit of Helana is yours, the heart of Helana is yours; but she also shares love with many others, friends, family, etc. You John, need to understand that the Spirit never forgets so that when the minds of you become as one, then you should not fear or be confused, by the thoughts in Helana's mind.
Do not let human emotions stand in the way of your relationship. Helana will be completely faithful, dedicated and devoted to you. She has opened up completely to you; you share a closeness of perfect love. Helana was asked by the Spirit of Philip not to forget him, she does not break a promise, the memories of Jack are within her conscious mind. You need to understand this and all will be well. Your three Spirits have been together in many previous Lives.'

KEYPOINT HR23
It is possible to regress to learn about previous lives.

5.42 'Rejoice today John, for the Spirit of Jack has been released for this lifetime, it will now sleep, and the pathway is clear ahead for Helana and you. The man Philip has chosen not to progress spiritually in this lifetime; he has built so many barriers and will now need to learn when he passes to Spirit.'
I begin to feel a fullness in my Stomach, an ache. This I am told is my Spirit awakening and beginning to rise. I will also become aware of Helana's Spirit within me; this may lead to an awareness of previous lives.

It is necessary to bring-out all the past unhappiness and sorrow through tears, so that the Past can be cleansed and healed.

'You have found total love with Helana, both Spiritual and Human.'

KEYPOINTS HR24

a) We are all originally from the one GOD-SPIRIT.

b) Everyone needs to know that they are loved and cared-for.

c) We, even Hitler, or starving Peoples, or Cripples, chose this life for the experience it offered to them or to Others.

d) You can choose NOT to progress Spiritually, but then you must be prepared to accept the consequences of that decision.

5.43 KEYPOINTS HR25

a) Give love and you will receive love

b) Give pain or hate and you will receive pain or hate.

c) Everything you give will eventually return to you.

d) Always look for the Good in Everything and Everybody:, every Action, every Deed, every Thought.

e) What goes around, comes around........is a true dictum.

f) Everything happens for a reason. All is given to show and to teach so that you, your Soul, can learn and can develop.

5.44 I become aware of a 'hat effect' around my head. This I am told is representative of me being a 'soldier of Christ' and shows that teaching and learning is taking place. It may also be caused by Spirit sitting too closely on my head, I can request them to withdraw.

KEYPOINTS HR26

a) Beware what second-hand Objects are brought into your home; these hold the imprint of previous owners and their experiences.

b) Objects can attract their previous owners' Spirits who may bring sadness or unhappiness etc. and may affect your personal relationships...even a programme or a letter may be sufficient.

5.45 KEYPOINT HR27

Spirit take words literally. Be very cautious before you WISH for anything, and do not use the word NEVER. Remember every thought and word is heard as well as your actions seen.

5.46 In response to my question of Spirit. I am told that the Pope and the Archbishop of Canterbury only pay lip-service to their positions of power. They could do so much to change the World for the betterment of Humanity and for Spirituality; but they do not. This is their Choice.

5.47 Both John Lennon and Princess Diana come regularly to Helana, their presences' have helped Helana to improve her Spiritual Awareness whilst she was alone. John Lennon's music was a comfort and he became a spiritual companion to her.
John Lennon requests that I should not be jealous, and asks my permission to give to Helana a rose for her garden when she returns to Spirit. I agree.

5.48 We are told that there is a great deal of healing work to be performed in Ireland; clear instructions and guidance will be given. We are to achieve peace and calm within so that we can receive the messages. I need to find time to sit quietly so as to develop my communication skills. It is a balance between my free-will, and the need for me to understand about Spirit...I need also to learn to read my heart so I know what feels right.
KEYPOINTS HR27
a) There needs to be a balance between living the Human life and achievement of the Spiritual need.
b) Communication with Spirit is influenced by our ability to be 'at peace within.' You need to be calm and peaceful to achieve good accurate messages.

5.49 I am told that: 'I need to slow down the pace of my life in all its aspects. I need to show to Spirit that I can cope with a slower pace of life. I need to slow down and find calmness in my driving!...I must tell Spirit what I wish to achieve, what I NEED to achieve, and to ask for their help and guidance. It will not be possible for me a live a Spiritual life unless I slow down. Changes in little ways will bring big rewards.
KEYPOINTS HR28
a) You need to Ask, Inform, Request, Pray to GOD, for what you desire and seek to happen.
b) Politely, tell your Spirit Guide what you wish to achieve each day.

5.50 On the night of Saturday 30th May, we are woken at 03.00hrs.by the sound of strapping (ten lashes). We are told that both Albert (father) and Richard (me) used to beat Catherine. Helana wakes-up coughing and her Spirit is in distress.
I have the vision of a sword raised by one arm...It is said to represent my need for strength and protection; ready for the Battle which is about to commence on the Earth-Plane between the forces of Good and Evil. Helana hears the sound of the hymn 'Onward Christian soldiers'.

5.51 On the Sunday, we travel to Weston-Super-Mare and visit some friends, on-route we stop at the Catherine Wheel Pub and sit in the garden. There is the sound of Church bells, and a blackbird sings. We are told that our Spirits are together as one and that our marriage has been made in Heaven.

We choose to travel via Bibury, where Helana has a conversation with the Spirit of her deceased father, Tom.

We pass by the Tetbury Arboretum and are asked to re-visit Westonbirt. Helana passes-out between the A46 and the M4 - a reaction to Spirit presence in the Area. On-route, we stop at the Full Quart Public House, and are told of Spirit plans for us.

We are to establish a HOME-FARM in Ireland, which is also to be a Spiritual retreat, to offer bed and breakfast accommodation, a Healing centre, a Guest-house, a childrens' Farm with Donkeys and an Animal Sanctuary. We are to establish a cottage industry operation, and to live off the land, Guests will also bring produce to us.

5.52 That evening Helana has a vision of 'pulling back a child and saving its life'...this is representative of a change to her Destiny. She hears the song 'Silent Night'.

We catch the last few minutes of the TV , which shows the film 'Dancing with Wolves', I am asked to watch this video and to draw parallels between the leaders of the Indian Tribes and the leaders of the Churches in Ireland.

5.53 On Sunday 31st May...I travel to a Rugby Referee Course in Taunton, Somerset. During the day Helana drives around and returns with a photo of King Arthur's sword held in a stone...see AppendixII. One Soul, Past Lives.

5.54 We decide finally to use the Spiritualist Church in Bloxham for our wedding, Judith is to be a matron-of -honour. We agree to use the music Jerusalem, Imagine, You are my Man, etc....we agree to ask Abel, Helana's son to arrange the music.

A message is received from Jesus:

'Do you John, wish still to continue with the Spiritual work?..

I respond yes. 'Then, you must be careful not to hurt Helana with your words, your thoughts or your whispers. Everything is heard. You will experience the pains of childbirth. Healing will be given to your Spirit, as requested by Helana. You must clarify your thoughts and ensure that what you ask for is what you really need. Do not joke so much, as this can lead to misunderstandings. Remember what you do affects Others. Allow your lives to flow, keep your hearts pure. I am always with you to guide and support you.'

You have begun to climb the 'ladder of life'. You will be together now and always. Helana holds the future of the World in her hands'.

KEYPOINT HR29
Everything is known by Spirit, Every thought is known, If we joke, our words can be taken literally, so it is necessary to be careful in every sense!

5.55 We stay-over in Weston-Super-Mare at a bed & breakfast Guest-House chosen by Spirit, this was quite an experience of what NOT to do:
* the toilet did not flush
* there were no drinks in the room
* the shower rail had broken, and was half-off the wall
* the room was very shabby
* the towels were ragged and worn
* there was no toilet paper in the toilet
* there was a water-leak on the sink in our bedroom
* the Owner was too apologetic, and ate humble-pie, to the extent of disgust...uhg!!

5.56 We visit the City of Bath, the Roman Pump-Rooms, the Royal Crescent, Abbey etc. We are asked to return for another day as well. I feel a strong 'presence' when standing at the end of the Abbey. Our attention is drawn to the 'Jacob's ladder either side of the entrance (the ladder of life). It is a cold day and a steep walk back to the car parked at the Crescent; Helana asks for help and warmth; we are blown up the hill to ' An Irish Blessing'. I definitely feel warmer!

5.57 Helana has a vision of her riding on a Swan through the Sky.... pure, white, graceful, beautiful, with strength from the wings. I am riding on an Eagle alongside her...strong, hunter, fighter.... We are to fly with the birds and ride the clouds together!.

5.58 On Monday 1st.June, I am given a 'cough' to cause me to listen to Spirit whenever decisions or choices are to be made. In this way my awareness of what is right and correct will grow.
(at this time I do not feel confident enough to listen to Spirit, but I am confident to write down 'my Thoughts' and in this way receive the information necessary.)
It is still my choice whether to listen, write or to obey the advice.
I am advised to tell Spirit what I wish to achieve in any day. I am advised to read the book ' Embracing the Beloved', so as to advance my understanding.
KEYPOINT HR30
As we eat we can nourish Others in the World who are in need. Provided that we ask for this to happen:
a) When we chew on the left-side of our mouth this is for our own family and loved-ones.
b) When we chew on the right-hand side of our mouth this then is for the World.
I am told that I need to eat more slowly to allow this to happen! And that there are many Spirits, who feed upon our words of love and sit with us to learn.

71

5.59 The spirit of Phillip comes close to Helana, it is in need of love and protection. I am told that there is no need for jealousy on my part, no harm is done, Helana needs to ask for the Spirit to step-back; it comes to her as a child in need. 'Do not let this incident cloud your judgement!' Praise and blessings are received from Spirit for our progress to date. We will encounter many difficulties, but we will rise above them. We will be given help and guidance.

5.60 Judith predicts that we are to arrange a farewell 'Bash' at the end of September 98, and that we will leave England for Ireland in October 98.
Many people will be jealous and bitter and will call Helana names.
I will lose some of my family!
A warning is given by Judith, for us always to protect ourselves before we do any Spirit-work. She tells tale of a lady who gave crystal healing and ended-up with problems in her shoulder, chest, leg-joints and ankles. Judith was able to relieve her symptoms.
KEYPOINTS HR31
a)**Always protect yourself with the Light and Love of True Spirit before you give healing to anyone...say the words:**
'**Heavenly father, protect me with the Love and Light of GOD. Only allow those who come with love for Mankind to draw near.'**
b)**Before you commence Healing, ALWAYS ADD THE WORDS:**

'**If it be thy Will, according to the Individual's needs.'…where the words 'the Individual' are replaced by 'their' or the name of the person/animal.**
….**for remember, you are not GOD, and it is not your decision that someone, or some creature, is to be healed!**

5.61 Judith's Relationship with her husband Damien is coming to a close.

##

CHAPTER 6. THE PREPARATION

6.00 It is Tuesday, 2nd June 1998, when Helana and I meet with Judith and we meditate together. The following points emerge:

a)Helana is to help me with my work, telesales and letters, so that I can become more financially secure.

b)We should arrange a holiday in Ireland as quickly as we can; we need to decide where we are to live; we need to establish contacts in Ireland.

c)We should fly/drive, using a hire car to minimise Public awareness of our presence.

d)There is a short, thin lady, approx 65-70 years of age who we should buy a property from, we should buy direct (no Agent); she is shrewd and loves animals...I am to become the son she never had.!

e)We are to move in about three months time.

f)Judith is to move also to Ireland and to live close-by to us.; we are all to work closely together.

g)I should aim to achieve Practice Buy-out from my Work as quickly as possible.(*this is a procedure where IF I qualify, I can sell my Financial Business in order to raise Capital ie.a retirement package)*

h)Helana is to try-out the motor-bike with me.(she is reluctant, I have a Honda 750ccVFR)

i)There is a female, a lively, vivacious, blonde, in her twenties, who is about to pass to Spirit as she has reached the limit of her pain threshold. She is to choose to return to help me with my Spirit-work.

j)Helana is to attend Cooking classes, so that she can teach when in Ireland.

k)Helana should learn about Environmental Health, Hygiene and Safety requirements; all required for running a business.

KEYPOINTS TP1

a)Nothing happens without effort and application.

b)It is necessary for US, by OUR own actions to help to bring about what is intended. Spirit can tell us what is expected, they present the choices, but WE choose the Pathway and the timing.

6.01 In order to develop my Awareness, my spirit Hearing, my spirit Vision, I need to prepare myself so that I:

a)Allow time, space, quietness for reflection. I must ask for this learning and these gifts. I must be patient, and must be diligent.

b)Gain peace within my heart...I have been specially chosen

c)Demonstrate patience, love and kindness to myself, and to Others

d)Say to Spirit 'Take my life, I give it Lord to thee'

e)Be humble, subservient, show respect and acknowledge the privilege shown by Spirit to me.

f)Do not carry Guilt, accept situations which have occurred during my lifetime as they were intended for understanding.

g)Forgive myself, LOVE MYSELF for what, and for who I am.

h)Ask my Spirit Guide to resolve and heal certain situations. Let them go.

i)Look inside myself, and see the loving person inside.

KEYPOINT TP2

It is necessary to devote TIME and to demonstrate the qualities of: REFLECTION, LOVE, SERVICE, PATIENCE, DILIGENCE, KINDNESS, DEDICATION, FORGIVENESS, HEALING, INTROSPECTION, HUMILITY, ACCEPTANCE of THE PAST without carrying the GUILT...if you are to be able to gain your Spiritual Awareness.

6.02 Spirit sees the way I am, I am told that I am not seen as someone who will turn-back. There is a tremendous amount of work necessary for me to do. Much time will be necessary, and much painful self-analysis and examination within, if I am to be able to achieve that which is desired. But Spiritual help and love will be given, and it is expected that I will achieve the Goals set for me.

6.03 Judith, in vision, sees Damien, her husband, walking away from her.

6.04 On Wednesday, 3rd June 1998, we are both feeling upset by an altercation and dismissive words from a couple who live in Hook Norton. On the positive side, Helana learns of a £500 legacy due to her from her 'Uncle Grampy'. It has also been arranged for three Estate Agents to value her family house in Kings Sutton; and I feel Spirit presence under my rib-cage for the first time.

KEYPOINTS TP3

a)A sharp pain can be felt beneath the Rib-cage, to the left hand-side for light Spirit, to the right hand-side for dark Spirit, when they come to enter your body. This pain only lasts for a few seconds.

b)The principle point of entry to our Being is located at the lower end of the nape of our neck. You may be able to feel a 'burning sensation' on occasions.

c)You can block Spirit entry, by requesting a Door-Keeper to protect you.

6.05 On Friday, 5th June, at 00.30 hrs, it is my birthday, and greetings are received from Spirit, a beautiful card from Helana, and a present. We are asked to move forwards and to forget the Past. We have been chosen to carry out the work necessary in Ireland...a beautiful land of Mountains, Lakes, Rivers, Trees and Hills...so I am told:

'Helana's love for you will not falter, She has given you her All; her Heart, her Love, her Spirit, her Mind and her Being. She has climbed Mountains and overcome many obstacles to be by your side.

'It has been a struggle and she has shed many tears. Her beautiful eyes have seen much sadness and loneliness, but now, we can see happiness and love of a true kind. No other can fulfil your needs in the same way. Support her in every way, do not falter, do not flirt with others. Do not underestimate the depth of her love for you, nor her beautiful nature. She is a child of Nature, and yours to treasure for the rest of your life. Her love protects you, where-ever you are, her thoughts are never far away from you.

You share such closeness and beautiful love; this is exactly what the child needs so that it can grow in love of a true kind, and find understanding of its place in the Universe. Without this new purpose in your life, John, it would have ended in tears and grief. You have been brought together for the special needs of the World and its People. You have both discovered the love needed at the same time. All is as it should be, the healing process has begun; your lives will now be entwined together for eternity, by a Bond so strong that it cannot be broken; nothing can come between you. ONLY your individual free-wills can change this.'

6.06 'Spirit give to you today, the gift of your Spirits coming together for all Time. The feelings within are a preparation for this day. You will know immediately that Helana's Spirit is within you from the beautiful feeling of warmth, love and peace inside your body. Peace is synonymous with true love...There cannot be anything more wonderful than when your Spirits entwine for the first time.

You John, will be unaware of the greatness of this moment until a future time when peace can be found. You have shared many lives together, but your Spirits have remained separate but within. Once entwined you can never be separated. On another day you will be entwined at an Earthly level.'

KEYPOINTS TP4

a) Spirit talk of two levels of love, the typical Human level is mainly of a sexual nature and is not considered to represent true love in any way.

b) Spirit say FRIENDSHIP is a better indication of true Love.

c) The most powerful Bond is when the SOULS entwine, for then you achieve a completeness of Spirit, Mind and Body which will last FOREVER, through every existence.

d) Whether subsequently the bodies are together is not that important, for the Souls can unite whenever they wish to, every night in your sleep for example.

e) A beautiful feeling within your Body, of warmth and peace will be evidence of the presence of Spirit coming to you in true love.

6.07 'There are special times ahead, reach out, bring to Helana the glory of your love, let her see the Spirit in your eyes, raise yourself to her level. Do this, and Helana's love will be complete; this will enable Helana's Spirit to advance and to help Others. These words come from true Spirit, we sit by Helana's side and have no doubt that you, John, will succeed.

You John are the Spokesman, the Letter-writer, the Messenger, the bringer of Healing to those in need. Your frivolous nature amuses us. Do not lose this, as a lightness of Spirit is sometimes necessary to put across the message. It makes Helana smile, she has laughter in her eyes and smile. We thank you John for bringing Helana into the true light of happiness, and true love. Peace be with you both, allow us to take your words; strive for what is good and beautiful. Go now with peace in your heart, all is to be beautiful. We wish you again a happy birthday and the gift of love is yours.'

6.08 'Helana will have a tough time ahead. Many will wish her un-beautiful things, blame and darkness of thoughts; be it family or friends, dismiss them as friends of the Past. A wealth of knowledge is to be gained from the Hook Norton experience. Let this experience pass, it is their loss.' (this concerned the presence of a dark Spirit called 'Dan', who was becoming a threat to the children living at the house. Jesus had requested us to visit the property and to clear it of this Ghost from the Past. It was necessary to follow a special procedure to achieve this, but the folks living there were dismissive, unbelieving and rude, so the exorcism never took place.)

6.09 I am given a coughing-fit by drinking too much wine! July 17th is given as the date for us to go to Ireland. I am to explore the possibility of a transfer within my Organisation to their Northern Ireland office. We are to consider an immediate move from Aylesbury to another location near to Enstone. Helana's feet are tapping rapidly, a sign of progress, and the need to move-on. (Aylesbury and Banbury are both poor locations for spirit reception)

KEYPOINT TP5
Certain locations are poor for Spirit communication. This has been caused by their dark history, which has created a covering shadow and shield to the Light, and so blocks and restricts the ease of communication.

6.10 At 12 mid-night. A message is received from Jesus, he is pleased with our progress. There is to be no turning back. I feel my Spirit raised within me. Jesus speaks through Helana:
' Helana is crying, sobbing profusely, in need of your strength John. This is a sad day for her, '

'You have no idea of how great is her Spirit, and how it suffers and bears pain for so many and still protects you. We struggle with our words, for Helana does not wish us to inform you John, of the conflict within her. However, you need to gain an understanding. Be re-assured there is no need for jealousy.'

6.11 'The tears shed by Helana are for the Spirit of Jack. It is the parting of the ways, they were born as twins and they remain as twins; with the entwining of your Spirit, John, with Helana's, this is no longer possible. They will remain as brother and sister, but there is to be no more physical contact in this lifetime. Jack (Philip's) Spirit knows this.'

6.12 'You John, will now begin to feel the pain and suffering and other emotions which Helana feels. The love shared between you will bring to you all the healing which is necessary at this time. There is a great deal to be achieved in the next few days; not only in your daily living, but also in your sleeping hours. Strength will be given and rest assured. You will be protected at all times. Helana will need your support and tenderness at all times, but especially at this time.'
KEYPOINT TP6
When the Spirits are entwined, the human Emotions are shared also.

6.13 'Your work for Spirit has begun. Your work is to be shared with Helana and with Judith. A greatness of achievement will be obtained in this lifetime; your work together will create a Community and a History. It is for this reason you have been brought together, and the presence of Helana in your life has enabled this to be.'

6.14 'Go now in peace, with calm and serenity at your side. You are to be placed in the land called Ireland to perform certain tasks, these will be given when needed. You will be guided in every way. Remember, Helana is a fragile flower, but, so strong...there are many things you must learn and understand, but all will be given'...
Helana sighs and I feel the sigh within me.

6.15 Helana is given a vision of the 'Book of Life', in blue with gold writing. This book for-tells the future of the Universe, and is also mentioned in the New Testament...(John)
KEYPOINTS TP7
a) There exists a Book Of Life which outlines the future of our Universe, and which is used as a reference to all significant happenings.
 b) Your Spirit 'flips' when it recognises Spirits that it has known previously; in previous lives. Spirit recognition occurs throughout our hives. Our eyes change when this occurs.

77

c) Everyone needs to be very careful not to confuse Spirit recognition with Human emotional feelings. Many relationships fail because of this confusion in our Minds.

d) Spiritual love can confuse and affect human Feelings, your Relationships and your Perception of Others.

e) Our Spirits always search for PERFECT love. Your Partner should be right for us in every respect. If you find that you have made a wrong choice, you should leave that relationship, and continue to search for true love elsewhere.

f) Without SPIRITUAL AWARENESS it is impossible for you to know that you have made a correct choice. All that one can do, is to learn to know oneself, so that you are aware of your criteria for the future.

g) Forgive yourself for previous Relationships which have failed. Learn from your past Relationships.

(I need to review my past Life, to forgive myself. This is the key to Spiritual progression. Everyone is searching, Everyone is doing the same...In previous lives I have been Helana's child. Philip has been our child.)

6.16 It is 7th June, at 00.30 hrs. A message is received from Jesus.
'My dear ones, do not forget who I am. In many ways you think of me as the Great One, but I am just a Man. Do not forget also that you have the strength and the power within your Spirit to perform the Miracles; which were performed in my lifetime on this Earth-Plane.
I have seen many lives come and go, but none so great as this one. You have travelled far my dear ones. The time has come to bring you together in a way which will last for Eternity. We have asked you John, many times to confirm:
(a) Do you wish to share your heart with Helana?...my answer 'I give her my lifetime.'
(b) Do you wish to change your mind? ..my answer 'No'

Jesus continues: 'Helana has made the same choices, in this way the coming together of both your Spirits will be...Slowly you will feel the presence of each other within...John, take the same position as Helana. (*this refers to the way I was sitting)* .The bells are ringing in Heaven.... A purity of heart and mind will exist between you...Share not your bodies with another....imaginary rings are placed upon our fingers,....Helana first....Your families are present with us today in Spirit to witness this Ceremony....The child will not be born out of wedlock....

A meal is prepared for you.....Helana can see this....the fruit represents your labours.....the gates of Heaven are now open to you both.....indeed it will be Paradise! Together you will reside in Spirit and on the Earth... I, Jesus, will always remain by your side...'
'Take our love, and the light of true Spirit who bring to you these words of Truth, Wisdom and Understanding....May your hearts rejoice with the love that is found, as ours do on this day.....Sleep easy now, with your Minds at peace....All is as it should be.'

6.17 'You John, are trying to prove something to yourself; this is not necessary. You have a choice to make. How much easier would your life be, if it was not one of providing for Others. Let go the guilt...the pressure for you to work the way that you do will be considerably reduced. With pressure such as this, what chance have you to relax? It is not possible. ....

(I have been paying maintenance of £ 300- £700 per month for many years.)

To alter your situation will cause a great deal of animosity. Your mother will have a great deal to say, Helana will be blamed. This is not emotional blackmail. We cannot say stop working! but if you change your lifestyle, then you will not be surrounded by people who take and give nothing. You have the capability of loving perfectly, for loving sake...not for reward. You could choose to continue your work as a source of introductions; you need to use your initiative to solve these problems'.

KEYPOINTS TP8
a) As you give, so you shall receive
b) You always have the choice of changing your lifestyle. It is not necessary, nor desirable, nor intended, that you sacrifice your own life totally for the benefit of Others. You must also have a quality of life, so that you can pursue your own objectives.
c) Spirit will not do everything for you, only by your own struggles, and your own suffering, do you learn and retain the value of the lessons.

6.18 'See your life John, as it truly is. Spend as much time as you can dealing with the guilt within your head. There is always more than one-side to any situation. No one does anything without a reason, even though they may not be aware of what that reason is. Take-off your blinkers, you also have the right to live your life.'

(these words refer specifically to why Elsa chose to become pregnant)

KEYPOINT TP9
No one does ANYTHING without a reason, even though they may not be aware of that reason in their conscious Mind when the event occurs.

6.19 'Do your utmost John, to ensure that each of your children realises how much that you love them. Have no favourites, they are all individuals. Your mother has the deepest of feelings for you, it is sad that she cannot convey this to you. She has not always approved of your lifestyle'

KEYPOINT TP10

Not everyone has the character or capability of demonstrating their true Feelings. This is so sad, for sometimes opportunities are missed and misunderstandings occur which can live with us throughout our lives and can affect all of OUR feelings and relationships.

(this message refers not only to my mother, but also to the man Bryan who took his own life through a failure to express his true feelings for Helana)

6.20 Jesus continues.. 'You John, must slow down your pace of life. Slow down your hands, your mind, your car. A decision will be taken in Ireland. You must demonstrate a willingness to accept the slower pace of life. Do you love Helana enough? You must follow her guidance and have trust and faith in her. There is no need for jealousy or anger. Accept the moment, leave behind the Past and everything you have previously known. Are you prepared to accept the new life, and trust in Spirit?

KEYPOINTS TP11

a) Should you wish to live a Spiritual life, it may be necessary to change the pace of your lifestyle to one which is more in tune with Spiritual requirements; additionally it will be necessary to lose the guilt from the Past, to heal the Past, and then to leave behind the Past.

b) You cannot walk forwards and still drag with you all the baggage of emotion and feelings from your past life. How can you form new relationships while you are still injured by the old ones? You will always keep the love, the memories, and the good times; but when you decide to 'move-on', it is necessary to break with the Past. However painful this may seem to be at the time.

(IF, the Past is serving only to restrict your progress. remember what you do affects all those about you and in your Peer-Group)

c) Accept that the Past has brought YOU to the Present; without the past experiences, YOU would not have the ability, nor the motivation, nor the opportunity to move-on. Be thankful and be grateful to those who have brought you, and helped to prepare you for this new decision, new choice, new Pathway. ALL IS FOR LEARNING!

6.21 On 11th June, Jesus writes: 'A time and a place have been found; you will find the joy of living within this time and place. You have discovered many things this day; the closeness between you both has been found satisfactory to both you, and to Spirit'

'It has taken many tears, but we feel these have not been wasted. The oceans of your lives will now start to fill with fishes. The nourishment of life, and calmer waters.

Dreams will be found in this land of Ireland. Think now towards your future and all will be blessed. We have realised in Spirit the true nature of your Souls, and for this reason will allow you to continue. There will be no parting of the waves unless you allow it to happen. Find peace, let our guidance guide you safely on your journey. You will always remain in the light and love of true Spirit. Take the hand John of this lady, many times, and allow her to guide you safely. Go in peace now'

KEYPOINTS TP12

a) **High Spirit continually monitor your thoughts, feelings, actions, and objectives. All are taken into account before any chosen Pathway can be successfully followed.**

b) **Should your motives be wrong or misguided, then you will be deflected to an alternate pathway until the necessary lessons have been learned. In the same way that you must not build a house upon slippery sand, for it will surely collapse. You will be tested at every stage of your progress, temptation will be placed in your pathway and the choices given to you, to test your sincerity and to verify that you are worthy of the final construction.**

6.22 'I, Jesus, am here with you, to help you make the right choices...the World is in need. You John, have a special relationship to Helana who washed my feet when I was on the Cross. She helped me with my suffering when it was needed; now, I am here in Spirit World, and she on the Earth-Plane acts on my behalf.'

KEYPOINTS TP13

a) **Jesus is confirming that our Souls live many lives, and that nothing we do is ever forgotten.**

b) **Spirit will guide and help us to reach our Goals. The Goals may be personal to the individual Soul, or they may have far wider repercussions as is suggested here.**

c) **High Spirit tell me that this point in Human History is a water-shed; the choices made in this generation, by Humanity, will decide forever the PATHWAY of the EARTH and ALL the life-forms on the Planet.**

For this reason, the SOULS of those who contributed 2,000 years ago have chosen to return now. It is crucial to change, to lighten the Aura of the EARTH; this must happen, and WILL happen with or without Humanity.

(Spirit construct our Experiences to present us with the learning opportunity, not all is always as it seems. The roles played between Helana and Constance were initially reversed, in historical context; so as to convince me of the suitability of Helana to be my partner, and my tutor)

6.23 The following morning, Helana is very distressed. Her Spirit is bruised and crying. She fears the loss of me, and the spirit of Jack is coming too close to her, causing her to be distressed with feelings of rejection. Helana feels sick and has heart-pain and a headache. She sleeps for two hours before she recovers. We then plan our trip to Ireland and the day progresses well. Helana's Guide tells her that she needs to learn to raise her Spirit above that of Jack's. She will need to use music, will-power, and activity to dismiss him from her mind. We travel later to Worcester for my business, and Helana is affected by the Spirits we encounter on our journey.

KEYPOINTS TP14
a)Many Spirits have chosen to remain on the Earth-Plane. These Spirits may be disturbed by man-made works; such as Road or House construction or alterations. These Spirits need help, and it is to be part of Helana's work to help recover them. ...(we call these lost Spirits, 'Ghosts')
b)All Souls, eventually Everyone, will need to be recovered in order for Mankind to progress.
c)Keeping the Mind busy, helps to detract from self-pity and outside Spiritual influences.
d)There is a power struggle between Helana's and Jack's spirits. Jack's spirit can only influence Helana if she allows it to. Her mind needs to be stronger and to TELL him to go away, but will she? There are many other things she can do…..see Appendix IV

6.24 We have arranged a party at our home on 7th June. It is a combination of my birthday and an engagement Party. I am disappointed that some fifty people do not attend, but I am delighted that TONY does. It is forty-five years since we last played together as children when I lived in Mansfield. It is good to see Tony who has suffered badly recently. Both his wife and mother have recently died of cancer, he has suffered depression and has had to sell his building Business. Tony was the man Cain who killed me when I was Abel.
…see AppendixII. One Soul, Past Lives.

KEYPOINT TP15
There is a coming together now, in the Year 2,000, and in the near future, of many Souls from the Past. These Souls can choose now if they so wish, to contribute to the profound changes due to occur on the Earth-Plane in the new Millennium.

6.25 I have decided that I need to lose weight as my blood-pressure is border-line high, and I do not wish to commence to take tablets. *(my weight has crept-up to 225lbs.from a more comfortable 200lbs).*

Spirit tell me; ' Do not over-ride Helana's words or actions as often as you do. Lessons are to be learnt for the good of both of you. You John must listen carefully to everything Helana says, it will stand you in good stead for the future. Your ways are spiritual, but a channelling of energies in the right direction is necessary. You must speak clearly to your Guides. They hear, they see, they know your heart. You will be guided, helped and comforted in your Journey through life. You and Helana are as One, you see as One; you have a special responsibility as well. Listen to Helana's words, watch her actions. The Book of Life has been re-written to allow for your coming together. It will be shown to Helana again'

6.26 On the Tuesday, 9th June, 1998, on route to London for business, we visit my Auntie GRACE in Feltham, Middlesex, she is 90 years of age and the last surviving member of my Father's immediate family.
She gives to us many plant cuttings and we obtain a picture of GERTRUDE ALICE my father's Mother 'Gertie'.
I book the Irish hop, via Liverpool, for Dublin on June 22nd...
Spirit tell us :
a) I am not to worry about my work...it will be sorted
b) Five days will be sufficient time for our visit to Ireland
c) Jealous Spirits are creating 'space' between Helana and me.
....(Bryne and Jack)
d) Helana is also needing to cope with my father Ted's Spirit which comes very close.
e) Helana's mother will soon pass to Shadow-Lands, as she has not progressed, and has restricted Tom, Helana's father in the development of his Spiritual Awareness.
f) Anne's mother is also about to pass to Spirit.
KEYPOINTS TP16
a) Your attitudes and feelings may be affected by the presence of other spirits
b) To restrict or cause another to turn away from Spirit is a SIN.
c) The timing of 'Death' is known, and prepared for, by Spirit.

6.27 To help me relax, I should press my third index finger with my thumb and hold the pressure for five seconds. We experience:
a) Continual ringing of my telephone at home, when Spirit wish me to cease working.
b) My volvo car tape-deck plays silently when Spirit wish to communicate with us.

83

c) My hearing sensitivity is increasing...the clock ticks are getting louder, it is becoming painful, with the noise, when I wash the dishes!

6.28 A message is received via Judith. 'Your Spiritual work will not be within the confines of four walls...You are struggling with many problems in your mind...You need to relax to enable Spirit to be of assistance...There is a problem John, in your workplace....There is someone there who does not have your best interests at heart.. Beware!..it will not be the end of your world if this financial work ceases....You have so much to offer in other walks of life...Many choose to use you for this purpose, but there are those who can manage without...
viz. Elsa...We see many £'s disappearing without benefit to you.....This is not correct...You need to choose now where your duty lies...Do not turn your back, merely assess what happens to the money given to Elsa. *(maintenance money paid for the children, Edwin and Helen)*

6.29 Albert comes to us again, via Helana, and he asks for my forgiveness for the past suffering he has caused. I concur with this request. Helana is also asked to forgive the spirit of Jack for the stress and pain which his actions have caused to her, and also to me.

6.30 On Saturday, 13th June 1998, we are told that there are many feelings around us of jealousy. We are asked to rise above these, and not to allow them to influence our relationship. 'You need to understand the seriousness of this time together. Is your love-Bond strong enough to carry you through all the changes that are necessary to your lives?. Can you John, accept the new life and all which this implies? The children to be given are needed not only for now, but also to bring healing to your lives. Are you ready for this change? Do you have the strength in your character and the compassion in your heart? Spirit wish you to continue, but the choice is yours'

6.31 'Spirit has no doubt that your love is beautiful and strong enough, but, the love needs to be felt in your heart. Helana has made the commitment, for this reason only are you John, allowed to continue. There will be so much gained by you both for future lifetimes. Helana will be strong enough for you both to climb to the greatest heights. Helana's happiness is Spirit's main concern...if she is not happy, it will prevent her from sharing so much with the World and its People'.
...(throughout this period of Time, I have felt as if I have been walking a tight-rope, If I do not achieve the depth of love within my heart, the compliance with Helana's and Spirits' wishes, the personal commitment, if Helana is not happy, if she decides to walk away, then I will not be able to continue!!)

KEYPOINTS TP17
a) Souls retain their Personality and Feelings when they pass to Spirit-World.(ie.Character)
These are retained until the necessary lessons have been learned. It is incorrect for us on the Earth-Plane to believe that all is perfect when we pass-over.
b) There are many levels of existence in the Spirit-World, and these are associated with the individual's level of understanding...
(this agrees with the Spiritualist Churches understanding of seven Planes of Existence, with Heaven situated at level three)
c) Happiness is a desirable feature for you All to achieve. If you are not happy or at peace with yourselves, how can you then offer love and light to Others?

6.32 Helana has a vision of 'stormy waters' ahead.
She is told by her Guide, that our relationship together will have many trials and tribulations. We will need to discuss our feelings and talk openly with each other, so that we are able to resolve differences when they arise. Helana will not be dominated by me.
(Helana's Guide is very protective of her)

6.33 We are told that High Spirit do not always fully understand Human Emotions.
KEYPOINT TP18
There exist a number of levels of Hierarchy in Spirit-World, as there are on the Earth-Plane. The difference in Spirit is that as you rise to the higher levels, you become more remote from the every day, minute-to-minute influences of relationships and emotions. Consider the Chairman of a large multi-national Company, he is often quite remote from the Trade Union Official or the Chargehand on the Shop-floor. Add to this the feature that it can be many thousands of years since the last contact with the 'Shop-floor' and you begin to appreciate how this 'distance' arises.

6.34 We watch the video 'Ghost', which we are told is a good representation of what happens when we 'pass-over'.
KEYPOINTS TP19
a) Death, and the mechanics of Death, is a process which we all must face, when the Soul permanently leaves the Human Body, for the Body to return to the Earth. But, remember that the Soul can leave the human Body throughout the Day and every Night!..(but it is still then attached by the thread)

b) The knowledge that our Soul survives the death experience, and all Pain, Suffering, Disease and Disability is healed; I hope will reassure and comfort many.

c) Death can also be a wonderful, loving Experience when you are re-united with your loved-ones who have gone before.

d) Remember also however, there is no 'Death-Bed' forgiveness of Sin, whatever suffering you may have caused to Others will need to be acknowledged and truly repented. Following, note only following, a suitable period of remorse, then and only then, with an acceptance of light and love as the way forwards, a recovery of the Soul from the depths of depravity and darkness will become possible.

(I have been told of the hundreds of years for my Soul to be fully recovered following the lifetime as 'Alexander the Great'.
....see AppendixII. One Soul. Past Lives)

6.35 We visit my brother Edward, in Worthing, Sussex, his children are present and Evelyn my niece is pregnant. We talk about Spiritualism, our plans and our experiences. We meet opposition, rejection and disbelief at what we say.

KEYPOINT TP20
The Spirit of a child resides inside the mother some 4-6 weeks BEFORE conception. Remember, all is foreseen, all is known in advance, all life is given.

6.36 I am told: 'The life you should lead is to be similar to that which Jesus performed on the Earth-Plane. Is this not to be worth more than any piece of paper, which will buy only Material possessions?
Think deeply John, we see a great nature and gentleness within your Spirit which has been buried deeply for many, many, Earth years. Allow us in Spirit to carry the burden of your guilt; in this way your mind can be free of guilt and restrictions... Your Spirit can be saved, and can be free, and can be present within your life. Love can only exist in freedom. The chance of a peaceful lifetime for ever after is yours. Allow it to be. Love yourself, who you are, what you represent, what you can be. Hold your head up high to allow others to see. Let your mind be free, let the glory of this World become yours.'

KEYPOINTS TP21
a) Spiritual gain is worth much more than material possessions.

b) The origin and composition of your Spirit John, has long been a cause for some concern and reservation by High-Spirit, especially in view of the history of your previous lifetimes on the Earth-Plane.

c) What is now said, is that you have the opportunity in this lifetime to redeem yourself, and to cast-aside any lingering doubts about your Purpose. The union of your Soul with your true Spirit is now within sight.
d) The ultimate aim of life is for our Soul, the imperfect Sector, to be re-united with the perfect Sector and thus become at one with GOD.

6.37 'Your son Ford progresses. Many hearts are to be healed, many smiles will be found on many faces. Simple days lie ahead, simple things, meaningful and important. Allow this to be.'...
We are told that we have a duty and a responsibility to Others which is beyond the norm. I realise for the first time in my life that it has a purpose. Spirit tell me to use the following words when in discussion with another, when the conversation is leading nowhere...
'Do you feel you have a purpose to your life?'...' Do you know what that purpose is?'...Do not give an answer, leave them to ponder the questions.

6.38 We are told that we must spend time alone together, so that we understand each other's vibrations. In this way, when we are in company, we can relate to others and protect our relationship. A quieter time is necessary, do not fill our time with visitors and places.
Allow Spirit to guide people to us. Whenever Helana clasps her hands close to her heart, this is a sign that Spirit are close-by. At these times I am to watch and listen closely to her.
KEYPOINTS TP22
a) Others' Emotional and Spiritual needs can affect you, your Spirit, and in turn your own personal Relationship.
b) Beware of these influences from others.

6.39 We three are to form a new CHURCH.......Judith, John, Helana

6.40 Helana takes a crystal wine glass, it is blessed by Jesus, we then share some of my son's wine. We are only to use this glass when directed to. It is wrapped in a napkin and placed inside a water-jug.

6.41 We share a meal with Judith,
- she lays out a pink table-cloth which represents love,
- a brown urn with vegetables which represents 'from the Earth',
- a silver candle which is a gift from Judith to us,
- the green china harp represents Ireland,
- eight pieces of bread represent the giver of life.
- Water is as rain, symbolic of Ireland also.
We will prepare many meals in the future, for Travellers who will be brought to our doorstep by Spirit.

a) Rain cleanses the Earth and the Spirit.
b) Rain promotes new life from the Earth.
c) Rain helps to wash away and purge the land of the
negative and darkened influences left by Man.

6.42 Helana's Spirit regresses to Biblical Times. I, then John, looked
after Helana (then Rebecca) and a child following the crucifixion of
Jesus. We were followers of Jesus who had to flee for our lives, and
were banished from the land. I loved and cherished the child even
though it was not mine. The child was Jesus's son Christopher.
He was beautiful to see, but alas we were hounded by the Romans, and
to avoid the child being taken by the Authorities it passed-over to
Heaven. We now have an opportunity to produce a child ourselves,
which will be ours. We as parents will need to be strong and courageous
to protect this child in whatever way we can. It will be given what we
need to do, we will understand.

6.43 On Monday, 15th June, 1998, Helena receives a message from
Princess Diana.
'I am glad to see you, but sad of what could have been for me. Helana's
thoughts are welcomed for my children. I come with the strength that
will be needed. Helana is to do work similar to that which I did.
It is so sad to see so much suffering on the Earth-Plane, it is so sad to
see the suffering, so sad. So many cruel things happen to so many
people. There are so many in need of kindness, and of thought, and of
love, and of prayer. A little love and tenderness, a thought is all that is
needed. You John need to help also. Helana and I have had similar lives;
parallel pathways, so much loneliness. We are close now and will remain
so. I am pleased to see the love between you. I have been asked to
come this day for decisions have been made'.
KEYPOINT TP24
Spirits of those departed can choose to come to you, but
also they can be <u>asked to deliver messages</u> by High
Spirit. This implies Instruction, Tuition, Order and
Free-will in the Spirit-World. Princess Diana has been
asked to bring the message for her Spirit comes
frequently to Helana and the relationship is already
well established.

6.44 'I bring a message also for you John, I see what is in both your
hearts. Do not miss this opportunity, your time together is so precious to
you, but also to demonstrate to others a Spiritual Life. It is so necessary
for parents, for people and for teachers to show the way. I tried, but did
they see? They blunder and think only of their selfish-ways. Do they
see? Do they hear? Do they listen to other peoples' needs?

'It took me some time to see this and to break-away. I could not stay in a love-less marriage. My children have suffered since, but they would have suffered more if I had not parted. It is your thoughts that matter to them. Distance is nothing. It is Spirit which counts. I give my love to my children, my Spirit is side-by-side with them. I come to them. Your Spirit's presence can be felt by your children. They will be aware little-by-little; their Spirits are raised by your presence.

Helana too has walked away from her boys. She has a heart of gold, it broke her heart to leave them, but she has now recovered.

She can now reach-out in other ways. You have been told by so many. understand, your children have a whole lifetime to find out what is needed in their lives. Do not fear, they will begin to show the look of love in their eyes. Your child Edwin is special, he has a wealth of knowledge in his Spirit; he will be a Guardian Angel to the new child. He will bring comfort and peace to your heart, he will make a difference. Open your eyes and your heart to all that you can see. If you do not, not only will it be a loss to me and for my family, but also to the World. It is only a matter of time before your mind is free. Let it be in this lifetime, there is so much to be achieved.

I wish dearly within my heart that you achieve this.'

KEYPOINTS TP25

a) **There is little point in staying in a love-less relationship, for you may well block the opportunity of finding your True-love. Your children sense your happiness, they know whether a situation is loving or not. It is often better to part to find new happiness for them to share in.**

b) **Your children must make their own lives. Do not use them as a prop, or excuse for your own actions!**

c) **The achievement of freedom within your Mind and Soul is what is required. I,(John) have called this Spiritual Awareness, when full two-way communication occurs between your Mind and your Soul.**

6.45 A message is brought from Helana's guide (Samuel), to me. 'Consider all the options open to you. If you do not make the correct choices in this lifetime, they will be represented to you in a future lifetime. All can and will be healed. Trust in your heart. Your Spirit is somewhat sad, for it knows also of the life that would have been lived without the choice. Your Mind is not aware of this, but is influenced by your Spirit. Consider all the changes necessary and come to a decision, having reflected deeply, as to what you wish to happen.'

KEYPOINTS TP26

a) **This lifetime is all about making choices. We have been given this facility by God. We choose our pathway through this life. We choose the timing of Events.**

b) We choose our level of learning, our level of understanding, our level of suffering, our level of happiness, the love which we aspire to. We choose our partner, our relationships, our friends, we make our own opportunities, we decide whether to help Others and whether to serve GOD.

c) Remember, that by our attitudes and thoughts we attract to ourselves similar Souls, similar People with similar aspirations.(like attracts like).

d) YOU can choose to change your life TODAY.

e) Our Minds are influenced by our Souls.

f) If we make the wrong choice today, we will have to re-live this lifetime, or that experience, until we make the right choices. BUT, in so choosing YOU are condemning ALL those relevant Souls in your Peer-Group to return to that situation also.

g) When in Spirit-World the Soul still retains its free-will and choices can still be made.

h) Spirit is the life-force of the Soul. The Soul comprises:

- the Spirit
- plus the Character,
- plus the Aura Energy Field which surrounds you.

6.46 On Tuesday,16th June, We are told that:

a) Today, PURE-LOVE has been found between our Hearts, and between our Beings, and between our Souls.

b) It is now necessary for me to protect myself against less-good Spirits, who can occur in all living things...Trees, Animals, Plants, etc.

c) I am to try Spirit-writing.

d) I am to picture myself as having climbed half-way up the Jacob's ladder of life, as seen on the front of Bath Cathedral.

KEYPOINTS TP27

a) Spirit is the life-force of God, all life-forms therefore have Spirit, Lighter or Darker Spirit.

b) Spirit drawing, followed by Spirit writing, is an excellent way of progressing your level of communication with Spirit.

c) Visualisation is a useful tool, I appear, at this time, to have only progressed half-way along my Spiritual Pathway.

d) You are vulnerable to influence from ANY other Spirit, be it in Human Form or any Other.

(I should point out that throughout this Book I have also needed to live a 'normal' life and to earn a living. This record is not about my business life, but I wish to say for example that on the Tuesday, I also completed three business appointments, taking me some 150 miles around Oxfordshire)

6.47 On Wednesday,17th June, we visit Judith who is staying at a friend's mobile home near to Cirencester. Judith prepares for me a display, which reads 'LOVE can only exist in FREEDOM'. She also says that I need to allow Spirit more into my life; it is not a problem of Spirit connecting with me, rather of me allowing them into my life. The rapid SPEED of my thoughts and actions is creating difficulty for them.
A blue candle is lit for me. There is a lot of hurt within me. I need to think about this and try to establish the reasons why some people hurt me. I have also hurt some people. I need to forgive myself for these actions.

KEYPOINTS TP28
a) Colours are significant and represent our emotional state. We should wear specific colours to help us when we are in need:
- **Lilac/mauve/pink for Spiritual Love,**
- **Yellow for Learning,**
- **Green for Growth,**
- **Blue for Healing,**
- **Black for Strength,**
- **Purple for Love.**

b) The PACE of your life can restrict Spiritual assistance and guidance, it is necessary to slow down at times.
c) Do not carry guilt for what is history. You cannot change the Past, but you can choose to learn from it.

6.48 That evening, Judith receives a message from the Spirit of my father Ted. He is feeling very sad and melancholy at the present time, he feels that he did his best for his children, what was expected of him. He foresees problems ahead for Helana and me. He is unhappy at the friction which existed between Leonora, my mother, and him. He says bitter words to Judith who responds ' There is no point in feeling bitter and being unpleasant. We all have choices to make, you chose in your previous life, and should not have been 'trodden-on' by your wife. Go forwards now, it is time for you to choose again. Walk over the bridge which leads to Spiritual progression.

KEYPOINTS TP29
a) Spirits at level three (Heaven), can choose whether or not to progress to higher levels. They can also choose whether to remain close on the Earth-Plane, to await the arrival of their loved-ones; or to progress to other learning or activities.
b) Spirit at level three can foresee a suitable distance into the Future at a local level, but they have no knowledge of the wider view.
c) The level of foresight is related to the status of the Soul.

d) Many Mediums and Clairvoyants do not allow
sufficiently for 'human freewill' in their predictions.
d) When Souls pass-over, they still retain their
Characters and their Earthly feelings; whether these be
good or bad.
d) We choose in Spirit to be born again, so as to learn
the lessons our Soul needs to, in order for it to able
to progress more rapidly.
e) Some can choose to return for a special purpose, such
as to help Others.(ie Jesus)

6.49 I am asked in the middle of the night, by White Eagle, the words
come through Helana:
'What is more important, one man or the future of the Earth?
I respond that no one individual is more important than the whole of
Mankind.
I am also asked: 'Where would I prefer to sit? At the head of the table,
or to the right of Jesus?'
I do not fully understand either question, but respond that to the right of
the Lord Jesus is acceptable to me.!
KEYPOINT TP30
All seated at the Table are equal. The 'Table of Life'
is where all decisions concerning the Earth are taken.

6.50 Judith tells us in trance, that one of my previous lives was as
'Running One', Chief of the Minowa tribe of Red Indians, some three
hundred years before Christ. She continues:
' A couple WILL be found to achieve the work necessary in Ireland; three
couples have so far have fallen by the way-side, for their own personal
or relationship reasons. Helana and I now have this opportunity; but, we
must be of the correct mind to make the right choices. We cannot
pretend.'
KEYPOINT TP31
The best laid plans of mice, men and Spirit can be
thwarted by human Free-will, and Personal, Emotional
priorities! But Spirit do not give-up easily, they try,
try, again and again.

6.51 Judith teaches me her way of opening of the Chakra's. The
opening of the Chakra Energy Centres increase our sensitity to
communication with Spirit, and the receptivity to the healing Energies.
Before you meditate use these procedures.

KEYPOINTS TP32
You <u>must always protect yourself</u>, and ask for low Spirit
to be kept away, before the Chakras are opened-up. Use
the Words:
a) Heavenly Father, please protect me with the Light and
Love of True Spirit. Please allow only those Spirit who
come with love for Mankind to draw near, and keep all
low Spirit away from me.
b) I ask for my Door-Keeper to be present....I ask for my
loved-ones to stand-back so that my Guide can
communicate with me. (both optional)
c) Imagine then the Light Energy, flowing upwards from
your Base Chakra to your Crown Chakra, as each Chakra is
opened, visualise a 'Cog' engaging on a vertical Shaft,
or a Rose in Bud opening its Petals...
d) Work through each of the main Chakras, one-by-one:
Red, Orange, Yellow, Green, Blue, Indigo, Violet.
At each stage visualise the colour in your Mind, as each
represents the raising of your vibrational Energies, and
the raising of your Spirit.
Ask your Spirit to rise within you...(You may find
coloured flash cards useful, initially)

6.52 I need to learn to LOVE MYSELF, I am not second-best to anyone
else, neither am I unloved. Nothing else is more important to my Spiritual
growth than to achieve this.
*(throughout my childhood I have felt unloved by my parents, and
second-best to my brother...In my relationships with Helana, it would
seem that I have also felt second-best to Jack for her love and
affections, as is shown by her current struggles)*
KEYPOINTS TP33
a) It is essential to love yourself, to be happy with
your Being, to be at peace with your situation, to clear
any past guilt, to accept your history, to come to terms
with your life, if you are to be truly ready for
Spiritual growth.
b) Spiritual LOVE, more the love of the World, is
different to Emotional LOVE, which is more the love of
an Individual. Spiritual love is more friendship and
complete giving, without expectation of return.
Emotional Love can sometimes be solely sexually based
and superficial.

6.53 On 19th June, Helana is asked by her Guide, to buy the baby-
clothes which Judith has in-store. Helana's tummy is now getting larger,
and she is asked to have a pregnancy test.
(The test answers nothing, not yes, not no!)

Helana is also distressed by the influence of Jack's Spirit, which she believes is restricting her Spiritual growth.

I am asked to try and sit quietly on a regular basis.(to meditate) It is necessary for me also to spend two hours per week with Judith, so as to progress my Spiritual Awareness. Helana agrees to this.

Problems have been caused to her Peer-Group by Helana's Spiritual Awareness progressing so rapidly.

(Life becomes more complicated when you are Spiritually Aware).

KEYPOINT TP34

As any one individual in the Peer-Group progresses spiritually, so this causes the Spirits of the others in the Group to be raised, and so their attitudes and outlooks, needs and desires will also change.

6.54 White Eagle asks, when I am half-asleep in bed: 'If you could invite some people to a dinner-party, who would you like to invite?

I think back to my previous relationships, and do not wish to upset Helana or offend anyone else by leaving them out. I think for ten seconds, and respond that I would like to invite all those who love and have loved me!. I then fell asleep.

Little did I anticipate the problems and antagonism that my response would create, in retrospect, perhaps I should have taken ten hours to decide upon my reply!.

The Banquet took place, without my mind being aware of this. I am told that at a future time, when my full awareness has been achieved, that I will be able to recall this occasion.

Some two hundred Individuals were present, stretching back through Time over my seventy-seven human lives. Chaos, Jealousy, Hate, Spite, Unpleasantness was present, for many there had not met with their adversaries or protagonists, since their original involvement with me took place. Wives, ex-wives, lovers, mistresses, Helana was put-out, Spirit were not too pleased, I was surprised, as the order of seating at the table reflected their depth of love for me.

...see AppendixVII.for the Seating Plan.

6.55 The following day, Helana brings to me the following words from White Eagle:

' John, we wish to say all is as it should be my dear man, and your thoughts have been noted on many occasions. We brought to you last night-time a lesson in the power of Thought, what is needed now is for you to apply your mind as to how this meeting will have affected those who were present at your table.

The Lord Jesus had prepared one similar in past Times to share with his Disciples all that he could offer in the way of re-assurance to these men of life-everlasting; and to emphasise his continued presence in their lives even beyond all that could be seen by their own eyes at that time'.

'We had hoped my dear man, that your speech to those around your table would have contained a gift for the future years, which would have helped these Spirits find reassurance within their own hearts for their future Pathways....

We feel for the time your lady is absent from your day, in the future days to come, you should reflect on how your thoughts and actions can and do affect the lives of Others, and how much in this life has changed from that of past-lives,...to change what has become part of your true nature.'

KEYPOINTS TP35
a) Thoughts on the Earth-Plane help to create our future World and future experiences.
b) Thoughts in the Spirit World act to create the Present.
c) Thoughts are as powerful as Actions, accordingly they need to be controlled.

6.56 On 20th June, at 02.00hrs, a message is delivered from Jesus:
' Be patient John with Brian and Ford, both are spiritual and receptive, but they do not understand. Helana has seen what they need in terms of love and understanding. Allow her to guide and to help these children. Listen to her words. Rome was not built in a day. You are soon to discover in your awareness many things: Who, what and where you are to be. It is to be a time of Revelation. Many things have been said which you do not understand fully, but you are aware of the need for and importance of your presence in Northern Ireland at this time.

So many are in need . We are all one family, all is shared. The Creator of the one family is GOD in Heaven. There is so much that you do not understand at the present time. Allow yourself to be free. Allow the knowledge of who you are to bring about an understanding.

Ask...Why am I here?. Why did I choose it to be now?

You are aware that you sit at the 'Table of Life'. All which happens on the Earth-Plane is governed from this Table. The choices were so important as to cause you to leave this Table to enable the work to be done to be achieved.'

KEYPOINTS TP36
a) We all originate from the One GOD.
b) The present Time in Mankind's History is of great significance.

6.57 'You have been given this lady, (Helana), to guide you. Your Awareness is buried so deep at the present time. Once it is released, you will not stroll away, you will run forwards. It is all there ready to be found. The work to be done is indeed important, you are not fully aware of the extent of what is needed. Little by little you will understand. The work will be completed by the children you leave behind. It is all there, when their full potential is liberated. It takes many years to bring to them the compassion and direction which they will need to find.

You will teach your children. You will be a great Teacher. A gentler manner is necessary, this will come in time. Wise ways, true ways, will rise to the surface in you. This lady is gentler.

Your children will become Healers, the previous lessons were necessary to prepare these children. At no time will a trail of unhappiness be left behind.'

KEYPOINTS TP37
a) Your Mind can completely suppress your Spiritual Awareness, it can take much application, determination and Spiritual assistance for the Awareness to come to the fore.
b) All is planned, all experience has a purpose.

6.58 Jesus continues: 'Allow your mind to think in terms of a preparation, in order that you gain a fuller understanding. There is no reason for you to feel guilt if you think in these terms. There is a Grand Order of things, all our lives are inter-dependent, all are needed for any one life to be complete and for the objectives to be gained. Helana has an understanding. You, John, should allow yourself the time to gain an understanding also. We in Spirit have been surprised by Helana's knowledge, she has acquired this herself without any 'special help' from Spirit. It is her hard work alone, which has brought her to her current level of Awareness. You must quickly do the same, it is needed at this time.'

KEYPOINTS TP38
a) All lives are inter-dependent for the experience to be gained.
b) It is possible by shear hard work to gain your Spiritual Awareness, if your will and application are there.

6.59 'Your complete understanding of Northern Ireland will be gained in a short time. We see your lives coming together and are pleased. Now, there remains only the question in your minds of whether you will achieve the friendship and the strength that is needed within your Relationship. It remains a mystery to your Mind as to why this is important, but, happiness is all-important within both your Mind and your Spirit. Your Spirit is in need of all the data for it to be able to rise. We can see within your eyes and heart that the feelings for Helana are deep and true. However, more evidence needs to be available in your Mind, for your Spirit to see this.

It is more than being together, it is a question of sharing a new life, a new direction and a new outlook on your life.'

KEYPOINTS TP39
a) Happiness plays a key role in our lives and in the direction we follow.
b) Evidence of love and true feelings, are seen in our Eyes and in our Hearts.

c) The Mind acts as a doorway to the Spirit. The Spirit sees the Thoughts, and monitors the Feelings, assesses the true Affinities, before deciding on any reciprocal Actions.
d) Your Spirit, in conjunction with your Spirit Guides, oversee and control the direction of your life.

6.60 'You John, have an affinity with London; there is no such place in Ireland. Can you survive without this? There is very little entertainment within the places you will go, but you will meet many people. A clear Mind is needed. Habits will be abated. Speed is not necessary.
Blue skies are fewer, aggression is not needed. There are so many things that will be different. These are the questions you need to ask yourself in all honesty, upon your return to England.
We will wait a few short days following your return, for you to come to terms with all that you see. We will give you time to find your true feelings. Allow your time spent in Ireland to be free. Listen to the people, enjoy your visit, we will leave you free to enjoy your time together.'

KEYPOINT TP40
All experience is for Choices to be made, and for understanding to be gained. Time is allowed for the Mind to analyse and decide upon preferences.

6.61 'We understand your needs, to be with Helana and the child. But, more is needed, the love has been found, but, the choices were made here, at the Table, to come to Earth to achieve at this time. The work is needed. But, without your happiness also, the work cannot be achieved in the same way. We understand your free-will to want this to be. We will allow this. It is to be if all else is settled in your Mind.
We do not expect miracles, but what we need to see is your conviction and compassion for the people of Ireland. That you feel within your heart the help that is needed. The love of your life is to be second place at this time. Your relationship is safe. You need now to find a freedom from love, to allow your Mind time to explore, and to question, and to find in your Mind what is needed.
Peace and serenity will surround you both....go now in peace and allow this time to be free and happy. We know you have the strength to achieve this. Our love surrounds you at the present time and always. Remain seated for a little while for the words to register deep within you. Understand this is also difficult for Helana, who also requires your love.'

97

a) All life has a purpose. It is planned before we are born.
b) There exists a controlling hierarchy of High Spirit.
c) If your motives and commitment are not correct, a greater purpose will not be allowed to continue.
d) Our lives can be monitored and controlled from above.

6.62 We have planned our first trip to the Republic of Ireland, and on Sunday, 21st June, find ourselves staying overnight at the Park Hotel in Aintree, near Liverpool. On the Saturday, 20th we have attended the wedding Ceremony and celebration for my nephew, Timothy, which was held in Croydon, Surrey. Subsequently, we drove back home from London, and then up to Liverpool, by car, some 200 miles away.
We intend to explore Ireland, and to return home on the Saturday of the 27th June. It was an uneventful, pleasant drive north on the Sunday morning. I have checked the prices and costs and have decided to drive my car, and to cross from Liverpool to Dublin (Dun Laoghaire), using the Packet Steam Ferry Company.

6.63 It is 22.00 hrs., we are staying overnight, waiting for the Ferry to leave on the Monday morning at 08.15 am. I am sitting on the bed, writing, when a message is delivered from Jesus: ' Your lives can be heaven on Earth if you so choose. Every moment is special, and every moment demonstrates that you are part of Nature. Love yourself in all that you do. It is no good if there is distress or unrest in anything that you do. A release of anxiety in your Mind is necessary to allow you to begin. It is within your grasp, but a peaceful Mind is necessary.
We understand the importance of your Journey, take care to know that we have your interests at heart in all that you do. Our love and light surrounds you both at all times'.
(we are excited and apprehensive about this 'leap' into the unknown, and worrying about being able to find the Ferry Terminal, and to arrive to Board in time).
KEYPOINT TP42
A quiet, peaceful Mind is essential, to be able to communicate clearly with Spirit.

6.64 'A strange place, a strange room; understand Helana, that all is well within and around you. I bring to you peace and understanding. Do not be distressed in your days together, you have a greatness of Mind and Spirit to achieve that which you must do, to enable the work for Spirit and for the World to continue. Your eyes have met, and your Spirits entwine to enable this work to continue. You have a greatness of Spirit and Mind my dear, you have been chosen for this work. Do not put yourself down my dear. We bring to you peace, to know that this will be.'

'Your Mind will be sufficiently peaceful to enable your Spiritual growth. Spare your Spirit the agonies of the Past, and allow yourself to move forwards. You have a charm which only you can use.

You will succeed. You were always intended to be the mother of this child. The child needs a mother with a love so pure, and a gentleness and loving nature, which cannot be found in many. Only you will see the beauty of this time, no words can describe this.

KEYPOINTS TP43
a) Spirit bring peace and love to quieten your Mind and fears.
b) There is a greater purpose to our visit to Ireland, which is beginning to emerge.

6.65 'John, in your mind, your Spirit will rise, and you will see in Helana's eyes the mother and lady of your life over many, many, years. You ask of the places to visit in Ireland. We have given many places, these will suffice. Upon arrival you will have time together, you may share this with Spirit if you wish, work will begin the following day... Dublin is where you will begin, a more suitable place to your needs will be found later. Your sights will be set on Mountains and greenery, these will bring about what it is necessary to see every day of your lives.

A feeling of euphoria will be found. This land offers warmth and comfort and beauty which you have not previously found. You may share this with one another, but also speak to the child within Helana, and allow it to know, and to share in the Beauty.

The child is within, to share and grow with the knowledge of the love ever-lasting which you share. To experience and to share all of the precious moments which happen to you. Acknowledge the presence within of the child. It is your child John, you have been given the seed to make the child into so beautiful a person in years to come.

All is given, it remains now only to see, and to accept this Land.'

KEYPOINTS TP44
a) Jesus is confirming that Helana is pregnant, that I am the father, knowing that as far as I am concerned that I cannot father a child, because of my vasectomy.
b) A child within a mother is receptive to all Emotions and Feelings which the mother displays.
c) Love is visible in the Eyes; Strength is a feature of the Spirit; Compassion comes from your Heart.

6.66 'The child's home-coming is welcomed in Spirit. The child will blossom, beautiful in face, in body, and in mind. Do not speak of this, it is important. Many others will wish to see this child, it must be kept a secret. It must live a normal life, to avoid the passions of jealousy and greed etc. which will arise in many people.

We ask you John, do not reveal this to anyone other than Judith...You are a team of three, a strong band to fight the cause of TRUTH, HONESTY and SPIRITUALITY in its truest form.'

'I know, believe these words, we will be with you to guide and to help you. Allow your Mind to be free, to see what there is to see...this is necessary in order to combat all the forces of those in opposition.'
KEYPOINTS TP45
a) Should any child be born who has special gifts, How then, would it possible for a normal development without the pressures of publicity in our Society today? If such a child is born then it will need to happen outside of the Public domain, if the normal relationship lessons are to be learned.
b) Jesus refers to the war which is raged on the Earth-Plane between the forces of Light and Evil.

6.67 'Helana will find that there are many times when she cannot go on; but, the love of this child will be with you. She will have a strength all of her own. She has promised to Spirit that she will not let go. Her love for the World enables us to see her true strength and character.
She may seem a little confused and silly at times, but she has a true strength to pull you through; we have seen this strength. Bring to her John, the knowledge that she needs...these words come with the true depth of feeling from my heart...I walk besides you always. You have succeeded in friendship and a bond that will not be broken...this will enable you to carry-on with a greatness of strength. Understand, I am high Spirit and your friend at all times.
Allow us to guide you;...go in peace. God places his trust in us....
we are one family, we are true friends.'

6.68 Helana is asked to read aloud Psalm 83

6.69 Jesus continues:'
Bring to these people of Earth the knowledge of the one GOD.
Bring to these people of Earth the knowledge of your love.
Bring to these people of Earth the knowledge of sharing, and of Nature.
Allow them to see the beauty of your love
Let them understand the purpose of your life
Tell them about the beauty that is around people at all times.
They do not see, They do not feel the breeze, They do not understand the rain.
Their lives are filled with pain and suffering
Allow them to see the beauty of all things and Nature.
Do not let your Mind cloud your Judgement
It has to be your own choice, your own Judgement.
We bring only the knowledge and hope that they, and you,
will see the beauty that surrounds you.
Go now, and let us know.!'

6.70 Jesus brings the knowledge that:
a)Mary, my mother, is alive in the Land at the present time. She will not be known to you until you return to Spirit'
b)IRELAND is the Heart of the World.....Heal the Heart and then you can heal the Body, (ie.the rest of the World). The rest will fall into place once Ireland is healed.

KEYPOINTS TP46

a)Affirmation that history is to repeat itself, that the current time in Human History is very significant. That the Souls from Biblical Times are gathering again for the New World.

b)The conflicts in Ireland are viewed as a cornerstone to solving ALL the problems throughout the World. The Heart needs to be healed and strong for the Body to be capable of being healed.

###

CHAPTER 7. IRELAND The First Visit.

7.00 We rose at 06.00 hrs. on Monday, 22nd June 1998, there was no time for breakfast and in any event the Restaurant was still closed. I had previously asked the Hall Porter for directions to the Ferry Terminal, but on leaving the Hotel, with all the traffic and dual carriageways, we were quickly lost. Eventually, we arrive at the Sea-cat Terminal on time, only to find that the Ferry was out-of-action for two days following engine failure. We are asked to drive to Anglesey, North Wales, where a reciprocal travel arrangement has been made. I feel frustrated and let down by Spirit, who seemingly did not guide us.

Before we leave Liverpool, we have a good breakfast at Frank Smith's Cafe on Dock Road.. He tells us of his problems with the local Council and 'Mafia', who wish to close-down his Business. Upon returning for breakfast a year later, I am disappointed to find the Cafe is shut down.

KEYPOINT TFV1

Always ask for help from your Spirit Guide well in advance. Keep a peaceful mind, if you are to be able to receive messages.

7.01 On route to Anglesey, I decide to take the Coast road, and to drive via Rhyl. In the Town Hall is advertised a Bible Exhibition, organised by the ChristaDelphians, who I learn are strict believers in the words of the Bible. I am told that they do not believe in Reincarnation or that the Spirit of non-believers in Christ, lives-on.

Helana refuses to enter the Building, or to even look-at the Exhibition. She accepts at a later date, that it is necessary for her to face these situations in order to learn how to deal with the people involved, and to learn of their beliefs.

KEYPOINTS TFV2

a) To believe that those who are ignorant of the Bible and Jesus will be Damned forever, I find difficult to accept.

b) Equally, to believe that any of the great Prophets and Godly People who lived prior to the life of Jesus are also Damned, is equally unacceptable.

c) To believe that when Heaven is established on the Earth-Plane, as it is to be! that at that Time all the Bodies of all those who ever lived, will rise from their graves, I find to be interesting concept, and at the very least a preposterous proposal.

7.02 We just make the Ferry at 13.25pm. I park-up my Volvo car, and we board as foot-passengers. It is good journey, it is almost as if the Liverpool, Seacat, was deliberately out-of-action. The traffic in Dublin and leaving Dun Loaghaire by bus is diabolical. The traffic delays us by over one hour. We eventually manage to collect the hire-car, and proceed north to Drogheda.

We are tired, but upon reaching Drogheda, are directed by Spirit to look at an Angel statue with a broken wing, this takes a further thirty minutes of heavy, frustrating, traffic-driving. We are then directed away from the town centre, alongside the riverbank of the River Boyne, down small country lanes which seem to lead nowhere. After several miles of countryside and no sign of any Guest-Houses, I begin to feel uncomfortable with our close proximity to the fast-flowing water and decide to turn back to the town centre. I am once again, annoyed and upset that Spirit have not helped us more. My expectation of a pleasant, relaxed, friendly holiday and time together, seems to be going out of the window!

KEYPOINT TFV3
All is a test, a test of our resolve and perseverance, the strength of our Relationship, and our determination to succeed.

7.03 We eventually find a Tavern, it looks reasonable from the outside but is scruffy inside, and in dirty surroundings. I turn to leave, to look elsewhere, but words from Helana cause me to change my mind. It is a wrong decision; the breakfast and service is very poor, but the rest of our stay in Drogheda passes quite well with a good evening meal in the town and live Irish music.

We are told that tomorrow we must start work. I am specifically told that I MUST OBEY any Spirit instructions if we are to succeed with our visit.

KEYPOINT TFV4
Obedience is a key requirement to enable Spiritual work to be completed.

7.04 On leaving the Tavern, on the morning of Tuesday, 23rd June; we are both aware of the need to comply with Spirit's directions. However, I personally, have found difficulty in knowing when Helana is talking, and when Spirit is talking through her. The need to obey Spirit at all times is paramount, so I propose a system of hand-signals in order to clarify the situation. My natural inclination is always to offer my own viewpoint and opinion. This apparently is not acceptable when Spirit are giving directions to us which might be critical to our personal safety, or which they wish me to follow for the learning experience to take place.

(I talk to Helana as my partner, and our normal relationship is fine, however, I am not aware of when she is merely acting as a spokes-person for Spirit, for she does not necessarily go into Trance, or change her voice, or her presentation in any way. Neither, am I used to, or compliant with agreeing totally to everything she says, without comment. I might just as well be a rag-doll or puppet!)

The following finger-code is adopted:

- Forefinger and thumb brought together and apart, Helana is delivering a Spirit message.
- Forefinger and thumb touching together to make 'O', this is a Spirit instruction which MUST be followed.
- Hand wave, fingers brought to palm, Spirit advice, it is our choice whether to follow.
- Hand on her chest is Helana talking
- Two hands, knuckles together, I need to protect myself and ask for my Door-keeper.
- Hand upright, I must cease talking, as a Spirit message is due to commence.

7.05 We must drive at no more than 45-50 mph, if we are not to miss-out on directions.
(*this, I find particularly difficult to do, to drive so slowly*)
When Helana drives the car, the steering-wheel is directed for her.
The purpose of our visit is given as:
a) To establish whether I am happy to accept the slower pace of life, which we can expect when in Ireland.
b) To meet the people,
c) To visit the places and to assess whether I can be happy to live in Ireland
d) To experience the way of life in Ireland
e) To consolidate our relationship.
f) To find an Area which we would like to settle in.
KEYPOINT TFV5
Spirit do not impose a lifestyle upon you. They do not do that. It is your personal free-will and choice as to which Pathway to follow.

7.06 We find lovely lodgings at Letterkenny, and dine well in the Town. The Landlady's sister has become a Nun after an ' Psychic Experience' and a useful discussion follows.

7.07 We enjoy our time in LondonDerry. Helana cries as we approach the City and feels movement within her Being. We have reacted to the places we have passed through on-route. I have felt pressure on my ears and heat through my arms and upper-body. Helana has felt pins and needles in her feet and pressure to the side of her face. Helana is given the message 'welcome home'...Helana's Spirit is sad from the absence of Jack's Spirit.
(*people say LondonDerry if they are Protestant, or Derry if Catholic*)

7.08 On Wednesday, 24th June, we find ourselves driving-up the west Coast of Ireland towards Donegal, and are directed across the Mountain Drive. Without warning and without a map, we end-up driving from tarmac road to mountain track; no houses, no support services, and no evidence of other life other than sheep, derelict Crofter Cottages, and heaps of cut and bagged-turf. Dusk is falling, and the weather looks as if a Storm is brewing; with black thunder Clouds reducing the visibility. If it does rain then I am fearful that the track will become un-passable, for the road is so steep and little more than rough-land in places; neither do I know where we are going nor whether there is a destination.!

Helana becomes afraid, and I become apprehensive, but for some reason believe that we should continue. Why should Spirit send us into the Wilderness? Is this another test of our resolve?

7.09 There is a strange beauty to the barren Moors, heather, rocks and streams with occasionally an abandoned Crofter or Shepherds' Cottage. I stop to free a sheep, which has become entangled on the wire fencing. Then suddenly life! a new house! and evidence of living people, the track becomes a road and mud and grass are replaced by tarmac. We see a sign, we have crossed the Red-Way ! It is a beautiful land with lakes and trees and valleys.
KEYPOINT TFV6
Indeed a test of our resolve and faith in GOD, we are told that this experience was similar to that which Jesus was presented with in the Bible Wilderness.

7.10 At 23.00 hrs a message is received from Jesus...
' You have experienced all the feelings of this Land, and its emotions of hate, sadness, despair, warmth, bleakness, mountains and fear. It has been a good day, we are pleased. There is to be no turning back for either of you. You will share a lifetime in this land and bring forth the child in this land. The child is within, stirring, and will bring great joy to your hearts. So much good and understanding will come from this time, there is now no separation between you.
Dream not, for Reality has become Fact. You can see the beauty of this land, but what is lacking within others is love and understanding. There are so many who do not see. They see peace as only a means of materialistic gain. They are in need of guidance and understanding. To gain the respect of these people a friendly manner is essential. We have seen this. You shine so brightly amongst the darkness of their Minds. Amongst all the clutter and the devastation of their lives, you have brought a ray of Sunshine. They wish to touch and share with you these feelings. Your eyes will see so many things when you begin your work in this Land.'

'You and John are as one, this message is for you both, you have a togetherness of a unique kind. At this time be aware of these steps, you will then see and hear many things which will disturb you. Helana is aware of these thoughts and feelings, they are necessary for her work. You need to understand the workings of your own Minds, so that you can appreciate other peoples' views. You, John, must not try to possess Helana, allow her, her freedom, to do and to act as she chooses!'.

7.11 'Do understand these words come from Jesus, who walks beside you and cares so much for the work ahead.
I wish only to guide and help you, and not to enter your lives. We understand the pressures are great upon you. We have given you a journey for you to enjoy and to see the sights, it has also been combined with lessons. We try our best to fulfil our needs with your own needs. Time is so short on the Earth-Plane. No definite plans have yet been made, because we needed first to be sure of your feelings. You will be shown again places, to allow you to truly decide where your heart lies, for both you and for the children.
We understand isolation is not needed, but peace, water, trees, mountains, and aspect are. You share the same views and feelings. There has been no disappointment, and no greed with what you have seen. A working together has been seen. Reach-out with both hands and grasp what is on offer. You will be shown many places. A togetherness has been found in every way, and we share with you everything. You have put the Past behind you...you have walked away and taken on-board the challenges. Now, open-up your Hearts and let Spirit in. Go in peace, knowing we are beside you at all times.
Let your Hearts be filled with what you see. Take care to know that these words come from a true friend who walks besides you.'

7.11 We return to Donegal where we eat 'fish and chips', before finding an Irish Bar with live music. The musician asks who here is Irish? There is no-one! The Bar is packed with perhaps seventy people, all Tourists, from across the World. We comment on the excellent bungalows we see and the care with which people take over their maintenance. In general, we consider that Northern Ireland is far 'brighter' than the Republic. There are localities we also like in the Republic. We are impressed by the beautiful Countryside, but are aware also of the 'concrete jungles' and animosity of certain areas we pass through.

7.12 On the Thursday we return to LondonDerry, to confirm our choice of Area. nb; LondonDerry if you are Protestant, Derry if you are Catholic' Helana is aware of the presence in the car of my casual jacket, a present from Lorna. Helana tells me that Lorna is in difficulty with her life, through her obsession with money and her refusal to share her life and love. I hand-in the 'new' jacket to an Oxfam Shop, which lifts the atmosphere in the car.

We travel to the Giant's Causeway in the North.

On-route we both feel the effect of the atmosphere in the towns we pass through, Coleraine and Port Stewart are particularly, heavy and oppressive. The absence of trees, Nature, and beauty is apparent. We visit St.Patrick's Well and the lovely Beach nearby; Helana is told of the prosperity, which lies ahead for us both. We experience body heat, feelings of elation, sensations to our arms and ears dependent on the nature of the Areas, which we pass through.

KEYPOINTS TFV7
a) Nature is visible. It will respond and react to the surrounding Environment.
b) The health of Nature, the number of trees, plants, flowers in any Area, and their condition, is indicative of the emotional level appertaining at that Time and previously....viz. trees dying, an absence of wildlife, or wild plants, or Birds is indicative of a negative environment of 'Hate' and 'Evil'.

7.13 Whilst we stand on the Causeway Stones, (supposedly created by Nature), Helana receives a message from Jesus: 'Spirit was impressed by the perseverance of the Spiritual People who built the Causeway. They lived in caves(now washed away), overlooking the Site. They believed that if they could build sufficient 'steps' from the sea to the horizon that they would be able to reach Heaven. The time was 15,000 years bc. These peoples were not Humans in the current sense, but forefathers of your Race, John.'

KEYPOINT TFV8
The Giant's Causeway was constructed by Ancient Peoples (Aliens), who travelled to the Earth before modern Human Times commenced.

KEYPOINT TFV9
In Northern Ireland, today, the year 2,000ad. and to a certain extent in the Republic of Ireland; the Place names you use, the Places you visit, your own Surname, the Flags you fly, the Organisations you belong to, where your child goes to School, whether you can get a Job, whether you need to pay Protection Money, whether you can get legal Permission to build a house.
All these basic Human Rights are restricted and controlled in the UK, if not by the Authorities, by the Terrorist Groups and reinforced by the individual and tribal hatred. They and many more segregating features are indicative of Religious and corresponding Political Divide. It is Apartheid in the United Kingdom; the only difference being that the majority are white skinned!

a) What is also noticeable is that you do not hear on the Radio, or you do not read about in the Press, or you do not see on Television, many of the Political or Church Leaders, openly or repeatedly, condemning the violence, or the other features of Apartheid.
b) You do not hear about the 'knee-cappings', the beatings, the house burnings, the intimidation, the threats, the real fear that still exists.
c) Is this still a free-society? Or is it so common-place that it is no longer News-worthy?

7.14 On Friday, we visit St Patrick's Grave, at Temple Patrick.
Messages are received from Jesus:
'We ask you John, to bring the Masonic Order into the 21st Century'

Afterwards in the Cathedral, whilst looking at the picture of St.John holding a book, the words are brought.
..'You are more blessed if you give, rather than if you receive'

We stop at the Round Tower at Donaghmore and hear...
...' Free the Minds of these People'

We pass on to Newcastle which we both like, but we then register the hostility when driving over the Mountains of Mourne, on route back to Dublin, IRA flags and graffiti are evident everywhere.

7.15 Helana is up writing late that night. She is sad, sad because of the sadness in this Land, and also has spent two days coming to terms with the sadness of Jack's Spirit. Helana picks-up the sadness of Ireland which, as it is the Heart of the World, reflects the sadness of the World.

We have chosen to stay over in Antrim, where we have found excellent lodgings and food. Helana is approached by the Spirit of the lady who used to own the Hotel, and still resides there as a Ghost. Her name is Emile and she is very unhappy about Events in Ireland, 'Can we help?' We respond that we will do whatever we can. I am feeling sensations and energy-flow through my hands throughout the day.

7.16 Jesus states ' Sleep is needed to bring you both strength; as the peoples of this land drain your Spirit, as they are so in need of Light. Recognise these feelings, as they will help you with other people. John also has felt in a different manner. Working together, you will find it useful to understand the feelings of others, and to agree between you what is needed at a later time. We have asked you this day not to work for Spirit, but to understand the feelings so that once you live here, you will be able to immediately relate to the people.'

'Remember their history, they are blinkered. Their towns reflect this; in many Places you have felt sadness and tears. Understand the needs of these peoples. You have been shown many beautiful things...places, objects, colours, trees. We hope that you have gained memories which are stored for future years, so that you can look back and remember once your life begins here. Already you have begun to fill in the gaps and crevices, which were filled with darkness and sadness and so in need of life, love and uplifting. Remember these times and experiences.'

KEYPOINTS TFV11

a) **Thoughts do interfere with people's lives; they are transferred into the Minds of people. When those people return to the Spirit-World, they will have gained an understanding, which will help to change their situation for the future.**

b) **Others can drain the energy from your Spirit. This can be re-charged when you are asleep and at rest.**

c) **High Spirit can take your Spirit away for healing, such that when you awake you may feel fully refreshed, or drained and exhausted, until your full Spirit is returned.**

d) **Should you wake feeling very tired, this could be the result of the work and travels which your Spirit has accomplished whilst your body slept.**

7.17 Spirit tell us that it has been difficult for them to communicate with us in this Land, as our sensitivity has been closed down to protect us. It is important that our Spirits are kept at the correct vibration to enable effective communication in the future.

KEYPOINTS TFV12

a) **The achievement of Spiritual Awareness, and the ability to be able to communicate with Spirit, is related to the level of vibration of your own Spirit.**

b) **Raising of our Spirits is therefore not only the raising of the physical position within our Bodies, but also an increase to their vibratory rate.**

7.18 It is Friday 26th June, We have been directed by Spirit to avoid certain towns such as Attica, Hilltown, Newry, Dundalk, Drogheda and Belfast, as Spirit are protective towards us. I am told to expect a Spiritual surprise by Helana. We return to England via Liverpool. Spirit tell us that all that was needed has been achieved on this trip...
' Do not fear that a house is being prepared for you, and this will be shown to you on a future occasion.' My Guide comes to me for the first time through Helana. 'Helana is an instrument for Spirit as you are. Take Helana's ways as true ways. The writing you have done is not from your Guide. It is not possible at present for you to directly communicate.....'

'Trust in Helana, and allow her the freedom to be your Guide. Have trust and faith in Spirit. Helana knows true Spirit. She is unhappy, for her awareness is being restricted by your attitude and actions John. You need to accept her as a more spiritual person.

Your Spirit John, will remain buried, unless you let go of your Earthly Mind. Learn by the lessons that you have been given... you have so short a memory! Share your food with someone else in need, in this way you will not feel uncomfortable afterwards. Keep your back straight, this will help with the communication. Do not worry about leaving food on your plate...it is your choice.'

KEYPOINTS TFV13

a) Other Spirit can come to you and pretend to be your Spirit Guide, you need to find a Mentor to help you to avoid interference.

b) Your Mind is powerful enough to prevent your Spiritual growth. It is necessary for you to convince your Mind that you wish to pursue the route of Spiritual Awareness before real progress can be made. A straight Back helps to assist reception.

c) If when you eat, in your Mind you nourish others, you will not then feel so uncomfortable afterwards. Do not always eat food because it is there, stop when your Body tells you to.

d) Do not try to communicate with Spirit on a full stomach, you need to feel comfortable, to be able to relax, and to 'switch-off' from the physical senses.

7.19 Jesus continues: 'Listen carefully to these words. Understand, do not think that it is fiction or tales. Read the book 'The World Unseen'. It takes a brave person and frightening experiences to be able to learn, and to progress, and to understand. Allow us to continue to bring the knowledge to Helana, so that she can continue to grow. She can bring so much good to others. Helana has expressed a wish to share her life with you. Listen to her. Do not tell her what to do. Do not rule her life. Allow her, her freedom, it is love she gives to you of a true kind. She is there in pureness of Faith and Spirit to enable you to grow your Spiritual Awareness. She has seen many lives taken from her, she does not wish this to continue. She has the trust and faith that your Spirit will continue to be raised, to be at One with her is all that she wishes. Allow her this happiness to see your Spirit raised. She will not remember these words. All that she does is for your Spirit. Do remember this, Do read and re-read and remember these words.'

(it would seem that my actions are still causing problems to Helana)

KEYPOINTS TFV14
a) Jesus is confirming that High Spirit are assisting Helana's Awareness to grow. He also states quite clearly that one of Helana's purposes is to assist my Spiritual Awareness to grow.
b) It needs a brave person, and some perhaps frightening Experiences, for growth, learning, and understanding to take place.
c) It is necessary for my Spiritual Awareness to grow, in order that Helana's can grow, in order that I may grow. Our progress is linked as we are of the same Peer-Group.

7.20 'Release the misery and pain of your past-Lives. Shake-off the guilt of your Past. Move forwards with your Heart, and your Spirit, and your Mind. Words alone are not enough.'
'Do not doubt these words, I am of High Spirit. There are great works to achieve. Your work is precious for the people of this land (Earth). It will be a sad day if the opportunity is not taken in this lifetime.
You have been given a lady to love you, and to support you, Helana also has different work to do. This will continue with or without you.
Your work John, will continue, and you will father another child, but Helana's life will be shared with another, if you continue not to understand these words. This is not wished for, but Spirit need to see a greater commitment from you, not just words. Two people are ultimately better than one. We leave you now with peace in your heart. Read these words often. Helana does her very, very best. You cause her so much pain. You do not realise that her life is a spiritual one, she has a beautiful nature. You will learn so much from her, allow your Spirit to grow.
Take these words into your heart. We are with you every moment of the day. It is truth, it is not a fairy tale!'
KEYPOINT TFV15
Simply saying that you wish for your Spiritual Awareness to grow is not enough. You also need to clear the guilt from the Past, and to commit with your Heart, with your Spirit, and with your Mind.

7.21 John, read frequently, the words displayed in your hall, given by White Eagle:
' If you live Tranquilly and Patiently, always with the Consciousness of GOD's love upholding you, you will find that all your Life will be Heaven. Whatever has crept into, and seemingly spoilt your Life will all gradually be resolved. But this won't happen if you harbour Irritation, Fear and Chaos in your own Heart.
Let go these futile worries and fears my Children. All things work together for good for him (or her), who loves GOD.'

7.22 'Be yourself, be that person with a raised Spirit. Let it be, care not what others say, be they family, friends or people in the street. You are who you are! Believe in your allegiance, but first listen, live and breathe in Spirit and in the one GOD. The well-being of Helana's Spirit concerns High Spirit if she continues as she does now. Helana must be allowed to be more spiritual. You must be careful what you say to her, and how you say it. Almost all of her decisions are made by Spirit.
Helana has chosen to continue to help you against the wishes of her Spirit. She struggles because your mind is so strong, but your short-term memory is so poor. Remember the times when your Spirit is raised. Aim for the skies, they are within your reach. Let our arms enfold you, you are in need. We wish you peace in your Mind and success. Allow it to happen.'

7.23 I am asked to arrange to meet with Judith regularly, every week, and to read the book the 'Power of Thought' by HT Hamblin.

7.24 My thoughts are:
- If I cannot become Spiritual enough I will lose Helana
- If I cannot satisfy Spirit enough, so as to enable Helana to grow, I will lose Helana
- If I choose not to pursue the Spiritual Life, I will lose Helana
- If I lose Helana my Family progression, my own personal Spiritual Growth, my mission in Ireland will all fail; therefore I MUST SUCCEED!

7.25 We visit the Bugle Horn Public House, in Aylesbury, I am asked to note the construction of the garden furniture and childrens' climbing equipment, so that I can become capable to manufacture for sale, these types of equipment, when we establish our 'Home Farm' in Ireland.

Some children in the garden are are singing ' Ring-a-ring-a Roses' the tune reminiscent of the Great Plague of the 17th.Century. Spirit point out to us that the Plague, the Great Fire of London, and the Great Flood, were all given by GOD, to purge the Earth because of Man's evil actions.
KEYPOINT TFV16
GOD will only allow Mankind a certain amount of freewill. If our Actions and lifestyle reach an unacceptable level of Sin, then we must be prepared to accept the consequences.

7.26 We are told that we need to be in Ireland for our own safety! Helana is asked to join the Womens' Institute, and to develop her Tapestry skills.

KEYPOINT TFV17
Spirit are aware of certain Events due to occur, and can
warn and protect us, through direct communication,
visions, premonitions, or even in dreams.

7.27 We play a Patsy Cline CD, this brings her Spirit to us, she is still lonely and sad. We offer a blessing and she departs. I am left wondering has she accepted that she is dead?, has she passed over to Heaven? or has she become another lost Spirit and a Ghost?

KEYPOINTS TFV18
Mankind has free-will when we live on the Earth-Plane.
Our Souls also have free-will when we pass-over, the
Soul completely leaves the Body and the human Body dies.
The choice then becomes whether we:
a) Accept that our Earthly existence has ended, and,
choose to pass-over to Heaven to be healed and to
commence a new existence; or,
b) Refuse to accept that the human Life has ended,
pretend to continue with the human Role, refuse the
opportunity to move to Heaven and to meet with your
loved-Ones; and, become a lost-Spirit and Ghost.
c) Prayer will Heal.

7.28 On Monday, 30th June, I have suffered upper-jaw and ear ache; my ears have felt funny, as if open to the elements. Whenever I breathe or swallow, I feel my ear drums. It also feels as if my upper-jaw is being re-shaped. Helana goes to bed with a head-ache. I heal her with my hands. We make love and I enjoy a wonderful, double climax, both physical and spiritual (above my heart). A wonderful sensation is felt in my chest for the first time.

7.29 Jesus states: 'That which can be found on the Earth-Plane is kept forever by the Spirit and is more valuable than lessons learned later in Spirit-World. The hurdles you John, experience on the Earth-Plane are there so that you gain knowledge, so that when returned to Spirit-World, High Spirit can learn from these lessons, and use them to help other Spirits...
Your Mind John, is strong, so that the lessons can be learned, so that on your return these lessons can be used by Others. Remember, these days of learning are for the benefit of Others, as well as for your own Spirit. The knowledge will enable Others to progress more easily. Look upon these days, as days of hope for Others. If you succeed, you will bring to Others this hope. You have chosen this life, so that you may gain all that is needed. You must examine and understand the purpose for your life.'

a) There is a purpose to everyone's Life. When you achieve Spiritual Awareness, you will know what your true purpose is.
b) It is easier for the Soul to learn the lessons needed on the Earth-Plane.
c) The lessons needed are presented to you, for you to learn. Every day and every Event is there for you to learn.

7.30 My Spirit Guide continues 'There are additional goals to achieve, you will learn of these in the days ahead. You need now to accept, and to try to live the life of Jesus, and to walk in his footsteps, to walk away from all material possessions and to start a new life in Ireland. A new simple life, with simple effects, simple food and a simple style of life. The rewards will be far richer in the Spiritual sense. You should pray and ask for guidance.'

KEYPOINT TFV20
Guidance can come from asking GOD for help in prayer.

7.31 I agree for Spirit to start to specify the food which I eat, so that I can start to lose weight. I am told that Helana still needs to forgive me, for she still blames me for the miscarriage she suffered in the 18th Century, when I was known as Richard Cookson.
I also need to forgive Helana for the loss of our child then. This situation is a barrier to my spiritual Progress and Awareness. A repeat of History has occurred. I need to forgive Helana now and to cry for the loss of our Child. I must think deeply and in a universal way as to how to forgive her.

KEYPOINTS TFV21
a) Situations, guilt, and occurrences from the Past can restrict and prevent your Spiritual growth.
b) History will repeat itself, lifetime after lifetime, until, and unless, the correct lessons are learned. If you can identify a repeating pattern in your lifetimes, or in this lifetime, ask the question;
Why? Only in this way can the solution be found.

7.32 On Tuesday, 1st July, we three sit in discussion with Judith, the message is received from High Spirit that
'Helana and you, John, must be prepared to work together now, if you are to be able to progress together to Ireland. The relationship must be right for both of you, you must like each other and you must be mutually supportive. Helana must live a more Earthly life. Choices need to be made by all three of you! Helana must decide her own priorities, and tell Spirit these. She must listen to this advice. Part of Helana is afraid to offend Spirit, and so she allows far too many other Spirits to come close to her.'

'She must not allow Spirit to take over her life; she must shut them out in a definite, positive manner. Otherwise, it is difficult for your own Guide to communicate. It is not good for Spirit to have constant contact; they can be refused. Helana allowed Bryan too close; she refused to enter the Exhibition in Rhyl, she has walked away from other situations. Often the work to be done cannot be achieved unless she faces-up to any situation. Her own Spirit-Guide would not have said no.

KEYPOINTS TFV22
a) It is necessary to be able to shut-out other Spirits who may try to interfere with your life and who can restrict access by your own Spiritual Guide.
b) Spirit should not be allowed to completely rule your life, you have your own free-will and must live an Earthly Life as well as being able to know, to understand and to try to achieve your Spiritual Goals. It is all about Balance.

7.33 On Friday, 3rd July, I meet locally with Trevor, an acquaintance, who is severely crippled through a swimming accident which broke his neck. I am told that the accident was given because of his behaviour to Others, in this, and in his previous three lives. We are told that appearances can be deceptive, and we need to look beneath the surface to the person and to the Spirit within. I suffer a groin pain for three days, which I have collected from Trevor.

KEYPOINTS TFV23
a) If we repeat a set of circumstances which are negative in their impact to Others about us, then we must be prepared to accept the consequences.
b) Give unto others as you expect to receive. Sooner or later; retribution will take place, if not in this lifetime in the Future.
b) You need to protect yourself at all times, to avoid collecting physical pain and suffering from others. Additionally, you can ask for a Doorkeeper to protect your Spirit from interference by Others.

##

CHAPTER 8. DREAMS

8.00 It is Sunday, 5th July, 1998, when we receive a message of encouragement from Samuel, Helana's Guide and also from Jesus.
' All is to happen as previously given. Your relationship has been tested and found to be satisfactory. Your Awareness will now grow. We ask you to view the videos 'Highlander' and 'Abyss'. You need to find peace within your minds and beings'.

KEYPOINTS D1

a) It is necessary for your relationships to Others to be satisfactory, for you to find 'Inner Peace', for you to 'Love Yourself', before your Spiritual Awareness can develop.

b) Events and situations will be brought to you to test your relationships, your determination, and your commitment.

c) Messages and understanding can be gained from some films and the words within songs.

8.01 My feet are still burning, my neck is burning, there is a tightness around my head and some new feelings in my hands. The pain in my groin is reducing. Helana is told by her Guide, that she needs to find more self-esteem and direction in her own life. It is necessary for her to find the correct balance between 'faith' and 'healing.'

KEYPOINTS D2

a) Many feelings we experience are given by, or the consequence of Spiritual influences, and, as such it is often your MENTAL ATTITUDE and APPROACH which can resolve the DIS-EASE or affliction, rather than to need to use a chemical or a drug solution.

b) This question of BALANCE is a critical area.

- Whatever, or however, we relate to Spirit, we still need to lead a human life.

- If you do not lead the human life, why then are you here on the Earth-Plane?

- Our Soul has chosen the experiences it needs for the understanding to be gained.

- If we do not live the life, if we do not play-out the role, then the lessons will not be learned!

c) When we are able to communicate with our Guides, we are then able to avoid the same mistakes over and over again, and progress to new learning and understanding.

8.02 We visit the Bicester, Oxon, Spiritualist Church and meet with Rita and others:
A vision is given to me by the visiting Mediums, Olive and Len Foster.
I am seen standing at the top of a ladder, painting a white house with a thatched roof. I am to beware, for the ladder is faulty. Both hands are needed to hold-on.
(I need to watch every step I take, and be careful that I do not fall-off, I am not to be distracted)
A Labrador dog is seen, and then a Boxing Match.
(the Boxing Match indicates the fight which is to take place with the Church Establishment.)...
A Jewish gentleman is involved. Spirits will get closer as my hearing improves.

8.03 On Monday 6th July, we meet with Judith, and I am told that:
* I should try Spirit writing when it feels right to.
* I should sit quietly and invite my Guide to be present.
* I should try for the same time each day.
I feel pressure on my ears, and am told that: The left ear alone signifies NO to any question, The right ear alone signifies YES.
(nb; the order can be different for different people)
KEYPOINTS D3
a) Spirit can communicate through physical stimulation of the Body, through Sensations, through Feelings, through Pain and through other forms of Discomfort. They can also communicate directly into our Thoughts, or through any of the normal Human Senses.
b) Spirit can take any Form. Any Being you meet may well be 'unreal', just as Jesus chose to appear to the Disciples, so GOD, or GOD's Agents, can choose to take on any form to bring to us a Lesson or Experience.

8.04 On Tuesday 7th July, I buy the book 'Past Lives and Present Dreams'. Jason at the Hawk and Partridge Public House, in Bloxham, Banbury, Oxon, talks of chasing a Spirit-Cloud around his Bar with a broom. He then categorically states that he does not believe that Ghosts or that Spirit exist.
KEYPOINTS D4
a) Some people close their minds to ANYTHING which they cannot rationalise, or which is outside their previous experience or accepted Beliefs.
b) Despite overwhelming evidence to the contrary, they simply dismiss this, and choose to ignore a fact, an experience or a happening.

117

c) They are blinkered, and cannot be helped. We are asked not to waste too much time on these individuals, we must use our efforts to the greatest effect on those who are prepared to listen.
d) They will need to learn when they return to Spirit-World, and then to return, to re-live the experiences on the Earth, so that they can then make the correct choices.

8.05 Jesus states: ' You have earned this time together, and you should use this to repair the damage of the Past. You will gain a great deal of understanding through your time together. Many lives were lost by you in the Past when you stepped backwards; but now, even in your short time together many steps forward have been taken. As leaders of a Church a great deal of progress will be made. A strength has been found, which will carry you forwards, tripping only on small stones. Larger ones can be overcome if a spring in the step can be found. You have both a great need and strength of Mind and Character to prevail in all areas. Courage, tenacity, surefootedness will be with you both. What is needed will be found in your hearts and in your Spirits...you will remain together. We see the shear determination, courage and friendship, growing steadily and surely...like trees in the ground, standing the test of time, we feel sure the roots will hold you in place for many, many, Earth years. Every step which you take in this life brings you closer to healing the Past. You need to soul-search and find reconciliation of your past lives; but; only refer to these memories at certain times.'

KEYPOINTS D5
a) A Church is to be formed...The Church of God on Earth.
b) It is possible, through the wrong choices, to fall backwards away from the Light. This has happened to us both in previous lives.
c) It is also possible to heal the Past, to ask for forgiveness, to stride forwards towards the Light and Love of GOD.
d) The Mind can be viewed as a Film Projector. The films are already made; it is only the order of play, or the repetition which we choose.

8.06 'Be aware, do not falter, do not stray. Do not take each other for granted, do not get lazy, for all can change at the blink of an eye. A moment's disturbance can upset a lifetime of dreams. It has been given that a marriage in Spirit has taken place, understand the vows are held in great esteem, to be listened to and to be understood at all times. Care not what others may say. Forget your past lives, we see no return to your old ways. It is needed, it is asked for. Rebuild your lives, strength and positive ways are called for. You both are to work alongside the highest realms in Spirit to bring this about.

We have chosen wisely and believe it can be achieved. We have seen the determination in your hearts to continue.
Step aside from the hurts of the Past. Dream only about your future together. The treasures of the Earth can be found in your hearts'.
KEYPOINTS D6
a)Marriage, and the joining together of Souls is held in the greatest esteem by GOD.
b)A hierarchy exists in the Spirit-World, there are ascending levels of Purity, Understanding and Wisdom to which you can aspire. The seven Spiritual levels of Achievement imply this.

8.07 'The skies rejoice in what they see. Bring sunshine into the lives of Others so that they can see what can be achieved in their own lives......
A Blessedness, a Glory, a Haven, a Beauty, many, many words can describe what we hope will be achieved. Do not allow Others, or memories, to put aside the treasures that can be found in your lives.
See the light at the end of theTunnel. It can be seen. It can be reached. It is long, but it can be travelled quickly without faulting. But, remember my dears, there is much to be seen along the way. The Tunnel is lighted by candles to show you the way. It is not dark, you will not be weary. You will travel the miles on many Backs who will carry you safely in times of need. Shoulders also will be present to bring to you strength and support. They are wide shoulders. Reach out also for the Hands which will guide you through theTunnel'.
KEYPOINTS D7
a)Spirits are there to help and support us on our Pathways through Life. We are never alone.
b)Always pray and ask for help and it will be brought to you. If YOU do not ASK, how can YOU hope to receive?

8.08 'Speak only of this my Dears to friends of a true kind. Announcing to the World is not necessary, it will be read in the pages of a Book which will be written. (this book!)
Allow your children to see in the lives of their parents how great thou art.
You have promised that you will continue to bring about this Work for Spirit...Each one a different Role.
Your Efforts are needed so much. You will be given the strength to continue this Work. Fear not; Peace will reign; you will be Guided. Take only that which is offered; no more, no less.
Speech will come to others who are in need of Guidance and Trust. Go now in peace, and remember we are by your side in all that you do. Angels surround you as you work. Go in Peace.'

KEYPOINTS D8
a) The writing of this Book has been predicted by Jesus,
some two years earlier. Caution has been stressed
throughout this time, the dilemma being, how much to
tell those around us, without telling them too much, but
hopefully enough to explain our actions as rational
Human-Beings!
b) White Eagle has also predicted the writing of this
Book in 'The Living Word of St John', and 'The
Lightbringer', both written in the early 20th century,
and published by the White Eagle Publishing Trust'...see
appendix VI.
c) We are reminded to take ONLY that which is necessary.
We are reminded NOT to fall into the trap of Greed,
Possessions, and the Material life.
d) We are told and re-assured, that the Strength,
Guidance and Words necessary, will be brought to us to
enable the Work to proceed.
e) ANGELS exist and come to us in times of need. Many
miraculous Events, when lives are saved are the
consequence of Angelic intervention.
f) We all have a Guardian Angel, with us at all times on
the Earth-Plane, it is sometimes possible to see your
Angel. Our Guardian Angel will replay to us all the Key
Experiences of our Lifetime, before we pass-over.
g) Angels are a separate Species, who work tirelessly for
the one GOD. It is possible, by exception, for Humans to
progress to become Angels. The Arch-Angels direct and
control the activities of the Angels.

8.09 Helana struggles with the relationships to her step-sister, her
mother and her son Steven. I am asked to look to the skies for strength
and an uplift of my Spirit.
I am requested not to sell Helana short in the battle with her ex-husband
Mervin, for a Divorce financial settlement.
KEYPOINTS D9
a) Every aspect of our Human life is known and monitored.
Fairness in all things is expected.
b) Look to the Skies, the Heavens, and the Stars, for
strength and an upliftment of your Spirit

8.10 On Thursday, 9th July, Helana's Guide, Samuel speaks :
' Give all that you have received to those that you love and wish to love.
They will see the joy, pleasure and trust in your eyes. They will feel the
love that is being given. What you give, you will receive. It is so simple.
Show compassion, not sympathy, for others in need. It needs to be felt
by the heart. You have found compassion many times before in your
heart, and it has been gladly received by your Spirit.

120

Think of a Soul's journey. When you look at a Baby, think compassion for the Soul within, it cannot communicate or see properly. Your Spirit is like a child, it needs to learn and to understand, so that it can grow. Every aspect of talking, walking, reading, all needs to be understood before it can grow. Take one subject at a time. Think about it before you move on. Set your mind, the task, of reviewing 'the Ways of Life.'

KEYPOINTS D10
a) Your Eyes are the gateway to your Soul.
b) Feel compassion with your Heart.
c) Without Spiritual Awareness we are likened to a Baby. We need to learn the ABC of Life, before our Spirit can grow.
d) The Spirit will learn from the Mind, and from the Experiences. Reflect on each Aspect, one-by-one, as part of an overall learning Plan.

8.11 Samuel continues: ' Understand the life of Jesus, look at what he gave, at what he endured. Put yourself into that situation. Learn to give. Learn to put other peoples' needs first; but, do not let them walk all over you. Learn to give and to receive love. Look at every situation to see what you can give. Do not expect. What will be given, will be given, when the time is right. Question any situation, in that way your Spiritual Awareness will sharpen.

KEYPOINTS D11
a) Do not give to receive.
b) Do not expect to receive. You will receive when the Time is right.
c) Put others' needs before your own, BUT, do not be walked-over...(Respect and love yourself)
d) Understand the life of Jesus, try to walk in his footsteps.
e) Spirit Guides are not GOD, they are Instruments of GOD, in the same way that we on the Earth-Plane are. Guides are appointed from those who have progressed to level five of their Spiritual Growth, and who wish to return to assist Others.
e) In every Situation, or Meeting, or Event, ASK:
• What is there to See here?
• What is there to Learn here?
• What is there to Hear here?
• Who is there to Meet here.?

8.12 On Sunday, 12th July, it is face-off day at Drumcree, Northern Ireland, when the Unionists and Orange Order, try to force their march through Catholic Areas. We collect my mother Leonora, and drive-up to visit her brother in Norfolk, we also visit Norwich Cathedral, Great Yarmouth, and London. Helana seems to be pregnant, judging from the shape of her tummy and the corona around her nipples.

8.13 On Monday, 13th July, we receive some lovely words of encouragement and praise from Spirit. I feel a shiver through my whole Body, said to be the arms placed around us, so as to help us through the Tunnel. I do some Spirit writing from Offrey, an eight year old Spirit Child. (....see appendix VII, scribble drawing)

8.14 On Wednesday, 15th July, a message is written from Samuel, Helana's Guide:
'Soon there will be the presence of a bright light around you to guide you. No other humans will be able to see this. You will understand and see the light as your Minds clear. You, John, do not understand the full extent of your Minds being as one. Helana now sees a great deal of what is in your Mind. It is now time to clear the waves and to understand completely what this means. You, John, have this ability also. You need to look, to hear and to see. You do not understand at the present time... I, Samuel, have great joy that you are together in many ways. You are amongst the tallest of all the trees, you have the ability to raise yourself above the rest. Reach to the skies; think of the trees. You have no idea what is in store for you together in the Future.'
KEYPOINT D12
The linking of two Minds as One, is possible when true Bonding has occurred, and Spiritual Awareness has been attained.

8.15 'This message is for both of you. You are to see how strongly we feel for this World. Your eyes and your ears see the needs of the People. We feel that you are strong enough in heart and courageous enough to bring about these works. You will need strength, and courage, and guidance of a special kind, this will be given. Many, many, times we have said this. We can see in your hearts the joy that it brings to your Spirits, that your lives will bring growth to your Spirits, and help to Others. Think positively and courage will be gained. Allow Helana to enjoy her chores, they are caring and giving, and they are needed. Your work also John can be mundane, and similar, in some ways. Share your lives in every way.'

8.16 'Love, and the love of a Child is to be shared by you both. Two loving parents are needed, to teach skills and understanding of a different kind, you will be guided and you will both be able to see and hear your Guides at this time. You can have no doubt that this child is given. There is no greater love than that of a Child. A Child's life represents the love and teachings of its parents. A normal life of growth and understanding is necessary; we are pleased to have found the right parents. Obedience and teaching is necessary. We understand the confusion and the busyness of your Minds...this is necessary to gain understanding at times.'

'In many ways, you two have been pushed together. We understand it is hard, it is difficult, it is not easy. The Bond between you will not be broken. You will gain strength from each other and your understanding will improve with time. Remarkable as it is, these changes in your lives are for real, are for keeping, are for recording. It is important for People to understand the beginnings of true life, very little is known about Jesus's parents, we wish to change this'.

KEYPOINT D13
Spirit, once again, are confirming that a special Child is to be born to us.

8.17 'Keep the knowledge of the child to yourselves, no other is to hear. You have a special task ahead. Safe in our hearts, are your hearts my dears. We care and protect those who believe and who will see the beauty and light that surround you both. There will be many who will visit your Church. Each of you has a special task to perform. Both of you are all-important for Spirit. No one job is less important than the other.'

8.18 'Scrape away the social Teachings. Tear away the chains of your Past. It is not for your lives to be bound by these restrictions. A freedom from these chains will be present in your lives if you allow it to be. Understand these words that have been given.
Safe now in our hands are your lives; you have the protection of true Spirit surrounding you at all times, this does not mean that you must not take care that you are not taken, for there are tests and lessons to be learned. Go in peace and rest your weary minds. Lessons have been learned. It is only a matter of time, before all will become clear. I will leave you now with peace in your hearts and understanding.'

8.19 'You are now joined together by a golden ring which protects you both. (a spiritual band of gold) The Ring cannot be broken, unless you wish it to be. Go in peace.'

8.20 On Thurday, 16th July,1998, Helana has a pregnancy test, the result of which is negative. Judith says we must have faith. I am asked to try sitting quietly on my own. The toilet is suggested as a good place to begin.

KEYPOINTS D14
a) Prior to sitting, (meditation), you should try to avoid electrical disturbances in the vicinity.
b) Appliances like the Television or Washing Machine create fields and energy disturbances which will act to negate communication with Spirit for up to two hours.
c) This is why the quiet hours between mid-night and 05.00 hrs, when human activity is at a minimum, is the best time to try to communicate. Equally, if you ascend to a high point, the top of a hill, or a mountain, then you are clear of some interference.

d) An open-space will serve the same purpose. Preferably somewhere with Beauty and Nature, and at peace. LOOK TO THE HEAVENS!
e) Avoid the vicinity of Electrical Pylons or Transformers, which create their own energy fields.

8.21 On Saturday, 18th July, I try Spirit writing for the first time, and Geoffrey comes through. Judith tells me that Offrey has been blocking access to Geoffrey, and he needs to be told to stand back. A long talk follows with Helana, She has felt neglected the last few days, and is told that the success of our relationship is paramount to any Spiritual progress.........
Helana's Guide asks her if she wishes to move back to Jack!!
Helana tells me that she wishes to persevere with me, provided that our relationship is okay!! My younger children, Edwin and Helen, have been very good, helping Helana in the garden and with sewing. I have spent my time reading for most of the day.
I am told that I must accept Helana as my Earthly Guide, I must listen to her words and respect her opinions and advice. I need to remember what is given, and to refer back to it more frequently. Helana tells me that she has cancelled our appointment with the marriage Registrar. I am told I am too prickly, and can feel a distance opening between Helana and me.
KEYPOINT D15
a) The close presence of any one Spirit, can and does restrict access by Another.
b) It is often necessary to ask for Friends, Relatives, or other loved ones to stand back, to allow your true Guide or a named Spirit, to draw close for communication.

8.22 Saturday is perhaps the most dramatic evening and night to date.
I sit alone with Judith, and Judith's Spirit Guide states that Helana and I are not 'soul-mates', and that perhaps we are not suited.
She tells me that three years down the line I would be bored with Helana and that she would feel dissatisfied.
I am told that I need to think very carefully about our relationship and the future which lies ahead for us.
I feel the energy flow through my feet, which feel very hot, I have tightness and pressure to rear of my head, and tingling hands.

8.23 At 23.00hrs we are re-joined by Helana, and our sitting continues to 04.00hrs.
Judith tells of receiving a vision of a lake, which all three of us need to cross. We will each take a different path, but, we will all meet up later, on the far-side, provided that each of us individually, progresses in the way intended.

I am told that it is necessary for me to review the whole of my life, and to clear away the guilt which I carry from this lifetime, and from previous lifetimes. Unless I am prepared to do this, I will not be able to progress my Awareness. Judith tells me that one of my previous lives, was as Zechariah, the father of John the Baptist. Her present Guide is John the Baptist.

KEYPOINT D16
We three have a common Goal, but our Pathways will take different courses until we finally meet-up again.

8.24 We send healing to Ford, my eldest son, and are asked to envisage him washed and surrounded by white light each day. Ford has been depressed and has withdrawn within himself, from normal Society. Doreen his mother fears that he will commit suicide.

KEYPOINTS D17
a) The Power of Thought and Prayer is such that it IS possible to HEAL by remote will-power, and my asking GOD, the Heavenly Father, or for one of the Revered Saints, such as Jesus, to bring healing to whosoever you wish to mention.
b) IT IS ESSENTIAL that the words ` If it be thy Will, according to their Needs' are used. For, it must not be forgotten that the experience of this lifetime has largely been pre-chosen before birth, or given for the lessons necessary to be learned.
c) There will however, also be incidents where other's free-will, does alter your individual life-plan...viz car accidents etc.
d) If you bring Healing to someone against their wishes, then you may waste their purpose for this life, which may then need to be repeated.
e) It is also necessary to heal the Spirit, before any Physical Healing can occur.

8.25 On Sunday, 21st July, I sit to practice Spirit Drawing, and find that I am able, for the first time, to receive Spirit Writing from:
Offrey, Geoffrey, John Gurdon, Oliver, Peter Grant.
I can choose to write or not to write.
I think that John Gurdon is my Guide but I am told by Judith, that he is not.
I later learn from her, that all of these Souls reside in SHADOW-LANDS.

KEYPOINTS D18
a) A useful way to attempt communication is to try Drawing, and to simply allow your hand to flow. Blank-out your mind from controlling your hand, and watch the results! When the pictures make sense, progress to the alphabet and then simple words. If you get nonsense, stop, tell the 'Influence' to go away, and then ask for your own Guide to direct you.

b) Once again, I say that there is no Death-Bed, forgiveness of Sin. If you commit Sin, then you will need to truly repent in your Heart, and demonstrate this through your actions, AND through your Thoughts, before recovery from HELL or SHADOWLANDS can be considered.

c) Shadowlands is at level TWO. It is a Dark, Damp, colourless Place, no natural Light, no natural Warmth, in company with other Dark, Selfish, Sinful Souls.

d) Souls who reside in ShadowLands, can still influence the Minds of Souls upon the Earth-Plane, especially if those Beings are receptive to that influence.

e) Some Higher, Enlightened, Souls dedicate their time to the recovery of Others from Shadowlands and Hell. They visit as a 'Florence Nightingale' and those who choose to, can establish contact. Following an appropriate 'Period of Remorse', a Recovery and Evaluation Phase can be entered.

f) HEAVEN is at level Three. Heaven in many ways is similar to life on the Earth-Plane, except for the absence of Imperfection, and no Disease. The colours are brilliant and almost everything can be achieved by the power of Thought.

g) Should a dark Soul show little sign of remorse, then it may be appropriate to reconstitute the Entity. When this happens a proportion of a lighter Soul is 'fused' with the darker one so as to assist with the recovery and so improve the chance of rescue.

8.26 John Gurdon wishes to rescue his daughter, Joanna who we learn was killed by the kick from a carriage-horse, outside the Church Doors, at Great Tew in Oxfordshire. We visit the grounds later that week and try to persuade Joanna, who is still playing amongst the Headstones and Trees, to go with the Angels, who will take her to Heaven to join with her relatives. But alas, she waits for her father and refuses to leave. We then learn that John Gurden cannot collect his daughter, for, as a Medical Practitioner, he assisted a patient to die. His punishment for this Euthanasia, was to be sent to level Two, and from there he is prevented from communication with Joanna.

A tragic example of human free-will at work.! Joanna has been playing in the Church-Yard for over 150 years, she has no concept of Time, or that she is dead...another example of a lost Spirit or Ghost!...

I am delighted to report that John was subsequently rescued, as a direct consequence of his actions in trying to rescue his Daughter, he was then able to collect Joanna who accompanied him to Heaven. He now works in the Recovery Hospitals and Research Laboratories in Heaven.

(this message was received on 21st July 1999!!...exactly one year later)

KEYPOINTS D19
a) **The deliberate taking of life, however kind and sympathetic, or for whatever reasons deemed to be ' in the patient's or 'loved-ones best interests' is wrong.**
b) **The Soul has chosen its experiences before it was born. If you choose to negate any experience, then it may need to be repeated, in a later life, with all the implications on the rest of your Peer-Group.**
c) **Equally, if we choose to prolong life, with mechanical means, transplants or drugs, Is this meeting the needs of the Soul? Is this preventing the learning?, or is this not simply creating more problems?**

The dilemma does not arise if artificial Life extension is withdrawn, or stopped.

8.27 A message is received by me, in writing, from the Spirit of a Peter Grant. The message asks me, implores me, that I should contact Peter who is in danger of taking his life because his best friend has been killed in a motor-cycle accident. I am given an address to visit on Ladder Hill, in Wheatley, Oxon...some twenty miles from my home. Over the next few weeks I try to find the address, only to discover that the property no longer exists, the telephone number is not available, and the surname is not known. I learn from the Station Hotel, that the Property used to exist, but the site was re-developed some twenty years before.

KEYPOINTS D20
a) **It is possible to be asked to help Souls.**
b) **Care must be taken not to waste too much time, as sometimes the contact seems to be in a 'Time Warp', from a bygone Age. In a similar way to the girl, Joanna Gurdon, time stands-still for Spirit on the Earth-Plane, or in Shadowlands, when the Human Life ends.**

8.28 On Friday, 24th July, a message is received by Helana, whilst we drive to the Magistrates Court in Oxford. A difficult day and the female Judge is an unsympathetic 'Bitch'. This is the initial hearing of the financial settlement between Helana and her ex-husband. Helana is told:
' Listen to your man John, for he is a good man with a wealth of love for his lady, he has no guilt left within his heart for past ladies, and does not wish to communicate with anyone other than you in matters of the heart. Helana my dear, your message is written with truth and clarity, for it comes to you from your true Guide and mentor. John is your man my Dear, for many years he has waited for your return.
His Spirit my dear has been awakened, and all is now to become reality. You need now to remember all that has been given and keep it close to your heart. You are in no danger of losing your man John, or the Child, and help will be given to help Jack to progress along the pathway he has chosen.'

'Today, my dear, you will see many changes within your daily routine. Let them be, and continue to be yourself in all that you do. Signals will be given and recognised by you to help you with your understanding. Believe my dear you have a great gift of love to give to this World. Go in peace and serenity, and know that we are with you at all times.'

8.29 Helana is despondent because of apparent contradictions in messages received from Spirit. We realise that whatever may have happened in the Past, it does not affect our present feelings and desires. Our relationship is becoming very intense, and she now wishes to marry me. We agree to move to live in Ireland.

KEYPOINTS D21

a) It is important to record even the slightest detail of messages from Spirit. One small word missed-out can completely change the meaning. We jump to conclusions too quickly, so as to meet with our own expectations and aspirations. Take care to ensure every sense and meaning is considered.

b) Not all messages are transparent, Spirit wish us to ponder and to consider, and to reach our own understanding, so that learning can occur.

c) The timing of Events is not that well understood and allowed for by Spirit.

- **What is given will happen, eventually, but often not when expected or at the given Time.**
- **The Prophets have often been humbled by the timing of Events! (It is given that Human Free-Will can and does cause delays to occur.)**
- **Outside factors and influences can and do occur.**
- **For any one situation to occur, perhaps a thousand, Free-will, choices need to be predicted with accuracy!**

8.30 Judith is also annoyed and frustrated with so many changes, the slowness of developments, and the apparent unreliability of messages from Spirit. Judith has spoken to her husband about a separation from him! *(their relationship has been tottering for years, she admits that they should not have married, their child is now four years old. His life is now a financial disaster, and he gives her next-to-no money to support the family, or to pay the mortgage. She believes he gives money to his ex-wife through guilt, at the expense of his current marriage. He is a qualified Counsellor and Hypnotherapist who wastes his talents, and works as a static Security Guard.)*

KEYPOINT D22

If you do not accept the Past and lose the guilt, you will almost certainly destroy the Present

8.31 On Saturday, 25th July, 1998, we visit Bath, the Cathedral, the Roman Pump-Rooms and Weston-Super-Mare. Helana identifies a lifetime of her's on the tomb of Romulus and Victoria Sabina in the Roman Baths. A good day, but Helana is being bothered by a Spirit. (we later learn a contact, Trevor, from a previous life)
Over dinner I ask ' If the overall level of Spiritual Awareness is improving, why then is it still necessary for Mankind to be punished ?' The response from Samuel, Helana's Spirit Guide, is that answers will become clear in due course of Time. Our safety in Ireland is confirmed. The role we are to play has been chosen over many previous lifetimes. A dramatic confirmation of our future role in teaching and guidance is given. We are told that a succession of natural Disasters, which is necessary to cause Mankind to re-think its role on the Earth-Plane has begun.!!

KEYPOINTS D23

a)Mankind is responsible for creating its own Environment. Nature and GOD will not stand idly-by and allow the forces of Evil to destroy the balance of Nature.

b)We are entering a time of retribution for past errors. We are given the choices, to act with compassion and understanding, and respect for other Species and Nature, or, to learn the hard way by suffering, until or unless we change our attitudes and actions.

8.32 Sunday, 26th July,1998, is a good day, we have stayed overnight at a bed and breakfast Guest House, in Weston-Super-Mare, and then travelled to Bristol. We visit the Navel Volunteer Public House, in King Street, which was very emotional for me, for I recalled the last time I was there with Connie. We sing and listen to the Accordianist, we then visited Bristol Cathedral, a few words with the Verger and I sense a feeling on the back of my head. The frequency of messages to me from Oliver is increasing.

8.33 It is a busy week ahead, meeting friends and client appointments. I have also spent time looking for the man Peter Grant,(see 8.27), and in visiting a local 'Jesus Man' to introduce myself and ascertain his views. He publishes a news-letter which causes many to think and to re-evaluate their actions. In discussion the couple do not accept the concept of Re-incarnation, or the life thereafter for the Soul. I have been warned previously that I would meet a religious man, but there is no point to wasting my words on him.

KEYPOINT D24
**Many people are entrenched in their Beliefs, and in this
situation there is no point in wasting your breath! Is
it better to bring enlightenment to fifty others, or to
perhaps waste your Energies on one? There are only so
many hours in the day, and there are so many Others who
will be more receptive, and will be prepared to listen
and to learn.**

8.34 On Thursday, 30th July, we meet-up with Judith, and my true
Guide 'Razeem' comes through for the first time, via Judith. I am told
that I need to find calm within to allow my Guide to enter. He has been
waiting for many, many years and will continue to wait to embrace me.
I am asked to ' Avoid the television, avoid the radio, slow down my
walk, and to slow down the pace of my life.
KEYPOINTS D25
**a) It is necessary to find an 'Inner Peace', before
effective communication can take place.**
**b) The Mind needs to be cleared, the 'busyness' needs to
be quietened...This is why the practice of Meditation is
so helpful. Once however the clarity has been attained,
and the link is truly established, then our Guides can
communicate in the normal run of daily life...then
Trances, or Meditation, or other means, may no longer be
essential, except for special occasions.**

8.35 On Saturday, 1st August, my Guide Razeem comes via Helana,
with the forefingers making a circle. 'John, you are to trust in Helana,
listen to her words. Helana needs to avoid the man Trevor.(a past life
negative connection). You are to sort Peter Grant yourselves. Your
Spirit, John, has the knowledge, it is still hidden by lifetimes of
Darkness. When these are all released, the light will enter very quickly.
Helana has learnt by blood, sweat, tears, and contemplation; it has
taken her a long time to achieve her Awareness. She has achieved this
alone, without any help from Spirit. Helana gives to the World the love
of a child, the child will then be given to the World. Can you imagine a
greater gift than a mother to give her child away, so that others can be
saved? Can you imagine the strength and love that is necessary? There
is no greater love to be found than a mother's love. You will then
perhaps understand the greatness of her Spirit...
Do not under-estimate this lady'
KEYPOINT D26
**It is possible to achieve Spiritual Awareness, on your
own, by contemplation, by self-examination, by turning
to GOD and to Nature. By loving, by questioning, by
pondering all experiences, by studying, by listening to
music, by helping Others, by praying for help.**

8.36 'All life is a preparation. You are prepared to let this child go! An understanding has been reached. The sooner man realises that compassion is necessary, and that our thoughts and actions cause ourselves suffering and pain, then the sooner perfect Beings and peace on this Earth will be found. Mankind chose its path, like moss around a ball; Mankind is getting further and further into the mire.'

8.37 'Consider Adam and Eve. Man was created without clothing from the Earth. Instead of accepting differences as Nature, they chose to place leaves on themselves. This was the beginning of disaster for Mankind, just as you are tempted each and every day with the knowledge found. We do not expect you to wander around with your skin alone. All that is necessary is the understanding, the Spirit then retains the knowledge through life everlasting'.

'It is one thing knowing, it is another doing. We understand it is not practical to walk around naked, but let the Spirit remember, this will bring the inner strength to help others, and to realise, that your actions can cause pain and suffering to others. You are Nature. You are as that Child. There is no need for conflict between Animals, Man and Nature. You are from the one Spirit. Complete understanding can be found. You, John, already have this understanding. Understand the differences. You have this knowledge, it can be found. Read your notes, and understand them fully, before you move on.'

KEYPOINTS D27
a) Adam and Eve did exist, the story is not fiction.
b) Alien Souls were introduced to the Earth-Plane for learning and understanding to take place.
c) All situations and events are created for the Soul to learn.
d) It is Mankind's Free-Will Choices which have created the problems.
e) Knowledge, and the use of knowledge, is the source of much Evil. It is necessary to use knowledge with compassion, so that we do not bring pain and suffering to Others. This is the key to peace on Earth.
f) It is not necessary to act. Understanding is enough for the Soul to learn what is necessary.
g) We are a part of Nature. There is no need for conflict between Mankind, Animals and Nature. We all originate from the one GOD.
h) GOD is the creator of All, including Mankind.
i) All Species, All Life, All Creation has a life-force and a Spirit.

j)All is Energy, All is a different arrangement of Molecules and Atoms, what we perceive and understand on the Earth-Plane is because our Senses have been created and given to us for that reality.
Consider the Fish or the Dolphin and the World they live in. They must look out of the Sea and see the Universe of Air and Space beyond their comprehension and understanding, in much the same way that we look at the Stars and the Heavens around us.

8.38 On Sunday, 2nd August, 1998, we visit St Albans, the Verulamium Roman Theatre, St.Michael's Church and the Cathedral and then walk through the Park. Helana feels 'feet' beneath her rib-cage for the first time.

- We notice the window to King Oswin 'Let us die manfully for our Brethren and let us not stain our honour.'
- We notice the military Altar and the words 'Take up thy Sword' above one of the Doors is the ' Banner of the Lord'
- 'This is to be the banner of the CHURCH OF GOD ON THE EARTH which you are to create'. The symbol of an Indigo-coloured Shield bearing a gold diagonal Cross is to be the Emblem and Motif. ...See AppendixVII
- We are impressed by the picture display by the Artist, John Reilly.
- The Epitaph to Charles Maynard 1665, is symbolic and we are told is representative of the three of us, Judith, Helana, John.

KEYPOINTS D28
a)We are to plant a new Church, to be called
` The Church of GOD on Earth'. (cogoe)
b)The Emblem and Motif for the new Church is to be an Indigo coloured Shield, with a gold diagonal Cross.

8.39 On Monday, 3rd August, a message is received from Princess Diana. She tells us that she can now come in voice, in Spirit, and in presence, but she is not yet fully healed. (Princess Diana was killed in a car crash on August 31st.1997)
She brings a message of strength to us both. We are told that we can call upon her if we wish to. 'Do not fear the Past, these fears are now taken away, have confidence in Helana. She will become a great Medium. Shut the door on the Past. Jesus is keenly interested in the progress of the Child. John will share in the love of trees and Nature which Helana aspires to. Save the tears of the Past until a later time, when you can look back with true clarity. I bring to Helana a clarity of vision and understanding'.
KEYPOINT D29
It is possible for Humans to call upon the Spirits of those in Spirit-World to help them.

8.40 A message is taken from Samuel, Helana's Spirit Guide: 'The tasks to be achieved are difficult, your lives are to be difficult. All is good within you, and can be achieved, and will be achieved, as far as we can see. Rest assured that it is our wishes, that you will be received in this Land with open arms and in the hearts of these people'.

KEYPOINT D30
Not everything can be predicted with accuracy. Dependant upon the level of the Spirit Guide, will decide as to how far into the future they can see.

8.41 A message is received from Jesus... 'Use the experience of past Relationships to help you personally, and also to help others. An understanding has been gained from past lifetimes. You need to relate first to those relationships in this lifetime. Ask yourself...'What went wrong?.. How did I deal with that situation?..How did others react to me?...Look at yourself, take a deep breath. Look in the mirror. You are what you are. You are loved by this lady for all your faults. Helana sees the person you are, and loves that person without change. It is for you to see Helana as she is'.

'Accept her as she is with all her faults and short-comings. It is a coming together of the Spirits. Accept one another as you are...Let situations flow and deal with them as they arise. Do not let them fester. Work through the difficult times knowing in your hearts you are perfect together, knowing you are 'designed' for each other. You can and will grow together. Look back only in difficult times, in stress and in anger. Ask: What is wrong? ...What can I do?...What can I say?.......Do not face these moments alone. Allow it to be so. Fresh air and breezes can bring a wealth of understanding. They also bring knowledge, trust, and faith, that there is nothing that needs to be discounted. Truth and honesty is of the utmost Importance'.

KEYPOINTS D31
a) Accept that the Past has brought you to the Present.
- **You now have the Opportunity, presented by your past Knowledge and Experience.**
- **Accept who you are.**
- **Do not live in the Past, it cannot be changed.**

b) Examine and ponder on the Experiences of this lifetime, learn and understand, but then put them behind you and do not carry the Guilt.

c) Do not allow Situations to fester. Deal with them as they arise.

d) A walk in the fresh air, with Nature, can bring a wealth of Understanding and a new insight. Remember, all is for learning.

e) Truth and Honesty are essential features to any Relationship.

133

8.42 'Open up your Heart John, allow this lady to see inside. She has seen on occasions. Kept within your Spirit is the knowledge of these past Relationships. It is necessary, in a small way, for you to restrain the burning heart-felt feelings of these times, so that understanding can be gained to help you in this Relationship. We do not see a cause or reason for this to end. But, as in all life, there is temptation, and devastation can be caused by this alone. Work through them. Do not allow the actions of the Past to creep in and end the beautiful time which is now. Close the door on the Past. Only in times of stress draw upon your past knowledge. Dig deep John, to help you to understand what was wrong then, and transfer that experience into understanding in this Relationship. This will also help you to understand what are the needs of the World. You need to accept the Past, as a necessary preparation of learning for the Future. To love is to give, and to accept your Partner's freedom. viz...Helana's Spirit has accepted that you will return to the Table, and she will not.'

KEYPOINTS D32
a) **Temptation and Evil are ever present, to deflect us from the true Pathway.**
b) **To love is to give, in every sense.**
c) **Freedom of Action is essential for love to grow... Jealousy, Possessiveness, Violence, Insults, Lack of Respect, Avarice, all of these can combine to destroy Love.**
c) **Each of us has a role to play, be it in this lifetime or the next. We cannot always be together for all of the time, there will be occasions when essential work has to be completed elsewhere, and we are parted from those who we love. Jesus, and the Disciples, sacrificed their family lives, for the benefit of the greater purpose.**

8.43 On Thursday, 6th July, Helana has a period. That evening we visit Judith, who conducts a psychic operation on Helana, as she lies upon her kitchen table. Under guidance from Jesus, Judith reaches into Helana's stomach, performs the necessary surgery, and then closes her up. Judith also treats her thyroid gland. Words are given: 'You must rest and will feel sore for a few days. Your Faith and Belief are a credit to you. You are needed in Ireland, and physical body ailments, cannot be allowed to cause a problem'.

KEYPOINT D33
a) **Spirit are determined not to allow physical problems to prevent a move to Ireland.**
b) **Psychic Surgery can occur, without external wounds being visible.**

8.44 A message is then given to Helana from White Eagle: 'Look at the World as a whole; a small happening, which is happening to you, can change the World. You can heal Ireland alone with your love. You will need to visit each Area, to heal that Area and that Community. Both John and you have a vital role to play. I apologise for past misrepresentation. To explain fully about the child would take a long time. It may be that a child is not necessary; each action of each person dictates these things. Continue with your faith. We wish to prepare you for the coming of a child, in case that child is necessary. We cannot say whether a child will be needed or not. World Events are such that we need to be ready. It is complicated my Dear. We only ask that you live your life, and if we feel the need is there, then it will be you to whom the child is sent. We talk also to you John in this respect. Do not allow it to mar your relationship. Do not feel used. I cannot fully understand the human Emotions involved, it is many years since I came to Earth as a living being. Rest assured my Dear, no outside Spirit will be tampering with you'.

'If you feel this is so, look again, and understand yourself more deeply... we will be with you and will be watching. The Spirits who have troubled and invaded you and been a nuisance to your body will not trouble you again'.

KEYPOINTS D34
a) Healing of Spirit and Body, can take place merely through the presence of God's Healing power, as, at this time the Holy Spirit was present within Helana, it was simply necessary for her to pass through an Area, in order for Healing to occur.
b) By allowing People to feel the presence of Love, their Attitudes can be changed, and so the possibility of change and reconciliation between Peoples can occur.

8.45 'We ask of John a little more study, a little more calmness and a little more discipline in his Mind, and in his lifestyle. Not to change his lifestyle, but more of these things will enable him to see, and to hear, far more quickly. We look forward to the time when he can bring these messages. We ask that he does his utmost to stop Earthly things taking so much precedence; we realise these are important, they can be achieved, but also, at a moment's notice he can be with Spirit. It is of great importance that he hears every word and brushes nothing aside. In this lifetime, each meeting, each person, each event will be of importance. In order to hear and to see, do try and calm your Mind. It is easier to help others in a spiritual manner, if they see a calmness in you. Allow others to see this, you may then bustle-off.!'

a) A calmness in your Mind is an essential feature of good communication with Spirit.
b) Spirit can and do arrange all key Meetings and Events; they can even control the speed of a vehicle to ensure a key Meeting or Event takes place, nothing happens by pure chance or coincidence.
c) A balance is necessary at all times between Earthly and Spiritual work. Spirit wish me to commit more fully to their work and the learning necessary for my Spiritual Awareness to develop. This is difficult when I still need to feed and house myself and Helana, pay maintenance, and service my debts!

8.46 'We thank Judith for her hard work. Look and see the time that was necessary to bring forward Helana. We ask you three to do this for others. Earthly things are of minor importance once you have taken the steps necessary. We wait to welcome you fully to the spiritual life. It is also the time now, to tell you that we are withdrawing Judith for a period of time. She is not aware of this, but there is work to be done elsewhere'.

'Be of an understanding if she cancels an appointment, or is unable to see you. She looks forward to coming to Ireland and working with you, John. This may be the case, but if she is successful with the work elsewhere, she will not be with you in Ireland'.

8.47 'You may now rejoice, as we do here in Spirit, for the love found between you both. You will be as one from now to Eternity. No man will be able to put aside this coupling. We wish you both love, peace, understanding and clarity of Mind at all times. Thank you for your time, and follow the words given'.

8.48 'Helana's presence is needed in Ireland. The need is now. Make plans to be in Ireland as quickly as possible. We ask that you work hard to be in Ireland. Time is limited. I reiterate the previous words...This is a major necessity to World Events. A place of residence will be shown. We ask this of you John. A greater understanding will be given of anything which is not clear at the outset. If you live frugally, your expenses can be met. We ask: ' What is better? The World and all that you know, or, a full meal on your plate within your own home? This comes as a dramatic request to your Minds...The need is thus.
We would drop pennies from Heaven, if we could to help you.
Go forwards with haste. A great happening is to come about.'

a) Timing is of the essence. To be in the right place, at the correct time, is sometimes necessary when Events of Worldly magnitude are likely to happen.
b) High Spirit have told us that they do not trust in the decisions which the American President, Bill Clinton might take. The wrong decision could lead to an explosion in World Events, which could precipitate a reaction from Russia, China, Iran, Iraq, Korea, or Nature itself. High Spirit wish us to be in Ireland not only for the Spirit Healing, but also for our own safety.
c) Your World is also under threat from Alien Forces. Not that they seek to overpower you. But that the Aura from the Earth is dark and negative, which is blamed for Others' problems. It is therefore necessary to convince these Aliens that steps are at hand on the Earth-Plane to combat the forces of Evil, and to lighten the Earth's Aura. In this way the Human Race, and the Earth, will be allowed to continue.

8.49 White Eagle continues: 'You have a slight vision of a new World emerging. That World... the time allocated for that World to come into being, runs short.
You merrily strolled the roads and lanes in Ireland, little comprehending the major necessity for your presence. We do not wish to strike fear in your hearts, but, the cogs which turn are wearing-out. The work is to be done from this moment. Spend time Helana with your visions, and your heart focussed solely on Ireland and Eire as a whole. We thank you for this evening, recognising: How can a Heart Centre be sliced down the middle?. It will not beat.! We realise that you need also to live your Earthly life'.

8.50 'We ask that you, Helana, set aside at least one hour per evening to concentrate your mind, your body and your whole being on the heart-centre of the Earth.(Ireland) ....that you walk and continue to walk in Ireland, until your days on Earth are over. There is much afoot beyond your comprehension. The state of Ireland is dire, and this is indicative of the situation on the Earth-Plane'.

KEYPOINT D37
Ireland is at the Heart of the World. If the Heart is healed, then the Body has a chance to be healed. The Heart will not be healed fully whilst it is divided. Ultimately, the two halves will need to unite.

8.51 'We ask of John too, that he will allow you to concentrate on this work. He too is needed in Ireland. We are pleased, although we jest and joke and send strange messages.'

'We are very delighted by the progress he has made. Do not lose your strength of character, John, but we ask that you seek the calmness within, and show to the outside World a jovial, and likeable character. Judith has given to us that you do slowdown your pace of life and Mind. We require of you a Jeckel and Hyde existence. Do not speak of these matters until a signal is given. We need calmness, for our benefit, to allow us to hear you. You do not appreciate the difficulty we have, the draining of our energy it takes to come to the Earth-Plane. Your Planet is so low in energy vibration, it is so difficult to come here, I puff, I pant, it is so dark here....but, I come because I work for the true-Being, I work for the Holy-Light, but of a brilliance so great you may be blinded.'

KEYPOINT D38
It can help High Spirit to remain close, more easily, on the Earth-Plane, when a candle is lit. Remember though, that candle-light will attract ALL Spirit.

8.52 'If I sound pompous, forgive me for I do not wish to...only to explain the differences. Imagine if you will, I walk normally in the most brilliant of sunshine; I come only in matters of great importance to the type of light you may find at dusk. You are both the loveliest of people who come together in unison'.

'Things have been said of you which must have hurt, but you still continue to move forwards, and when your eyes are truly open, we look forward to welcoming you. The importance of this mission is beyond your comprehension. Do not fear that you will both be protected and cared for'.

8.53 'I am not able, here in Spirit, to completely comprehend the human emotions and needs related to you as a couple, blessed by Spirit with a love so profound. There need never be any doubt between you as to where the other's Earthly heart is placed and will remain. I have returned with a message, in the hope that John will understand most fully'.

' When two Earth people come together in the way that has been blessed by the highest of Spirit, then there can be no time apart from each other, but that is not in a bodily fashion. Your Spirits are entwined forever, so have no doubt that if Helana is not within Earthly vision or presence, it simply means her body is not there. It is the case that each of you is being asked to work for Spirit. At any given time, each of you could be doing entirely different Earthly or Spiritual work; but trust John, that your whole Spiritual Beings are together. If one is doing an Earthly job and the other does not approve, it matters not.! Neither of you should question what the other does. It is to be the case that we require Helana to sit and think of Ireland...Do not be put-out John, understand that as two vibrations working on a single task, they may become blurred. Compare this to a Radio Frequency, an overlap of Stations can occur. It is the same with two Spirits, they will not concentrate in the same manner. We ask you John to sit alone...uninterrupted.'

'We ask you to do Spirit work at that time...do not allow any feelings of hurt to enter any part of your Being, that is not the case.
The great work will enable the Spirit of Helana to rise and to reside in the future with you John'.
KEYPOINTS D39
a) There exists around our Being an Energy field (Aura) which reacts to and is changed by other Energy fields...People or Machines or Nature. Whenever you pass close to or beneath Electricity Pylons for example, you need to ask for a protective shield to surround you.
b) Your own Aura and Spirit may be affected by, or may become dependant upon, another close to you. It may be necessary, when each of you needs to contact their own Guides, or to work independently, for you to physically separate for this work to continue.
c) Your Spirits may be together, even though your Bodies are not.
d) Each Individual has an Aura; the collective combination of all Humans produce an Aura which emanates from the Earth-Plane and affects other Planets throughout the Universe. The Aura which emanates from the Earth is dark and negative and indicative of a dominance of Evil. This is why the present Work and the need for change is so pressing.
e) If you have a bad Apple in the Barrel, what do you do?...The Earth-Plane is viewed by Alien Species as the bad Apple. Fortunately, we now have time to heal the Core, and to grow a new healthy Apple! If we do not succeed, then the Earth-Plane will not continue to exist as such; we can then expect another Atlantis or Noah situation developing.

8.54 The sixth of August is to be a date to remember as the anniversary of the coming together of our Spirits on the Earth-Plane.

8.55 The coming together of many people of like and good Minds and Spirits, can create sufficient white light and positive thought to change the whole World, and to counteract all the negative Thoughts. These People are to be brought together, at the same time, in the near future.
KEYPOINTS D40
a) Do not under-estimate the effect that YOUR contribution can make...consider the Nuclear Explosion; whenever a critical Mass is established, the whole will rapidly change.
b) The ONE, (You) can make all the difference.
c) HEAVEN ON EARTH will be established when the Critical Mass of LOVE and COMPASSION is established on the Earth-Plane.

8.56 On Saturday, 8th August, 1998, a message is received from Mary, the mother of Jesus. The original words were written by me in red pen, at the request of Mary. We are still living in Aylesbury, Bucks, England. The text reads:

'Have you felt different today?

A pleasant day felt by many in this land. Look at the brightness of the Sun, the Moon, and the Stars! Your wishes to become loving to others, will be returned in the next few days. You will see a marked change in your daily routine. You may if you wish to, remain the same; but we feel you will welcome a more peaceful existence for your time in this land. Swiftly you will move forwards and experience a different and enlightened way of living in the new World which is opening-up. Ireland will bring peace of mind to your daily living, and your sights will be set upon achieving that which is within you. A difficult time ahead will be remembered, but this is necessary to achieve a " tidying-up of loose ends".

'A step-back needs to be taken from your families and friends...this does not mean that you will lose them entirely. Ships that pass in the night can be seen with the lights full-on. Nothing is missed, all will be seen. They will remember in their minds, what they have seen, and felt, in your presence. They will be remembered in your minds. Many will fall by the wayside. This is not due to lack of care by yourselves, but by necessity. Extravagance of words is not needed.'

8.57 'A carefree style of life will be attained in time, putting aside the time for work for Spirit...The lifestyle will be different. A peaceful existence, ordinary days. Set aside also time for music and laughter. You have a need for these times. We see so clearly your dedication for Spirit and the work which lies ahead. We wish you well and success in what you wish to achieve. This is not all that we ask you to do. There is the need also to achieve many things on a personal basis. Rest assured, times will be allowed for these, it will not benefit Spirit if you do not have the time. Today was set aside, a comfortable existence, conscious of Spirit and aware. We do not wish to take up your whole day with Spiritual matters. Your own lives are needed, to be together as husband and wife, mother and child, these are important. You need your own time also, for the closeness of being together, it is a question of balance.
KEYPOINTS D41
a) Funds, Space, and Time will be found for this Venture. Once again the need to satisfy Earthly needs and relationships is stressed.
b) A Balance needs to be found, to complete the tasks for Spirit, but also to lead the Human Life and to satisfy our personal Goals.

8.58 'Within the home a nesting period has begun. It is satisfactory but it is not complete. We understand it is temporary, and appreciate the need for a more permanent existence, a safe home is to be found. Safeguard this knowledge.
 Memories of this Land will not fade away, they will remain'.

8.59 'Your future is to be so profound, I cannot explain in words alone, your lives will be guided accordingly. You will set aside a time and a place for Healing. Healing hands, for the work are needed. A testing time has achieved the process of bringing you together. Your Hearts, your Souls, and your Minds, will share so much. We ask you to keep it within your Minds that a swift departure will be necessary.
We understand the need for a temporary residence, one will be found. You have shared this time here with us. We thank you. I come softly and gently, I do not wish to harm the confidence of this child (Helana)'.

'So much is shared my Dear in your Mind. I will come to you in times of need...there is a strong possibility this will remain a necessity! I praise your name, you are a brave and a beautiful Spirit. You have seen the need, you do not fully understand quite what there is to be. Do not be afraid, we are here at all times, to comfort you in your times of need, and bring to you the support to guide you safely'.

8.60 'A little of your future, is known to me. I come to you as a Spirit that has an understanding and need to be close to you at times. To bring you gentleness, and to safeguard your Minds. An affinity is also felt within your child's Mind. See not the dangers of life in this Land. Believe in your heart that you will be protected at all times. There is no danger for the Child if this is to be. Faith in your hearts my dears will bring to you an understanding of what is needed. All will be revealed in time, to guide you along the way. I will leave you now in peace, and it remains only for me to say 'GOD be with you in all that is to be achieved'.
I remain close to you at many times, comforting you, and stroking your brow. Do not fear this'.

8.61 'Safeguard these hands John, they are beautiful hands which safeguard the World, as do your hands as well! (I am sitting, facing Helana, and holding both her hands) Allow these hands to touch your face from time to time, feel the love within. You cannot see, but believe me when I say that these hands will do no harm to any living thing...Plant, Animal, or Creature. Those who touch these hands will be healed in a way of love and peace. Allow Others to come as necessary, you will lose nothing. A love that is shared is one so powerful, there is nothing lost, but all is gained by sharing. Gifts of love are showered upon you both, to give you strength in your hearts.
Speak only these words in confidence with special friends. Not many now, but many will understand in years to come'.

KEYPOINT D42
Much is to be gained by the sharing of Love, Knowledge,
Understanding, Compassion, and the material benefits
with Others. Give and you will receive, but give
willingly, without expectation of reward.

8.62 'It is hoped that you will act as a father figure to ARJUN.
(Arjun is my lodger, just 21 years old, who is a Management Trainee,
locally at Rothmans).
He is now in need of direction, of compassion, of companionship, of
caring, of love, and of confidence in himself. Cleanse his mind of
previous Religions. He needs to have courage and bravery in his heart to
go forwards. His family respect his needs, they are a good family. Arjun
is needed to spread the Word in the new World. He has been chosen as
a helper. Give time to his cause'

KEYPOINTS D43
a) There is no Evil in money and wealth in itself. It is
the pursuit of these Assets at the expense of Others
which is wrong...viz Greed. How can it be right, for one
Person to have so much, whilst Others suffer and die
through neglect?...viz the Biblical Story of the 'Eye of
a Needle'
b) Those who have much, MUST use a significant portion of
it for the common good, if they wish to be redeemed.
Otherwise the wealth will be removed from them in
subsequent lives. Consider the following:
c) Arjun's Grandfather is a case in point. He acquired
much wealth through his own diligent work and effort. He
has then used some of this money to establish Schools
throughout India for those who are less well-off. It is
therefore acceptable to Spirit that he keeps the rest of
his wealth.
d) In many of my previous lives, I personally have had
much wealth...for example as the Duke of Westminster.
I did not use this wealth for the benefit of Others. In
my present life therefore, it is intended that I should
experience being poor, so that I learn more compassion
for Others.
e) A local man in Oxfordshire is destitute, and feeds
himself often by eating turnips and vegetables he takes
from the fields around Banbury. It is 1998. He claimed
to be the Lord Syon, and that he owned much of the
Queen's Estate. We discussed this claim with a local
Barrister, and I even wrote to the Heraldic Office in
Edinburgh. He was dismissed as an Eccentric. In fact he
WAS a previous Lord Syon, but, because he abused his
wealth, he must now suffer accordingly.!

8.63 A message is received from Helana's Guardian Angel. 'We bring to you this message on this night, to enable you to be prepared for what is to come in future years. There will also be visions and pictures to help you to understand. Many tears are to follow and you will be kept in the company of Angels. Smile my Dears, for the days of testing are at an end, you have overcome many trials and tribulations. Treat these days as lessons in your lifetime, for they have been hard and wearing on your Minds and on your Spirits'.

'You have accepted these well, and have gained Courage, Strength and Understanding. I am a gentle Spirit, I wish no harm and come as directed by your Guide, to enable me to speak. I am different in a way that you are beginning to understand.

I will come to you in vision also. I may appear to you a little strange, but, believe my Dear you know me well. I see the Spirit within, I make no claims upon the Spirit, but I am aware of your presence within me. I caress you in your sleep. I have no wish for tears in your Eyes, precious woman'.

(Helana feels the presence of Wings on her Back)

8.64 Your son Ford's Spirit, is with you always, and also with Helana. His Spirit is battered and bruised. It will in time create a stronger Spirit; it is for this end alone we ask you to understand. Do not fear, for this time in his life is needed. He has done well considering the efforts of his Spirit. The Mind alone now, is all that is necessary to be corrected. He is very caring. Do not doubt the actions of many at the time his Awareness was beginning to grow. Understanding will be given, and the work that is to be completed, will be achieved. Ford is a chosen Helper in this lifetime.

8.65 Your other son, the brother Brian, is twinned with Ford throughout Eternity. Together they have been children shared by your two Spirits. It matters not that the mothers have changed, the Spirits are still the same; joined together as your Spirits are entwined. The children will return many times, fear not intrusion of Others' lives, they remain the children of your Spirits, they each have a particle of yours within them. Brian has many tasks to achieve in this lifetime.

KEYPOINTS D44
a) It is the Spirit Origin, Learning and Progression which is significant, not the Human Genealogy. Consider the Body as merely the vehicle which gradually wears out, requires maintenance and needs servicing. When it is beyond economical repair, it is discarded, and the driver (the Soul), moves to a new vehicle.
b) Today's Queen could have been yesterday's Beggar! The Body, the Family, the Lifestyle, is pre-chosen for the learning the Soul needs

8.66 On Sunday, 9th August, 1998. we start to tell our children, our families and our friends that we have decided to move to live in Ireland. We have decided to be married in Ireland, rather than in Bloxham. We had previously looked at the possibility of a wedding in the Spiritualist Church in Bloxham, followed by a Horse and Carriage drive to a local venue for the Reception. Spirit tell us that Others cannot understand the change in my Life, and that they will blame Helana. Helana is asked by Spirit to make an Altar-Cloth, to represent all aspects of Nature.(she has never done this!).

8.67 I feel throbbing inside my right index finger; I glimpse a blue square with my right eye. Judith asks me to help her to re-do her Will. She is asked to leave her husband by Spirit and to join with the man BOB. She says that they both have an equal share of the Spirit of John the Baptist, and have Mind contact. They need to be together for the Spiritual Work to be completed. We are told that Judith and I are due to achieve this level of communication when my Awareness has developed.
 Later in the day, I drive with Helana, as directed by Spirit, to RAF Halton, there we see the Squadron Fighter sign with a 'Crown' above it. Perhaps this is a call to Action? When we return, Judith tells me I am short of salt, which is not helping my Awareness develop. My Mind is clearing slowly, and she sees a green Aura on my shoulders. The 'burning' which I feel at the base of my neck is at the entry-point for Spirit.
(The man Bob is a surgeon who is married, and eventually chooses not to leave his wife!)
KEYPOINTS D45
a) Green is the colour for growth.
b) John the Baptist is Judith's Guide, he was also my son when I was Zechariah.

8.68 On Monday,10th August, a message is received from Mary: 'Your work in Ireland is so important, it must come first before anything else! It will be completed by your Children. The decision whether to give the special Child will be made, and will be reviewed, time and time again when you are settled in Ireland. The child, a girl, has been given in Spirit and will await the final decision, as to whether she is to be born in this lifetime, or in your next. Your need is heard and Spirit is aware and compassionate. Your sorrow John has been felt. Helana sees the girl in vision, I am told that I will be able to do this when my vision has cleared. (Helana has a heavy period, her tummy starts to normalise, the doctor says she needs Thyroid tablets for six months.)
I feel many cob-webs around my face when I sit. My ears are becoming more sensitive, when I blink, I sense a running water effect! Later that evening, at around 23.00hrs, we are asked to step outside to look at the stars in the Sky. We see four Shooting-Stars within five minutes, and are told the display is for us!.

8.69 On Tuesday, 11th August, Helana is feeling sad after the weekend. My Guide, Razeem tells us that we should target 1st November, 1998, for a permanent move to Ireland.

A message is then received from Samuel, Helana's Guide:

'I try so hard to come in this way, I have not yet mastered the voice control. This lady Helena allows me to be within her. I am her Guide.

'Her trust and faith enable me to do this, I will speak slowly and clearly so that you John, can write more correctly. The trees are so beautiful at this time of year; we give you both a vision of these at this time. You may not see this John, but your lady can share it with you. It is a tunnel of trees, guarding your way against danger. They are the essence of your life here on this Earth-Plane. They are beautiful.'

'We ask you: Do you feel the peace that these trees bring? We ask you to relax and to go within yourself; visualise the trees to bring peace...

I feel a deepness of calm within. 'You John, will not understand these words fully, however we ask you to retain them within your Mind for future learning. I come to help you this day, for there are many Helpers around you at this time, and your Doorkeeper will be present shortly'.

'Your Doorkeeper allows you to mingle with Others...ie. in a Spiritual Circle or at a meeting.. to protect your Spirit from other psychic People. It can also be necessary on visits to Spiritual Church as there are many Others present who can see. It is not necessary always to ask for your Doorkeeper as he comes automatically'.

KEYPOINTS D46

a) A Doorkeeper is appointed to you when you become Spiritually Aware, to protect your Spirit from invasion, control, or attack by other Spirits.

b) When a Medium sits in a Trance, their own Spirit is raised and leaves their Body. A visiting Spirit can then enter and use their Body and their Voice. It is prudent to restrict the Host-Occupation to no more than forty minutes at any one time; it may then be necessary to provide physical and verbal stimulation to the Medium, to cause their host-Spirit to return.

c) If you visualise a row or tunnel of trees, these can help to calm your Mind.

8.70. Samuel continues: 'We wish you to understand. This has been a traumatic evening for your lady, she has borne the rigors of the day upon her shoulders so bravely. You have not understood completely, the meaning of the divide of her Spirit with another. It is a step backwards for the World. She knows this. It is her dearest wish to unite the families of the World as one. When One has been united, and then divided, it is like the divide we talk of in Ireland.

Perhaps you do not see the significance of this, the Knowledge in this child is so great.

'She now suffers the loss of this Spirit as physical pain within her body. (reference is made to the Spirit of Jack) We do not wish you to send healing, this situation has been given for a purpose.
It will be remembered by her Spirit, for as and when it is needed. She will understand the pain of parting a Land, on it being divided, and draw the parallel to the split with Jack's Spirit.'

8.71 'Do not doubt these words, they are felt within you, but in a different manner. So much has changed within your lives. Do not despair over your children. We have felt the anguish and pain. It is yet to come, the treasured years, when you will share their lives once again. Be patient, allow them their freedom, they will return. Helana has done this to Steven, her eldest son. There was no greater pain and divide. He could not find the mother he once knew. He was confused'.

8.72 'You John, have now the same problem. Your gentler ways are beginning to show. The divide gets greater. Do not change your personality too much however, you are what you are. Your children have many lessons to learn. Consider carefully what you bring into their lives. It is your duty to show them the gentler ways. When they are with you, they need the comfort of a gentle father. Your humour need not be lost with them or with anyone else. We do not need you to be a 'boring old fart'. You have the greatness of Spirit to bring to them all that is necessary within their lifetimes. Allow them their freedom'.
KEYPOINT D47
It is necessary sometimes to let go of your children, to allow them their freedom of Choice. By allowing them their Freedom, you may well find that they come to respect and love you more.

8.73 'As Helana's child was allowed this, he has returned in fullness of face. His mother is still his mother and is welcomed within his heart. She is a wise woman, listen to her words in both trivial and in most important matters. These words are given to enable you to succeed in all walks of life. A high regard is set to achieve. Life is not easy, but we can help you if you listen to the words spoken. All can be comfortable and carefree if you will let it be...I come as a friend to help you with this thought. These lessons, this need to be present in the moment and to allow your children to be free are of the utmost importance at the present time. You have gained sufficient knowledge, and have been given directions by Helana.
All knowledge has been gained by Helana's Spirit and her Mind. We cannot say how delighted we are, in words to say about the greatness of this Spirit...The works that can be achieved by her actions and love are very great. It is difficult within a marriage to accept all that is given and to see what is required of you'.

146

'You must feel at times that you cannot 'win', or do anything right! but understand, there is no selfishness in Helana's Spirit. We hope that you fully understand, for it is necessary for you to know this. Take these words into your heart and understand what this means'.

8.74 'We ask that you advise us now on what questions you would ask. We wish to help you in any way we can, if there is understanding needed. Please ask.'
'It is important for you John to practice sitting quietly, you need to be able to do Trance work, and to be able to bring messages. You are protected at present by a 'Band of Light' which allows not others to see within. The knowledge which is within your Spirit is not for those who can see, nor for you to pass-on to those who can hear. It is difficult, but understand the importance of this message'.

8.75 'A message is received from my Guide Razeem, via Helana:
'My Dears, so much has been said this night, we wish you now to rest and your Spirits will be together even then. Rest assured, your visit to Ireland will be safe. You have no understanding at this time, of what is expected of you upon your return. A pleasurable trip, one of many, is all that we foresee at the present time. Your journey will be pleasant and without mishap. My Dears, rest assured you are in our safe care and loving arms every step of the way. Go now to your rest and allow your Spirits to be together in space and freedom...free from restriction, like the stars in the sky you will shine. Go now and rest'.

8.76 On Wednesday, 12th August, I awake in pain. I suffer pains from the Past, Chest pain to the front of my arms and chest, caused by the Spirit of Trevor; Shoulder-ache caused by the Spirit of Elsa. Both are alleviated by praying; by bathing; and by washing the pain away. We are told that Helana is to bond with my son Edwin. A new Guide comes to her. Jesus we are told is not the highest of Spirit. It is suggested that we should buy a Lottery ticket. We are asked to delay any decisions until the time is right, a message will be received from my Guide as to which way to turn.
KEYPOINTS D48
a) There is a correct time to make decisions. Allow a situation to unfold fully. Do not act in haste...The saying is true: ' Act in haste, repent at your leisure'.
b) It is also true: 'Do not put-off until tomorrow, what can be achieved today'...If some task needs doing, do not delay. Complete it and move-on.

8.77 Outside Spirits can cause you physical pain and suffering. If the pain is not yours, tell it to go away. There are ways in which you can protect yourself and minimise interference. Recognising the problem is half the solution.

KEYPOINTS D49
a) Say prayers for any invading Spirit.
b) Forcefully, TELL any invading Spirit to go away. Open the window or door and 'Shoo' them out.
b) Wash and bathe away the pain.
c) Say the words: ' Heavenly Father, Protect me with the Light and Love of True Spirit'.
d) Visualise yourself completely surrounded and protected by a sphere of white Light, a shield, which will repel any unwanted Spirit or evil Thoughts. Evil Thoughts are directed back onto the sender.
e) Be aware of the Thoughts in your Mind, every Thought is given to help you to achieve an understanding. If you do not at first, it will be represented.
f) Think on every situation, it has a meaning to be found. Analyse every situation.

8.79 Razeem tells me that I must allow my young children, Helen and Edwin their freedom. ....'Do not deny any child the freedom to find its way and its own Spirit. Every Spirit has its own pathway to follow. Do not tie it down, this is possessiveness.
Helen and Edwin do not receive the love they need from their Mother alone. If love is not found in a marriage, then it cannot be shown fully to the children of that marriage.
A child is given with so much love, it is the most beautiful thing in the World. Only good can then come from the Spirit of the child.
KEYPOINTS D50
a) A baby or child can have a very old and wise Spirit.
- Treat all with respect and love.
- Every individual has their own pathway to follow.
- As a parent you have chosen to have the child and your responsibilities are to nurture, love, teach, educate, and protect until at adulthood, the individual can then follow their own pathway; you must then take a secondary role and allow them to make their own decisions.
b) If love is not found, and demonstrated and alive in a marriage, how can the child then learn these values?

8.80 Razeem continues: 'There are to be many children in your life together. It is important that you show no favouritism, and give as much love as you can to all equally. Understand how love is shared. You John, have achieved this before. Helana has so much love to give, it is enough. This is important for the love of the whole World. Another child is to be given to you both, a girl, She awaits. Have faith, feel it in your Hearts, you are the most important people to this World. We need you here John, here and now, with this lady to gain your Awareness and raise your Spirit.'

'We will do whatever we can, but, you must also play your part...the man must change! You are part of this World's history...you are needed at this time!'

8.81 Judith gets a pain in her Heart when Helana thinks of her. Helana gets a cold Face on one side when Judith thinks of her. Judith's Spirit is closely entwined with both of us, and always has been. Judith's Spirit comes with words, through Helana in her sleep for the first time.
KEYPOINT D51
Thoughts can create physical sensations; pain and suffering in Others.

8.82 'There are many different kinds of love, for each person, for each child, for each animal, for your family...all is love, but varying degrees of love in each situation. A love shared is a love gained.
Allow this freedom of Spirit in this marriage and in this lifetime; your Journey will then be complete, the Earthly chains will then be broken. Possessiveness is not true love, it puts boundaries on the Spirit. True love cannot be achieved, if it is to be, if boundaries are placed around it. Save yourself anger and pain by allowing yourself freedom in this marriage. It is freedom within the marriage which brings true love without boundaries. Jealousy destroys, there needs to be trust for love to exist. If Truth and Honesty are present, these emotions need never be returned to. They have destroyed your previous relationships and your previous marriages. Go now in peace, and rest in peace, in the knowledge that you are safe in the light of True Spirit. You are protected by the light of True Spirit, guiding you safely along your chosen pathway in future years. Save only your tears for Mankind. Let them fall, but do not take on the worries of this World. You are being moved forwards. Your faith and trust are our hope for future years.
(There is an opportunity in the this lifetime to break the chains of misery caused by jealousy in previous lifetimes, which has destroyed our previous marriages)
KEYPOINTS D52
a) Our Spirits strive to achieve and learn about love, all the different types and aspects of love.
b) We choose our lives before we return to the Earth-Plane, but free-will and the effect of Human Emotions can alter our chosen Pathway.
c) Honesty, trust, and freedom from boundaries, allow Love to flourish. Jealousy and possessiveness destroy Love.
d) A primary purpose for our life is to Achieve and to Experience, all the different aspects of Love.

8.83 On Saturday,15th August, there have been many messages over the previous Evening and Night. I have seen the vision of a Tunnel of Trees. We have experienced a beautiful love-making session. I am asked to write a passage on love and feelings:

8.84 I write: Love is.........
Allowing freedom to the Spirit, so that it can complete its Karma.
Your whole Being yearning to be as One with another,
Your physical Body linked, your Hearts, your Minds, your Souls and your very Beings.
A feeling of Euphoria inside, complete satisfaction, the overpowering Desire is satisfied at that moment inTime, but not Possessiveness.
Your Heart is overcome with a complete sense of Love, and Delight, and Pleasure. There is no Lust, your physical need is satisfied throughout your whole Body....contact from Head to Toe outside; and inside your Minds are linked, your very Will,

There is no thought, nor need, nor wish for any other Person, nor Event, nor Happening. Everything you aspire to achieve, and need is satisfied. The place, the moment, the warmth, the love, the entirety of your whole Essence.
You are complete, two Souls as One, two vibrations linked, two lives shared and entwined forever...
I lightly touch your Body, completely from Head to Toe, and massage your Spirit with my Hands...the shape of your Body, your Back, your Breasts, your Mind...

8.85 I protest to Helana:.........How could I have lost you for 2,000 years? We have loved before at a physical level, and lived many lives together, but our Spirits have not been Aware or entwined together as now. Our feelings for each other have never been so deep before. How can I not feel possessiveness now, when I love you so ?
Helana responds:..
'Possessiveness is insecurity, we must trust each other, there is no need for jealousy. The feelings of another (Jack) can be felt, but you need have no concern of my love for you. In this lifetime, we will build our life and our future together as One.'
KEYPOINTS D53
a) Human Love and Spiritual Love are different. Spiritual Love is felt within as your Spirit becomes Aware, the feelings are difficult to describe, but amount to pure Joy above and beyond the normal Sexual climax.
b) Spiritual Love is more akin to Friendship, it is nothing to do with sex,
- **It is total commitment to your Loved One, and to all living creatures of Nature.**

150

- Giving of Yourself, without the expectation of receiving,
- Being unselfish, being caring, respecting your Loved One's wishes.
- Respecting the sanctity of your relationship,
- As you come to Love, you will find inner Peace.
- As you come to Love, you will come to appreciate Nature, and the harmony of the Universe,
- You will come to glory in the Love of the One God, and all of Creation.
- As you come to Love, you will begin to become more Spiritually Aware, and then you are opened-up to an understanding of the reason for our Earth-Life, and how we fit into the total Universe.

8.86 We listen to the Words on CD from John Lennon; his Spirit tells me that he is delighted to have them reproduced in this Book.

LOVE is Real, Real is LOVE
LOVE is Feeling, Feeling LOVE
LOVE is Wanting to be Loved.

LOVE is Touch, Touch is LOVE
LOVE is Reaching, Reaching LOVE
LOVE is Asking to be Loved.

LOVE is You Feeling Me
LOVE is Knowing we can be.
LOVE is Free, Free is LOVE

LOVE is Living, Living LOVE
LOVE is Needing to be Loved.

##

CHAPTER 9. AWARENESS BEGINS

9.00 It is the first week of August 1998. I have tried many times drawing, and trying to receive messages from my Guide. Now I can do this in written form, now that the interlopers have agreed to stand-back. Now I can begin to accept messages myself, and to build more confidence in their accuracy. It is possible for the first time, for me to receive messages and to verify their accuracy with those received from Helana or Judith, separately and independently. This is important, as it is an essential feature of building my confidence.

KEYPOINTS AB1
a) If you are to become Spiritually Aware, then it is essential to your learning process that you can verify the accuracy of Messages received. Part of the problem of accuracy is that the Mind is a powerful force and your own Thoughts can over-ride and shutout the true messages from Spirit; this is particularly true when messages of a personal nature are given.
b) It is essential that everyone has a Mentor, someone who can provide an independent 'second source of data'........
c) Remember, there are many rogue, jealous and dark Spirits who may wish to mislead you, or try to prevent you from achieving your individual Goals. These Spirits may even pretend to be your true Guide.
d) The forces of Evil will always attempt to prevent the achievement of Love and Goodness.

9.01 My Guide Razeem writes ' The week of 31st August is satisfactory for your next trip to Ireland. Your journey is to be accomplished via Stranraer to Belfast; your friend Steve will help to drive the van which needs to be a 3.5 tonne Luton vehicle. Contact your Company for the best rates. Allow Helana to lead you, as to where you go and when; you will be able to home in on your chosen area and will feel a lot more comfortable about things. Bangor will be a good place for you to seek temporary accommodation. Look when you visit Bangor, for an Estate Agent who will offer you a property'.
(Bangor was suggested to us by an ex-army friend who was based nearby in Holywood and worked at the local Rugby Club in Banbury.)
KEYPOINT AB2
When the timing is correct, all will fall into place.

9.02 It is Thursday, 13th August,1998. Razeem writes: 'Try to sit and relax for thirty minutes each day, at the same time, so that I can communicate with you more easily...Today is indeed a momentous step forwards. We can now progress rapidly with your Awareness. My friend, you have done well and so has your lady. Your Spirit will now begin to rise and we will be able to complete your understanding.

Take heart, for events are proceeding well and soon we can embrace each other. Your Mind will be prepared, so as to allow your Spirit to gain complete Understanding. Well done my friend'.
(Helana and I spend a lovely night together).
KEYPOINT AB3
It helps with Spirit Communication, if you choose to sit regularly at the same time. In this way they can be prepared for you.

9.03 Helana lays-out on the breakfast Table a willow-pattern cloth, and explains that the freedom of the birds in the picture, is the freedom she has given to Jack's spirit. She explains that in January 1998, that she was visited by my Spirit; and also that of Jack (now in Philip).
(nb: we did not meet in this life until March!),
A tussle took place inside her with the Spirits arguing, pulling and tearing her apart inside.
My Spirit was the stronger, and so she agreed to release Jack's Spirit, but Jack's Spirit has not accepted this.
The Spirit was fighting to remain with her, but the Mind of the man had rejected her in view of their age differential (only five years!), her spirituality, and her strong personality..
(.It should be remembered that Jack and Helana's Spirits are twinned. This allowed one-to-one contact at all times, mind-to-mind, and also a sexual relationship. To reject all of this, was an extremely traumatic experience for Helana).
KEYPOINTS AB4
a) Twinning, or in this case the same Spirit dividing, allows for an extremely close contact between the individuals involved.
b) Not only can the Spirits communicate, but with Spiritual Awareness in both parties, the Minds are also linked.
c) This will then allow Thought connection.

9.04 Helana lights a single candle in the centre of the table; she tells me she loves me and that I must put Jack into the Past, he has gone not to return.! No longer do I need to feel second-best! No longer does my Spirit need to be held back from Growth. The restriction of Jack has held back my Spiritual Growth for many hundreds of years! Helana tells my Mind to release my Spirit and allow it to fly!!. Helana now does this to Jack (Phil), and Constance also did this to me. I feel euphoric, I feel taller, my Back feels straighter, there is a release of tension. Helana sobs profusely.
KEYPOINTS AB5
a) Any one Spirit in your Peer-Group can restrict your Spiritual Growth.
b) An Emotional block is created, which needs to be released before progress can be made.

c) This block can be created by Jealousy or Hate or any other strong Resentment.

9.05 Razeem sends his congratulations. 'Your Awareness can now progress. As the Relationship between Judith and Bob progresses, so too will develop the Relationship between Helana and you John. Your Love and Progress will be felt by the World, and Others too can also now progress! This is how Ireland is to be healed. You John, have the Knowledge inside your Spirit, it is only a case of releasing this. Have Sympathy and Compassion for Others who will struggle so much more to achieve this learning. You are being helped by Helana and by Spirit. Others' lives will not necessarily be so easy!

Dig deep on important Issues, these will be given in Visions and in words in your Mind. Allow the Thoughts to drift in and out. Let them flow; if they are needed they will be held. Turn the Energies of these Thoughts into something good; instead of anger and frustration. Calm your Spirit and send love to the World. Stand back, breathe deeply, and think of Helana and the love found. It is these Thoughts that can be sent to Others and in this way share your love with the World. In this way, no damage will come to your Spirit. It is freedom to share what you have found which is important. Your love shared without jealousy. If you share this love with the World, there will be no-one who will take it away'.

KEYPOINTS AB6
a) All is given for Sharing.
b) If you have a Talent or Ability and do not use this to help Others, then in subsequent lives it will be taken away.
c) This applies to any gift,...Love, Wealth, Wisdom, Musical Ability, etc.
(I have been told of a Lifetime as a Cathedral Organist, I chose not to use this talent to its full potential; so in subsequent Lives it has been removed.)

9.06 On 14th August, a message is written from Razeem my Guide: 'Your Ears are being prepared for Audio-Reception, so be ready! Your lady is correct when she tells of the interference last night when you tried to sit and meditate. There may still be interference but this will now rapidly diminish. *(I had had a discussion on the telephone with my brother Edward about his 'beliefs'...or disbeliefs! and I had posted to him writings received from our father TED in Spirit; I felt very agitated inside, rubbing on my leg and was unable to relax.*

An immediate sense of relief was obtained by sending Edward a thought message of Peace, Love, Calm and Light. I subsequently sent Edward a book to read so as to try to modify his Beliefs...he had previously agreed to read the book but then returned it un-read.) .

(Revelations are coming fast and furious it would seem)

154

'Take notice of all that happens so that it can be recorded for the future. You will soon enjoy the direct contact (seeing and hearing).
Do not fear this; it will be an initial shock but you will quickly come to terms with this. Visit your mother tomorrow and take your lady to see the sights. Accept that progress is being made and that Events will develop quite rapidly now. Allow your Mind to be still and I will come to you later this evening. You should be able to gain far more tonight. Your friend Razeem'.

9.07 Razeem continues:
'In our eyes, LOVE is the greatest treasure. If you are possessive it is taken away. Think of your past lives, riches were taken away, as also your musical Talents.
You have lost Gold, Silver, Love, Music etc... Do not Possess!!
Everything is a gift from God.
GIVE and TAKE. Do not fear you will lose this child (Helana) Her love is so profound and so is yours. It is the only way to find freedom in your lives, to progress fully. We hope that you have gained an Understanding. Now that you have found each other, it is necessary to allow the freedom and to understand what this means. Think carefully John, we do not wish to see any anguish or pain in your lives yet again.
We have tried many times to explain...We feel that now you are at a level of Understanding to retain what is given, and to retain what is in front of you. Do not lose it.!
KEYPOINTS AB7
a) LOVE is found in FREEDOM.
b) POSSESSIVENESS and JEALOUSY destroy LOVE
c) LOVE is the greatest TREASURE
d) SHARE your TALENTS or you will lose them.

9.08 Over lunch the words come through....
'There are now more wasps and fewer bees, this will continue as the nature of Man becomes harsher. Ants are also beginning to invade Mankind's space. NATURE will rebel against the hostile actions of MANKIND. Moths who have an aggressive side are attracted to a light-bulb and are blinded. In the same way Man can read from Nature, if only he allows his Eyes to see.
KEYPOINTS AB8
a)MANKIND is a part of NATURE. If through our own Greed, Ignorance or Intolerance, Mankind disturbs the balance of Nature,Nature will respond to correct that Situation.
b)ACTION creates RE-ACTION!. GOD created the balance and the power. It is Mankind who chooses to create the re-action, not God.

9.09 We discuss the Video we have just watched called 'The Mission'. Razeem responds:

'Picture the scene of the Jesuit Priest who had more courage and faith than those who fought...Remember also the soldier who stopped in his tracks, but then allowed others to stand in the way of the truth he felt. Do not be afraid of what Others may think of you.

In that one second there was hope for the World, *(when the Soldier hesitated)* Do not be swayed by the actions of Others.

(I was tearful at the remembrance of the video and went to the toilet to hide my tears).

'Allow your children to see you crying...the nature of this man has changed. Allow the gentler side of your nature to be seen, knowing in your heart that you are right. The man who found his faith...in the end all was lost by his final actions. You John, are now a member of the Army of God. Do not allow Others to take this away from you.'

KEYPOINTS AB9
a) Many Spiritual messages are apparent in songs, films and videos, if only we listen to the words and appreciate the messages which are presented to us.
b) Do not allow Others to deflect you from what you believe to be correct.

9.10 At 04.00 hrs, Razeem speaks through Helana. 'Allow the spirit to settle with the lady Helana, she is brave and trusting. Questions can be answered in privacy to avoid any upset to Helana. You John, are not aware of Helana's work this day. I come in her Voice to avoid any more tiredness to Helana's body or Spirit. You will recognise me from the gestures of my hands. Believe, it is I, Razeem'.

KEYPOINTS AB10
a) The bringing of Messages and Trance work can be physically and mentally exhausting.
b) Time is necessary to allow for healing of the Spirit and recovery of the body.
c) If your own Spirit is removed from your body for too long, it may well need to be persuaded to return...The experience of enjoyment and pleasure outside of the Human form, free from the aches and pains, may be such that the individual Spirit is reluctant to return...If it does not of course, then the body will die!
d) It is necessary to have someone with you, to talk or shake you back to Human Reality, as soon as the visiting Spirit departs. A few minutes should be allowed before a vigorous stimulation is applied.

9.11 'I take the Hand of this Child, on this day, and bring you together as man and wife. I cannot say how glad we feel to see this Event take place (touching the second finger of her left hand).

The realisation, of the entwining of your Spirits is about to become a Reality, not just a Manifestation. Through the Ages your Spirits have been divided, you have come together now in Spirit (and bodies also occasionally!). Understand that we have little understanding of your Earthly ways...These are memories only, as the Emotions are long gone. The pleasure of sensing the Spirits coming together is all that we need.
Safe in this Heart is John....(pointing to me)
Safe in this Heart is Helana...(pointing to her)
There can be no Other in this lifetime. The Spirits are entwined for Eternity. Watch my hands....(Rotational and circular movements are made above our heads with the hands clasped together).
Believe this in your Heart and in your Spirit....We have tried to explain...You cannot fully grasp....We ask you to accept this as time goes by...We hope that you will pass on this to your lady'

KEYPOINTS AB11
a) The entwining of two Spirits in Love is the ultimate goal. Once achieved they are joined forever.
b) It is not necessary thereafter for the physical bodies to always be together, for there are many other Relationships, and forms of Love to be experienced.
c) A joining together and bonding does occur in the Spirit World, which is held in great Sanctity and Respect.
d) You are held Accountable and Responsible for all of your Actions on the Earth-Plane.

9.12 'I heal this child's Body....(pulling strands away from her stomach). I will take away all that is needed to be gone, so as to allow her the freedom for her Spirit to grow....(the hands are used four times to pull strands from Helana's Throat as well as her Stomach)....She has a role to play; it is for this reason she has been also given today, the re-union of this Spirit on this day. She has had many a broken Heart, and the Spirit of this Angel, Christopher, as we shall call him now; has been present in this lady's life for many Ages, to bring to her the love that is needed for her to survive'.

KEYPOINTS AB12
a) The Human Body is an Energy form, as is everything we perceive in this Earth-World.
b) It is possible by changing the Aura Energy field, to modify and change the physical Body within. Conversely, the Aura itself is an indication of the physical state within.
c) Some people can see Human Auras, and can accordingly diagnose physical problems, equally some people can actually see within the Body to directly identify any Physical defects.
d) Psychic surgery is the act of modifying the Aura and the physical Body.

e) There are many books available to the reader, which identify and list the Chakra Energy centres.
A block or distortion to any of these centres, will restrict and affect your Emotional, Physical, and Spiritual Relationships, and Feelings.
f) What Actions we take as Humans, directly affect our Auric Energy Levels, which in turn directly affect our physical well-being.
(In the year 2000, I have been for Healing to a clear a blocked, distorted, Chakra. This Block occurred in a previous lifetime, when I lived as a Roman General)

9.13 She will not entertain the loss of Jack's Spirit gladly, for this reason the Angel's Spirit has been returned to her on this day. You John, do not understand what is being said now, but retain these words for future Understanding. You, Helana, have seen my dear who this Spirit is…you have no idea now, but all is returned this lifetime for the work to be achieved. He is beautiful and will remain so!'
There is silence for a few minutes and the words 'John, my dear man, forgive us this privacy'….I continue to sit in silence facing Helana who is in Trance.
(Helana senses and feels the loss of Jack's Spirit, my own Awareness is insufficient for me to be able to direct and control my own Spirit, so that it will remain within Helana to fill this void. High Spirit have accordingly introduced Christopher to help until my Awareness is great enough.)
KEYPOINTS AB13
a) We are Spiritual, Energetic, Physical Beings.
b) The fact that the majority of Humans, cannot See, Sense, Feel, or Hear Spirit, or many of the other Energy Forms, simply indicates that their Awareness has not yet developed enough.

- As Spiritual Beings, we are affected by the presence of other Spirits.
- As Energetic Beings, we are affected by the presence of all other levels of Energy, seen or un-seen, felt or unfelt, sensed or un-sensed…Heat, Light, Radiation, Thought, Emotion, etc.
- As Physical Beings, we are affected by the presence of our Physical Environment…….the Chemistry, the Form, the Senses, etc.

9.14 Words are then received from Christopher….
' I am now here as your Guide and Mentor; I am not Razeem, forgive my passing through your lives, you are not yet ready for a full explanation, but I am a little one from the Past and will assist you for what is to be.

'I come in disguise...my ways are hidden....fear not John,...I have loved this lady for so long...she is my mother and my treasure. I have waited so long for her to recognise me.'

'I have stood by her side for so long and now see her in her true light. I will assist you now in all that is to be.
I am to be a Helper, and come to you in words and memories of a past life. I am by your Side at all times. It has been given that I would not return, but matters of great urgency come to the Earth-Plane. Perhaps now John you will understand the feelings within me, and not feel a jealousy of any kind. I may be within the body of a man, with ordinary Eyes and Ears, but the Spirit within me is that of Christopher.
I too have lessons to learn. I will return on another occasion and bring to you the Knowledge of my Being within your lives.
I will return again in a future life, in disguise, as an Angel. There is much to be achieved...it has begun, but another life is needed. We will all return quickly. It is for this specific purpose only that I return for, "needs be" as the saying goes "all hands on deck" are needed. I will leave you now in the safe hands of this lady who loves you dearly...as I did on the Earth-Plane, and will continue to do so.'

KEYPOINTS AB14
a) Christopher is the Spirit of the son of Jesus, who was rescued by me in my role as John the Disciple.
b) Jesus did have one son Christopher, a Child with Rebecca. (the Spirit of Constance).

.(At this time Helana was Ruth. When Jesus was crucified, the Romans, encouraged by the Jewish Priesthood, treated this Act as one to apply to all the Band of Followers. We were all pursued as Terrorists and had to flee for our lives. Jesus had previously asked me to take care of Mary, Rebecca and Christopher for him, as my own.
We managed to escape the Holy Lands but were relentlessly followed where-ever we went. When Christopher was six years of age,...(He was four when Jesus was taken), we were cornered by the Romans, and GOD decided enough was enough. The child was taken to Heaven on a cloud, by Angels, to avoid slaughter by the soldiers, we were then able to depart anonymously and to escape).

9.15 On 15th August, as she drives me home, Helana tells me that our car is being driven by the Spirit of Christopher. Later that evening, I receive answers to many questions asked by me about the nature of Spirit, these are dealt with in the chapter on Spiritual Awareness. Before we left to visit Judith, Helana has previously laid-out a meal for the Spirit of Jack...(a final supper).
Upon our return she destroys the table-cloth, washes the napkin, and sprinkles the chair and cutlery with purified water. The cutlery is then taken outside of the house to be washed and cleansed by the rain.

KEYPOINTS AB15.
a) Rain water purifies and cleanses the Land, it is also a necessary ingredient for almost all Life-Forms.
b) Any object placed in the rain will be purged. The light from the Sun can also serve this same purpose.
c) A Person's depression or negativity, can be helped by placing their Image in the rain or in the Light.
In the same way that Energies from the Sun can transform a dark, dull day, into a beautiful experience. When the clouds lift and the Rainbow shines through the cold, wet, rain, so our Hearts and Minds and Spirits can be lifted.
d) Positive Thoughts and Prayers, do help to change Attitudes.

9.16 On the Sunday morning of the 16th, my Guide Razeem writes: 'Your Sitting last night did serve a purpose, but you are not aware of this. Do not lose heart, as all will become clear in the next few days. Do not struggle John for anything, as all that is needed will be given if you have the Trust, the Faith and the Love. Your Spirit is indeed entwined with Helana's and the recognition of this by you is about to commence. You can now go to your work (11.00am) appointment. Helana is now to go her own way for the rest of the day.'

9.17 'We wish you to understand how the great question of how the World is to change is to happen. Even now developments are still in flux, however, we are now close enough to 'D' day for us to convey to you both news of the arrangements as they stand, but remembering that timings can still change if the situation warrants this change. We are pleased with your progress and wish your full comprehension to follow as quickly as possible. It is necessary to move forwards swiftly if we are to gain the initiative before Events take-over, and cause step-changes to the existing status-quo. We wish you to appreciate the urgency in every way.
It may be necessary to drop everything and go to Ireland at a moment's notice if Events spiral 'out-of-control'. At present your plans up to Christmas look reasonable. When you visit Ireland you will establish the Area and Contacts to enable you to find Accommodation.
Your work Interview, John, will proceed as planned. Do not waste any time thereafter in making arrangements for your move. We would prefer you to be in Ireland during October,1998, if at all possible. The more that you plan a quick move the better. Pack now as much as you can. Take everything you consider essential for your new life together; further guidance will be given day by day. World Events are dictating the final time-scale, as is Man's will and choice! So, we cannot be more specific. You will not be in any danger, but appreciate that anything can happen which could precipitate a crisis'.

(The messages at this time concern the urgency of our departure. This appears to be important not only to protect our Earthly Lives, but also for Spiritual reasons to provide healing to the Peoples of Ireland).

9.18 I ask of Razeem the question:, 'How is the World to Change?'

KEYPOINTS AB16

a)Mankind's Actions will precipitate a crisis of Nature. There may be widespread devastation which will change the Economic Situation. Throughout this period you, and your families, will be protected. Your actions throughout this phase will be as a bystander, without drawing undue attention to yourselves'.

b)Not all Events can be accurately predicted by High Spirit. The timing is often determined by Human Actions. If these Actions continue, widespread devastation will result.

c)Some families can be protected, but this may mean fleeing a location or an Area.

9.19 Helana feels a 'restriction' within, the message is received that she is being 'probed' by two Spirits, those of Jack and Bryan. She is told that her thoughts have attracted these unwanted guests. These Spirits are lost and still seek answers. Helana is told that she must rise above these Spirits and tell them firmly to move-on. Helana feels a pain in her right side, her eyes change and she starts winking, this is the presence of the Spirits affecting her.

(winking is a habit of Philip/Jack)

Helana is asked to say prayers for them, and to send them on their way. Helana's Guide, Samuel continues:..

'The Spirits of these two men have been in chains for too long. Jealousy has destroyed their inner strength of peace and calm. The chains have been broken by this child, for now she is no longer the keeper of their Light. It is only her love that has kept them walking in this life-time. They have been in Shadowlands and have been retrieved by Helana. It is the walking away by Helana which has brought to them destruction. They do not know how to progress themselves, they have no direction in this life, hence they seek Helana, it has always been so.

Do you not see Helana, why they come so close? It is not to be, you are fully protected. They will not be allowed to harm your Spirit or your body. We ask you to understand that this will be repeated, at the present time, for they are in need of prayers. You are of an understanding of this and you will be asked to do this, for they know of no other with love in their heart to offer them comfort.'

KEYPOINTS AB17

a)The presence of other Spirits can change your Appearance and your Mannerisms.

b)Thinking of Others does attract their Spirits to you.

c)Jealousy destroys.

161

d) Prayers will comfort and heal.
e) It is possible for Spirits to be recovered from Shadowlands.

f) PAIN can be caused by other Spirits, either deliberately, or to announce their presence, or out of ignorance. Should you suddenly feel a pain or discomfort, ask yourself ` Is this mine? or is it given to me? Try to think of any loved-one or recent acquaintance, who has, or had, a similar pain or discomfort. Tell the pain firmly to go away. Say prayers for the Individual. Should the pain ease, repeat the words until it goes completely, or simply ask the Individual to step back and to stop bringing you the discomfort.

g) PAIN can also be given to you as a direct consequence of your Thoughts, or your Actions. This pain is for you to learn and to UNDERSTAND. As soon as you accept that you have been: Cruel, Heartless, Nasty, Bitter, Racial, Prejudiced, Spiteful, Critical, etc....and, you repent these Thoughts, Words or Actions, your PAIN may well ease.

h) My legs and feet itch terribly, through the presence of Spirits from previous Relationships. This is removed by applying a lotion or hand cream, and acknowledging the presence.

h) PAIN it must be remembered, is also the mechanism whereby the MIND, is persuaded to allow the SPIRIT to permanently leave the Body when it is time to depart this Earth-Plane.(die or pass-over)

i) PAIN should not be feared, it is necessary for your Body to protect itself from outside Agencies, or for the Mind and Body defence and repair Mechanisms to be brought into play. The Body is a wonderful Being, self-regulating and finely tuned. When it is invaded or harmed, the defence Mechanisms are stimulated and triggered by the Pain response.

9.20 Later in the day, we are told: 'Your prayers have been heard and compassion felt. Do not doubt these words are from True Spirit. We will remain by your sides, an understanding has been gained to send these Spirits on their way. There will not be a repeat of history!
Remember these words for another occasion. Do not fear all has been completed at the present time. You are now free to remain at peace, working for Spirit of a true kind, and of a gentle nature. The mens' Spirits, have now finally left your presence.'

9.21 I suffer pains in my legs.... 'John, my dear man, you have been given the 'legs of this man Philip/Jack' to remind you not only of your dedication to this lady, but also that the Spirit of Jack is in need.
The prayers will come best from you, for in this way you gain forgiveness in your Heart for this man, and he gains forgiveness in his Spirit that will enable him to progress.
It is also hoped that you will find an Understanding for both these men, and, that they also will find an Understanding. Do not fear this message, it is given with Truth and Understanding of the needs of Others.
A reminder to say prayers for this Spirit.
KEYPOINT AB18
- **Prayers are Heard**
- **Prayers can bring Harmony and Forgiveness.**
- **Prayers can cause Healing and change Attitudes.**

9.22 On Sunday,16th August, 1998, I am asked to sit quietly:
Razeem tells me that the time is right for me now to begin to Hear properly. 'Concentrate your Mind on a favourite recreation, this could be Rugby. Allow the ball to pass quickly from player to player.(visualise)
Alas, Razeem tells me later, my Mind is too busy for any progress to occur. The Exercise is accordingly postponed for a later date.
KEYPOINT AB19
A busy Mind will negate any progress towards Spiritual Awareness.

9.23 Helana has a Vision involving three pale-green suitcases.
She is back in her home in Kings Sutton and is being guided as to what to pack. She knows the destination is Ireland. Spirit is getting impatient for her to leave. She wishes to take a delicate trinket, but finally decides to leave it behind. Packing the trinket and then walking back to leave it on the Bed. She is dressed in black.
My Guide Razeem interprets the vision as:....
'The three suitcases represent her sons Abel, Steven, and her ex-husband , Mervin. The journey is to Ireland. The trinket represents the memories of the Past, which she leaves behind. She is dressed in black for strength, so that she will accept more readily the departure and separation from these People and the past Situation.
A complete break is needed, with no Guilt, no Remorse, and a positive step forwards. The suitcases also represent all that she can carry, and she leaves behind most of her Effects and Valuables...Take heart, the pain of this time will soon end, and your future life can begin in earnest. Helana will not be able to switch-off completely until a financial settlement is made with her ex-husband.'

a) Many messages from Spirit, are given in Visions and
Dreams. Always record these, and seek interpretation.
b) Often later Events will show you the significance of
the Vision. They are given for us to understand our own
Lives, and to be able to help Others.
c) Many passages in the Bible are figurative; they
require interpretation and should not be taken
literally.

9.24 'Helana carries the burdens of your Spirit, John, as well as hers.
This is her gift to you. A complete act of Love on her part. This means
that you do not need to dig so deep into your life, and that as she
progresses, so will you too. This is one reason that she suffers so, for
she takes on the burdens as indeed Jesus did. For this reason she will
sit at the feet of Jesus, when she returns to the Spirit-World. Do not
fear that where she treads is not pure. These were her words and a
bargain with GOD. These were the words actually spoken by Helana to
GOD.
................" I wish to tread in the footsteps of Jesus".....................
Her ways will be your ways; listen to her Heart, she is within you. You
will be guided along your way to follow in the footsteps of Jesus. Your
baggage is lightened, free from the Burdens of many life-times. Helana
will take on board the Past. She will sift through the Past to resolve
these issues, as she has done many times before. Understand John,
these words are from True Spirit and will not be repeated. We wish you
now to Understand that this is the true nature of this child. Sufferings of
the Past will be dimmed, in this way Helana has helped so many in the
Past'.

9.25 Jesus states 'She has even shared the burdens of my Life. It is for
this reason, we set aside a place in the highest of the Heavens, to bring
to you both, the rewards that you deserve. We are delighted to see the
coming together of these wonderful Spirits, we could not have chosen
better.! We see you growing stronger and stronger by the minute. You
are a powerful force in the World, and will continue to be this one great
Spirit throughout Eternity. Understand John, why it is so important for
Helana to be in Ireland. It is a great act she does for this World. Sleep is
now necessary for her Spirit to recuperate, and to be still. There will be
many tears. Understand, this is because of her nature and feelings for
other Peoples'.

KEYPOINTS AB21
a) It is possible for one Spirit to take on-board, to
share, to help to resolve, the Burdens of another, but
only with the approval of High Spirit.

b) It is possible to make a bargain with GOD, if you are prepared to devote your present Earth-Life for the benefit of Others, then you can expect some advantage. Some, perhaps deferment of Karma, in this lifetime. *(the bargain is normally with High Spirit, who act on behalf of GOD.....BUT BEWARE IF YOU DEFAULT!)*
c) ALWAYS be extremely cautious of what you wish for.
d) The POWER arising from the twinning of Spirits is far greater than that from two separate Spirits.

9.26 My Guide continues: 'Every day of this Child's life is given to the Peoples of the World. As in Visions of the Lord on the Cross, understand that the Spirit of this Child receives this treatment every day of her life. It is her choice. It in no way affects the true nature of your relationship, but understand, there is so much love for the World and its Peoples. She now brings to you John, this euphoria and love. You have a treasure in your heart. Do not walk away or discard it, for there is no finer one to be found. The heart of this Child is equivalent to that of Jesus. She has the abilities to Understand, and to Suffer. She is still learning to channel the gift of love she has for these Peoples.'

9.27 We ask John, for your help and assistance. We ask you John, to allow her to be free, to channel her love. Understand, it does not affect your Relationship. Throughout all your Lifetimes you will not experience a higher love. Understand this; Eternity offers this constant love. For your lives on the Earth it may be necessary to bring about a parting of body only, but your Spirits will remain entwined forever. You will not be parted from this lady. She has given so much to this World and will continue to do so. It is understood by Judith, the nature of her Ways. This message comes to you from True and Honest Spirit.'

9.28 'This Child is a free Spirit, she needs this to be able to send out love to other People. She is one of Nature...a deer...the clutter of the Mind is not necessary in her daily life. For this reason we bring you together so that the load can be shared. You are as One. You, John have the ideas, to set them down on paper. This Child has the Actions and Emotions to bring to people what is necessary.
As your role, John, is clearly seen, so too is the life of this Child. If all is shared, the pattern of working can be achieved. One is Teacher; one is Scholar. One is Giver, one is Taker, etc.
All can be reversed and all is shared. Pen and paper is your forte'...this is not Helana's, Hers are always the Hands, the Mind and the Heart. She is like the Breeze, the wind in the Branches, she needs the freedom of the Trees. Freedom is necessary and is important for her Spirit to be free to travel to where she is needed. Understand John, this work continues daily and does not stop at any moment. In sleeping hours also, she is here in Spirit to help and to understand the lightness of the ways in which they can communicate'.

9.29 'It does not stop on the Earth-Plane; it happens universally throughout all Levels, there is so much to achieve. The Spirit of this Child never dims and never stops working. Your Spirit John, also continues to work in different Spheres. Each has their role to play, different, but both equally important. Do not judge others by your standards, John. One is of speech, one is of writings. The rest is within each of you. Your Spirit sends out messages of hope and love, taking away fears of this World and the Universe.

Have an Understanding, that:
* not Everyone is the same.......
* not Everyone needs pen and paper..........
* not Everyone has to achieve the same..........
* not Everyone needs to be able to Communicate, for some are within Spirit already.........
* You have the gift of Communication also, necessary for your Earthly Life.....
* You are here as a Human Being and also as a Spiritual Being. Combining both lives is possible and can be achieved. A balance will be found.
* Do not force your ways on Others, Understand their Ways are also important.
* Allow Freedom, and Love is yours.
* A cluttered Mind is incompatible with an Awareness of Spirit. It is not possible to work together, with Helana, or with Spirit, if your Mind is cluttered.
* You must allow the Spirit to achieve what is to be achieved in this Lifetime.

KEYPOINTS AB22
a) Everyone is different, their Purposes and Goals are different, so their Needs and Skills need also to be different.
b) Respect Others for what they are, recognising that they too have a purpose to their Lives.
c) The Mind needs to learn to accept that each person has a Spiritual Purpose to this Lifetime. Through the attainment of Spiritual Awareness, it is possible to determine your individual Purpose. Through Prayer you can be guided, but only if you genuinely seek. Seek and Ye shall Find. Ask and Ye shall be given.

9.30 I feel a tightness in the base of my throat, I ask Razeem if this is a signal:..
' I am Razeem, I come to you today to see whether it is possible for you to make conversation with me. The pressure on your throat, is caused by me trying to speak through you.'

166

'This is difficult because you are still resisting this in your sub-conscious Mind. We will continue to try to break through this barrier.

Do not give up hope, it can be done with practice. Practice makes perfect. The words form okay, they are coming directly from me, but via your Mind. Please continue to write in this way. The only way forward is to continue to try to overcome your Body's fear of any intrusion. It is good that you are able to write now in this way.

'It means that we can proceed to communicate with you on paper and in a short time without writing.

Allow your Mind to accept the Words and Speak them as well as Writing at the same time. In this way your Body will become used to accepting this practice, and then we can dispense with the Writing. We can continue as long as you wish to co-operate. This procedure is quite normal for people to get used to Spirit Communication.'

KEYPOINTS AB23

- **Spirit are quite logical in their methods.**
- **I began to learn with drawing pictures, then letters, words, followed by sentences.**
- **We progressed to written messages, to be followed by the spoken message.**
- **A signal is given to promote a Response, in my individual case a 'cough', this can now be pressure on my throat, or around my body, a stiff finger, a thought, a particular feeling under my chin, etc.**
- **My own sub-conscious Mind is resisting any attempt by Spirit to enter my Body, so I am unable to carry out Trance work. I sometimes hear noises or single words. Occasionally, I see Spirit 'Clouds' or Groups. All is progressing gradually and steadily.**

9.31 Razeem continues: 'I do not know how long it will take for you to move to direct voice response. Your Ears are now ready to receive and soon you will begin to hear Noises and Voices. Do not be afraid of this. You are surrounded by True Spirit who wish you no harm, and are preventing anyone else coming too close. All is as it should be. Your Throat is now ready to talk in the same way as your Hand writes. I would like to write some more if you are agreeable....this procedure is the only way forward. Your Spirit is now aware of what is necessary, it is only necessary for your Mind to accept this'.

'Try to concentrate on the words and see them in your psychic-Eye. We will try again on another occasion. I am happy with your progress so do not be despondent. Relax now and go to your bed...your friend Razeem.'

(The psychic Eye is positioned mid-way between the Eye Brows, it is where you visualise from)

9.32 The morning 17th August, 1998, 'Hallo John, this is Razeem here. 'The story unfolds my friend, you must be somewhat amazed. It has been so difficult to await your Awareness, and it is so pleasing now that significant progress is being made. Allow Helana to lead you forwards to your full Awareness and to heal the past memories. Later tonight we will try again to come closer. Listen now to these words;..bucket, spade, God, animal, friend, foe, Razeem...that is good, we now need a sign to let you know that it is me.

What do you feel in your right hand?....my response ' A stiffness in my third finger'.

'We will try this signal for you to realise your thoughts are from me. Relax now and we will consider further.'

KEYPOINT AB24

Agree a signal with your Guide if at all possible. This will then provide you with confidence as to the origin of any message.

9.33 'You ask about secrecy; indeed, you are surrounded by a force-Field, in the form of a 'Band of Gold'; this prevents lower levels of Spirit from accessing your Minds and your Conversations, or your Spirits. In this way we can talk privately and prevent others from learning of our plans. You have done well to ask this question. You have a good Mind. The light which you both emit is so beautiful, it attracts Others, like a Moth to light...for this reason you need to have the protection. Only the chosen few are aware of the plans. Loved-ones will know something special is afoot, but little else.'

KEYPOINTS AB25

a)We seem to be involved in a special Project, which is privy knowledge to only a few Others.

b)All is possible with High Spirit.

- **They can protect you.**

- **They bring to you only those people who you need to meet, for the learning and understanding.**

- **They predict and plan the Experiences. They can even selectively cause you to hear remote Conversations.**

- **All is known. The names and whereabouts of murderers and their victims, the location of Arms-dumps, the plans, the Evil intentions.....If the Authorities were more willing to listen to advice from Mediums and Clairvoyants, many more criminals would now be in jail, and many millions of pounds of Public Expense could be better utilised.**

9.34 Razeem tells us: 'Your wedding rings are to be purchased shortly; they are to be used sooner than you think, however, this will not be in your current lifetimes!'

(I did not latch-onto this remark at the time, or question its meaning).

'Christmas draws near and it is a time when Spirit relaxes and conducts its own festivities. What you two need to achieve is important, and so cannot be delayed.

Christmas, is also a good-time to work, for people's Minds are filled with Goodwill, and we can more easily bring to People the Peace and Love which they need. Plan a meagre Christmas, to be shared only with the chosen few. Your Spirits will be with your loved-Ones'.

KEYPOINTS AB26

a) The true Anniversary date for Christmas, the birth-date of Jesus, is September 25th. The December timing is incorrect through Calendar changes. Jesus's age is also wrong as he was six years older than the Bible relates.

b) Spirit celebrates the fourteen days around the birth-date in September; Spirit treat the six days before and seven days afterwards as a Festive Holiday.

During this period of Time, Human Communication with the Spirit-World is greatly reduced.

c) Whenever any Spirit-message is ambiguous, or not fully understood; always question, always clarify. Always follow an Answer with a Question, to confirm what has been said. The statement " This will not be in your lifetimes" was a warning which at the time I did not grasp!

9.35 On Monday, 17th August, Razeem gives the message: 'The Spirit of Jack has had many lives shared with this lady, but he has had these lives taken away because he has not allowed freedom to her. The final recollection will now be shared. You will perhaps recall parallels to your choice of ladies in this lifetime. All your lives have not been wasted. You have learnt about many lessons of understanding. You have learnt about the values of:

- Respect for Others.
- Allowing Others their Freedom, without which Love cannot survive.
- Compassion for Others
- Understanding of Others' Viewpoint

9.36 The Spirit of Jack has featured in many of these lives. We call her the Lady Helana, because she is a beautiful Spirit and a true Spirit with a gentle nature. We ask you to respect this at certain times, when you feel she is a little despondent to your ways. In her heart we feel the pain. It is not her true way...The Spirit of the child Jack, he is indeed a child, is not as ancient as your two Spirits. He remains a child and will always be so. It is for this reason you need to understand the lives shared. There are many aspects....you are part of a jigsaw....each One making up a whole'.

KEYPOINTS AB27
a) All Life is for learning, so that either the Soul can learn, or the Experience can be provided for another Soul to learn.
b) The Learning is necessary for the Soul to progress, or for the Karmic Debt to be re-paid.
c) The key aspects of life to be learned are:
- Respect for Others, Peoples and all of Nature's and GOD's Creation.
- Compassion for Others
- Understanding of Others' viewpoints
- All the various Aspects and Types of Love, Relationships, and Sharing.

9.37 'Do you not think a child will bring a simplicity to the World?.....for this reason Jack will remain a child. Even a child can learn Respect and loving Ways. It is not necessary for all Spirit to progress to Adult Lives. All Aspects are necessary to bring the World all that is needed. This child of the Universe, was given to this Lady, to comfort, to heal and to teach. She has done her work admirably, no-one could have given so much. Many Earth years were spent in Spirit to bring light into the life of this child, who had ended his life in a tragic way and had no idea how to retrace his footsteps'

KEYPOINT AB28
Not all Spirits progress to higher Levels, or to greater Understanding. Some Souls remain as a Child.

9.38 'An outstretched hand was offered by this Angel, but progress does not exist in the Spirit of Jack. He has ended this life in a different manner. He cannot progress without breaking the Chains of the Past. We wish you to understand the detail of this lifetime, to uncover the many truths that lie there. Remember they were born as twins, not identical, a boy and girl. Times were hard, very little money, what there was, was drunk away by the father Albert, a hard man with many cruel ways. His Spirit had a great deal to learn, his wicked ways caused a great deal of suffering, many beatings, for she was a girl amongst brothers, a slave, she was not wanted, just another mouth to feed and less money for beer!'

9.39 'At the tender age of nine years; she was raped by the father who continued to do so. The mother was aware but did nothing, it was looked upon as a duty of the daughter to bring comfort to this man. The eldest brother also treated her in the same way (Spirit of Bryan)
When she was twelve years old, she was befriended by Jack her twin, and true love was found. Freedom was found in the trees. They became lovers and children were given.

170

9.40 'The elder brother Bryan acted as an informer as to the happening in the trees...he was jealous as he saw the love in the eyes of this lady, for this man Jack.

The information passed to the father caused such rage and outcry..... what was good for the goose was not good for the gander!, the child was sent away in disgrace, and Jack was not told her whereabouts. Can you imagine the anguish? They were twins not only in body, but now also in Spirit. They could talk to each other in their Minds.'

KEYPOINT AB29

The achievement of Spiritual Awareness and the twinning of Spirits, allows two Minds to remotely Communicate. (Mind 'A' to Spirit 'A', Spirit 'A' to Spirit 'B', Spirit 'B' to Mind 'B')

9.41 'The Child when heavily pregnant, walked many miles to find Jack. She suffered greatly, heavily laden with two children, bare feet, living only on berries found on the way, and water from streams. The father turned her away again, but now Jack knew where she was. They met half-way and then together approached the father; he again refused to allow them to be together. Time passed by and two girls were born, then without the knowledge of the mother, one-by-one they were given away. She was so distraught.

Jack then decided to find again his beloved, but he could not bring himself to do this....for the shame and fear of a brother and sister living as man and wife was unheard of at this time. We cannot say whether he could have proceeded or not. In the eyes of Spirit this love would have sufficed. It is possible surely, if true love is found. Is it not worth rescuing and holding onto? whatever the reasons or circumstances. Then the lives of these children would have been saved.

As it was the Spirit of Jack ended his life in the trees.

(Helana took me to the site of the tree in Oxfordshire where Jack hanged himself. The Spirits of the children who were given away are known to this day to be those of two daughters born to Philip....the Spirit of Jack.....who today lives close-by, some two miles away from where Helana grew-up.'

9.42 'This lady, the very same day, had returned free from the burden of pregnancy and the children. She had decided again to ask her father to allow her to return....bearing in mind that she knew of the slow death of Jack's Spirit. She found Jack dead, hanging, in the trees. Jack had hoped that she also would take her own life to be with him...but alas for him, the Spirit of this lady had an understanding that this is not how we thank our GOD. The Spirit of Jack passed to Shadowlands. Many years passed, a succession of tragedies, until at last you John were found, to hopefully bring comfort to this lady's heart. She had suffered so greatly'.

9.43 'She was employed by your family, as a house-maid, to work long and hard hours. Yet again she was raped by the gardener. (now George in this lifetime). She had beautiful hair and face and was outstanding in every way, she was graceful compared to her family who were rough and uncouth...they alienated her. At this time her name was Catherine'.

9.44 'The Lord of Over Worton Manor, had a son, Richard Cookson, (your Spirit, John). You took a fancy to this child and decided that it was her duty to give you sex'.
'It was expected, you were powerful and had Wealth, she had nothing. As love grew, you decided to elope together and to become one in marriage. You did not realise that your father would disagree so strongly. You were treated badly and disinherited. You were offered a house and a small amount to live-on. Still more than local people, but indeed a lesson to lose wealth yet again. Yet it was necessary, it was hoped that you would find true love and a perfect life. Unfortunately, it was not to be so! Richard could not come to terms with the depravation of his lifestyle. This created so much bitterness, anger and hate. Yet, there was this lady offering so much at this time. She had decided to move on, and to leave the Spirit of Jack in peace'. (Over Worton is a small Hamlet in Oxfordshire, England)

9.45 'Richard blamed her for his loss of Wealth and all that he deemed a treasure. A child was given, the spirit of Jack had entered your lives to bring to him the mother's love that was needed, and also to help Richard understand the importance of the life which was a part of you. Richard could not forgive this lady. He would stand and watch her beautiful ways...talking to flowers, talking to trees and bees. He wished to be part of this but knew not how. He did not allow her to explain; he did not talk to her. She became ugly in his eyes, for the wealth that had been lost. The baby was lost, the lady wasted away...she grieved for the child, she grieved for Richard's Spirit....her love was so great, but he could not share it, he did not know how to. She spent many years shut-away in her room, she was not a Lady of Standing to be at the table. Richard blamed her for the loss of the baby, a possible heir to enable him to retrieve the family wealth'.

9.46 'We hope that this story brings a new Understanding. Helana has now forgiven all these men from her previous lives. It is for you now, John, to forgive and lose the guilt of the Past, so that your Spirit can progress'..
KEYPOINTS AB30
a) Your Soul cannot progress when 'Chains from the Past' exist. It is necessary to clear the Guilt, to find Forgiveness, to heal the Past, before you can move forwards.

b)We live many Lives until the lessons given have been understood and accepted. History does repeat itself over and over until or unless something changes, we are locked-into a 'Cycle of Events', with essentially the same group of Souls, until we have learned the necessary lessons to enable our Spirit to move forwards.

9.47 'You are unaware of the work done by Helana, not only in Spirit has she worked hard, but also on the Earth-Plane. She has waited many years in the hope that Philip would achieve the level of understanding. He has not taken away this lady's love, for you now have it all. 'Understand that you are not second-best, this Spirit will not again be your child. It is hoped that you John, can find forgiveness in your heart, by understanding the love that Jack has for this lady, and why he has been a part of your lives for many years. A tragic, tragic tale.'

9.48 'Helana's life has been hard and long, but she is strong and delicate. She has had to come to terms with many aspects of her life. She has been abused and used in all of her previous lives. Understand that she now progresses .She has dug deep and has found the forgiveness necessary, for her to end the pains of the Past. The tears that have flowed have filled the Oceans of the World. You too John, can now achieve this, by finding forgiveness and understanding for the lessons of the Past. You can begin, by forgiving the Spirit of Jack. We do not expect sympathy, but compassion and understanding. Different actions are necessary to avoid a repeat of past lives. Healing has been given to so many lives by Helana, Forgiving those who have contributed to her suffering. We ask you John to do the same'.

9.49 'Call John, upon Helana's Spirit for strength in this matter, for there is no finer person to take on these burdens, for this reason she is so necessary in Ireland. She will take on the burdens and in this way many people can progress, and healing can take place. She can forgive and ask for compassion for all of these peoples. Do not ask her to do so for herself, for she is a humble Spirit, and accepts her role as one of love and not glory. She understands so deeply the pains of the Past'.

KEYPOINTS AB31
a)Forgiveness, Love, and Freedom are the keys, only by Forgiving and Understanding the Past, can our Spirits progress.
b)Jealousy and Possessiveness destroy all that we strive to achieve.
- **Bryan killed himself over Helana, in this lifetime**
- **Jack killed himself over Helana, in a previous lifetime.**

- Helana has displayed possessiveness for the Spirits of both Jack and Bryan, which has prevented freedom of their Spirits, and destroyed the possibility of love.
- You John have always been jealous of Helana's love for Jack, and this has destroyed your own love for her.
- You John lost the love of Constance by restricting her freedom.

9.50 'The Spirits of Jack and Bryan must now stand on their own two feet, without the light from this lady. They will not return. There is no more Helana can do to help these Spirits.

She has accepted this, only saying that they must stay in the Light. You John, have always had Helana's love. If you forgive Jack now, then in the next life you can achieve pure and true love with Helana.

She will then be your love alone. If Helana's Spirit is at peace, just think how that will benefit the World. She has sufficient love alone to heal the entire World.

(this is explained by her being given the Holy Ghost)

KEYPOINTS AB32

a) **Spirit Guides will normally only help someone on the Earth-Plane, if when the help given, it helps their individual Soul, not necessarily the human Person.**

b) **You the Human are not forgotten, but High Spirit do not act solely to prove things to you.**

c) **Your Prayers are heard, but the results will depend upon the Spirit's progress. ... 'We only help someone if their Spirit needs help.'**

d) **Some Spirits choose to return to the Earth-Plane for sacrifice.....viz Jesus, in order to help other Spirits on the Earth-Plane.**

9.51 I write the following words: The Past is the Past. We are here and now. If Helana can forgive these injustices of the Past, and love these People, knowing that it is their Karma, that they have themselves to learn before they can progress; then who am I not to share in this Compassion and Understanding? I wish these Spirits to learn, to be comforted, to feel the virtue of Love, so that they may know what they miss.

- So that they can aspire to the Light.
- So that they can Learn.
- So that they can Change.
- So that they can Progress and Learn the Lessons necessary.

I ask for Understanding and Compassion for these Souls, so that they can see the error of their ways and can raise their Awareness.

- I accept my Guilt from the Past, and the errors of my ways in this Life.
- I accept the Lessons learned and wish to come to terms with the Understanding necessary.
- I ask for your help for my Spirit to be healed.
- I ask in the name of the Heavenly Father to allow me to find the Peace within and in so doing to join with Helana and complete her Awareness and Understanding.

JOHN

9.52 Later that night, I receive the following message from Razeem: 'The words written will allow you to move forwards and to place the Past behind your Door. Do this now.

Unbolt the door and place the memories of these People and these Events on the other side and bolt the Door again. Forgive yourself, and forgive the Others who have caused you anguish, pain and suffering. We will visit you in your sleep and give you a fuller Understanding. Rest now and renew your Energies. Your Friend Razeem.'

KEYPOINT AB33

- **If you picture a heavy, thick Door in your Mind, with three heavy barrel bolts, and this Door is the only escape for anything placed behind it; then it is possible to put behind that Door anything that you wish to shut-out from your Life.**
- **We can place behind the Door those People who create the guilt, those who disrupt our Inner Peace, or those who hold our Spirit back from progressing.**

9.53 'The pressure on your left foot is a sign that you should be moving-on and forgetting the Past and not concerning yourself with the History. This can be visited when the current climate has relaxed and you have your Awareness. Your feet are hot because you are discussing travelling to Ireland and the love shown is expressed in heat. Nothing to worry about my friend. Take heart that your Trials are now behind you and you are moving forward.

(Future events will unfortunately prove that this statement is not completely correct).

KEYPOINTS AB34

a) Every physical Sensation or Feeling should be questioned, to see whether it is caused by Spiritual, rather than a Bodily problem or Dis-ease.

b) I can identify with several instances of a sharp, stabbing pain, beneath my Foot, to tell me to move-on, to leave a meeting, to rise out of bed, etc.

9.54 'Live for the moment...Let go of the ME and the I... be gentle...ask for help and guidance for yourself, so that you may gain an Understanding, so that you are not Selfish...put yourself in the other person's shoes...how would you feel in that Situation?...put the other person first....Is one man's love more important than the World?... Do you understand the nature of Selfishness?...are Helana and Judith selfish?'

KEYPOINTS AB35
a) Do not be afraid to ask for Help and Understanding for yourself. Ask from the Heavenly Father (GOD), or from Jesus, or from your Spirit Guides who act on behalf of GOD.
b) Live for today, and for the Moment.
c) Consider the other person's point of view. Do not be Selfish. Be gentle with Others.

9.55 A message is received from Razeem: 'Inside this child is a Spirit equal to that of many trees. She has exceeded our expectations, beyond the realms of Understanding. Many lessons are to be learned from the nature of this child.
Not only the child which is to be given, or the one who is to be with you, but also by yourself, John. We have asked you many times to listen, and to adhere to the ways of this lady, I am Razeem your Guide, I am hardworking and stern. It is necessary. Slight not the words of this child as I wish to call her, as she is but a child of Nature. Many others upon this Earth-Plane have gathered her in, but allowed her to be free at times of her choosing. You are not perhaps of an understanding of this'. *(on the one hand, we are to create a new life together, to work, to meet people. On the other hand, Helana is to do her own thing, to have her own freedom!)*

9.56 'You have been given that she has within her the Holy Spirit of the Most High.(The Holy Ghost)
It has been given for a purpose John. It is not given to anyone who is not deserving of this gift. We ask you to understand this, for you doubt her words so. We feel, we see, we hear the words spoken, the actions given. She is not a daughter of High Spirit; but the One and only True Spirit of the World resides within her. There is nothing but Truth and Honesty within her. Remember this, do not doubt, it will be given again if necessary. Her life has been given to Spirit for the work, which has to be undertaken in this Land by so many. You do not allow her to do this work, you do not allow her gift of purest Love, to be given in the purest way.'

KEYPOINTS AB36
a) The Holy Ghost is only given to the select few.
b) The Holy Ghost, also known as the Holy Spirit of GOD, is the only, One, True Spirit of the World.

c) In Essence, the Spirit of God divided, back in Time beyond Comprehension. The one Part, the Holy Ghost, represents Purity and True Love. The Other Part became the opposite polarity of Negativity and Evil.
d) All Life is composed of opposites, both Positive and Negative Facets.
e) All Matter is Energy arising from different polarities and combinations there-of. The Holy Ghost strives to re-Unite with itself again. As the Soul becomes closer and closer to unity with GOD, the percentage of the GOD LIGHT within becomes higher and higher.

9.57 'Relax your Mind John. All that was is past. All that is, is now present. All that will be, will be given. You see, you hear, you accept the words from me, your friend Razeem. You accept the words from Spirit, why then do you disbelieve, and push away the one you love. It is hard perhaps in a Relationship.
'Perhaps if the male/female Roles were reversed, it would be easier. This lady is your Teacher, not your Keeper. She gives you the freedom, for she loves you so much. You would gain little if we gave you the answers to the questions before they are asked.'

9.58 'Helana is guided in every small way and in every large way. She has a mind of her own, but she trusts and has faith that all is well. We are all working towards you achieving your Awareness as it should be. But this will not be before the feelings of anger, and suppression are cleared from your Mind. These are felt by this lady. Not only do you suffer, but she does too. Understand this. Remember to forgive. These feelings are not necessary in this lifetime, there will be difficulties, you will be given choices. On this occasion, you refused to go for a walk when invited to by Helana; this created so much pain and anguish, a rebuff!'
(I was feeling tired, and was reading a Spiritual Book, whilst also watching a Video. This need to comply with almost everything said by Helana, I found to be very difficult to follow. I, at that time, still believed in a normal relationship, one in which there were choices and 'Give and Take'. To expect me to do anything which Helana said, would be tantamount to me being little more than a lap-dog).

9.59 Razeem continues: 'Do not walk away from this child in any way. Believe that her Spirit is that of the Holy Ghost. Do you think John that she would tell you lies, or mis-lead you in any way.? Our task is hard my friend. Do not fight and struggle, we can then lead you with peace in your heart and bring to you what is needed. Gentle ways and understanding are needed to be seen, for the moment, when love is offered so clearly. The idea of a walk was requested and agreed to by Spirit. Helana does have a mind of her own, all is not given from Spirit.'

9.60 'You are requested to say prayers for the next seven days, for the Spirit of Jack which comes in need of forgiveness and reassurance. Pray for a helping hand from the True Light of True Spirit to help Jack. Then send this Spirit firmly on his way. Do not feel irritation or anguish at his presence, rather offer compassion and understanding. In this lifetime, Jack has made his choices, to walk away from Helana.'

9.61 'My friend, we need your full co-operation, every moment of every day, until we have achieved the full Awareness you need to have. The time for amusements is passed until you have reached your goal. Allow Helana to guide you'.

9.62 'You, John, have gathered your Aura, over the years from various places on visitation. As each place is visited, a piece of your Aura is left behind, it can be collected and this is necessary on occasions, to collect your Aura from the Past'.
'You are John in this lifetime, in the Past, you have been in the body of Jesus, and also that of Abel. There are still some parts of Jesus's Aura to be gathered. It is hoped that you will understand the need for the Aura to be collected. You will understand more fully at a later Time.
(I have given much thought to these words, as to their accuracy and the true meaning. I rationalise this statement on the basis of a Past-Life twinning of the Soul)
The total love of Christ resides only in the chosen few, were it different, it would be to the detriment of the World'.
KEYPOINT AB37
Whereever you travel, a piece of your Soul, the Aura, is left behind. It is possible to return to collect this Aura even many Lifetimes later, sometimes it is necessary to do this, as the total Soul and Spirit then become stronger.

9.63 'It is said that the Spirit of Jesus is spread amongst many. It is not within each and every person; but his way of life is within All. The thoughts of this man and his Crucifixion were transmitted around the World. It is not the actual Spirit, but the memories of the Spirit of the man, at this Time, which are within All.'

9.64 'It is for this Reason, that we bring you this message, for we need you to understand the work which Helana is to perform. Her thoughts transmit around the Earth-Plane bringing love to all, not only in Ireland and the World, but also to the Universe.
All that is needed is Pure, Truthful, Honest, Love.

KEYPOINTS AB38
a) Thoughts are as powerful as Actions.
b) Thoughts can travel throughout the Universe.
c) It is the combination of the sum-total of Mankinds'
Thoughts throughout the World, which can and do
influence the rest of the Universe.
d) At the present Time this influence is negative and
hostile; that is why we must CHANGE THE EARTH'S AURA for
us to be able to Survive.
e) Pure, Truthful, Honest, Love, can act to solve and to
resolve All of Mankind's Problems.

9.65 The Earth is like the bad-Apple in the Barrel, if we are not careful
we will be discarded and destroyed. We are part of a whole, we are not
the whole, there are many Others. If we do not change, the rest of the
Barrel is at risk. What do you do with a bad Limb? You try medicine, you
attempt healing; but if the limb gets more and more poisoned,
eventually, it is necessary to chop it off, so that the whole can survive.
KEYPOINTS AB39
a) There are many hundreds of Alien Life-forms and
Species throughout the Universes. (300+)
b) What happens on the Earth-Plane affects Others
throughout the Universes.
c) Mankind has no absolute Ownership of the Earth. If we
do not comply with the Laws of Nature and GOD, then the
Race will not survive in its present form.
d) We have been granted by GOD, a limited time-frame in
which to get our house in order. This time-frame is
sufficient, provided that a pro-Active Stance is taken,
to demonstrate to Others that the virtues of Love and
Light are to be upheld.

9.66 Razeem continues:' The Spirit of the Child which is to be born to
you both, is part of the Spirit which you have shared at an earlier time
when you were not man and wife. It matters not, the child was born in
love of the purest kind.
The child's Spirit is divided amongst many, but not too many.
My Dears, you have a great deal of understanding to take on board. We
have not given you the full story, we will remain silent to allow these
words to be understood.
The Child to be given is the Son, of the Son of Man'

9.67 I am asked to give healing to Helana. A signal is given, as to when
to begin and when to stop. A few seconds only are necessary. I am told
to remember who I am. The Spirit does not forget at any time.

KEYPOINTS AB40
a) It is not necessary to touch in any way, when you Heal.
b) Thoughts alone can travel and bring Healing. A few seconds only are necessary.
c) ALWAYS REMEMBER the words to be given.
' If it be thy Will, according to their Needs.' for, not Everyone, or every Being is ready for Healing.
d) It is necessary for Spirit alone to decide when Healing is to take place.
e) Healers will be guided upon hearing, upon feeling, upon seeing. They will become aware without the need for time limits, it will come naturally.
d) The Spirit never forgets anything, the nasty videos and films which we show to our Children are all remembered by their Spirits.

9.68 Razeem tells me that there is no sex in the Spirit-World, but there are special needs. These start with forgiveness in the heart.
KEYPOINTS AB41
a) There is no sex in the Spirit-World.
b) Forgiveness of Others wrong-doing is a special requirement in the Spirit-World.

9.69 Razeem continues: 'You are aware that the Spirit can divide, and the Spirit can travel. It is also necessary to understand that Opposites reflect, and exist. There is another in the Spirit Realms of your child to be. There is also a living person with the same Spirit as Helana (Connie) It is hoped that these two children (yet to be born) will unite as One, as the parents have.(Helana and John)
The Child to be is a replica of the Mother (Helana), she has the Spirit of the mother within her, as we see her on the Earth-Plane. In this way the strength of the Holy Ghost is increased, but only when the child reaches maturity.
KEYPOINTS AB42
a) Spirit can and does divide, so there are therefore, normally two Beings with the same Spirit.
b) Spirit can and does travel throughout the Universe when appropriate.
c) All Spirit originates from the one GOD. In this context all are related if you return to your origins.
d) Left-Handed People are one of a pair.

9.70 'You John, are asked to collect the 'Aura' of Jesus, there are still a number of parts on the Earth-Plane which need retrieval. You can do this work as your origins are very close to those of Jesus. The same Planet, the same Time, the same Spirit which divided. In fact back in history you were Twins!'

9.71 Jesus tells me that when he was in his mid-teens he knelt down and prayed to GOD, using the Words 'Heavenly Father take my life, do with it as you will, I dedicate my life to your service'...all followed from giving this commitment to GOD.

KEYPOINTS AB43

a) It is a pre-requisite for any person who wishes to serve GOD to be prepared to walk away from all of their Worldly possessions, be these Material or Personages of any kind.

b) The pathway to Glory of the Soul is not an easy one, it will involve many hardships and many tears. But the rewards are everlasting and cannot be lightly undertaken.

c) Every Soul has a purpose, every Soul has a role to play, be this for one minute Understanding to be gained. Remember all is pre-chosen, the Parents, the Events are created. The Mind will then decide whether or not to follow the Pathway.

d) Many fall by the Wayside, many are far too Ambitious. It is far better to adopt a lower Objective and to be successful in that Achievement, than to target the Skies and then to fail and have to face the ensuing Consequences.

e) This is not a solitary Choice which affects only you individually, remember you are part of a Peer-Group of Souls who all need to play their part if the Objectives are to be achieved.

f) The achievement of Spiritual Awareness will enable you the individual to become aware of what Purpose you the Soul has chosen for this Lifetime.

##

CHAPTER 10. BITE THE BULLET

10.00 It is still August 1998, Razeem mentions that it is essential for me to achieve my Awareness as quickly as possible, so that Others can be brought into the Light. 'Judith is always your Father, You are the Son and always will be. The other Son is not yet known to you; but he will soon appear in your lives. Fear not John, History will not be repeated in terms of your death. Allow Events to flow and all will be revealed when the time is right. Helana is the Holy Ghost. You three have returned at this time of Crisis to help the World from its wayward state to a new Beginning.' (these words refer to our Souls of course!)
KEYPOINT BTB1
The new Millennium is to be a time of change for the Human Race. Many Souls have chosen to return at this time for a re-enactment of Biblical Times. Our task is to prepare those on the Earth-Plane now, so that Attitudes and Relationships are receptive to the coming of the New Messiah.

10.01 Helana and I are to plan a further visit to Ireland. We should travel due west from Dublin and visit the places on the West Coast. There are many beautiful places to visit, the visit is to be free from stress and relaxed. We are told that it is only necessary to reach Bangor for the Wednesday, so that we are available to meet the contact necessary, to enable us to choose our residence.
KEYPOINT BTB2
When the Time is right, all will easily fall into place, but ONLY if we play our part, have faith and trust in Spirit, be obedient, and grasp the opportunities when they arise...something as simple as my tendency to drive too fast, can throw-out the timing for any meeting!

10.02 I have been suffering from a shoulder pain which now clears; a flicker commences below my left eye. I am asked to send prayers, and send forgiveness and love to the Spirit of Jack.
Razeem continues: ' His Spirit is like that of a ten year old child, he blames you John, for walking away from him. A reconciliation has now taken place, this has taken many years to achieve. Now that Jack has his freedom, your own children in this lifetime can now draw close.
KEYPOINTS BTB3
a) Release the guilt from the Past, be it in this Lifetime, or from a previous Lifetime...
(actual words....however distant!....however close!)
b) My Relationship with my own Children, in this Lifetime, is dependant upon healing the problems created almost 2,000 years previously. Barriers were established then, which have affected present day attitudes and restricted love.

c)If those who are given Light do not see, the ability to see can be taken away.
(This refers to the partial blindness of the man Phil in this lifetime. This has been given because he fails to see that he has gifts of Healing, and psychic Ability which he rejects. In a similar way, Helana's mother is gradually losing her mobility, because she refuses to try to walk and to help herself.)
d)All is given, All is planned. The way in which we are now, is controlled and regulated by our Spirit Guides, it is a consequence of our actions or thoughts in this lifetime, or the choices our Soul made before we were born, or it may be caused in this lifetime by interference from other Spirits.

10.03 I am given by a Medium at the local Spiritualist Church the number seven.
KEYPOINTS BTB4
a)The World was created in seven Days! A fact not a fable!
* There are seven Days in a Week;
* There are also seven Years in a Life-Cycle;
* All the cells in our Bodies, replace themselves every seven Years.
b)Divide your age by seven to find out when your Life is due to change. I am 54 years of age, so my life is due begin to change in two years time!
(of course this is a gradual and continual process)
c)Our Lives are governed by the number seven. Every seven years a change can occur to our nature, our Body and our Attitudes. This can be reflected in our work and in our Relationships.

10.04 Razeem, my Guide, tells me: 'You are to write a book John, (this Book). It will tell your life-story, the Book will be written both to provide understanding for you, and also to teach Others about Spirit, and to awaken them to Spiritual Awareness. The Book is to be a true book of Revelations, passed-on in a language that people can understand...not like the previous Book which you wrote! It will be a devastating time for people who read these words, but a necessary time to give understanding to Mankind.'
KEYPOINT BTB5
The experience of History, with the different interpretations of the Old and New Testaments, has shown that any words written, need to be without ambiguity, and written so that they can be clearly understood, by All who care to read them.

10.05 'You are puzzled John, as to where you have been this night. Believe me that a great deal of work has been achieved whilst your Bodies have rested. We take your Spirits to the Lands and the Places and the Peoples and to the Worlds where we need you to be. You are protected so closely, do not fear this is not so. Remember my dears, you are our hope for the future. Trust in Spirit, and have faith that you have been chosen to guide the many to freedom and to peace. Go in peace my dears and understand that this day has achieved a great deal within your lives on this Earth-Plane, and within the Universe. Trust in Love, and trust in GOD is the key to your heart.'

KEYPOINTS BTB6
a) Our Spirits can and do travel extensively throughout the World, or even throughout the Universe, whilst our Bodies rest.
b) We can Choose where to go, or we may be directed and guided as needed.
c) There are many Life-forms throughout the Universe, but, All originate from the One GOD.
d) Love and trust in GOD, are the keys to your Spiritual Growth.

10.06 We are asked to read '2-Kings-6', an interpretation is given by Razeem.

King of Israel/ People	= Jesus
Chariots and Horses	= Spirit
Bread and Water	= Forgiveness
Israel	= People
Axe-Head	= Man's Greed
Do not chop down trees	= Be satisfied with what you have
Prophet	= Good

KEYPOINT BTB7
The true meaning of much of the Bible is lost without understanding of the words used.

10.07 Razeem continues, and the words are summarised below:
KEYPOINTS BTB8
a) What you do to yourself, and your actions, are your personal Responsibility.
b) It is not only your own personal Actions which cause pain. Pain to you individually, can also be caused by any of the Others in your Peer-Group. Your Life is governed by not only your own Actions, but also by those of the group of forty or so Souls in your Peer-Group.
c) It is your Mind which causes the pain. There is no need for pain and suffering if All in your Peer-Group see the good.
d) Love is the greatest power in the Universe.

e) If you can find compassion and forgiveness for Others, this will also be present within your heart.

- Help Others to See.
- Do not be Selfish.
- Do not Pity.
- If you bring help to Others, in so doing you help yourself...GIVE and you will RECEIVE.

f) Your Peer-Group are those Souls with whom you travel for almost all of your many lifetime experiences. The roles are interchanged from lifetime to lifetime, so that you can learn all the lessons of love necessary to your Soul's progression. If of course you do not learn the necessary lessons, the lifetime experience will need to be repeated...and repeated...and repeated. So in this lifetime you could well be the female child, but in the next you might be the male father, or the friend, or the brother, etc.

KEYPOINTS BTB9
a) The Body is made from Matter. The Spirit, which provides life, is Energy that has a bounder-less freedom, and can choose to travel anywhere. (except to those Realms where-in the extremes of Light and Darkness are incompatible or too hostile)
b) Nourishment is Love;

- Nourishment is not necessarily the act of eating the gift of food;
- Nourishment is a gift of Love from Spirit.
- You too can share nourishment and Love with the World;
- You too can give anything to the Spirit of any Person in this way. A flower will be received by the Spirit of the individual, when love is sent to them.

10.08 'Helana has cleansed her Body from head to toe. Like the rains that fall on the desert Plains, if so wished an abundance of flowers can be produced...within the hearts of many are barren Lands.
The fields are given as a message, all is relevant, all is there to be seen, the reaping of the corn, the ploughing of the fields, the planting of the seeds to grow in Spring, the rains which wash-away. All is understood by this child, she has a wealth of knowledge, all you John need to do is to ask her. Trust her words, we will guide them.'

10.09 'When Helana eats on the left-hand side of her face, she eats for the Spirit of Jack, this also represents the children from all our lives, the Present and the Previous. When she eats on the right-hand side of her Face, she eats for the World.'

KEYPOINT BTB10
**The process of Eating, how you eat and your thoughts at
that time, can be used to nourish Others.**
- **The left Side of your face is for your own Family,**
- **The Right-hand Side is for Other People.**
- **You need to consciously direct your thoughts as you
  eat.**

10.10 Razeem states that 'The Mountain isolation in Donegal, was given
for Helana to feel the isolation which Jesus felt. If you John, find it
difficult to follow in the footsteps of Jesus, then you should follow in
the footsteps of Helana. Helana requested this way of life and it was
given. Helana requested the Holy Ghost and it was given. Helana was
given to you John, to help you to learn, and to teach you. You are now
beginning to understand how her special, beautiful Energies, can help
the peoples of Ireland and the World. Jesus was also given the Spirit of
the Holy Ghost, he was given a larger slice than most men. You John,
have a role to play in this lifetime, you are to be the hands of the Christ.'
KEYPOINTS BTB11
**a) Helana's choices have been made following a direct
request to GOD, to allow her to pursue a Holy Life...She
has been granted what she wished for! One of her roles
is to teach me.**
**b) The percentage of the Holy Ghost which your Spirit
has, will determine your capabilities.**

10.11 We purchase matching wedding rings in Aylesbury, and are told
that a time will be given when they are to be worn. 'They are to be
worn and blessed by Spirit before a Earthly service is given; no human
guests will be necessary at this time, for there will be many from Spirit
present. The rings have been chosen for you by Spirit; the two parallel
lines on the rings represent your Lives.
The 'Band of Gold' will unite you together as One. Your Wedding will be
the 'Wedding of the Year'...
Your Spirits are truly great, we bow to you. You unite as a new star in
our Universe, a diamond in the sky looking down on us all, as the
diamond engagement Ring.'
KEYPOINT BTB12
**We were taken to a specific shop in Aylesbury; and
directed to specific rings. Spirit do indeed choose!**

10.12 Hallo my friend this is Razeem here. 'You are beginning to
appreciate the extent of the commitment necessary to this way of life.
Understand, nothing is impossible, and everything will and can be
achieved. Continue with your studies and acceptance of the words of
Helana. Judith will also continue with your Awareness training.'

KEYPOINTS BTB13
a) Nothing is impossible.
b) Everything can be achieved if your motives, your
attitudes, and your trust in GOD is true.
c) You will also need to ASK for help and guidance!

10.13 Jesus writes: 'Only in Healing was I different to any Others.
It is not necessary for me to perform the Act of Crucifixion again, but it
is necessary for you John, to gain a complete Understanding.
Helana's tears were for your Spirit, and sadness for the World.
You John, do not have to be alone in this World; you now have a
partner who will share your burdens, your tears, your fears and your
cries of anguish and pain.
You John, are the only man the Spirit of this child has loved fully.
You John, will never be more loved by another in the Universe. You are
united in understanding and love throughout Eternity. The rings placed
on your fingers will not be removed for all Eternity. As a man you do not
realise this, but upon your return to Spirit all will be revealed.
Helana has not fully recognised your Spirit in previous lives. Think,
ponder and surmise upon these words in the deepest way possible!
In the years to come, you will realise the greatness of the Spirit within
you now. The Work to be done has been needed for so long.'

10.14 I am beginning to wonder about the nature of the Spirit within
me!, and why do I need to understand about the Crucifixion?
Is this all about Sacrifice ?
I have previously been asked by White Eagle: ' Is one man more
important than the World? My response at that time was to say that
'No one man is more important than the whole of Mankind'
KEYPOINT BTB14
Love when established is never lost, once it is achieved
by the Spirits, it will thereafter exist for all
Eternity.

10.15 Friday, 21st August 1998 is a special day for us, we are told of a
Child to be! a new Star in the Heavens.

10.16 Razeem tells me that my Spirit still needs to come to terms with
the fact of walking away from my children. Helana also feels this
sadness, but she blames me in no way for the Past.
I need to lose this guilt and gain an understanding in this lifetime.
Jesus was just a man, with the same powers of thought and
understanding which Helana has, he left his child when he took-up his
mantle and the work for GOD. You too John have left a child in all of
your previous lifetimes. 'Understand John, there was no loss by your
actions, only gain.
Listen to the Words of Helana, Watch her actions, See her beauty.

187

Aim within this lifetime to achieve the beauty, tolerance and patience which she displays. You may think that you are becoming less of a man, do not fear that you will lose your free-will.

When you have achieved your Awareness, then and only then, is the time for you to establish your independence of choice and actions. Watch, listen, feel...allow all your Senses to be involved.

Release your Earthly ways and you will make real progress.'

KEYPOINTS BTB16
a) High Spirit are fully aware of all your Thoughts, they knew that I felt Guilt through separation from my Children.
b) Sacrifice is sometimes necessary in order to achieve the common good.
c) All is known by the Souls of the Children before they chose to be born. It is not necessary therefore to carry the Guilt.
d) Guilt will restrict your progress towards Spiritual Awareness.

10.17 'Hallo John, this is your Guide here, I am not Razeem, my name is not important. We wish you to realise that Helana is giving to you all her energies, but that you are not fully aware of this.

The situation will improve as you gain your Awareness, and we can direct you in an easier way. Please persevere with the current situation, this will improve as everything is resolved. You will shortly be in Ireland, and these learning days will be past memories. Allow Helana her time and space to do things her way......................................

At times, certain chores could be speeded-up, but we all have our ways and we need to be considerate of others' needs. It is a testing time, as so much is being devoted to Spiritual matters. When you are fully Aware and established in Ireland, more of your life will need to be spent on Daily, Earthly, mundane tasks. At the end of the day, you are still humans with a human role and life to live; we appreciate this....'

10.18 Your children can learn as much by assisting you in your daily tasks; it will not be necessary to devote hours of time in playing and feeding them; when you also need to be washing, ironing, feeding, and making the daily routine of visitors and friends welcome.

Do not fear that you will be able to cope with everything asked of you, in both Earthly and Spiritual matters. We are fully aware of the conflict in time, and will plan accordingly. Trust in our ability to plan and to direct you, you will find that all will slot into place. We wish you well and every success...Your Guides.'

KEYPOINTS BTB17
a) As your Spiritual Awareness develops, you may be allocated different Guides.

b) You may also have Guides for a specific purpose such as Healing, Technical Queries, Training, Direction, Protection, Surgery etc,

10.19 It is Sunday, 23rd August 1998, ' There are Angels all about you. My dears, you may feel their presence. We bring you and all Mankind glad tidings, the blessings of this Child to be conceived this night, within your sleeping hours. You will be aware of this time. You have been given the Star, now you are given the Child in Matter. You will be told of many dates by those on the Earth-Plane, but you will be told the true date by Spirit. You may if you wish treat this message as one from the Angel Gabriel, as appeared to the Shepherds in the Past...all is a little different, but all is the same. You will be told of the arrival of the Child when necessary. You will not lose this Child, but care is necessary to allow it to grow in its mother's Belly.
We do not use romantic words. It is to be understood that these words come from Spirit of the highest Plane, who come to you with great understanding of the needs of you both on the Earth-Plane. Visions of the Angel Gabriel will be given in time.'
(A bright Star is seen thereafter above our Home, I can only presume this to only be visible to those with psychic Abilities)

10.20 'Human love upon this Earth-Plane is for many an accepted thing, such that they do not allow it for any reason to go deeper than the throat. It does not even touch the heart. This is not so within your hearts, we see a love so profound and so beautiful. The Child within will feel this love, we repeat WILL FEEL THIS LOVE.
Many words may be spoken to the Spirit of the Child. It is a living Being, already on this Earth-Plane. It grows within, like a nut on the Tree, a kernel or outer shell, but the nourishment comes from attachment to the Tree. The Tree is then nourished by the Earth. This lady is the Tree.
They are beautiful and majestic on your sky-lines, this is a time for beauty, and freedom of your given Land.
Trees are the lungs of the Earth. The mother Earth is the shell. You are the kernel...as an acorn you are small to begin with; but consider the beauty of an Oak Tree after many years; the strength and form of the character, is a joy to see. The Earth needs the Trees to bring life to the ground, so that it can breathe the air.
KEYPOINTS BTB18
a) There are different levels of Love.
Many only pay lip-service to the name. Love can only be felt in the Heart.
b) The unborn Child is aware and alive in every sense, and can be communicated with, and should be communicated with when inside the Womb.
c) The Spirit of the Child which is yet to be conceived, is given up to six weeks before conception, and resides thereafter in the Body, to await conception.

d) Abortion is murder and should not be supported by the State.
e) Trees are a necessary feature of Nature, to allow the Earth to breathe.

10.21 Your Lady is greatly tuned to the love of Trees, she has an understanding, to her they are people; they speak to her in a language not known to you John. She speaks in a language of love and beauty. Watch John, when Helana greets a Tree; the light within beams out to bring love to the Tree. She is guided, but she has a love of her own for Trees, whether single or plural. Mankind is as the Earth, you were created from the Earth. You feel the hands of this Lady, which caress your Body and leave you in no doubt of the love within. It is this love she feels when amongst the Trees. It is not necessary for you John at this time, to understand fully why this is, only to appreciate the wonder and mystery of all life.

KEYPOINT BTB19
Trees have Spirits and can be communicated with by some People.

10.22 We bring to you John a message of Understanding, safe in the knowledge that this lady will not be aware of the words spoken, for she is in a trance-like State. We speak for her but we do not use her voice as the vibrations are not good in this house (Chesterfield Place, Aylesbury, England) We can only say that your hearing is to be so profound, you will indeed hear the words of Spirit, but to begin with it will be an impression on the Mind...as you do now with writing. All else will follow. Remember, what lies within is so beautiful and clear, you can be in no doubt that with healing, your Awareness can be adjusted to suit the life that is needed.

Your Spiritual Awareness is beginning to take place. The Eyes have been lifted to open-up the lids that have shielded so much. The Ears have been opened, to allow you to hear all there is. Your musical Ear will be opened slowly to enable you to sing more clearly in tune. Composing will not be given, but a musical Instrument will be given, do not force this. Remember the words of your lady, this will help you to understand.

KEYPOINTS BTB20
a) All Talents are given.
b) Physical changes may be made by Spirit to assist your growth.
c) Your rate of Spiritual Growth is a feature of your Thoughts, your Actions, your individual Goals and your personal Needs.

10.23 ' Upon request we will ask you to lay down your possessions of the Past and to start a new Life. It does not matter that you will leave your Material possessions which make your life comfortable.

Ask,....

"Is it to be my wife and child, or my house and chair? Your house or your home?"

The home may not be grand, but it will be comfortable and filled with warmth and love. It may be bland in places, but look beyond the colour of the walls. Allow the lady to guide you for a short while only. A home of a more permanent basis will be found in time. You need to find accommodation that will please you both at this time, not a large place....but one that is comfortable at the present time. Do not split too many hairs. Take stock of the house that Judith resides in....all rooms can be occupied; bear this in mind, you will move-on when matters in-hand are settled. Dream only of the home, on the land, given in Vision.....the one that will be known as 'Home Farm"

10.24 'We leave you now with Angel Wings sitting on your Backs, to guide you whilst you live on the Earth-Plane, all around you is brightness with wings with which to fly.

Rest in peace my dears upon this night, with the beauty of love within and around you. The Child within sleeps peacefully, content with the love that has created her Being.'

10.25 'Razeem, your Guide, is to progress to higher Planes, and your new Guide is called Ahizar. We wish you to be happy and content in your new life together in Ireland, we express our sincere wishes for your future together. What you do tomorrow will depend upon the moves Bob makes in terms of meeting with Judith. Your financial worries will soon be resolved. We have needed to progress your Awareness as quickly as possible in view of the Child's coming, and the pace of World Events. Whilst Mankind has free-will, you should realise that our actions in order to meet our Objectives can be dependant upon the choices of one thousand People. Each individual choice affecting the subsequent decision.

This is the complexity of the situation we have to cope with.....We are now in a situation where we can progress and move forwards with increased certainty, as many obstacles have been overcome....

Pack and stack now is the order of the day. You may need to react quickly, and if schedules get out of hand, be prepared to leave for Ireland at a moment's notice. We hope that this will not be necessary, but you should be prepared for any eventuality and be prepared to react as we dictate'.

KEYPOINTS BTB21

a) Every choice and action we take as Individuals, can cause an Effect and different Choice by Another.

b) We are all inter-related...Consider the pebble dropped into the lake, the ripples spread-out and can cause an effect and a reaction MANY TIMES GREATER than the initial effect.

c) Relate to any one act of Love or Friendship to another....could this cause them to act differently in a different situation?

- If your one act of kindness could cause a Leader, or someone in a position of Power to change their staunch; your one act of Kindness or Compassion could CHANGE THE WORLD.
- What one Act, or series of Experiences, was it that caused Hitler to have a vendetta against the Jews? A few kindly acts by a few Jewish People, would this have saved six million Lives and Souls?

10.26 Ahizar writes: 'Carry your writings, and pen and paper, with you at all times, so that messages can be brought. Your hearing John, has been restricted by a shortage of salt, this has now been rectified, but you should take salt regularly as you sweat so profusely. It is good that you recognise the finger signal to write, as this is less intrusive than pressure on your ears.*(I get a stiff third finger when Spirit wish me to write)*
Your headache was indeed caused by your exposure to Anne's mother, and is a warning to you to stay clear of any further healing efforts.
(I had been asked by Judith, to heal her mother's arthritic Knee, this removed the pain and brought back normal movement.....but in so doing had caused her to recover from her illness, which if continued, would have changed her Karma, and also her influence on the rest of the family.)
KEYPOINTS BTB22
a) Your Abilities to receive communication with Spirit can be affected by your physical make-up...Your psychic Hearing, for example, may be affected by a deficiency of salt (sodium chloride)
b) You need to protect yourself when you Heal, so that you do not collect any symptoms from your Patient.
c) Not everyone is to be healed, all disease and suffering is given for a reason. Always use the words: `Heavenly Father, I humbly request healing for --------
If it be thy Will, according to their Need.'
d) Do not try to heal people who do not ask for Healing.

10.27 'You have your urgent plans to make, and your urgent tasks to achieve in Ireland. Do not delay your Departure for any reason whatsoever. It is essential that you are permanently in Ireland before Christmas. We wish to resolve all of your personal matters with the greatest of urgency. We are not happy with the way in which Helana's husband is refusing to compromise and to agree to a financial settlement. We have decided therefore to change his personal situation so that he will wish to settle more quickly.'

'Do not, Helana, allow him to brow-beat you, do not give way on your demands. The monies from this settlement; are needed by you both in Ireland.

Do not falter, do not waiver. Monies will also be forthcoming from both of your families in the New Year. Your Guide Helana, will tell you what provision to make for your children'.

10.28 We wish you to be able to purchase your 'Home Farm' and also to be freed from debts so that you can have a fresh start. We are to change your Karma John. We wish you both to be freed from Earthly pursuits so that you can devote your energies to Spiritual Matters and also have the monies to be able to travel extensively. We also wish you John to bring-up your children in Ireland, and to be free of any ties back in England. All these matters are to be resolved by Easter of 1999. The pace of World Events quickens, you can by-pass many Occurrences by living in Ireland.

- Your Work there demands your attention there.
- Your attention demands your Presence there.
- Your presence there demands your Actions there.
- Your Spiritual work is to begin next year. As your powers increase, you will be made aware of what is required.

KEYPOINT BTB23
Your Karma can be changed in any Lifetime.

10.29 Plan your move to Ireland using your friend Steve to help and a vehicle from your Contact 'Dick'. Do not waste time on other methods. Plan your move for November, 1998 and keep the lease on your house until Christmas. Your Friend Judith will move into your house whilst she awaits news from the man Bob. He will not leave his family until after the New Year.

10.30 A Message is brought through Judith to the three of us.......
'The Angel of the Lord circles amongst you, bringing Light, and Purity, and Love. Shared between you is a bond which has been made between you, and will never be broken. Much pleasure and joy and celebration is felt in these Realms, of the Acceptance and Understanding shared by the three of you joined together tonight. The closeness felt between you all will not be broken. As you have seen, Anne's role is that of the mother hen, clucking around the pair of you. She will continue to help and to guide you until such time as she must leave to pursue her own work. By this time you will be established in the place that awaits you.'

10.31 'Fear not, Contact will not be lost, and many good times of pleasure lay ahead. We wish to thank you for the opening of your hearts to allow us in...for without that we could not have achieved what we have achieved.'

'All that we ask now is that you continue to live your lives, allowing Spirit to enter in order that you may be guided along the path that leads to the Light that has been shown to you.'

10.32 'We cannot explain the joy here. This disputes the fact that we do not have Emotions once we are in the World of Spirit, such rot!!..... but, it is a different Emotion to that which Humans feel, for it is not tied-in to jealousy which destroys. Our Joy continues in the Purity and the most meaningful of ways in which a word can be used to describe a feeling. We leave you now and surround you all, individually and together, with the light shone down from the Lord most High.'

KEYPOINTS BTB24

a) Spirit do feel Emotions, but they are different to those which we experience on the Earth-Plane........

- **They certainly indicate feelings of Joy, Anger, Frustration, Annoyance, Happiness, Love, Hurt, Communication, Bitterness, Pride.**
- **They also remember their Earthly experiences, such as Taste, Flavour, Smell, and can inflict and cause Pain and Discomfort.**
- **The Memory of Earthly feelings is also dimmed by the passage of Time.**

b) Whenever you visit anyone, or, they visit you, always give them a gift......be it a Biscuit or Drink, a Kiss, a Hug, or even only a Smile.

10.33 Helana in Vision returns to her parent's home and 'gathers-up' that part of her Spirit which was left their when her virginity was taken by Mervin her first Husband. I am told that I am the true father of the Child given to us, and the mother is as a virgin...for her purity has been gathered-up and replaced. It is only my Spirit that has entered the seed that is in the mother of the Child....no other has entered in before this time. The pureness must remain intact, for it is only in this way that this pregnancy will be allowed to continue.

10.34 'There is to be no other in your many lives ahead, you have been told of this. Understand this, it is necessary for your Spirit to feel this, to Know this, to Understand this. All that has gone before is irrelevant. This lady is your lady alone.

No other will or can have this love, but it can be shared in many different ways with Others. You will always remain side-by-side. There will be, and can be, and has been, no Other. You have always remained close friends, relatives, lovers, spouses, but in this lifetime the coming together has come in a true way and will not be replaced by any other life to take-away what has been gained in this lifetime.'

10.35 'Know within, that you have the purest kind of Spirit, which will bring to the Peoples of the World a special beauty and love.
GOD is within the lives of each of you. As your Spirit grows, so do the Spirits of your children and your grand-children and thereafter, a continual stream of Holy Spirit.'

KEYPOINTS BTB25
a) Whatever we individually achieve in terms of our Spiritual growth and Awareness is never lost.
b) All following will subsequently benefit, in particular your children and their children will be capable of greater Understanding and Awareness....for do you not teach the young-Ones your values and understanding.?
c) But realise also, that their Spirits will contain a proportion of your Spirit, so that their Souls will be born at a higher vibratory level.

10.36 Isaiah writes through Helana....
'My Dear, you have learned many lessons of purity since the time that Jesus walked this Earth, for you know my dear, your Spirit is as the Mother of Christ, Mary. You have been given Mary many times now, we wish you to understand why the feelings have been so strong, and your understandings so great. Perhaps now your confusion will cease, and allow a more settled approach to the Holy Birth. ALL is the same as it was in Biblical Times, but all is different my dear. We learn by our mistakes and this is the reason for the differences, but the message is still the same. GOD bless all that you do my dear, and we see now a calmness within which will teach your Child well. Go in peace my dear, and remain our loyal friend who greets our Eyes with Purity and Splendour'.

10.37 It is still Tuesday, 24th August, 1998, Helana receives Visions of two weddings, the first, in Spirit, involves a Rolls-Royce, a beautiful white gown and many guests we cannot see. This vision of this ceremony is to be brought to us at a future time.
'The second Earthly wedding is to take place shortly, the dress is cream...the colours are significant, cream means 'a softening of the edges'.

10.38 As we drive back at midnight, from Banbury to Aylesbury, Helana sinks into a trance and my Guide Ahizar delivers this message:... 'The Star of Bethlehem we have seen in the sky will always travel ahead of you. When you move home it will sit above the rear of your home in Ireland. (the most brilliant of Stars appears overhead, I can only assume that this is only visible to those who can see in a Spiritual sense.) The Star will serve to guide those few who have the Awareness to your home'.

10.39 'The Child who is given will be as Jesus in Spirit. The combination of the Holy Ghost from Helana and the Jesus element from you John, will produce a beautiful, wonderful Spirit. The Child is not the new 'Messiah' but is in no way less important. The Spirits will be equal in their abilities to perform wondrous Works and Miracles.

10.40 'The parents of Jesus were not given an important place in History, but this is now to change. Joseph was a Carpenter, and it is hoped that you John, will use your hands, not only with wood, but also in many other ways.....to teach all of your Children, and those assigned to you, in the ways of the World, and how to travel, and to move around with the minimum of Publicity. Your Role, John, is to teach them to Heal and to perform Miracles....remember, that this knowledge is within your Spirit, yet to be released.'

10.41 'The History of the World is to be re-written with a new 'Book of Knowledge' and a new Order. You both have a key role to play in this making. History will repeat itself in the way in which the Child is born, in the Stable, but the Surroundings will be different. A wondrous Time is to happen, which will change the course of History. GOD be praised and let us all rejoice.'

10.42 'It is hoped that the Book will be read by many...and not buried away in some distant Past. **The Book of Truth and Knowledge** shall also be written, (this Book), and many will see the futile ways in which they conduct their lives, their selves, and their Beings. The message contained in the Book, offers to the World and its Peoples, a chance for them to inherit this Earth in all its glory....for at the present Time the Earth is only on loan to, and only borrowed by the Human Race. We wish to see a more permanent state of affairs, but this will only happen through actions of Respect and Responsibility in all aspects of Human Behaviour. Take care my dears, to realise that we are around you at the present Time, and will do so always, as your Guardian Angels and Protectors.'

10.43 '**The Book Of Knowledge** (Life) is referred to in the Bible, but has been largely overlooked by Mankind in its ignorance. This Book sets out the Future as agreed with GOD, and this Book serves as a working guide for all Spirits on the Earth-Plane to follow. This Book was written before the Earth and Mankind existed; accordingly, it was re-written when Mankind was created, and was re-written again when Jesus was born. With the Events planned for the New Millennium, it is necessary to once again re-write this Book. The Book is more about the Whole of the Universe than the Earth, but without re-writing this Chapter, the whole of the Universe will stand still. There-in lies the problem. Only you John, and Judith, know the location of the Book and are able to access it.'

'It is held on a distant Planet and guarded by hostile Beings who speak a unique language. It will require a special Key before they will release the Book. You, John, and Judith, wrote this Book and amended it at the time of the Christ, so the information about its location and access is known to you both. Unfortunately, you John do not have your Awareness necessary for you to remember.'

10.44 ' Judith's Spirit is refusing to impart this knowledge, unless, and without the man Bob physically joining with her. He has now delayed this decision until the New Year, in view of his personal and family commitments....
Alas, we cannot afford to wait that long! One solution would be for Judith to sacrifice her Earth-Life and to return to Spirit, but we cannot demand this for she is Higher Spirit than us. This information has been locked within her since Time began.! Judith is of such a loving nature that she will not force Bob to come to her. This is our dilemma, we wish only to request your help John, and to signify to you the strength of this lady's Being. Why else do you imagine that we allow her to give us such words of abuse, when she is not pleased with our using of her!'

10.45 It is Wednesday, 26th August 1998....I am suffering from a pain in my left shoulder. My Guide Ahizar says ' the pain is caused by the Spirit of your ex-wife Elsa who is jealous of your contact with your friends in Holland. You can ease this by praying for her Spirit and then sending it away; she is not a pleasant lady.'
KEYPOINTS BTB26
a) Other Spirits can cause you physical pain and suffering.
b) Always question whether a pain is yours, by telling it to go away, and being aware of any change to the intensity........
c) It is possible through the use of Prayers, protective Shields, and through 'raising your Spirit' to reduce and prevent this suffering.

10.46 'We have told you previously, that the influence of the Earth within the Universe is negative and hostile. This is how the Earth's Aura is viewed by other Worlds. There exists a Council of Representatives, from other Worlds and other Planets who serve to advise GOD. and can act to maintain Harmony, Peace, and Love, throughout the Universe. You see that you are not alone and that your actions CAN and WILL bring about your own demise unless the influence of the Earth is lightened and All is brought closer to GOD. We work tirelessly and continuously to bring Light and Love to Mankind.'
KEYPOINTS BTB27
a) The Human Race is not alone in the Universe.
b) There exist many hundreds of Alien Races, many of whom are far more advanced than Humans.

c) It is necessary to change the Earth's Aura to one of Love and Tolerance if we are to be able to choose our own Destiny, and not have Others decide it for us.

d) The Human Race does not have an absolute right to live on the Earth-Plane, we are here with the opportunity to redeem ourselves. It is necessary to earn the right to a more permanent residence.

10.47 'Your burdens John, from the Past, have been contained in a shaft of Light above Helana. They will be released one-by-one for analysis and understanding. We wish you to understand this beautiful act that Helana does to enable you to progress fully. It is hoped that most of these burdens will be lifted before you journey to Ireland. If at any time you see Helana's position change such that she is weighed-down, understand that this may well be the reason. Have compassion when Earthly matters are not achieved, for there are many burdens on this Earth-Plane to work through. It is this work that will be achieving Peace on the Earth and Understanding for all the Peoples of the Earth and other Planets. She has carried the Cross for Jesus in much the same manner.'

KEYPOINTS BTB28

a) It is possible to ponder and to reflect upon any situation, so as to able to Analyse and to Understand the Causes for any Event to happen. In this way it is possible to ask for healing and for forgiveness.

b) If you identify any patterns of repeating Behaviour, then you should also consider:

- How could I have acted differently?..
- What can I learn from this Event?
- Which Souls have been hurt or injured?
- How can I heal this Situation?
- Why?

10.48 'All Beings are not filled with hatred and warped minds. There is beauty on the Earth-Plane that needs preserving. Helana has been a Missionary and a Peace-Maker to other Peoples. The Journeys have been long and difficult at times over vast Space and Remoteness, it has been difficult to enter these other Worlds, but her beauty and strength have prevailed, and this has created a peace amongst other Beings of this Universe. Like your Friend, Judith, you John, are a Creator of this World. You will indeed discover your true identity in times to come'.

KEYPOINTS BTB29

a) There is beauty on the Earth-Plane worthy of protection.

b) There already exists Communication between different Worlds. As Mankind progresses, Some will become capable of this communication and Spiritual Awareness.

c) Some Souls already devote their Energies, to act as Missionaries and Peace-Makers between the Worlds.

10.49 'All your previous lives, John, have been a preparation for now. Since Biblical Times you have searched for fame and wealth in a Materialistic way, and you have needed to learn all about Human ways, but this has detracted from and squashed any Spiritual Progression. Hopefully in this lifetime that situation will be corrected. You, John, need to find love in your heart for the Peoples of the World. You have achieved this in a previous lifetime. Once released from your Mind, all Knowledge is there, this is our frustration.'

KEYPOINTS BTB30

a) The pursuit of EGO, the pursuit of Materialistic gain, the pursuit of Power and Fame, any or all of these attributes can over-ride the progression towards Spiritual Awareness.

b) It is necessary at all times to act with Compassion and Love towards Others, to give to Others, to share your Talents.

c) It is not necessary to go without, you can live a comfortable Life, provided that you share your wealth and help Others...In so doing you will not need, in the future, to LIVE the experience of others' Lives in order to understand their needs, and so to learn to feel Compassion for them.

10.50 'Do as you have been told my friend. Travel with Judith to Holy-Head, and she will accompany you on your travels in Ireland. Indeed this will be most useful as her knowledge and her Awareness will be of use to you. She will also gain an insight into many Places, which will enable her to choose a residence close to yours.

Anne's child will be cared for by one of her sisters, who will choose to stay at your house for the week. Monies will be forthcoming from your Lottery ticket to pay for all your expenses. Do not delay in sourcing a car, we prefer you to travel over as foot-passengers and to hire a car in Dublin with an Irish number-plate......the winning Lottery numbers are..3,8,11,14,38,41. Do not concern yourself with Earthly or work matters; use your time to pack, to talk, to source a car, to purchase your rings, to do your shopping.'

KEYPOINTS BTB31

a) Always be cautious of messages which are of a personal nature.

- **Judith did not choose to accompany us.**
- **We have not won anything on the Lottery then or since.**
- **Our finances have suffered through lack of attention to my work situation, and little help has been forthcoming from Spirit.**

I am forced to conclude that either the message was a deliberate lie, or dark Spirit wished to mislead-us, or my Mind over-rode any Spirit message...remember that the Mind is very powerful and can superimpose your own Thoughts.

10.51 'Allow Helana to teach you, to guide you. The ego of the man is large, your strength of Character must also be retained, it is necessary for your future work.....listen carefully to all the words of this lady; adhere to them, and find Understanding about the ways of Nature. We do understand, that within a relationship that it is more difficult to accept the words of a woman who is also your partner, but, it is only by doing this that you will learn the knowledge that is necessary.'...

(As my own person I naturally question what is said to me, and also express my own opinion. The difficulty arises as before, are the words spoken simply from Helana, to which I respond as a normal human Being, or , are they from Spirit, who seem to demand my acceptance without question!.....remember I speak of every moment of every Day and it is not always appropriate to give hand-signals to qualify.)

10.52 'If you read the words from ancient Churches, and learn of their customs, you will obtain a good knowledge of Spirituality. The messages have always been there, for they represent the houses of GOD. Alas, the understanding today falls deaf upon the Ears and blind to the Eyes of those who should know better....ie. The established Church leaders, Do they not realise that the true meaning has been lost?....Do they hear GOD's words ?, Do they see GOD's works,? .....No ! They parade around in their best clothes and consider they have done their duty and helped their fellow Man.'

KEYPOINTS BTB32
a) There is much which those in positions of Power and Authority can do to improve and to change Peoples attitudes and behaviour.
b) There can be, and is a role for those who teach and guide Others, but first these leaders must understand, and be capable of fulfilling their roles in a humble, loving and compassionate way.
c) The traditions of the Past have a part to play, but it is more important to bring the message of Love to everyone on the Earth-plane.
d) Jesus did not remain within the confines of a Church Building, he did not solely preach to the converted.
e) How can Mankind progress if you only talk to those who already Listen? No!
* **It is necessary to go down amongst the People, amongst those who will initially reject you.**

200

- To counter their words and actions, to demonstrate
  through your Actions that you do have Compassion, you
  do Care, you do give to Others, you do help the Poor
  and Distressed, you do help the Sick and the
  Suffering.

f) Much of what is related in this Book existed in a
ancient Times. There is much that can be learned from
Antiquity.

10.53 'Mankind is made from matter, the matter is always returned to
the Earth from which it came. Dust to Dust. Ashes to Ashes. When
placed in Fire you return to the Earth. When placed in Water you return
to the Earth. Yet Water and Fire, together with Air, are all necessary to
Life, or they can be used to extinguish it on the Earth-Plane. Reflect on
these Words.'

KEYPOINTS BTB33

a) We have in Life, the opportunity to learn, to
understand, to love, to care for Others.

b) We can also choose to use Fire and Water to comfort,
to make wonderful Foods, to Heal, to Purify, to
Grow......or,

c) We can choose to use these Forces to Destroy other
Humans or other life-forms.

d) The Choices are ours,

- the same power of Nature can be used to Heal or to
  Harm,
- to Create or to Destroy,
- to build immense or powerful Creations,
- to produce a loving Environment, beautiful Clothes,
  Buildings, Music and Everything we know,
- Or, to Burn and Demolish and Wash away every last
  trace of our Existence on the Earth-Plane.

e) Every last Individual has a PERSONAL RESPONSIBILITY
for the SURVIVAL of MANKIND.

10.54 'A few Spirits work to ensure that the balance of Nature is not
upset, for without this input to balance the structure of the Planets,
there will be no Earth for Mankind to walk upon. Be prepared John, if
asked to, to assist in this essential work. More understanding will be
given at a later time.'

10.55 'The Stars in the Universe belong to you. Your many lives as
Humans are nearing an end. Many years before the Earth-Plane existed;
you were together as " Other Beings". It is from this original Planet that
your love stems. It delights us to see this again, united once more. Not
only do you unite the Humans about you, but you also unite the Humans
of this Spirit World, and those of the Universe and of the Planet of Earth.

'It is to be hoped that the Universe will be as Love, as those on the Earth will find in Heaven. It is this work which Helana's Spirit is to achieve.'

KEYPOINTS BTB34
a) What Love is achieved on the Earth-Plane, has a
consequence and effect throughout the Universe.
b) Do unto Others as you would have Them do unto You.'
c) Everything is given to be Shared, your Wealth, your
Musical Talent, your writing Skills
d) Use or Lose' is the basis of Life; and the basis of
one of the Parables told by Jesus.

10.56 We Find two gift vouchers in the Lounge.....M & S for £ 20 plus Argos for £ 20.
We are told that the vouchers are a gift from Spirit for the new Child to be born. Praise be to GOD. Praise be to you both.

KEYPOINT BTB36
Spirit can and do remove objects, and can bring objects.
The transference of matter is a reality. I am told that
some of the maps used by the IRA Quartermasters to
pinpoint the location of Arms Dumps have been removed by
Spirit, and those aware of the locations also have been
removed, so that the knowledge has been lost.
......see AppendixVI. The Scole Experiment.

10.57 It is Saturday, 29th August 1998. Judith and Helana sit huddled-up against the 'cold ' created by the presence of so many Spirits. I am told that members of our families for the past 2,000 years are present, by invitation of High Spirit, to witness the proceedings. They are brought this Day together for them to understand what it is that we are doing, to give to them Knowledge of our Trust, our Commitment and our Belief. By seeing this, each one of them will rise higher in the Sphere of Spirit, having glimpsed the glory that can be. White Eagle is to speak through Judith, to his right hand side stands Bob, behind them stand four High Spirit, two each side. Jesus kneels before Judith.
' My dears, I hope that I may come fully with my voice, I have now come forward to bring such a message, even I do not have it, it has been two blinks of the Eye since I last spoke with my own voice...
This...that is better, the Child relaxes more that I may come more easily for you....Welcome, welcome, I look upon this....I am not happy with my voice....Forgive me..(.pause)....We will proceed regardless. (Judith stroking her throat)
I welcome you, I thank you and wish you to relate all to your friend upon her return. (Judith's Spirit has left her body and has been replaced by the Spirit of White Eagle)
My dears, your Trust and your Faith and Commitment and your Beliefs have been sorely tested......We welcome those from Spirit to join us to witness what is to be.....'

'The coming together of your friend's Spirit with that of the Man. Bear in mind the importance of this. These Spirit were first parted at the beginning of all of you. (*Adam and Eve as in Genesis,...see AppendixII)*

Do not however be fearful for each Human body will walk their chosen Path on the Earth-Plane, until such time they are recalled to the World we call Spirit. These two Spirits are to be joined as One, never to be parted. Together in every life...should they choose to return...they will find each other and know the other instantly.
The Human side is a little more difficult for them, only because they are Human, and each Human having their own very strong...it is the way of them....their personality, they have strong personalities, but each also has such deep love for Mankind.....this lady smokes...gestures!!! They will come together as a beautiful couple, but at times it will be tense...
...we will smooth the way. Try my dears...we are helping each of you as best we can....for their Spirits stand here behind Jesus....to be joined with such beauty, such love, such strength and such power.
Your Friends can see (hand gestures) the gold ribbon which signifies these Spirits remain together for Eternity...is bound around them by the Lord Jesus who comes as a symbol for the People gathered who are able to understand Jesus....For you, the things you are to achieve, relate so strongly to this Man who walked your Earth and died to be remembered, to never be forgotten. How sad he suffered for us...Now, to have to do this again.
KEYPOINTS BTB37
a) Spirits can Divide and can be re-United.
b) The Strength and Power of the combined Spirit is greater than the separate parts....provided that both Spirits have attained their Awareness.

10.58 'The way ahead will not always be easy. Earthly Emotions mar certain functions within you. We do all we can to help you to appreciate this, that your Earthly Emotions may be understood by each one of you, that you come to a clear understanding of yourselves. In this way all becomes lighter, the Burdens become lighter, the World becomes lighter. We now move-on.'
KEYPOINT BTB38
a) Your individual Actions can affect everyone else.
b) As you gain Spiritual Awareness and Understanding of yourself and your Emotions; So your Spirit becomes lighter, So your Burdens and Baggage become less, so the Aura of the Earth is lightened.

10.59 'My dears I am an old Man, this Girl's body does not fit me......I like laughter....I struggle.
I so wanted this to be completely my voice....to know that I would not come lightly to this Room. You are correct....there is a shadow which hovers over this Town.'

(Banbury has a darkness created by its History, starting with the Druids and continued by the Plague and Civil War etc.)

'We have first to say goodbye to the Visitors....we thank them for coming and hope they have enjoyed their visit, and have seen the joining of the perfect Spirit......forgive me Bob. I cannot lie " together you can move Mountains."

10.60 'Welcome Helana and John, I wish you were able to see we have another visitor brought here for the two of you. I introduce the Angel Gabriel, who is to pass his blessing on each of you. We, I am preparing to recede slightly that your friend may see the visitor and tell you later...but please in this instant try, try to see yourself. He has come to bring you the most precious gift known. Let no Man, or no Spirit tell you differently. Walk together along your chosen path.

But my dears we have chosen it for you. Do not let that detract from the Courage and Strength you have shown in letting us guide you. The gift of the Child is within. The Angel Gabriel encompasses the Babe that it may grow into the beautiful Child you have been shown. Who else put this loving Man as the Father?

I known to others as White Eagle, join you also in a love so strong that there may never be any doubts or concerns.

You are of the Earth. There will be those moments.....Do not let them fester so the wound is not too great to heal. All can be healed by love to enable you to 'make good' again' ....(I thank White Eagle.....He smiles and claps his hands)...'It is as old friends being re-united'

10.61 'Your Friend Judith is so joyous at meeting with Bob again after so long...I thought....I may not overcome that strong Spirit. This brings us to a most important part of these proceedings...the strength of the Spirit, whilst joined with the other half is all powerful. Therefore it follows that this....for instance, will only be possible should the joined Spirit fully allow another to enter the body. At normal times, a Spirit, particularly a higher Spirit can quite easily, not remove the Spirit of a Human Body, but lift it allowing the Higher Spirit to enter. A darkened Spirit cannot simply enter, it can only enter if invited and allowed to be there....whereas a Higher Spirit can uplift the host Spirit and enter in to give a message.....but even this is difficult if both the Mind and Spirit of the host Body do not wish this....but it can still be done. Helana had a problem only because she allowed that to happen....I only mention this as a comparison.'

KEYPOINTS BTB39
a) Dark Spirit cannot 'take-over' your Being unless you are a willing host.
b) Higher Spirit can, if they so choose, enter your Being by 'lifting' your Spirit for a short period of time.

10.62 'Again, we have to request that you continue to behave with your friend, Judith, in a normal manner.....for, the way she is on the Earth-Plane is most beautiful, maybe not to all men, but we see within her, she is pure Spirit, but for all that she still needs the Earthly love of you both.....as this has been a considerable amount for her Earthly Mind to contend with. (The Angel leaves having blessed each one and the child) I thank you for allowing this to happen, as I leave be ready to assist your friend.'

10.63 'I return my dears...Helana, John, have your Spirits not previously been joined? ...wrapped around with the golden Band. Did this ceremony not take place for you?
This joining on this Occasion....which I give my humble apologies for not making it more clear, was the joining of Judith with her half-Spirit Bob......... ' Now the Spirits are as One'
White Eagle continues: 'You may wonder as to why I did not refer to the Man by the name you know him on Earth.......He in a previous life was my wife! I therefore find it most difficult to refer to him by the name now chosen.....You understand that his Spirit was the lady I took for my wife.....I apologise, but however hard I try, I cannot think of that Spirit as a Man....that Spirit is so beautiful....I am sentimental, but take it that it is Bob. Do not forget that you John and Helana, are joined as these two are joined.'

10.64 I feel tightness around my head, it is the Spirit of Ted my father who comes with love. ' Hallo son, you are some lad aren't you. I can talk to you now as you know. I am happy now that I am on my way to more Understanding and Awareness. I am delighted that you and Helana are progressing so well. I do not know the full picture, but there is great excitement and anticipation here as to the future. I am delighted that you two seem to be involved in this and look forward to learning of your Exploits. You have a lovely lady son, look after her well and forget all those past Relationships. To have found your one true love is wonderful....you must be absolutely delighted. I am so pleased to be able to do this and will hope to be present when the Earth wedding takes place. Good luck in your new home together. I don't know why you're off to Ireland, but it is a beautiful Country but for the troubles. Take care both of you and I hope to talk to you again soon. I pop down every so often just to see how everyone is. They all seem to be suffering at the moment but life is sometimes like that. It can change so fast when you least expect it to. Good luck and love.........TED.'

10.65 Following a visit to the Museum at Daventry, Visions are received and an interpretation given by my Guide.

- Seven Faces of Man = the faces of Good and Evil
- A Dogshead   = The Old War-Dog
- A burning Sail   = Wars of the Past
- A Gauntlet, A Circle = Signs of Re-Birth necessary
- A Green-Mask   = Merlin

KEYPOINT BTB40
To conclude, unless Mankind changes its Attitudes, the wars of the Past will be repeated and Evil will take precedence over Good, and Evil will rule the Earth. This cannot be! The Earth will perish. The need therefore is for a new Arthur, a new Lancelot and a new Merlin...these my friends are you three.

10.66 Helana is in discomfort through the presence of the Spirit of Lorna. I am told that I am also being affected by the Spirit of Mervin.

10.67 White Eagle states that 'Helana is beautiful not only in Spirit but also in her Being.
She is:

- As the Deer in the Forest
- As the Breeze in the Trees
- As the Warmth of the Sun
- As a Light in the Stars
- As the Glow of the Moon

10.68 Jupiter is the Planet of Law and Order for the Universe.'

##

CHAPTER 11. IRELAND RE-VISITED

11.00 We had been told by Spirit that Judith and her Child, Joseph, would accompany us on our visit to Ireland. I had booked to travel by motor-bike, but at the last minute was asked by Spirit to change this to a car, a hire-car, with an Irish number-plate, so that we would be less conspicuous. Judith arrived in Aylesbury ready to depart with us, initially with the three year old Joseph, and then finally decided to leave for Ireland without him. Judith's marriage was on the verge of breaking-up and she arrived very distressed with evidence of bruising from battering by Damien her husband. Eventually she decided to stay in Aylesbury whilst we departed alone to Ireland.

11.01 It was Sunday 30th August when finally Helana and I left for HolyHead by car. *(I had hoped to travel by motorbike, a Honda 750cc VFR, but Helana was apprehensive about using the bike. She considered that she was also in the middle of a 'period', but Spirit say she is still pregnant, and we are given the name of the Child to be as 'Nhadia'.)*

11.02 An apology is received from Spirit for their indecision over our travel plans and whether Judith is to accompany us. They say that they find it somewhat difficult to understand our human Emotions and relationships, but they are prepared in the circumstances to allow a few months more for 'loose ends' to be sorted. We do not know whether Judith will still be in Aylesbury when we return.

KEYPOINT IR1
Spirit do not always fully allow for, or understand Human Emotions and Human Relationships. This can lead to inconsistency in their Expectations and a degree of unpredictability in the course of Events.

11.03 Our outline Route has been agreed with Spirit before we leave; there are certain areas they wish us to stay clear of, and certain places we are to visit. We have been told to head due west from Dublin and then to wind our way due north up the West Coast, across the North and back down to Bangor. I sit down and plan a detailed route and then ask for clarification, as to which places to visit and which not to.

KEYPOINTS IR2
a) Where-ever you travel can fulfil a purpose, your Mind may not be aware that the Spirit is working.
b) Spirit are capable of directing our every move and experience.

11.04 I join the A5 North from Aylesbury and head towards Holy-Head; after a few miles I stop to fill the car, an E-registration Volvo, with diesel-fuel. The tank has perhaps two gallons of petrol in it, when I fill it with diesel fuel! Not a good start to the week's relaxing holiday.

I manage somehow to keep the Engine running, and after a very bumpy half-an hour it runs reasonably well, coughing and spluttering. I reason that the solution is to progressively run down the level of diesel fuel in the tank, and then to mix in more and more petrol. I had not appreciated that running is so different from starting; a Vicar kindly gave me a push-start at the next petrol filling-Station.

(The journey is later compared to that of Joseph and Mary. They say that the 'accident' with the fuel-type was deliberately given by Spirit to replica the difficulties faced by Joseph and Mary in Biblical Times.)

11.05 On route, near the Site of the Battle of Bosworth, Helana assists Angels by saying prayers for the recovery of the Spirits of many hundreds of lost Souls who still remain at this location and have never moved on to Heaven.

KEYPOINTS IR3
a) There remain many thousands of lost Souls on the Earth-Plane who for whatever reason have chosen to remain here rather than to move on to Heaven.
When seen by Humans they are called Ghosts.
b) Eventually ALL of these Souls will need to be recovered, prior to the raising of the Energy level of the Earth-Plane. Angels carry out this work, but it may need a higher Soul to provide the initial trigger.
c) The majority of these lost Souls have never accepted that they are 'dead'; they wander as if in a 'time-warp' where Time stands still, not realising that many hundreds or thousands of years have passed since their original transition. As time passes these Souls may well become darker and darker.

11.06 Upon reaching Shrewsbury, I enter the town to find somewhere to have a meal and to relax. The car by now seems to be running fairly smoothly. Suddenly, Helana strides-off and she is frog-marched along the Severn Riverbank, around in a complete circle, across two bridges, along the Riverbank and back towards the car. Helana is in communication with the Spirit of Bob, who has come to protect her whilst we are in Shrewsbury. We are asked to leave the Area immediately....I know only that Helana is in danger, she can barely stand, and her voice and Spirit are becoming progressively weaker; I fear for her life if we remain too long. We abandon any attempt to find a Restaurant and return at once to the car. Will it work?

It eventually takes three lads pushing for over one hundred yards, to get the car Engine to re-fire' We depart Shrewsbury and continue our journey, as soon as we reach the perimeter of the City, Helana recovers as if nothing has happened. We are aiming to reach the Port of Holy-Head, on Anglesey, to catch the Ferry over to Dublin.

KEYPOINTS IR4

a) Once before Helana had been asked to collect her Aura from a particular Area and to leave quickly. This is because of her extreme sensitivity, and the recollection of Events in a previous Lifetime. She took a previous life in this particular location, and Spirit were anxious to ensure no repetition in this Lifetime. Remember the Spirit never forgets anything! The collection of your Aura is to build the strength of your Soul.

b) When you feel comfortable in a particular location, or with a certain person you have just met, this could well be the Spirit recognition from a previous lifetime. 'Deja-vous' in folklore to most people.

11.07 We still have not eaten when at 01.00hrs I find a Chinese Take-a-Way Shop, near Bety-y-Coed, Conway, Wales. The crowd of twelve people milling outside the shop are all speaking the Welsh language; inside the shop the three Chinese assistants speak one of their dialects; there is Irish music emanating from a window close-by. What a cosmopolitan spot! We eat fish and chips in the car before driving-on through the night.

11.08 Eventually we reach the Ferry Terminal and find the car-park. On the Ferry shuttle-bus, we strike a conversation with a young man called Peter who seems to be a 'spiritual person'. He is in the process of moving to the Sligo Area from Liverpool. Helana comments that he is a 'Philip' look-a-like.

11.09 It is a gruelling experience carrying our luggage from our car the Ferry, from the Ferry to Dun Loaghaire Terminal, from the boat Terminal in Dublin to the Bus-stop, and from there eventually to find the car-hire Company, in the back streets of Dublin. The traffic in Dublin is horrendous, but eventually we make our way out of the City and head due West. I am not too enamoured with the start of our holiday, we have been travelling for 24 hours with little rest and much hassle. There are many, many, tri-colour flags everywhere we go, many new Bungalows with nice gardens and cars. I wonder where the money has come from, for all these new homes.

11.10 It is daytime, and what is surprising is that there are so few people about, no children, no flowers in the gardens...flat, dark, hostile, atmosphere. Helana passes-out 3-4 times, as we pass through certain Areas. The People we see do not smile. It is striking that some roads have been re-surfaced and some have not. The Atmosphere does not lift until we reach the West Coast and eventually make our way North, to our eventual stopping place for the night, up past Sligo.

KEYPOINTS IR5
a) The frequency of Trees, Plants and wild-Flowers; the health of Nature's Creation, the absence of Disease...
b) The number of Birds and Butterflies, these are all a good indication of Mankind's degree of Compassion for himself and for other Species...
All of these features reflect the 'Atmosphere' and enlightenment of any Area.

11.11 My left fore-arm hurts. I am told that this is caused by the Spirit of one of my step-children who has learnt of my plans to move to Ireland and feels neglected and abandoned.
I am asked to send to his Spirit prayers of love and understanding, this will then relieve the pain.

KEYPOINTS IR6
a) Other Spirits can cause you physical pain and discomfort.
b) If you Pray for them and ask them firmly to leave, this can help to relieve the Symptoms...There are many other ways to protect yourself and many of these are listed in the Text and summarised in Appendix VII.

11.12 My left shoulder aches...caused by Jack's Spirit. My right shoulder also aches, given by Spirit, who say that I am harping back to using my motor-bike; if I change my attitude and gracefully accept the situation, then my discomfort will be relieved.

KEYPOINTS IR7
a) Pain and physical discomfort can be given as a teaching lesson; to try to cause you to re-consider your attitude to any Situation or to other people.
b) Arthritis is a typical affliction which can be relieved by a change in Attitude, or it may likewise be brought to you for displaying a hostile, critical, negative attitude to Others; or, by closing your Mind to Spiritual Awareness.

11.13 We learn, we then teach our children how to behave; how to react to others; how to talk; and how to communicate; how to love others; and to be at one with Nature....they then leave the home and go out into the World..........
They then teach their children and so the learning and the ripples spread out and grow.

a)We teach our Children their Attitudes,
b)We shape their future Behaviour and their
Relationships; ...in this way we shape the future of the
World.

11.14 Throughout our journey, Helana is suffering from Spiritual attack from many of those we know: Her mother who causes her leg-pain, Lorna, Elsa, Mervin, Colin, and in particular Connie, who gives her stabbing pains in her back and chest. As we travel through the various Regions, attention is drawn to the previous lives I have lived in this Land, with Helana, Connie, and Lorna, this draws the Spirits of these ladies close, and causes pain to Helana.

KEYPOINT IR9
When you think about Someone, you attract their Spirit
to you.

11.15 We visit the Hospital and Retreat at Cloonamahon, where we read the wonderful words displayed in the 'Prayer for Peace' and reproduced here.

Lord, make me an instrument of Thy Peace.
Where there is Hatred, let me sow Love;
Where there is Injury, Pardon;
Where there is Doubt, Faith;
Where there is Despair, Hope;
Where there is Darkness, Light;
And where there is Sadness, Joy.

Lord, grant that I may seek rather to Comfort, than to be Comforted;
To Understand than to be Understood;
To Love than to be Loved;
For it is by Giving that One Receives;
By Forgiving that One is Forgiven;
And by Dying that One Awakens to Eternal Life.

11.16 We visit the Church, walk in the Grounds, and then find a Seat facing the trees. We exchange our gold wedding Rings, and then Helana talks with the Spirits of two of the Trees who congratulate us upon our Engagement. We leave the Hospital and look for somewhere to park, facing is a small side-road and an overgrown track; we need somewhere to stop for refreshments and I am drawn to the Entrance of a 'Castle'.... nothing remains save the Entrance. I am told this is where I lived a previous life with Lorna.

KEYPOINTS IR10
a)Trees have Spirits and certain People can communicate
with them.
b)Helana had previously told me how she saw the Spirit
leave a Tree, as that Tree was engulfed by flames.

11.17 We give a Hitch-Hiker a lift. We have an interesting conversation, he is seeking a distant relative and has travelled from Scotland. He departs happily, stealing our new road-map of Ireland. We are told to trust no-one!

11.18 I arrange an Interview with the senior Manager of my Company, for the Thursday, to explore the possibility of transferring my Office to Northern Ireland. This is subsequently agreed-to for whenever I decide to relocate to Northern Ireland. I need to contact the local Branch Manager in Belfast, and my Manager in High Wycombe, to arrange the transfer details.

11.19 On Wednesday, 2nd September, we drive into Bangor at around lunchtime. We were recommended to Bangor by Steve, an ex-soldier who served nearby in the Holywood Barracks some years before; and whom we met in the local Rugby Club in Banbury.
The area looks and feels good. I pull into a shopping lay-by as we enter the Town as I had noticed several Estate Agents. We have allowed two or three days to look for a property to rent. Bangor is convenient for me to work through the Belfast Office of my Company. Bangor is also the holiday centre for Northern Ireland, and is perhaps one of the most tolerant religious Areas.

11.20 Most Estate Agents are closed for lunch, but I have noticed one which is still 'open'. The Agent has returned for some papers, he has only one Property available, one that has only just come on his Books and has not yet been advertised.
We arrange an inspection within the hour. We both like the three-bed semi-detached Property and immediately pay a deposit. We plan to take occupation from 1st November 1998. The location is superb, overlooking the sea and situated at a high-point; but within walking distance of local shops, the Town centre and the beach.
The Property is reasonably spacious with an Orchard and Garage to the rear. The price is about the same as I already pay in Aylesbury, in Bucks, England.
KEYPOINT IR11
Spirit can make your life very easy, provided that you accept their advice, and are receptive to their guidance.

11.21 Previously we have been given these words ' we see you today as reaching Bangor, for your base, while you explore the Locality. You will be guided as to where to stay. Take care on your journey to visit the Places given and to stop as appropriate. We wish you to feel the Emotions of the Peoples along your way. There will be a surprise in store for you when you reach Bangor!'...certainly there was, one House only to visit and accept, in a super location...the message was from my guide Ahizar.

11.22 White Eagle later comes through, we have checked into a Guest House near the Town Centre, ' All is as it should be. You have been guided and have followed well.'
'The house chosen by you to rent in Ballyholme (a District within Bangor) is the one intended. It is basic, but Helana can transform this. The choice of position will assist the clarity of your communication with us. This is only intended as a temporary home, for better things are to come. We are sorry that it was necessary to interfere with your TV reception in order to bring this message. We needed to bring this now in order to re-assure Helana. Helana has done well, her prayers have lifted the Areas you have driven through and many Souls have been recovered.
KEYPOINT IR12
Spirit can and do affect your Environment. TV reception, telephone bells, flickering electric lights, elongated candle-flames, to name just a few.
(Our TV screen in the Hotel was wiped-out in the middle of a film, to cause me to accept a message from Spirit. On other occasions, my telephone would not stop ringing, and my car radio tape-deck became silent)

11.23 I am suffering from a groin strain...given to cause me to drive the car more slowly and to listen more closely to words given by Spirit. I also suffer from a fore-arm ache...said to be caused by Connie's Spirit which has eventually realised the purpose of our journey and our intentions...my Guide Ahizar writes:
'She is Jealous of Helana in view of the revelation, (only recently given), about your lifetime together, many years ago, when you left her for Helana. This was the principal reason that she has left you in this lifetime, to get her own back! ....but now she feels some remorse for her actions. She also seeks reassurance from you that your previous lives together have not been a complete waste of time. This is not so. The timing of the previous lifetime was when you, John, were Lord of the Manor, at Placement, near Sussex.'

KEYPOINTS IR13

a) If you do not listen or heed the Advice and Guidance from Spirit, the lessons can become more and more painful.

b) Your Health may well suffer, you may have an accident, your agility may be restricted, rashes may appear, you could even lose your Sight or your Hearing.

c) Always examine your present lifestyle if you suffer a change to your Health. Ask, is there anything I am doing which is hurting other Spirits. Or, am I being particularly selfish or critical?

d) Karma of course could be the cause, for you may be suffering the consequences of what suffering you caused to another, in this lifetime or in previous lives.

11.24 I write the following words addressed to Connie's Spirit...... 'We have been together through many lives and have shared much love and happiness together. I do not regret this, I am thankful to you for this. We have loved deeply and we have raised children and have experienced the good things of life together. Think of all life as learning and progressing to your individual Goal. You have provided many lessons and stepping stones for me.....I hope that I have contributed also to your growth and your understanding. Do not regret, do not be sad; for we have shared much love and can rejoice for what we have gained. You are, and have been, a part of my life's jigsaw. Without you I could not have reached today and where I sit here. I thank you. We have needed each other so that we could learn and understand the roles we play in this lifetime.. that is so good. I feel sad to say goodbye now. Go with my wishes and blessings. Perhaps our Paths will cross again?'

11.25 Helana receives the following from White Eagle ' Helana my dear, your efforts are an example my dear of how great your dedication is to this man and the work for Spirit. Now we ask you to feel the comfort of your Homeland as now you have entered the coming of the promised Land. You have had a fractious journey with many hazards you have not been aware of. We say now that you will receive peace of Mind knowing that the rest of your stay will not be so fraught.'

11.26 'Your man is suffering at this present time, but Understanding is being given and we are pleased to see his acceptance of this. Your Journey is not complete, but understand yours is as one with that of Mary, and her husband to be. Understand there are many similarities and we wish you to record these! Your husband's pains (John) will disappear on understanding that we wish him to take more charge of his own life as regards to his Spiritual Understanding, and learning to help himself. We realise this is not easy but help will be given.'

'Go now my dear with new understanding in your Spirit and allow us to guide you safely on your way. Remember my dear that you are protected at all times and your husband also. He is suffering, but all is for lessons to be learned by himself, and these will be invaluable in the future years with his work to be for Spirit.

Let our hearts rejoice in your presence in this Land, for already your work has begun and the cloud has been lifted....Go in peace my dears and rejoice in the child who resides within your womb, awaiting the birth of this glorious Age; one to be treasured and remembered for all Mankind.'

11.27 It is Thursday, 3rd September 1998.... 'Today for several hours the Spirits of those you have shared your lives with will be allowed to approach and draw near, as a farewell. You may feel emotions and feelings, this will be for a short while only, thereafter the day will be yours.'....

I am short of Breathe, my Knee aches, I feel tightness about my Head; I feel a sharp piercing pain in the Crown of my Head, and cloaking of my Ears. I am told this is Elsa's Spirit and that I need to tell her forceably, 'to piss-off'!

Also, I have an Arm-ache, a Shoulder ache, an upper- Jaw ache and my Stomach muscles are is all tight.

My Arm pain is put down to Mervin's Spirit who is sending me continuous thoughts of pain and viciousness.

KEYPOINTS IR14
a) You can counter evil Thoughts by shielding yourself with the Light of True Spirit. Imagine yourself surrounded completely by a Sphere of White Light which reflects back upon the Sender any Evil Thoughts.
b) Tell unwanted Spirits forceably to leave. Open the Window or Door and tell them to leave and not to return.
c) Use the Words ' Please protect me Heavenly Father with the Light and Love of True Spirit.'

11.28 The Spirit of Connie is causing discomfort to Helana. Ahizar states that she means us no malice and only wishes to stay for a short while. She regrets her actions in leaving you John, and also of being jealous of the love you have found with Helana. She wishes to reconcile if that is possible. It is our choice in this matter. She asks Helana for forgiveness, and asks if she can stay to learn from us.

11.29 We respond that we are both happy to comply with this request and wish her every happiness in her future life...in the direction and with whom she chooses. I wish her well in her journey ahead and thank her again for the love and good times we have shared in the Past. We state that she must either come with compassion, friendship and goodwill, between the times of 10.00am and 18.00hours, or not at all.

11.30 Helana's Guide 'Samuel' responds; 'My dear your words are felt and heard on this matter. The lady concerned has received your words with gracious thankfulness in her Heart. Her actions were indeed malicious, but no damage will have been done to her Spirit, for forgiveness from yourself has been found. John needs to understand what great Acts of forgiveness have been achieved by your Spirit, for all his past ladies have come to you with malice in their thoughts.

Your great love and understanding has pardoned these Spirits and given hope and love into our World. Do not now feel that any more thoughts are needed for this lady, for you are now free from her influence on your lives. You have realised my dear the effect on your man towards you, when this lady has been present, but now my dear believe you will be free from her Spirit and any others' influence in the future years. Have peace in your Hearts for all is well this night my dears and a safe time will be had upon the morrow.'

KEYPOINT IR15
Your own Spirit can be healed or damaged by your Thoughts and Actions. Likewise you can affect other Spirits.

11.31 White Eagle writes: 'My dear, your man's Spirit is now with you in the fullest way; no more will you be sharing this man with memories of the Past or present life Situations. He has no understanding of the way in which his Spirit feels. We ask you now to pass on this message in its entirety for him to gain an understanding. Your love my dear has been constant throughout Time and History, never failing this man in any capacity. Believe these words John, to gain an understanding of the depth of love this lady has for you, not on any occasion will it fail you in any way.

A dedication such as this will be felt throughout the Universe my dear man; Look and see beyond the face; beyond the skin my dear man. Do you not see the true beauty of your woman who is and will be forever your love, forever your lady and always has been. No other can, has, or will be.!' Go now with this Knowledge in your Heart and do not ever give-up understanding fully this message.

KEYPOINT IR16
Your Thoughts and Actions on the Earth-Plane can have an effect throughout the Universe.

11.32 'My dear, your strength amazes us still. Will you now my dear understand why your presence is so important in this Land. We are expecting so much from your Spirit. We push and push not realising how much pain you can bear my dear, but still you seem to take on all that is given. Not only do you take on your own pains of the Past, but those of your man and this Land. Also, Understanding is not always present within your Mind, but in time this will be found more quickly.'

'You have now the feelings of all that has been within your past-lives with this man, and we feel that you are now of an understanding that sadness has played a major role in all of them. You can now go forwards my dear with the knowledge that all present within your lives in future years will be happiness and love.'

11.33 'Do not doubt your abilities in coping with what is brought your man. You are coping admirably. You have full protection my dear in all matters and we feel now your greatness in this ability to overcome obstacles will stand you in good stead for the Future..Your man's pains are those feelings of the Past which you have shared, for he still has more discovering to do about the past lives shared, for the Understanding is not yet complete.'
KEYPOINT IR17
The Spirit never forgets, and pain from previous Lifetimes can be returned for Healing and Understanding.

11.34 'You have been given all of these Spirits from your previous relationships my dear as a final clearing of the ways, to begin again, a new life, a new Spirit and a new togetherness that will be with you throughout Eternity and beyond all your comprehension. Do not feel endangered in any way, it was necessary to clear the ways before this new life could begin, and for the closeness shared to be seen in the fullest way. We now will see a marked improvement in the way your togetherness will come about and the sharing of your lives. Every movement will be a treasure to behold. Go now my dear with peace in your heart, knowing that all is clear for your pathway to be free from all obstacles. Let us now guide you through your years'....White Eagle.
KEYPOINTS IR18
a) Re-birth of your Spirit is a wondrous Event, when the Past is wiped clean, so that there are no restrictions on the growth of your Spirit.
b) Following re-birth, in the near future, you can expect to see Spirit, to hear Spirit audibly, to see Visions.

11.35 'Your love has now been found and you are joined together in love in this Land. You could have, and should have, achieved this in previous lives. You originally realised your love when you were brother and sister in a previous life. Now you can heal the Land and the Spirits around you....If you had come together in this way years ago, you could have done it then!'
KEYPOINT IR19
a) Love is the greatest power.
b) If you do not achieve in one Lifetime, it will be returned in another; but ALL your Peer Group will mark time until the desired result is achieved.

11.36 My Guide Ahizar continues:'The words from White Eagle express all our sentiments. Go forwards now together, forget these past Personalities and Experiences and travel your chosen Path together. Remember only the fond times in the Past, and the anger and suffering will diminish with time. Consider your Experiences as ones of learning how to protect yourselves and to cope with malicious Spirits which you will certainly have to face in the Future. This experience will be well learned and you can now have confidence in your Abilities to cope with these 'malevolents'. Your Spirits together, as your Awareness is raised, will in the future be in a much stronger position to 'brush-aside' deleterious influences. As time progresses you will also learn new ways of coping with these situations.'

11.37 'Relax now in the knowledge that the Past is behind you and we can now bring to you the increased Awareness that we wish to. You will appreciate that with all the debris of the Past that you have faced in the past few days, that it was prudent to restrict any new challenges of coping with each other's Spirits, until these influences had been cleared...this we feel is now so. You are far more aware of outside influences and will know and recognise them. Rest now and we will continue your journey tomorrow.'

11.38 'We suggest Helana does not go with John when he goes into his Office in Belfast tomorrow, as the time available does not allow for this. Proceed Helana to pack and leave for Dublin as soon as John returns from his interview. It will be useful to stop several times on-route to Dublin and to learn more of your past Lives....your friend and Guide Ahizar.'

11.39 It is Friday, 4th September 1998...We eventually regained Dublin at 15.45...All Routes into the City are blocked because of President Clinton's visit. Helana has suffered greatly during the journey from severe headaches; likewise, my body and arms ached badly. This attack was attributed to Connie, but in part it was down to Mervin. We needed to stop the car three times so that Helana could 'brush-off' the Spirit of Mervin.

11.40 In conclusion, the week went well, but the Spiritual attack was oppressive and coupled with the problems created by switching vehicles and carrying luggage, took the edge off the trip. Whilst waiting for the Ferry in Dublin we found a live music Bar and had an enjoyable meal. Eventually we arrive back home in Aylesbury, exhausted, at 07.00hrs.on Saturday, 5th September.

11.41 A few days previously, White Eagle had come with these words, whilst we admired the view in Killykeagh, Northern Ireland.

' Once upon a time there was a beautiful Princess. She became the treasure of the Land, her gift to the People was Love and in return her gift will be a home given with Love. All is returned, however many Lifetimes it takes, for all is remembered and nothing is lost but all is gained. Look around you my dears...this location could be Heaven on Earth if you so wish.'

(It is given that Helana was a princess at the Castle. As we approach the gates we are told of the detachment of soldiers in the Courtyard, who await her return. We say prayers for these lost Souls and send them home.)

###

CHAPTER 12. THE DEPARTURE

12.00 It is still Saturday, 5th September 1998, we have slept only a few hours that morning since returning from Ireland, my Guide writes: 'Your time in Ireland has set the foundations for the future, you can plan now to marry in Bangor for December 19th, 1998....this will be a joyous time for you both and will provide your families with the re-assurance they need to see. Prepare now to finally move and to re-locate in Bangor, we look-forward to this with delight, and will assist you in every way. Go in peace. Your Guide and friend, Ahizar'.

12.01 We have joined with Judith that evening. The following messages are received through Judith:

KEYPOINTS TD1

a) The purpose of our lives is so that our Spirit evolves in all the forms of Love:..........
parent/child, husband/wife, brother/sister, friends, teacher/pupil, grandparents, grandchildren etc.
b) You are your own judge as to whether the experience is satisfactory.
c) A Guardian Angel is also with you to judge whether you achieve what you set out to achieve. Sadly for many it never is...their Progress then continues whilst in Spirit World and their degree of Evolvement decides, how and when they will return to the Earth.
d) It is said, that it is the choice of the Spirit to come back to Earth and that the Life ahead is known to the Spirit on returning. But, we will say here that on occasions, a little push is needed. (in this situation a very difficult baby and child can result)
e) Eventually, Spirits who have attained level Five can choose to become Guides, or they can choose to stay on the Level that they have attained.

KEYPOINTS TD2

a) Some Spirits reach a Higher Level, whereupon they may wish to come back to help the People on lower Levels, viz...Level Three(Heaven) or on the Earth.
b) It is almost frowned upon for anyone to wish to achieve solely for themselves...it is not showing the necessary Compassion and Understanding for Others.
c) Very few wish to rise to the 'top'; it is more interesting and more rewarding, to stay at a lower Level to help Others on the Earth-Plane.

12.02 'From a High Spirit viewpoint, we tend to forget the bitter/sweet reasoning behind Earth Love, and we have tended also to ignore your Human Emotions which become so entangled.

Now that we are more aware of your Human 'Needs' we will attempt to make more allowance. You must appreciate that your individual Human Lives are insignificant compared to the Total Plan which we seek to achieve.'

KEYPOINTS TD3
a) There exists a hierarchy of High Spirit, who guide and control the Universe according to a Total Plan.
b) The Earthly Life is secondary to your Spiritual progression, not forgetting that:
.........the Choices you make,
.........the Thoughts you have,
.........the Understanding you gain
.........the Actions you take, will all Contribute to your Spiritual Progression.

12.03 My attention is drawn to an article printed in the Sunday Times Newspaper, which tells of changes in an individual's Personality following a Heart Transplant Operation. My Guide continues:

' So little is known by those who carry out Transplant Operations, they have no fundamental understanding of the workings of the Human Body, let alone those workings of the Spirit. Consider the girl in the Article suddenly being invaded by new Organs.

Do you think the Spirit does not remember?

Do you think the Spirit from where the parts came does not remember? The two Spirits can converse. What fun, what amazing fun to help jeopardise the use of these Transplants!

Could this girl wishing to drink beer be an attempt to persuade Others not to follow?

We are not saying all Medical help is wrong, but the extension of life in such a dramatic way is not necessary...remember, we are concerned about the Spirit. Could it not be the sole purpose of this Spirit was to suffer the pain? The Transplant could have caused the Spirit to be very sad and to stop its Growth.'

12.04 I am asked to allow some time for my own Spirit to talk to me. 'It is sometimes difficult to know what is wrong and what is right. Each person is however capable of healing themselves...The healing power comes from within, and from living the life which is right for you.'

KEYPOINTS TD4
a) Each Person is capable of Healing themselves.
b) Their own Spirit together with the Universal Power of GOD, can be called upon to provide Healing Energies.

12.05 'To live in the shroud created by Man on the Earth, in what is considered progress, so much is artificial. You sit and enjoy your meals at your tables...you know not in what circumstances these products have been prepared for you. The artificial contaminants used in almost all foods would make anyone ill'.

'The air you breathe my dears, Is this not what we are all concerned about on the road we are asking you to tread?.....There need be no illness, other than that which the Spirit pre-decided as a lesson to be learned. Examine the water through the tap. You have no knowledge of the damage done to you. The deterioration of your Body cells is immense. You have no choice but to use it. We require that in order to save this World that you start to give People the choice again. You see the Tractors spraying the crops...do you know the effect on the Human Body? Why do you all Age so rapidly?...there is no need. Many of the things you consider luxury items are harmful..

Do not be too concerned, or you would not eat or drink!

You see my dears, there is much work to be done, not by you in this lifetime, but each of you will return most rapidly so that you can prompt those around you, for you will remember what you have learnt.'

KEYPOINTS TD5
a) Our Bodies are being poisoned by the Environment we have created.
b) It is necessary to stop the contamination of all we Drink, Eat and Breathe, if we are to eliminate many of our ailments and also to extend our Lives.
c) There need be no Illness, other than that which we choose to experience before we are born.

12.06 Helana's kidney pain is caused by the Spirit of Mervin. Judith's discomfort is caused by her attitude to her family. As soon as she finds compassion for her mother and sisters, the pain in her leg will disappear. The ankle problem is different, this is caused by Damien who wishes to restrict her freedom. She can counter this by reflecting the pain back onto him.

12.07 The Giant Pyramid of Giza, and the Sphinx were built by Egyptian labour, but this was directed by Beings from other Planets.

KEYPOINTS TD6
a) There exist Other Beings throughout the Universe.
b) Some Alien Beings lived-on, and visited the Earth before our modern Civilisation began.

12.08 Many, many people are given labels, according to their Earth history, occupation, or the organisation they associate with. This Knowledge pre-conditions us in our attitude to them. It is necessary however to relate to the Spirit within, for only in this way can we truly know each other. You can only achieve this through achieving your own Spiritual Awareness......see Appendix IV.

KEYPOINT TD7
a) Do not pre-judge Others by their appearance, or their occupation, or their background, or by Others' words or rumour.
b) Judge people yourself, and look to their Spirit for Understanding.

12.09 Judith speaks to Helana, saying 'there are many guidelines to follow in the days ahead:
KEYPOINTS TD8

* **Give for the pleasure of Giving, without expectation of Reward.**
* **Do not always put Yourself first**
* **Stand-up for your own Rights, but, meet another Person halfway**
* **Do not take Others for granted**
* **Do not be dogmatic, but, be flexible in your attitudes and Relationships.**
* **When someone suggests that you do something, and it annoys you that they pressurise you...ask yourself ' would I have done it anyway? give it thought before you raise your Hackles.**
* **Expect of Others as you expect of Yourself**
* **Do not feel animosity, you cannot always ignore other People.**
* **Do not be rude to Others, do not be rude to strangers who do not ask particularly in the right way.**
* **In your Relationship with John, Helana, allow respect for each other.**
* **There are Many who will come to you for uplifting and guidance; they will not necessarily be Spiritual people. They will judge you on your Earthly manner initially. The Earthly Being needs to measure up to the beautiful Spirit within.**

KEYPOINT TD9
Evil exists when any one Spirit chooses to go against what is accepted as Love.

12.10 John, ' Tread your Path in a manner befitting your role on Earth' ..display these words so that you can read them on waking every day.

12.11 'It is quite an experience to come in this manner.....It is so heavy here......How any of your Spirits can feel uplifted in this Earth Atmosphere I fail to see!
Know please, and understand the importance of what we hope to achieve'.
'I send you the Blessing that each of you, and those within your knowledge who wish to see the Light, can be risen above this darkened Atmosphere. May the Light of the Lord Most High, truly penetrate the Atmosphere here, to bring All that is needed to Lighten this Planet once and for all...Isaiah'

KEYPOINT TD10
The God-Light is the Word used to describe the power arising from the All-Being and All-Creating GOD from whom all Life, all Spirit and all of Creation originate.

12.12 It is Sunday, 6th September, 'We see you moving to Ireland before the end of October, 1998. You should write and terminate the lease on your House in Aylesbury, from December 31st. 1988. We see Judith and Judy (a friend in matrimonial difficulties), moving into your property in October.

12.13 White Eagle writes.... ' The effect of the past days is taking its toll, and you need to recuperate and renew your concentration. You can ask for Energy to be given, this will be; your Spirit will still need however, to rest to recover to its full strength. You have had a difficult time in Ireland and in transit to and from that country. You have also had the problem of the message from Judith and the strain of the little ones. We suggest that you rest tonight and we will take you in your sleep to bathe and rest. Do not be distressed all is as it should be. You have done well and are making good progress. World Events unfortunately, set their own Agenda and we are obliged to react as quickly as we can. Forgive us my dears if we press you so much, you appreciate now the importance of your work and every support will be given to assist you, and to relieve the stress. Imagine yourself surrounded by a white Light and that Light pulsating slowly like a Lighthouse. Feel the Energy enter as the Light pulsates.
Clear your Mind of daily worries and troubles, and sit quietly to relieve your tensions. This will help you both to find relaxation. Go to your bed now, and we will talk later when you feel more refreshed.' (White Eagle is acting as a spokesperson for High Spirit)

KEYPOINTS TD11
a) You can Pray and ask for Energy.
b) You can condition your Body and your Mind by using your Thoughts to help you to Relax, and to relieve your stress.
c) Your Spirit becomes tired, and can need rest to recuperate, in the same way that your Bodily Being does.
d) Imagine yourself surrounded by a sphere of white Light which pulsates slowly. As the Light pulsates, visualise the Energy flowing into you.

12.14 White Eagle writes to Helana 'My dear, the People of Ireland cry out for your love and the peace that prevails whilst your presence is felt. You have indeed no understanding at this time what this Awareness achieves. We do understand my dear how much we ask of you at this time, but we feel your urgency to be within the Land of your chosen Pathways. All now will proceed and you will be within this Land in time for your Christmas celebration. All we ask of you at this time my dear Helana, is that your Thoughts reach out to the Peoples of this Land; bring to them the understanding that your presence has not been withdrawn, only halted for a short time. We hope this helps with your understanding, and we ask your man to contact his own Guides, for guidance as to what is to be achieved. All your lives my Dear, have been a preparation for this farewell end to a glorious life, shared with all the Peoples of this World. Go in peace my Dear.'

12.15 'Helana my dear, understand what is in hand, is very urgent to secure the lives of many people. Your apprehension is due to that knowledge of the work involved for your loved One. This knowledge is within but not known to his Mind. Do not fear this time my dear, for your protection is guaranteed at all times...you are aware of this.
The Children my dear, Edwin and Helen will perhaps have other plans which will enable you to see clearly what is needed. We ask a great deal of you all at this time, but understand the Earth and its needs will not wait. Your Guides are by your side my dear, and communications will become clearer very shortly.
Forget now my dear your personal problems for the time being, to see what is needed for the beloved Community of our Earth-Plane. Go with peace my dear'.

12.16 I ask the question: How can I 'draw closer' with Helana's Spirit? My Guide responds: 'You can finally join with Helana's Spirit by accepting her Spirit around your own. You may ask for this if you wish, but be certain this is what you wish to achieve, then say aloud the following words.'

225

' Heavenly Father, If it be thy will, I, John, do unreservedly wish my Spirit to be entwined with that of Helana, my wife. I accept her as my twinned Spirit now and forever. I forgive her past misdemeanours and wish us to become as One.'

KEYPOINT TD12

You can ask GOD to entwine your Spirits with your loved-one, but this will not happen unless true Love and forgiveness has been found.

12.17 It is 8th September......my guide Ahizar writes ' when you John understand the lessons given, your Spirit will be able to draw closer to Helana's. The Spirits of your past ladies will hover about you, waiting to see whether you have found the 'True Love'. When they see this they will be happy to release you and to move on their own journey's.
It is necessary for all to forgive, you to them, they to you, for all to be able to move forwards. You are all connected, You are all interdependent. It is ' One for All, and All for One!'
They will all find partners who can offer them the 'True Love' they seek, if they are willing to make their own correct choices at that time. You will have played your part in raising their Awareness, in offering them the life's lessons they needed, to help them to reach their present states. Do not be sad. Be happy for them to find their own 'True Love' elsewhere, and to fulfil their Destinies. Go in peace my friend.'

KEYPOINTS TD13

- **You do not travel alone through this Lifetime. You are only one Spirit amongst a group of 'Fellow-Travellers' who comprise your Family, Friends and Acquaintances in this Lifetime.**
- **The same Spirits have been present in your previous Lifetimes and the majority will be with you in your future Lifetimes. Here-after known as your Peer-Group.**
- **All seek to find their one 'True Love'.**
- **All seek to experience the range of Love, which is found through the living of many, different, Human Relationships, but all primarily within your 'Peer-Group' of Spirits.**
- **The roles may change from Lifetime to Lifetime with the same Spirit being ...father, mother, brother, sister, friend, aunt, uncle etc.**
- **If one experience is not achieved in this Lifetime, then it will be represented, in this Lifetime or in the next...an endless Cycle, <u>unless and until the lessons are learned and the understanding is gained.</u>**

- Above and beyond these Experiences, but also an integral part of the whole, is the need for the Spirits to approach towards the one True Light, to re-unite with the Perfect Sector of their Individual Spirits, and finally to become at One with GOD.
- What any one Person chooses to do, <u>will</u> affect the lives of the Others, it will improve or restrict their Choices; it will affect their Attitudes; it could <u>completely deflect them</u> from their pre-destined Pathway...perhaps through Bitterness, or Fear, Envy or Hate.
- When any One Spirit progresses towards the Light, all the Spirits in that 'Peer-Group' will also progress.
- As many, many Spirits are divided, sub-divided and re-combined, so you can envisage also that a change of any One can have immense effect upon the whole...as the ripples in a Pond!

12.18 'Forgiveness has been found by Helana for herself, and for the other people in her life.....in this way <u>all</u> the Spirits can progress. All the children in your lives have withdrawn from you, this has been a necessary phase for them to go through, to prepare themselves for the life ahead......their Spirits can now go forwards and progress.....both Ford and Brian are on their way. They have discovered in their Spirits that they need time to leave the baggage of the Past behind. It is necessary to lose all Material possessions, in order to find true love and understanding within your Spirit.'
KEYPOINTS TD14
a) Forgive yourself, and forgive the other people in your Life. In this way your Spirit and their Spirits can progress.
b) It is necessary to 'lose' all your Material possessions in order to find True Love and Understanding within your Spirit.

12.19 'Look at the way Helana has walked away from Steven and Abel! They will find their own pathways. Love them only...allow them to know that you are there for them. This is all that is needed. They do not come with pain, they come to you...but they need their freedom. Forgive them their lives, it is necessary for them to find their own way. If the light is strong enough they will follow...you John are their light. Allow them to see this by just being there. All your Children will return John...Ford, Brian, Helen and Edwin'
KEYPOINT TD15
Allow your Children to find their own Pathways. Love them, but then allow them their Freedom, and let them know that you are there for them, if they need you.

12.20 'It was hoped that Helana's mother would create a special bond with Helana, one of mother and child, regrettably, this has not been achieved. This understanding was necessary to Helana's Spirit, so that she could bring understanding to Philip's Spirit. It was also hoped that Helana's lives in Shadowlands would bring to her mother that light and knowledge necessary. It has not happened. This lady has been present in many, many of your lives; She has been given forgiveness, but she does not find it in herself to give anything.
She can see and hear Spirit. Her refusal to help Others is now reflected in her body.'

- curvature of her Back.........rejection of Spiritual ways
- lack of Breathe..................she chooses not to use her Spiritual Gifts.
- varicous Veins...................refusal to help herself.
- scabs on her Hands............refusal to help Others.

12.21 'We see each of her lifetimes as a complete waste of time and energy.
In each lifetime she has caused pain and suffering, for this reason the services of Helana will be withdrawn completely. The more Barriers she sets-up, the more illness she is given.
Her lack of living takes away the joy of living...therefore she experiences death on Earth. Unless she changes, her Spirit will 'die'.
All is chosen to enable you to achieve what you need to achieve in this lifetime!'

KEYPOINTS TD16
a) All is pre-chosen to enable you to achieve in this Lifetime, what you (your Spirit) has pre-chosen to achieve.
b) If you have gifts, (Talents), and refuse to use them, you will suffer the consequences....
- **for remember, you are not alone;**
- **What you choose to do, or not do, will affect all of those in your Peer-Group.**

c) Much Suffering is given, and is caused-by, and is a direct result-of your own Actions in this Lifetime; particularly when those Actions are of an Evil nature and hurtful to Others.

12.22 White Eagle writes... 'picture Helana as a flower in bud in the Desert, trying to grow without moisture, imagine the pain and suffering. You John, have the nourishment of her love, she needs the nourishment of your love before she can become a wonderful flower. The flower (Helana) is then able to nourish the World'.

'Your left-shoulder pain is given to remind you that the final piece of the puzzle is not yet fitted (ie my love for Helana), a small pain alongside that of the World. Helana has sacrificed and suffered much for you, she has been prepared to push you to your Awareness. Think of your leg-pains following the Company Charity wheel-chair push. If you John had walked away as Philip does, then you too could have ended up in a Wheel-Chair like the man Trevor!'

KEYPOINTS TD17

a) Our Human Choices can well affect the state of our Health!. *(the man Trevor is confined to a Wheel Chair following a diving accident and subsequent spinal injury. The accident was given as a direct result of his repeated philandering and the devastation he has caused to others lives)*

b) Spirit are aware of all our Pain and Suffering.

12.23 'We now see the 'perfect Being' arising out of Helana, for this reason we presented her with the **Holy Spirit**. Do not fear this. Do not worry that you cannot live-up to her expectations, she accepts fully that you are as you are.

With faith and trust, you John will not be made to feel above or below her. No harm will come to your Spirit. Open-up your eyes and see there is no judgement in Helana's eyes, only dedication and honesty. Trust her, look beneath the surface. You are her life, her one and only, she has no fear of this. Only sadness is felt perhaps for those left behind.'

KEYPOINTS TD18

a) The Gift of the Holy Spirit is quite exceptional, and should not be confused with our normal Spiritual Awareness, or knowledge from our Spirit Guides.

b) The Gift of the Holy Spirit imparts special Powers and a special Relationship with GOD...HELANA IS THE ONLY PERSON IN THE WORLD, TODAY, WITH THE HOLY SPIRIT.

12.24 My Guide Ahizar continues.. 'We wish you John, to enter the realms of Spiritual Understanding in everything, but first and foremost you must trust Helana in every way. You are as a Child within...so precious to Helana; she watches and waits for the Beauty to appear. The Heart Centre of the World (ie.Ireland) unites with Helana, and feels sadness when she departs, why then cannot you John? Trust her in this way, when you are by her side both night and day.'

12.25 'The peoples of Ireland do not know her face, but they feel her presence. They know her honesty, beauty, her love for them. They are as her Children, she is the mother Earth, her feet are the roots of the Trees, her eyes like the Sky. Trust, my dear friend, and all will be found. Do not pull away. Your suffering and pain is shared within. Allow your Mind also to share with this lady...she cannot and will not hurt you in any way. Understand that she has the knowledge within her body, her Mind, her Heart and her Being'.

12.26 'Do not pity those people who are disabled, rather try to make them Spiritually Aware so that they can personally influence and improve their predicament. Many will have been given their disability through their own intransigence in this or previous lives. When people choose to ignore the signs given, and the Opportunities presented to them, then we here in Spirit Realm have little choice but to cause them discomfort as a retribution for their reckless choices'.

KEYPOINTS TD19

a) Our Lives and Experiences are pre-chosen by us before we are born. We also accept, and our Souls are aware of, the Laws governing our behaviour, before we pre-chose our Lives and Experiences.

b) We have Free-will to accept or reject every Opportunity. However, our Choices also impinge upon all those in our Peer-Group and Others around us.

c) Life on the Earth-Plane is equivalent in many ways to a School, when we reject the Rules, we must face the consequences.
The result of 'straying' from our Life-Plan and in so doing harming other Souls, is to bring on ourselves retribution in the way of Pain, Discomfort and Suffering.

d) It all really comes back to Cause and Effect. We cause our own discomfort by our own Choices and our own Actions.!

12.27 KEYPOINTS TD20

a) Certain people will also choose their afflictions, in order to help the Spirits of those caring for them.

b) The Carers may need to learn their caring lessons in order that their own Spiritual Awareness can grow.

c) Those who suffer will also learn, and be able to progress their own Awareness.

12.28 KEYPOINTS TD21

a) Some afflictions can be caused by or given by Others on the Earth-Plane...ie physical pain and suffering resulting from evil Thoughts and/or Actions.
nb...Helana's tongue has length-wise lacerations caused by her past-Life Infidelities and her restrictions placed upon me in previous Lives.

b) My Spirit now does not trust her, and does not wish her to speak-out. Her Tongue will be healed when I give to her, her freedom!

c) The deformities in Beings can be either Physical, Mental, or Spiritual.

12.29 Consider John, Helana as a bird in a cage, with its wings clipped by you. You have not previously <u>ever</u> given Helana her freedom in <u>any</u> of her lives, she has been caged like a bird; and what happens when the door is left open...the bird escapes, and runs or flies away.! If freedom and trust is there, then love will flow. In this lifetime, you do share her with your friends and family; this is as it should be.(cf Richard and Catherine Cookson)

She is a being of Nature, we are all from the one GOD, Trust her and allow her to be free and as of Nature. If you fear she will walk away, then she will do so. Harsh lessons will result if you do not heed these words. At the present time Helana feels restricted. Both your Spirits are learning, but now her Mind needs to accept. We do not wish to give lessons which will spoil the beauty of your Relationship.

KEYPOINTS TD22
a) For Love to flourish their must exist Trust and Freedom. This must encompass both Mind and Spirit.
b) Fear, Distrust, Restriction and Possessiveness will destroy Love.
c) Love, and the achievement of Love, are more important than any Material gain, or any amount of wealth.
You enter this World with nothing material, you leave it with nothing material.
d) Be Honest with yourself. Do not cling to the Past. If Love is not there, Strive to find it elsewhere. Do not waste this Lifetime.

12.30 Today, 9th September, I confirmed to my manager in High Wycombe, Bucks; that I wished to transfer to the Belfast Office of my Company with effect from 1st November 1998.

12.31 In conversation at the Banbury Rugby Club, I am told that Helana's and my Spirit have been talking all day and have made love. Our Spirits have at last achieved the closeness necessary for our future together. Simon who works at Banbury RUFC offers to help us with the move to Northern Ireland (Simon was the Spirit of Tiberius, a Roman guard in Biblical times)

We return home from visiting Judith at 02.00 hrs. Helana is then aware of the presence of the Spirit of her son Abel, who is distressed and in need of love and comfort.

12.32 Immediately, we are faced with the logistics of:
* A move of House and Home,
* Collecting and identifying Helana's Effects,
* The Move itself and the Personnel to be involved.
* To notify all our Family and Friends,
* To arrange a farewell Buffet,

- To arrange our Wedding Day in Bangor for December 19th,
- To send out invitations and to arrange a reception and venue!
- Meanwhile the details of the financial Settlement and the Court battle with Helana's ex-husband need to be sorted.
- Additionally, I still need to earn a living, and to engineer the movement of my Business, Office and Client Files to Belfast.

12.33 We are told that a further visit to Ireland is necessary to help to prevent a terrorist planned Bomb Atrocity. The motorbike may well suit for mobility around Belfast, further details will be given later this week. I am asked to grow a beard to provide me with the necessary appearance for the Future.... 'remember that you re-live the Biblical Times'.

12.34 Helana in Trance brings words from Mary, the mother of Jesus. I am asked if I am strong and brave enough to be a **Prophet**. I will need broad shoulders to be able to face ridicule and rejection. I am flattered and accept the honour.

12.35 Ahizar writes: ' A change of HOME, LAND, APPEARANCE, LIFESTYLE and FAMILY. A change in my SPIRITUAL AWARENESS. A change to my JOB and my ROLE. A change is necessary for the future of Mankind.'

12.36 The Spirit of my friend Cor from Holland enters Helana; it is difficult for him to enter as the baby is so well protected. He has tried to come many times before, he comes with love and as a friend. The message given is that 'I need to find trust in Helana and in the Holy Spirit.'

12.37 We are asked by Spirit to carefully consider whether we wish to have twins, or for Helana to have two separate pregnancies.

12.38 I am asked to read the chapter on Desire in the book.. 'Embracing the Beloved'.. Ahizar writes: 'You John wish to lose weight, you wish to find your Beloved, you wish to be as one with Helana, you wish your children to be with you, you wish your monetary worries to resolved etc. Allow us to guide you, allow others to come first, allow Helana her freedom, allow your children their freedom, All else will follow.'
KEYPOINT TD23
Human desire puts the Mind first. Forget the I, forget the Me. If you can control your Desire all else can follow.

12.39 Judith has lost her Voice so that she cannot precipitate a crisis with her husband, Damien.'

'It is feared that if she has another verbal go at her husband, there will be a violent physical reaction which will cause a retreat and precipitate events too quickly for a reasoned response. Silence is best at this time!...(Judith lost her voice for two days)

KEYPOINT TD24

Spirit can and do act to protect us in subtle ways, particularly if our Actions are perceived to place us in danger.

12.40 It is Saturday, 12th September, I am told that I no longer need to go quickly to Ireland, so I can now take my son to Butlin's Holiday Camp. Immediately, Helana is told that she needs to remain in Aylesbury, because Steven her son, is in need of love and reassurance. A move to Northern Ireland in mid-October is predicted. I am asked to transfer my Masonic membership to a Lodge in Northern Ireland, and to cancel the Ladies Weekend, which I am already booked onto for February 1999, with Quality Lodge, 9356, in Bournmouth, England... contact is also to be provided to the Rosicrucian Section. (A.M.O.R.C.)

12.41 The Effect of our Spirits coming together in True Love will enable us to:
- Heal our past Lives and the negative Effects resulting.
- Heal all our Children
- Progress the Awareness of all those within our Peer-Group.
- Release those other Spirits to achieve their own Goals and to follow their own Pathways.
- Be an example to the World
- Create a special Healing Power.
- Connect Spiritually, and with our Minds, to our Guides
- Heal Ireland, and in so doing, to help to save the World.
- Prepare Mankind for the coming of the Messiah
- Fulfill our Destinies
- Be Happy and at Peace
- Share a wonderful Life together, and to share our love with our families and with the rest of the World.

12.42 I am told that Helana feels lonely and neglected by me. My Mind has been with the Spirit of Lorna who visited me overnight. I need to make a choice and to send Lorna away, she still clings to the memory of the Past...she always does this and has great difficulty in moving forwards. Her pride will not let go, this was a feature of our Relationship in this lifetime and in previous ones. I am asked to tell her forceably to leave and not to bother me again. My Spirit needs to come to terms with this final parting. I need to release the Past and trust Helana completely'.

'She has said goodbye to her Spirits, ie Jack and Bryan and is now empty without me. The Spirit of a Spiritual Being needs love and reassurance of a true kind; the withdrawal of my Spirit brings devastation and pain.

12.43 The Spirit of Christopher (Jesus's child) was asked to fill the void, but Helana refused as she was aware of my concern, and my Spirit's reaction to another Spirit within her. It is not enough for me to say the words, it is necessary for me to completely and utterly love her and to meld with her Spirit. If my love is not felt, then it cannot be given out to the World. It is now my choice, I have my Guides with me and I can ask for help.

KEYPOINT TD25
Before you can <u>give</u> Love you need to be able to <u>receive</u> Love.

12.44 Without Spiritual Awareness, it is extremely difficult for you to know what your Spirit is doing. I am asked to continue to feel love for Helana, I have achieved this. The difficulty arises when another Spirit from a past lady captivates my Mind...this causes my Spirit to withdraw. I need to stop this withdrawal.

The way to achieve this is to dismiss immediately any further thought and to tell my Spirit to wrap itself around a vertical pole. Forgiveness has been achieved by both Spirits, it is the withdrawal which is the problem.

KEYPOINTS TD26
a) Thought is very powerful and we should <u>tell</u> our own Spirit what we wish to achieve...your Spirit will follow your own Thought process.
b) When you commit to any one Person, it is necessary to <u>dismiss</u> the Thoughts of previous Relationships from your Mind.
c) Thought can be as powerful as Action and can change your future Life.
d) EVERYTHING which Mankind does in Thought or in Action is known to Spirit.
e) Nothing is missed, every Deed will determine a reaction for Good or for Bad. (Karma)

12.45 A message is received from High-Spirit, I need to sort out and to accept the role I have played in the lives of Ford and Brian, my first two sons. I need to accept that they pre-chose their lives and the Experiences. The Future is theirs, I served only to provide their Education and their Base, now they choose their own direction. I must not carry or feel Guilt.

KEYPOINTS TD27
a) In so much as our Lives are pre-chosen; our Children
chose to come to us in the knowledge of future Events.
b) We should not therefore carry personal Guilt for
situations which cause our children to suffer. (Having
said this it is not always easy to look back and to
accept the family disruption and to wish...if only!)

12.46 I buy a large bunch of flowers which I sort, one for Helana, one
for Judith, almost identical Gladioli. The ones given to Judith and placed
within her home are dead within four days.(twelve blooms).....The ones
given to Helana last for four weeks.
KEYPOINTS TD28
a) Life and Nature are responsive to Love. They respond
to the vibrations!
* talk to Plants,
* play music to Cows,
* some People do have green Fingers!
b) All Spirits are responsive to Love, they know your
Emotions, they sense your Concerns....Science has
demonstrated that Plants are responsive to Prayers and
Love.
c) Healing can occur when Love and Healing Energies can
flow.
d) Miracles CAN and DO happen.

12.47 I am asked to examine the relationship between my brother
Edward and me.....to think about the good and the not so good, and
why I feel the way that I do about our Relationship.
Do we love each other as Brothers?

12.48 My left shoulder ache is to ask me to review the relationship
between me and my children Edward and Helen. My eye tiredness is
given, because I choose to ignore those key issues which are restricting
my Spiritual progression.
I must **Ask---Question---See---Feel,** all which is about me........my
Guides state that sometimes they despair of me!!
KEYPOINT TD29
Blindness and Ignorance of the effect of Relationships
on the Earth-Plane, will result in physical pain and
discomfort...The man Philip who has the spirit of Jack
is already losing the sight of one Eye, for he chooses
to reject his Spiritual Gifts. If he continues to refuse
to 'see', then he will lose the sight of his second Eye.

12.49 It is Monday 14th September, I am told that my Spirit is within
Helana, but it does not move, so she is unaware of its presence.

KEYPOINT TD30
You can cause your Spirit to move by arching your Back, in so doing you will compress it and cause a reaction in another.

12.50 I am charged with reviewing all outstanding matters before the move to Ireland. This is to enable my full Awareness to take place. The time-span is short! I am asked to:
(a) Consider the Relationships between Edwin, Helen and me.
(b) Re-visit my relationship to Elsa.
(c) Consider the relationship between Helana and me from a Spiritual viewpoint.
(d) Convince my Being to accept the bonding between Helana and me.
(e) Allow my Guides and Helana to lead me in these matters.

KEYPOINTS TD31
a) Spiritual Awareness cannot develop unless we have found an 'Inner Peace' and learned to accept and to Love ourselves.
b) The key is LOVE , our relationships between male and female, must be ones of Caring and Sharing, with Compassion for the needs of Others.
c) If you do not love yourself, then how can you love others, and others love you?
d) If you 'put-on-a-face', then People cannot see you properly. Therefore your True Spirit cannot be seen and cannot be loved.

12.51 'When we accept that all is for learning, then we can put aside the burdens of guilt which restrict our progress. However, do not deceive yourself that this concept can be used as an excuse for Evil. Mankind has the free-will choice and must also face the consequences of cause and effect.

KEYPOINTS TD32
a) AS YOUR SPIRIT PROGRESSES, SO DO THOSE IN YOUR PEER-GROUP.....
b) Always send positive Thoughts for Blessings, Goodwill and Freedom to Others.
c) Whatever you do, whatever Choices you make, you are responsible for your Actions and the subsequent Consequences.

12.52 Consider your life, with a view to asking how the lessons learned, have contributed to and been necessary to bring you to where you are today, and to prepare you for the Work ahead.

KEYPOINTS TD33
a) All that we Experience is given for Learning, every Meeting, every Occurrence, every Event, every Relationship, be it a 'good' or a 'bad' Experience.

236

b) You choose this life for the Lessons necessary to your Spirit.

c) As you learn those around you learn as well. What you gain they gain also.

d) No-one is above or below you, each Individual has their own Path to tread.

12.53 I am asked to <u>tell</u> my Spirit forceably, not to be jealous nor possessive, nor to feel guilt, nor to criticize Helana. I must allow her Spirit to be free, to choose who she talks to, who she wishes to be with, who she wishes to touch or to connect with. Only through complete freedom can bonding occur, and true love be experienced. Helana has been suffering for two days, she has lost her voice, has a nose cold, her eyes are tired and her joints ache. I am told that all of these symptoms have been caused by my Spirit being too possessive and restricting Helana's freedom.

KEYPOINTS TD34

a) Any Spirit must NOT

- Be Possessive of Other Spirits, ie. children, family, spouses etc.
- Restrict the Freedom of other Spirits
- Carry the Guilt of Past or Present Actions
- Allow Jealousy to mar its Judgement or Actions.

b) Any Spirit must

- Give freedom to other Spirits
- Strive for pure Love
- Have compassion for Others
- Be prepared to help Others who are less fortunate
- Be prepared to sacrifice Time, Love, and Actions for the benefit of Others

12.54 'Your Spirit John, must be prepared to bond completely with that of Helana. At the time of Richard and Catherine, you John, were aware of the presence of the Spirit of Jack within Catherine...this was like a sore to you and soured your love for Catherine. Now, this is not the case, the way is clear for you and your Spirit. Accept this now and understand that the Past is over. **Open and Close the Door on the Past.'**

KEYPOINT TD35

If you do not walk away from the Past, it will prevent what you seek to achieve in the Present.

12.55 I am told by Jesus, that my communication link with Helana is due to begin in the near Future. My Spirit within her and her's within me will affect our Personalities. It will be two years before I progress to full understanding. At this time, when my Education is complete, Helana's Spirit will be free to progress along its own Pathway.

12.56 Helana links strongly to Brian my son.(they were married in a previous lifetime), my Spirit is jealous and possessive. I need to gain an understanding and be prepared to share Helana's love.

Guidance and help will be given to me if I ask for this. I need to sit quietly every day and to request a lesson each day from my Guides.

KEYPOINTS TD36

a) You must ask your Guides to help you.

b) You cannot expect help unless you ask for it.

c) Your GOAL must be for your Mind to be able to reach your Spirit. (This is what is meant by full Spiritual Awareness.

d) Live your Life in the Present. Do not carry guilt from the Past.

e) When your Mind accepts, your Spirit will accept.

12.57 When we talk of SACRIFICE it does not need to be animal slaughter, it can also be personal restriction. Sacrifice should serve to achieve a purpose..ie (diet), or to demonstrate your love for GOD..(time for worship), or to achieve something of importance..(a holiday) by giving-up other short-term pleasures. GOD never wishes for any needless slaughter, but at times there is the need to demonstrate and cause Man to suffer hardship, in order for him to learn the necessary lessons he needs.

In love, it may be necessary for you to give-up someone or something which you treasure, so that Others may gain.

(I consider that Judith did this to allow my Spirit to progress and to learn more quickly.)

KEYPOINTS TD37

a) Mankind learns through Lessons. Lessons come through Sacrifice, Experience or Suffering.

b) Spiritual Awareness develops through learning and understanding.

12.58 'It is sometimes necessary to stand-up to, and to fight EVIL or Aggression. If Good does not counter Evil, then all will be dominated by Evil. All means possible should be used to avoid physical contact, but, at the twelfth hour, when Diplomacy has failed, it is then necessary to choose either to submit to Evil, or to resist and fight by whatever means are available.

So long as you uphold your 'good principles' of behaviour and love and compassion in the execution of **War**...then the taking of life can be justified in **War**. For, what is worse? a lingering death, or to oppose, and stand your ground'....Ahizar.

KEYPOINTS TD38

a) War, and the taking of life in War, is permissible in the Fight against Evil, provided that all methods of Diplomacy have been previously exhausted.

b) Due Regard, Respect and Compassion should continue to be exercised in the execution of war.

12.59 There is a noticeable smell of smoldering in the room, similar to stale cigarettes about to flare-up. This is given to us as a sign of 'dangerous ground'. We are told that we are not in physical danger, but dangers lurk in the Mind and can influence our Relationship. The language is used to represent the confrontation which is occurring between Helana and 'dark forces'. Our Spirits are protected, but not our Minds, which can be influenced by jealousy from those from our previous relationships. Connie's Spirit tries to prise us apart, for it wishes a return to a past Relationship. I am asked to say words openly, so that she understands that she has her freedom.

KEYPOINT TD39
Understand yourself and your Attitudes, so that you are able to recognize whenever outside influences attempt to change your Personality.

12.60 My Spirit is apprehensive and worried, that if I join with Helana, my identity will be lost. I have always been a strong character, and by submitting to Helana's Spirit I fear that I will not be able to run my life as an individual. I am told that I can only gain from joining with Helana's Spirit; in no way will I lose my manliness or my strength.
By bonding with Helana's Spirit, I will gain extra knowledge and understanding.

12.61 On Wednesday,15th September, 1998, I declare and say openly the Words:...............
'My Spirit listen to me. Listen carefully. This is me talking to you through my Mind and my Body and my Being. I wish to bond completely with the lady Helana to the exclusion of all past or future ladies. I have decided to do this, for I love Helana with all my Heart, I love her Being, her Spirit, her Heart, her Body. I wish no other lady to split us apart. The Past is over, the choices have been made. Helana and I are now bound together on Earth, as in Heaven, and no other shall put us asunder.'

KEYPOINTS TD40
- **The speaking aloud of words, reinforces their meaning.**
- **Only speak aloud those words which you intend GOD, your own Spirit and Others' Spirits to sincerely believe.**

12.62 'Constance, you need to understand that my Spirit has walked away from all that has passed; and there is no room for your presence to be with me in this life, or in future lives' ...You, Constance, are free to go your way to make your own life in the future.'

'You have your freedom. Go with my fond wishes and find a new life for yourself. Our past lives are behind the wooden Door.'

KEYPOINTS TD41

a) **If you imagine a solid Wooden Door leading to a sealed Room , the Door has three heavy, horizontal, barrel Bolts.**

- **When you wish to remove a contact from your conscious Mind, you slide back the Bolts, and push the Memory/Person/Influence through the Door, and then close the Bolts again.**
- **This method is an excellent Protection to enable you to remove a Spiritual influence which may be causing you Physical or Spiritual Discomfort.**

b) **When you achieve or give Spiritual Freedom, then your own Spirit can grow and so can those Spirits in your Peer-Group.**

c) **As we are all inter-connected, all will then Progress.**

d) **Should you have had a relationship with the Individual concerned, then you may well be connected through your MIND, and/or your HEART, and/or your sexual ORGANS. In this situation visualize Chords connecting you at the various CHAKRAS.**

Now in your Imagination, sever/cut these Chords with a sharp knife/machete/axe and then burn away the severed ends back to the Individual and to Yourself.

e) **DISMISS any further THOUGHTS of this Person from your MIND.**

f) **REMOVE from your person or your home, and dispose of ANY possessions or objects arising from or associated with this Person.**

12.63 I am asked to:

- Think hard about everything associated with myself
- View every Situation from every angle...to Sit, to Ponder, to chew it over.
- Understand and know myself
- Look at myself as if I was someone else; be critical of myself
- Accept personal responsibility for my Actions
- Let go of Guilt, to forgive myself for the Past.
- **Love myself**
- Consider what has brought me to where I am today.

12.64 Ahizar writes....'We see that you have difficulty in Understanding what all the fuss is about! However, your lives in the Past have been filled with anguish and pain....We wish to help you to change this Way to one in which you are more gentle and responsive to others' Needs. This is not easy. You will need to become a gentler, a more quieter, listening Person than you have been previously.'

' We agree with you that to delve into past Situations will not help, accordingly we will examine new Situations as they arise. We do not wish you to surrender your Individuality, but to find a middle ground'.

12.65 It is 21st September,1998, We are told that Helana is pregnant, and is expecting Twins, a boy and a girl. ....
'We would like you to name the boy 'Matthew' and the girl 'Nhadia Elizabeth'.
(I have been previously asked to change my name from 'Dennis Brian' to 'John Oliver'; these names are more powerful and represent a few of my better previous lives. Alison is to move her name to 'Helana Bethany', I have used 'Helana' and 'John' throughout this Book for consistency....Helana is the Spirit of Helen of Troy)

12.66 'The Children within, await the Father to unite with the Mother, for they are One and the Same...the Holy Spirit!'

12.67 My left arm is painful, I am told caused by the Spirit of Connie which is in need of love from me. It is suggested that I say prayers for this Spirit and the pain should then ease. Connie is creating a barrier between Helana and me!

12.68 On Friday 18th, I have travelled by motor-bike to West Glamorgan for a 'Grail Retreat' weekend. Helana did not wish to come with me. It is an interesting Session and a beautiful journey through the Welsh Hills.

On my return journey I am asked by Spirit to visit the Abbey in Shrewsbury, here I learn about my lifetime as Roger de Montgomerie. Love was found in this lifetime. My Guides later apologize to me for their lack of contact. The vibrations from the motor-bike have made it very difficult for then to connect with me...(it can take up to two hours to re-establish contact)....some years later I learn that Helana was guided not to travel with me and that I was to be guided not to go. More urgent work was necessary with Judith.

12.69 We are told that it is **critical to be in Northern Ireland** at the earliest opportunity, even a day is important. We firm-up with our plans and decide to move mid-October 1998. I am told that my Guides will seek to trigger Communication with my Mind by means of a physical signal. I am subsequently given a number of signals, but the one which has been used most frequently is a Tickle and Cough in my Throat.

12.70 In the following few days we are visited by the Spirits of Jack, Bryne, Elsa, Connie, Lorna, Mervin, Barbara, Ford, and Abel. Helana is given a head cold to prevent her working Spiritually, she receives pain from Barbara who subsequently apologizes:

241

I talk to this Spirit.... ' I am curious to find out why you are moving to Ireland and what you will be doing there. Doreen has spoken with me and she is bitter about you moving away. I have always had a soft spot for you John and hoped that one day we might get together. Alas, time has marched on. I mean no pain to Helana, just having fun. I will go now. Cheerio!'

I am told..'The Lady Barbara has been on the fringes of your Peer-Group for many years. She was your wife when you were Zechariah...the father of John the Baptist.'

12.71 An horrendous Evening in Aylesbury when Helana's Spirit was threatened by Connie's. It took Judith to slap Helana's face, and take her into the garden, and to say very strong words to her; ...to cause her to fight off Connie and not to accept Connie's Spirit taking over Helana's Body. I was very concerned for Helana's life as she took on the mannerisms of Constance. Connie's Spirit is being very vindictive and spiteful. Words are given by my Guide. Helana's Spirit is very weak, she has been suffering all week from a head cold, cough, loss of voice and aches. I am suffering arm pain and a head cold which I put down to Constance attacking me, but my Guide tells me this is the Spirit of Elsa which is being equally spiteful and vindictive.

KEYPOINTS TD42

a) Spirit can, do, and are, capable of changing your Personality...........

Often, and this is when damage to Relationships can occur, without your Partner realizing that it is NOT YOU, but your Attitude, Voice, Words spoken and Personality which is being influenced and changed by Others.

b) In extreme cases, it is possible for another Spirit to replace the host Spirit, but this can only normally happen by consent....viz 'possession'...see earlier reference to Helana's possession by Bryan. What is particularly unique about Connie and Helana is that their Origins are the same; in fact they both originate from the same Spirit which was divided into two parts.

c) High Spirit can 'lift-up' a host Spirit and enter a Being if it is at a lower Level, but the preference is to do this by consent.

d) Trance Mediums allow this to happen and then the visiting Spirit can use their own voice and mannerisms to deliver a message.

12.72 The following message was received from Samuel, Helana's Guide on September 18th. The message was written by Helana, and first seen by John in June 2,000. It is included here to give an insight into the influences being brought to bear on Helana at this time:..'

'Your journey to Ireland will be with your man, John, he will be given the full two years my dear to re-gain his Awareness. We do not anticipate his failure, but we are concerned about your well-being in this matter...We see an inner weariness and frustration my dear, and you have seen how exhausted at times Judith becomes. We hesitate to bring these words to you. You have many tasks to perform in Ireland, and we wish to bring to your attention that a life without John can still achieve this work. Do not feel afraid for there are many around you bringing you the love you need, and a life alone would not continue for long...
My dear, you are aware that we have your needs in our hearts. Your bonding with this man John would continue, but on separate Pathways, and on return to Spirit you would again be bound together.
This bonding must not and should not be broken, you are bound together for Eternity. A short visit to your mother is necessary, but do not prolong this in any way. Do not tell her about the child within at the present time.'

KEYPOINTS TD43
a) Spirit plan and influence our Actions and Choices. Spirit know your inner-most Thoughts, Feelings and Attitudes.
b) When Spirits are bound together, that Bond is not broken by death of the Body, or by Reincarnation.
c) Spiritual Awareness can be gained in any lifetime, but, it can also be lost subsequently, by your Actions and Choices.

12.73 I make no apology for quoting this message in full, from Helana's Guide, at this time White Eagle. (12.73- 12.82)
' My dear, your bravery exceeds our understanding. We do not expect miracles from Beings on this Earth-Plane my dear, but your strength of Character far exceeds what we have believed possible for one so young to Spiritual matters. This man John has no idea as yet what a treasure he has been given. It was hoped your presence in his life would bring to him understanding of Spiritual matters to help him to progress. We have seen your dedication to this cause and have therefore progressed his Awareness accordingly. It was always intended to take place, that which has been given, but our hopes and expectations were for a new life in the next Lifetime, having learned many lessons in this.'
(This was a choice I have been given on several occasions, not to proceed in this Lifetime)

12.74 'The World's progress would have been halted somewhat, but plans were afoot to help this time, to support the lives of the People, until such time as you would have returned. It is clear to us now that this can be achieved in this lifetime. We apologize if you see this as a lack of faith in your direction, but miracles have truly taken place and your determination my dear sets a standard for all to follow.'

12.75 'Do not fear this, for it is possible for all Beings to climb the ladder of life if they wish, as you have shown to us here in Spirit. We do not expect this of many, but nevertheless it can be achieved. There is great hope in the hearts of all Beings in this Universe for what they see as real and promising, to allow the Peoples of the Earth-Plane time enough to discover what is needed.'

KEYPOINT TD44
a) All Spirit have the opportunity to progress their
Understanding and the level of their Awareness.
b) The passage tells of the existence of other Beings
within the Universe, and implies that the Actions of
Mankind are being monitored by some of these
other 'Alien' peoples.

12.76 'Your children within learn rapidly my dear, and will continue their mother's work into future Generations. Nothing is lost my dear and although your feelings are somewhat distant, do not doubt your worth, for your love is present and sent out to many Peoples at this time. Your sickness is almost over my dear, this has provided you with the time needed for your rest so deserved.

You are not aware of how much you achieve throughout your day my dear, constantly using your Spirit to project Truth and Honesty to all who will hear.
 Do not compare with Others my dear, for they too have their own ways in which they work. Understand, a life of giving has been for your Spirit, it is now time for those around you to give back something in return. Do not expect miracles my dear but understand and recognize what is being given'.

KEYPOINT TD45
Our Lives are pre-planned, and all that happens to us is
known and controlled...even to the extent of a Cold!

12.77 'The time now lends itself, to providing you my dear, a peaceful occasion where you may gather in all that has been lost along the way. Your Spirit sees a great deal and more is to be forthcoming. Lessons for John have been harsh, but it has proved necessary to bring to him these lessons in such a way, for his armour-plating around his heart is thick and strong.
We have found the only way to break through this barrier is to shock, and to show to him in vision what his actions cause, and what neglectful ways will create. Your suffering has caused him pain and anguish, but at last we feel we have broken through, and a fear of losing what is so precious to him, has now prompted his Spirit to rise from the depths of isolation. Understanding, that not to do so would cause such anguish and pain to Others.'

'One so beautiful in our eyes, would be such a loss to this World, and he has now realized the true wealth of your Spirit in his eyes.'

KEYPOINT TD46

The harshness of our Suffering can be adjusted, if this is necessary, in order to teach us the Lessons our Spirits need to learn! The more stubborn you are, the more resistant to change, the harsher will become the Lessons.

12.78 'All is now complete my dear, You will begin to feel alive again, for my dear you have been slowly dying within, encompassed by such loneliness and such feelings, yet again so alone. Your Spirit cannot survive my dear in this way, you are in need of constant love to enable you to feel alive. Your man must understand this and realize that if he cannot bring to you these feelings, then Others must enable you to survive. It does not mean he is in danger of losing you, quite the contrary. He will gain a great deal from sharing with so many, for as you are aware your love will be raised, and will be able to enlighten your man's Spirit, to the extent that his true feelings will be revealed'.

12.79 'He has not yet experienced the love of Spirit within his Spirit my dear, but it is only now a few short moments away, and when this has been realized, there will be no turning back. As you are aware, no love is felt as strongly as Spiritual Love....these words may be passed on to your man my dear, for he will recognize the signs as the words are read'.

'His Spirit is awakened my dear and his feelings for you deepen each day. It is hoped that a night apart, will bring to your man's Mind the true closeness felt by your presence, that has not been found with another Being that has shared his lifetimes.'

12.80 'We here in Spirit, John, sometimes have to make life so hard for you, for your stubborness of the Mind needs to be broken down. Understanding that cannot be found in a gentler way needs to be introduced in these hard ways. Understand that these lessons are given with love, for you to find-out what we know is necessary for your Spirit. Stubborness of Mind creates your suffering, and suffering to those closest to you, but in the end lessons are learned, and your true Spirit is found. It is hoped a greater understanding will have then been found for your progress with the work that lies ahead. '

12.81 'All is a preparation my dear man, but it is your Choices and the Pathways that you choose that can cause delay and suffering. But at the same time, all is needed for you to gain the Understanding and Knowledge needed for your ultimate role in the lifetime allocated to your Spirit.'

'You will be given a choice upon your return to Spirit, to either stay with your lady in a different form, or to return to this Earth-Plane......To visit again, and to retain your closeness, and also to help Others find the same. Your other choices will be either to return to your Host-Planets, or to become Angels.'

KEYPOINTS TD47

a) We do choose our Lives, and the purpose for our Lives, before we are born.

b) Some Spirits choose to return to the Earth-Plane in order to help Others.

c) Some Spirits originally came to the Earth-Plane from other Planets....The Human Race is formed from 'Alien' Spirits.

d) Some Spirits can choose to become Angels.

12.82 'Whichever Pathway you both choose to follow, understand you will always retain the Bond of being entwined as one Spirit, and not in any future lifetime will your journey be as long and as hard as it has been to find this beautiful Bonding that has now been achieved.'

'We hope now you will not become complacent and will continue to seek. Understanding fully all the implications that have been given, for nothing is secure unless diligence of Mind and Spirit are fully aware of how fragile life can be on this Earth-Plane. One slip of the tongue can take your Spirit back many paces, only to have to recover them again. You will by now, feeling as you do, feel a little relieved that your loved-one is safe from ending the life of this lifetime'.

'Always remember the fragility of this Spirit if love is withdrawn, but remember also the strength of her commitment to you and your life, even at the risk of her own. Go in peace now, and retain these words in your Mind for your Spirit to fully understand what has been gained that could so easily be lost.'

(this ends the message written by Helana and received from White Eagle).

12.83 I am feeling the Spirit presence of Lorna and Constance around my Head; they come to learn about my feelings, they know that they have lost my love and the chains of the Past are broken. They come for Understanding and Compassion. I am asked to say prayers for these ladies. Present also are the Spirits of Mervin, Abel, Steven, Helana's mother, Mary, Ford, Alan, Albert and Cleanort. I ask who is Cleanort?

KEYPOINTS TD48

a) Prayers can provide Comfort and Healing, and demonstrate Compassion for Others.

b) Spirit come to you to learn about your Feelings; for Understanding, to give and to receive Love, and for Compassion.

12.84 'Cleanort was your child when you were married to Helana and lived at a town called Tanthea in Greece. Your name was Andrecius and you were Governor of this Region...(206-144bc.), Helana was known as Percarnia and your other children were Marcia(Ford) and Adrenia (Brian). Cleanort was lost in miscarriage and has remained in Spirit ever since. The Child has never known a Human life; the trauma of the first miscarriage was too much for this Spirit to handle without extreme distress. He has now accepted the situation of a Spirit-life and is content. He can take any age or form, and you choose to see him as an 8 year old Child.'

KEYPOINTS TD49
a) Spirits are present within unborn children, and up to six weeks prior to conception the Spirit is within the mother.
b) The Spirit is affected by Trauma and Experience whilst within the mother, all Emotions and Feelings are detected.
c) Not all Spirit choose to come to Earth for their growth; not all Spirit choose to grow'

12.85 It is 24th September, 1998.....Helana and I are told that we were originally both twinned Spirits. We agreed to be twinned for the Earth life. We both originated from different Planets and were brought together, one to represent the Light (Goodness), one to represent the Dark (Sin). The Objective has now succeeded in terms of our original Spirits.

There is still more work necessary with my other Ladies, who were all originally dark Spirits, but our original Circle has been broken and a new Circle can now be formed.

KEYPOINTS TD50
a) The Human Form is but a Shell in which to house the Spirit, so that the necessary Lessons and Understanding can be learned, to enable the Soul to progress towards the Light.

12.86 Spirit Guides have always been present, initially from the Host-Planets, but then as more Spirit became available the current Structure was established, and Guides are now allocated according to your current or anticipated level of Awareness.

KEYPOINTS TD51
a) Spirit Guides are allocated to you as your Awareness develops.
b) As your Awareness progresses, so your Guide may be changed to reflect this.
c) Guides are chosen, monitored and changed to reflect your level of Spiritual Awareness and their own performance.

d) Guides must also learn their roles and be trained accordingly.

e) Guides may be allocated for many reasons, such as for your own Spiritual Progression, to advise on technical matters or to assist with Spiritual Healing.

f) A very special Guide known as a 'Doorkeeper' may be allocated to protect your Being and your Spirit from invasion by darker, jealous, or simply curious Spirits.

g) When a Spirit has risen to level Five, they become eligible to return to help Others as a Spirit Guide.

h) Your Spirit Guide will be aware of your Life-Plan, and will try to influence your Thoughts and your Actions, to bring to you those life Experiences which you have pre-chosen to Experience. Within this Framework you have free-will, which will cause changes to, and the immediate short-term direction, of your life's Pathway.

12.87 KEYPOINTS TD52

a) The Earth/Sun system is outside of the Spiritual Planes.

b) Other Beings from other Planet systems all travel to the same Heaven System when they pass-over to Spirit.

c) Spirit World is a place where all Beings can meet, can relate and can learn together.

d) There is no Racial conflict, and no Alien conflict, as these differences do not matter and anyone can take any Form they wish to.

e) All Creatures are from the one GOD-Spirit and language is not a problem.

12.88 My Guide continues: 'To resolve the question of how to handle the other ladies within your Peer-Group, it is necessary for you John, to **say the following words**.

' Take note ladies that History has been achieved. Your futures have been secured by the actions and determination of your man John. By forming an alliance with Helana, it has been possible to achieve a pure-love Bonding. Helana was always the intended soul-mate for John. It has taken 18,000 years for these two Souls to achieve what they have now achieved. You have played your part and are to be thanked. Now the Time has been reached for you to depart and to make your future lives with the Soul-mates who await you. While John was in your lives you could not, or would not acknowledge their presence; now you can proceed in freedom with your own lives........The Bonding of Helana and John is irreversible and for all Time. Go Elsa, go Constance, go Lorna. Find your own Peace, and enlighten your own Spirits to the Love, the Caring, and the lighter Ways....Go now and farewell.

You will also need to say prayers from time to time, for the Spirits of these ladies, to show them Compassion and to send them the Light.'

KEYPOINTS TD53

a) All that we <u>think and do</u> is known by those Spirit who over-see our Lives.

b) What we say on the Earth-Plane, as Humans, we believe is more important than what we think. However, we forget that <u>thoughts create actions</u> and they can directly influence our Future, and the interplay with all those who we communicate with.

c) Everything created in our Physical World was initially only a Thought.

d) In the World of Spirit, THOUGHT is all that is necessary to create immediate Reality. Even on the Earth-Plane our Thoughts influence the Spirits of all living Beings around us.

e) EVIL THOUGHTS bring Discomfort, Suffering, Disease, to those Creations of GOD to whom those Thoughts are directed to.

f) REMEMBER ALSO THAT WHAT GOES AROUND, COMES AROUND. WHAT WE GIVE WE WILL RECEIVE BACK UPON OURSELVES. Jesus said ' Love thy neighbour, Love thy enemy' knowing this simple Law of Balance and Nature.

g) We know that Plants and Animals respond to Love, we know that many of our Prayers are answered.

h) When a Dark, Nasty or Evil Thought enters your Mind, as quickly as possible, Dismiss it!........I visualize a Curtain of Water dousing the Thought and washing it away. These Dark Thoughts are brought to us to test our reactions, and for our learning.

i) It is always prudent and sound advice to check any Spirit messages received with another Source, or another Medium, or another Method,...to verify the accuracy.

j) In the case of <u>critical messages</u>, ie those which are likely to affect your Human-life, these are ideally confirmed by a minimum of three methods, or People working separately.

j) When we SPEAK ALOUD we reinforce our wishes so that GOD and our Spirit GUIDES and ALL SPIRIT about us are in no doubt that this is what we <u>WISH TO HAPPEN</u>. <u>IT IS</u> <u>ESSENTIAL THEREFORE THAT WE WISH ONLY FOR THOSE</u> <u>ACTIONS WHICH WE HAVE VERY,VERY SERIOUSLY CONSIDERED;</u> <u>AND, WE ARE PREPARED TO ACCEPT THE CONSEQUENCES OF OUR</u> <u>ACTIONS</u>.

12.89 I take Edwin my youngest son to Butlin's Holiday Camp for a weekend break. Helana chooses not to come and neither does Helen my daughter. I have chosen the dates for cost reasons and requested the children to take Friday and Monday off school. Elsa their mother, does not wish them to take **any** time off School

The children are also worried about completing their homework! Edwin does his homework in the car driving down to Minehead, Somerset. It is good to spend time alone with him.

12.90 This is the holiday which perhaps should not have happened.! I drive down from Banbury to Minehead, Somerwest, late on Friday evening.

- It rains all the way, some 150 miles
- I have two near-miss collisions
- I get lost trying to avoid the traffic-jams on the M5, M32, A370
- The check-in is a complete hassle, they cannot find my reservation, there are no documents and only one set of Chalet keys could be found, there is no luggage trolley, there is continual heavy rain. It is dark and wet, we are hungry and tired.
- No Holiday information pack, no pillow cases in the Chalet,
- no Chalet lights (power fuse failure)...and much difficulty in getting service!

It is not a good start to our holiday, I am not happy, but Edwin my son enjoys himself, and we spend quality time together. I am asked to visit the nearby Castle to learn of a previous life.

KEYPOINTS TD54
a) It is sometimes more beneficial, to be flexible and adaptable than to pursue our original plans.
b) If we do not 'Go with the flow' we can create even more discomfort and suffering for ourselves.

12.91 Upon my return, we drive to the Supermarket,Tesco; for household shopping and on the return journey I 'lose' my credit card wallet. I am told that the cards have been taken by Spirit as a warning to me, because I did not comply with Helana's wishes not to eat in the Tesco Cafe'.
I try to locate the cards at Tesco and then decide to cancel my six credit cards! My Guide Ahizar tells me not to worry as the cards will be returned. I am told to 'have faith'. Two days later I discover the cards in the ash-tray of my car.

KEYPOINT TD55
a) Spirit DO remove objects, viz map showing location of IRA weapons.
b) They can also blank our Memories, so that we do not remember where we have put items.
c) There are also documented records of items 'appearing' from nowhere!.....voucher gifts, Scole experiment
(see bibliography).

12.92 Helana has a heavy Period show for three days. We are told that she has not lost the babies, but she needs to become less stressed and to lie down for an hour every day.

The thoughts of others have not been allowed to influence the situation, or to put the babies in problem. The womb has been divided accordingly. I offer to do the ironing to relieve her workload. (Helana still does not have paid employment).

12.93 It is Friday 28th September...I wake-up with a pain in my lower back, my legs ache and my left arm aches. I am told:

- My lower-back pain (RHS) was the site of a spear entry in a previous life.
- My legs ache, reflecting the many miles my Spirit has travelled while I slept.
- I am asked to protect myself from the Spirits mentioned earlier, in particular also the vindictive thoughts by Mervin (Helana's ex-husband) are causing my arm ache. These pains will end as soon as I accept that Helana **alone** is to reach a financial settlement with Mervin.
- Helana and my Spirit have done much work overnight in our sleep, examining past lives and coming to terms with the understanding necessary. My Mind will become aware of these events at a later time. A good night's work we are told.
- The sensations in my ears continue, these are caused by Spirit coming to me, I am on the verge of audible hearing, and am asked not to be afraid.

12.94 On Saturday 29th September....my arm still aches! I am told this is caused by Lorna's Spirit who is aware of my visit to Butlins, I am asked to protect myself in the usual manner.

12.95 Helana has already had a miscarriage this year. The child who she knows as Peter was conceived in true love. Understand John, that your Spirit is within your children, as much as you wish it to be, and their's likewise with you. The Spirits' of your past ladies can be alongside you, but not so close as to influence your thoughts and your feelings.

KEYPOINTS TD56

a) **Your Thoughts cause your Spirit to travel and to connect with Others.**

b) **Your Spirit can enter other Beings and can influence their Feelings and their Emotions.**

- **Left-hand side below your Ribs is where lighter Spirit enter;**
- **the right-hand side is where darker Spirit enter**

c) **It is necessary for us to control our Thoughts.**

d) **We do not need to be possessive. 'LOVE CAN ONLY BE FOUND IN FREEDOM'**

12.96 Judith, Helana and I are asked to re-visit Ledwell, Oxon.
We have lived several lives at this place. We visit the village and are told that by walking through the lanes we have healed many Spirits there.

We have also collected our Auras. It was necessary for our combined energies to be present to release the Past, and to allow those Spirits there to now progress. 'We wish you now to proceed to Over Worton'.
KEYPOINT TD57
The mere presence of certain Spirits is sufficient to Heal, and to promote the Growth and Recovery of Others who have been overlooked by Time.

12.97 At OverWorton we are asked to walk to the Church for it is necessary for Helana to release the tears of the Past, so that her Spirit can progress. She is warned to avoid a repeat of history, when she isolated herself from my friends and acquaintances..... (as Catherine Cookson)......*She has already this year refused on two occasions, to come with me to visit my family and my friends.*

12.98 It is Wednesday, 30th September...I am told that I can tell my family the true reasons for my move to Ireland. I am to speak gently and with conviction:
'Take-up your Sword, John. The Fight begins Tomorrow' I feel a shiver for the first time throughout my Body, from my Neck down the back of my Legs. Judith sees a 'Halo' around my head.

12.99 We are asked to take a 'Spiritual' drive in my car. We travel to Edge Hill, near Banbury, Oxfordshire, at which location there was a famous first Battle in the Civil War, between the Royalists and the Parlimentarians. (23.10.1642) We stop twice and say prayers, to help to muster and gather together the lost Souls who still believe the Battle is in progress.
They can then be collected by angels and Others who do this recovery work. We then drive to alongside the house where Helana used to live with her first husband, her Aura trail is then collected, and prayers are said for the 'Ghost', a dark Spirit who inhabits the larder in the house.
KEYPOINTS TD58
a) Recovery work is possible for those lost Souls and Ghosts who still walk the Earth-Plane.
b) There is no Time frame for Ghosts.
c) Prayers can be used to help recover Ghosts. Certain Spirits can do this Recovery Work.

12.100 Later that evening we join with Judith, who delivers the following message to us. This it is said will be our 'Last Supper' together.
The message comes to us from GOD.............!

'From this Evening everything changes, the time has now arrived. We see the dedication within John and Helana...their Hearts already reside in Ireland.

252

'Continue with your Earthly plans, fear not when things do not seem to go as your Earthly plans. Now that you are working, all may not seem in your best interests, but on reflection they will be. John will need to continue to grow in the Spirit, but we are pleased with the achievements thus far. We see he is prepared, and will have no hesitation in applying himself. The work will be strenuous, not necessarily physical, but Spiritual work. He does not always recognise when working with Spirit, but this will come.
Helana needs to settle her Spirit; it is with some trepidation she journeys to Ireland. She will manifest by her presence, her beauty and her Love.
We will not allow you to stumble or to fall, we hold your hand. Settle your Mind on those you will be leaving, as they have no part in your new Life.'
'We have called the three of you together, so that you can celebrate the coming together of your Spirits. From this moment on, John and Helana will go forward, they will only be able to confer with Judith for a short time. It may seem difficult at times, but you will succeed and go on from strength to strength. This does not mean that all contact with your Teacher will end, this is definitely not the case, but understand that Judith, from this moment, her Spirit needs to set-out on a different Path. There have been many struggles, but later this evening we will show her precisely where she is to be and with whom.'
'There is to be much casting-aside of Earthly Beings, She needs your Love to help her'.

Now John and Helana, you will need to be supportive, and she will need lots of upliftment and encouragement. She has to walk away from all that is in this house. We rejoice for all of you, for you three, the Love will carry you on, and up to greater heights. There are no three other Beings with greater Love.'
'There are rivers to cross and mountains to climb. Know all of these things in the name of Spirit, for neither of you will ever walk alone again. We wish not to talk of babies at this point. They will arrive in their completeness when you have settled in Ireland. The body of Helana needs first to adjust and feel comfortable in the Land. We have placed you in a suitable position for this to happen rapidly. There may be times when you physically miss each other, but know that your Spirits will still communicate with each other.
Look up to the Stars, each of you will do so. Follow your own personal Stars, and walk with Love and Light in your hearts.'

'You have proved to be very brave in accepting the
messages brought, there are many who would have turned
aside. We thank you.
Forget not the road will be stony at times. The Earth-
Life was never intended to be easy, but you know it is
far easier with Spirit alongside you. Let Christmas joy
surround you. This is a special message for today.
Tomorrow matters will progress rapidly. Know always that
the Love and the Light flows in you and around you. Let
all know around you, who you come in contact with, to
realise and to see the Beauty and Love around you.'
KEYPOINTS TD59
a) The Earth-Life was never intended to be easy, but you
can ask for Spirit to help and to guide you.
b) The true date for Christmas is September 25th.
c) GOD can choose to communicate directly with you.

12.101 Helana then receives the following words from White Eagle:
' Walk the Earth with Light that will guide you. Let Wings be on your
feet for you to fly. You have many years together to change Earth's
History....I am honoured to walk with you.'

12.102 Judith then brings these words from GOD, she is portrayed
wearing a 'crown of thorns'....
KEYPOINTS TD60
a) Free-will is the key factor. It has been debated in
Spirit as to the merits of continuing to allow Mankind
to have free-will. It has been agreed that on balance,
that for the present, that so long as those in the Light
can continue, then Free-will will be allowed to
continue.'
b) It will be preferable for the Human Race to lose free-
will, if this is a choice between this and loss of the
whole Planet.
c) UNLESS your Actions promote Goodness, Compassion and
Love; you could well find that your freedom of Choice
and Actions are severely restricted.
d) Dramatic action may become necessary in the next few
years to ensure that all Beings alive on the Earth-Plane
are working towards the same Cause.
e) DEVASTATION OF THE HUMAN RACE IS PREFERABLE TO
DEVASTATION OF THE PLANET EARTH.

12.103 Helana receives the following words from her Guide, Samuel,
(these were not seen by John until May 2,000. Further messages are
summarised in the Appendix I.)
' My dear we have seen such a change in your smile and whole Being
my dear in the last few days. We are seeing now your true nature
coming forwards in every way. You have done so well my dear.'

' We have asked many things of you and many changes have occurred in your life's journey. We now ask you to know and to realise that your Spirit along with the man you call John, are entwined so closely now, and a parting of the ways will not occur in this lifetime'

12.104 'Your journey's my dear, will be completed together in the next few lives you share together. Children my dear will be given and many hearts will be healed. Sharing of love is very special and one way of sharing your lives is to be given in this way. You have seen my dear from the look in the eyes of your loved one John, sincerity and truth. All is given and what you see in the eyes of this man is Truth and Understanding and a necessity to be with you every minute of your Day'.

KEYPOINT TD61
a) To look into the EYES is to look into the SOUL of someone.
b) Our lives are planned, and CHILDREN ARE GIVEN, it is not pure chance which creates Life, all is given, all is known, all is planned.
c) LOVE HEALS ALL.

12.105 'We see now a coming together of such rarity, for the closeness you share with this man, John, is very special. You have combined the two paths of Spirituality and Materialistic ways of life so beautifully, we are so very pleased to see this taking shape within your lives. John has the ability to understand much of what is given my dear, and a true understanding on his part will take place shortly. After this period of Time your Healing Powers together will come into force'.

12.106 'We see this as a need and a special time in the lives of not only you together, but for all those around at any given time. Your Awareness grows my dear and many, many more wonders will take place within your lives.
You have seen a change in this man's Awareness already and his ways towards you also. We ask you now my dear to remember this man is to be your life, for each life, and all will follow.
Your Spirits my dear are entwined forever, and with this, healing of all hearts and Minds around you will take place. We ask you now to rest within the peace that surrounds you both and allow us to guide you through. All is as it should be, we see now this beautiful Spirit, Two as one with such Healing Powers coming into force as a rainbow in our skies. All now will be beautiful blue skies and sunshine, such that no-one, nor any one situation will create a division, as has occurred in past lives.'

KEYPOINTS TD62
a) A clear indication of both previous lives and future lives. The principle of REINCARNATION is a key aspect of our HUMAN Existence.

255

b) JESUS WAS BORN AND DIED TO BRING THIS KNOWLEDGE TO THE HUMAN RACE.

c) When one accepts that ALL IS BROUGHT TO US FOR OUR SOULS TO LEARN, AND THAT ALL OUR SPIRITS ORIGINATE FROM THE ONE GOD AND CANNOT BE DESTROYED, then the fear of Death recedes.

12.107 'The Spirit of Philip resides only my dear as a sleeping Spirit by your Side, and this will always be. You have tried so hard, but now this love you find within this man John will fulfil not only your needs, but the needs of Philip and all of those around you, be it in Spirit- Form, or Spirit of Man.'

' Remember my dear, I am always by your Side and your Spirit Guides of both you and John are working closely together, to bring you both the Awareness that is needed within your lives, not only at the present, but in future lives also. Take the love of our hearts my dear and surround your man and his Spirit with this love that you have found. Bring to him the Knowledge you have, show him your Ways.'

KEYPOINT TD63

Spirit Guides can and do co-operate and liaise with each other when the occasion demands this.

12.108 'Many times we have said that all is as it should be my dear. Your personal search for understanding of your past-lives is over my dear, you have obtained enough information for your needs; it is up to you now to bring this knowledge to your man. This we feel with complete faith you will do, with love in your heart, for he is indeed your treasure, but my dear you are also his'.

12.109 'You are both to become Teachers and Healers; in this way you will travel the World, giving an insight to others of perfect communion and love in the purest way. You have been together previously in many lives, and a gentleness of your lives will be understood and gained in the way of lessons learnt, and understanding given in words and messages from True Spirit. Everything will now progress accordingly, and a communication of Spirits between you will exist very shortly. Your man, John, believes most of what is said, it is only a matter of time before his understanding is complete. Allow us to guide you always, and remain yourself in every way, for freedom has been gained, and freedom also for this man is well on its way to being felt within his heart'.

12.110 'A journey of sorts is well under-way, to bring you both the Understanding needed, to direct you into your work ahead in this lifetime. Allow us to show you, look and see and place your trust in **how you feel, not in what you feel is needed.** Seek only comfort in one another, no other is needed for all is to be shared in this way. Your openness towards one another, and honesty is beautiful to see.

(*a warning for Helana)*

256

'We wish this way of life to continue. A peace has been found and this will be present throughout your lives together, you are as he is and he is as you are, and all sharing is second nature to you both... The love found is now growing rapidly and brings to you the faith needed to know that your lives now will be healed, and all that is needed will be found within your Hearts and Spirits...

Nothing is ever lost, only now will you find perfect love in the eyes of yourselves, and this others will see and this will bring to their Eyes the direction in which they must travel. All our hearts are overjoyed to see this Union of Spirits that exist within your lives now. Go in peace my dears and bring only joy and happiness into your lives and the hearts of many'

12.111 Helana writes prior to our departure for Ireland,

(Helana was also the soul of Elizabeth Barrett Browning)

'You're on your way to see this Land, Do not forget the task in hand.
Soldier on my Christian band of hope and glory, and a happy Land.
For this is where your dreams are made, and people's needs will be fulfilled.
Your treasures all are buried deep, way deep my children, and let us peep for we have all our Trust in you, to save this Land and climb that hill.
Trust and glory you will find beneath, the barren land that hides a multitude of hatred. War, my children do not let it fall,
Safe in our Arms and Heart.
We keep our loving children home with, see, a glorious day and lightened night, for Goodness sake , stand up and fight. The gentler ways will all be taught and victory now, with open thought will finally succeed, and love will reign.'

12.112 For some weeks we are pre-occupied with the necessity to prepare for a Court Hearing and financial settlement with Mervin, Helana's ex-husband. He refuses to compromise in any way, or to agree to any reasonable division of their assets outside of Court. I prepare and collate the information and agree to attend in Court to assist Helana, and so avoid any further legal costs. We take legal advice and the date is set for the Hearing. Spirit are anxious to ensure that Helana fights her corner and obtains a fair deal. Monies are expected to be approx. £30,000 and Helana is told to put aside some of this for her children. The majority of the remainder is to used as a deposit for our 'Home Farm'. Helana receives much advice and reassurance from her Guides as to the support she will receive in Court....On the day of the Hearing I am excluded by the 'Judge' and it is necessary for Helana to conduct all herself. Words are given and spoken by Spirit and a satisfactory outcome is achieved.

12.113 Helana is visited by the Spirit of Jack, who she is told is to be the Spirit of the child within. 'Our protection will be with you at all times, to allow you at this time to control this child....his possessive ways are only a show of affection...John needs to come to terms with this presence once more into your lives, and your child will need to learn respect for the father....this is what is needed in this lifetime
Both have a hard time ahead of them for they will fight for your affection. You have time now to resolve these issues between the two Spirits prior to the birth of the child, so that when the birth happens the family unit will be at peace! All love will be found my dear, but the work is long and hard, coupled with your Earthly life and the work needed for the World...We see your thoughts my dear but your strength will see you through! Go in Peace with our love in your heart for always, and be aware of our presence by your side at all times.
(These points were never discussed between Helana and John, I am somewhat surprised at this message and the tone of this message.....a test perhaps of Helana's resolve and belief in her own strength;... not one of her obvious assets and completely at odds with my and her expectations of a simpler and less stressful life ahead together.!)

12.114 Spirit state that both John and Jack are in need of a mother's love, but also is Helana herself...
'These men you see are your children in every way, not just within the Bodies you see, but also as Spirit at this time. A time will come when your man will see what your needs are, and all will be returned to you.'
KEYPOINTS TD64
a)All life on the Earth-Plane is about Love, and the Healing which results from Love...Husband-Wife, Mother-Child, Father-Child, Family Unit...our lives are lived on the Earth-Plane to learn these lessons to enable Spiritual Growth and Enlightenment to occur.
b)All, and everything, and everyone, are part of a larger family, THE FAMILY OF GOD. We know that our actions affect and change all of those within our Peer-Group; those in our Peer-Group inter-relate with other Peer-Groups, and affect them and so on.
c) IF NOW WE CONSIDER THAT SPIRIT NEVER DIES, AND ARE RE-BORN INTO DIFFERENT PEOPLES, OVER AND OVER AGAIN; AND THEN THAT SPIRITS ARE USED, MERGED AND CHANGED LIKE BUILDING BLOCKS, YOU CAN SEE AND BEGIN TO UNDERSTAND THAT A CHANGE TO ANY OF THE CORE SPIRITS, FROM WHENCE OTHERS HAVE DEVELOPED WILL BE OF A MAJOR INFLUENCE ON THE TOTAL !

12.115 It is October 2nd. 1998...We are formally requested by Spirit to change our Names from Dennis to **JOHN,** and from Alison to **HELANA...**
'Great works are to be achieved my dear from this day onwards...
White Eagle is with you.'

12.116 'All praise should be given at this time my dear Helana, for your great achievement in moving your Spirit from Darkness into Light in so few years....the Stars are yours my Dear, believe all that is written, for at no time will knowledge enter your Mind from others around you... many of whom are so jealous and have interfered with many of your previous life-times'.

12.117 'When you pray use the address... ' Dear Heavenly Father'.... All prayers are heard and acted upon. Take care with your requests, and ask only for guidance and assistance from the one Source known to you as GOD.'
(I have asked the question as to who prays should be addressed to, to GOD, to Jesus, to a Prophet?. White Eagle responds as here stated)

12.118 It is Saturday, 3rd October 1998.... 'All will now proceed with great haste, and lest all should fail, because others refuse to see the Light, believe that your togetherness and love will not be broken.
We do not give up all our hopes, but we mean by **failure** that your children will begin the new Race of Peoples on the Earth-Plane.
- **If One person can achieve this dream of our Lands and Skies, we have hope for future Generations.**
- **Our Hearts rejoice in the knowledge that all has not been lost....**
- **This Universe awaits, for as your success in this matter manifests, we see now renewed hope in the hearts of many Beings in this Universe....**
- **Your achievement of True, Pure, Beautiful, Honest, Love on the Earth-Plane....has provided a life-giving Force which may well save the Human Race.**

KEYPOINT TD65
LOVE IS ALL, THE ACHIEVEMENT OF SPIRITUAL LOVE AND
ONENESS WITH GOD must be the GOAL for every SOUL.

12.119 My Guide Ahizar tells me that I can inform my family and friends as follows:
(a) A baby is expected to Helana, but not confirmed, I am not to mention twins to anyone...the question of the egg dividing will be decided later.
(b) You have been asked to and have agreed to go to Ireland. This is a calling by GOD. Your precise work will be explained to you when you are there.
(c) You are to continue your Financial Services business in Ireland.
(d) You hope to commence a Bed and Breakfast and Spiritual Retreat Business in the Future.
(e)Allow us to speak the words for you and ask for help when specific questions are directed at you.

KEYPOINT TD66
It is possible to receive guidance from Spirit in all matters concerned with our daily life and experiences.

12.120 For some months now we have been preparing ourselves to establish a 'Home Farm' in Ireland. This is to provide our livelihood and a place to which Others can come for Healing and Spiritual Guidance; and around which the nucleus of the new Church can be nurtured.
Helana has been given specific guidance to research Hygiene and Fire Regulations with respect to Hotels, Treatments and standards of Veterinary care for Animals and Pets, and to educate herself in Food preparation and cooking.

I am charged with constructing toys, garden furniture, garden play-equipment....any items which can be sold. We are to consider Craft Item manufacture and sale. We are assured that monies will be found to cover all our needs.

12.121 We arrange a farewell 'Bash' for friends and family on the Saturday, 3rd October,
My Guide comes through: 'The evening will progress well, and we do not foresee problems.. ..Do not be drawn to say more than has been given.....Ask for your Doorkeeper to be present at all times...enjoy your evening. One of our guests is called Godfrey, I am told.... ' He has a lot to learn, he cannot continue to deny or reject.....He has to say yes in order to learn, or he can stay as he is and in so doing waste his life...Godfrey should now join a Spiritual Development Circle and ask his Guide to come to him. He will progress so long as he tells his Spirit this is his wish....We thank you for your efforts with this man which have proven worthwhile.'
KEYPOINTS TD67
a) **YOU NEED TO MAKE A PERSONAL COMMITMENT if you wish to progress.**
b) **You must ask God for help and then Act upon the advice given.**
c) **It is important to understand that your Motives for wishing to progress should NOT be entirely selfish.**

(Godfrey's background is the Police Force, as such he believes in only that which he personally can relate to. His wife died tragically shortly following their retirement; he has great difficulty in accepting the 'fairness' of this happening, and wishes now to contact his deceased wife before he can accept the existence of the Spirit-World. He also wishes to obtain 'permission' from his beloved, before he feels he can continue with his human Life and hope to form another man-woman relationship.)

12.122 Whilst driving on the Ring Road around Oxford, I pass an abandoned sit-on plasticTrain lying in the road, I return and collect this, as an intended present for Judith's young son. Upon our return I am told to discard the Train as it was previously owned by a darkened Spirit.
KEYPOINTS TD68
a) Every Object we identify with acquires our Spiritual Vibrations. The Object is not 'possessed', but the vibrations come together or 'tune-in' with each other.
b) Spirit can subsequently find and 'home-in' on this unique vibration.
c) YOU NEED TO BE CAREFUL BEFORE YOU INTRODUCE SECOND-HAND OBJECTS INTO YOUR HOME OR ABOUT YOUR PERSON.

12.123 It is Sunday, 4th October, 1998
I feel the presence of the Spirit of Lorna in my hair, and my deceased dog 'Peego' around my legs.... 'Helana has the Spirit of her mother with her, her mother's curiosity is awakened, she comes to see and to watch...There are many Spirits with you, this will be so now until your journey is completed in Ireland, they will then depart and will only return when your thoughts draw them..'
'Do not fear their presence as they come only to watch and to learn of your progress....We wish to bring to your attention that tomorrow is a day to finalise your packing and the arrangements to cross to Ireland with the car.....Judith will not be coming with you, she has her own situation to come to terms with... Steven, Helana's son, will not be available to help, and Ford, your son John, will choose not to come....Events are progressing well...your friends are intrigued by what you say and what they see...This is good for it will cause them to pursue their own enquiries which will help their Spirits to rise'

12.124 'Judith is in need of comfort and support...She feels isolated and in need of your companionship. Her situation will ease as soon as she moves and makes the break with her husband. This is the signal the man Bob needs, for him also to move.
(Bob is also married and is Spiritually Aware, he is faced with leaving his wife to join with Judith ....Judith and Bob have only met once, for perhaps an hour, on the Earth-Plane in this lifetime.)

12.125 'We foresee monies coming to you from your mothers' Estates, Helana's divorce Settlement, an Inheritance and a small lottery win. We foresee you both well established in 1999 in Ireland....It is expected that you will be joined by your Children and the twins will be born. The Clock business and John's Financial Services will flourish.
(Helana agrees to act as an Agent for a Clock distribution opportunity in Ireland...she insists that she wishes to do this alone.)...we are to buy a Lottery ticket tomorrow and on next Wednesday, use the numbers: ..1,5,8,13,24,36.'

12.126 On Monday, 5th October, we agree our wedding list, the marriage has been delayed twice and now it is agreed to proceed in Bangor, Northern Ireland, on 15th December 1998.

I hire and book passage for a 7.5 tonne Box Removal Van, plus 2 people, and also for my Volvo Car, driver plus 3 passengers. I decide to hire the vehicle via my Company connection and to cross via Cairn Ryan, in Scotland, over to Larne, Northern Ireland. Larne is some 30 miles from Bangor...this seems to me to be the most cost-effective option..

I have 5 agreed Helpers plus Helana and me.

Overnight, I experience for the first time my Spirit leaving my body, I am somewhat terrified! Most of my past ladies are about us, I ask for the names and write as follows:

Constance, Lorna, Elsa, Mary, Yolantha, Michelle, Barbara, Doreen, Crossley, Elizabeth, Agatha, Andrea, Colleen, Rebecca, Thania, Prolethia, Jaquelene, Paulene, Castran, Thesius, Oregano, Nedria, Alesius, Belinda, Xythia, Crassia, Draculania, Sandra, Rose.

'They come to wish you farewell from the past, and to wish you every happiness in the future. I am in pain from the thoughts of Elsa.'

12.127 I am asked to watch the Video 2001 and BFG (Rhoal Dharl), I am instructed NOT to watch 2010.

12.128 Judith is asked to relocate into my rented house in Aylesbury, when I move to Ireland. Her house is to be sold in Banbury, this will cause her husband to struggle, to move, to rebuild his life....Judith's family will then be forced to take care of the mother, and to learn their lessons.

'We wish to see the property on the Market within the month.'

(Judith's marriage is in tatters, she does not love her husband and acknowledges that perhaps they should have never married, but she is loyal and says her husband is not the same man she once knew. For the sake of the child, Joseph, she perseveres and tries to improve the situation. Her family have always leaned on her; she is the one who cares for and looks after the mother who has cancer, they all 'pass the buck' and avoid their responsibilities.)

12.129 'We wish you to be aware John, that as your Spirit is raised you will become as Judith and Helana. At that time, we will ask you to stop whatever you are doing, and to rest until the 'danger' is passed. Your ears are now tuned-in to receive Spirit words, so do not be afraid of any speech you hear.'*(I have felt 'sensations' in my ears for many months)*

12.130 'It is important that you are able to communicate with Helana's Spirit. The Spirit is at a higher level than the Mind. It is necessary therefore, for the Mind to raise itself above Earthly Awareness, to the place where it can communicate with Spirit.'

'The Spirit appears to be within the Body, but it is not so'.
KEYPOINT TD69
Allow your Mind to talk to your Spirit. When you have achieved Spiritual Awareness you will be capable of communication with any Spirit, from any age Past or Present, providing that that Spirit of course, wishes to communicate with you.

12.131 It is Friday, 9th October, 1998. 'Hallo John, this is your Guide Ahizar here, you have done well today with the packing and the farewells. Time now to move on, we see a new beginning as the week progresses...all will now fall into place'.
'Do not concern yourself with Ford and Brian, they will join you in their own time. Tomorrow, visit your brother in Worthing, Sussex, and follow your plans for Sunday. There will be work for you to do on route which you will find of interest. Allow Helana to pack at her own pace and you concentrate on your own areas, and some telephone work in the morning. We hear your thoughts and feel your anguish, but all will come good as the weeks unfold. A busy time is ahead, not only for your physical life, but also for the Spirit work. 'We wish you to allow time to sit as we have requested...this is important. Take time to relax, and you will feel the benefit. The work in Ireland will commence as soon as you arrive. A meeting will take place with a friend, this will introduce you into a new circle, and help also with your financial Business. As the week unfolds more will become clear. Your Helpers will enjoy their week and friendships will develop. Helana must not be allowed to lift...this is essential! She should quickly establish a doctor and a dentist in Ireland, and register for tests which this time will be positive. The man Bob will contact you next week, and a meeting will be arranged.'.....(Bob never made contact).

12.132 'Take note of my handwriting John, my name is Adrian, and I am high Spirit working alongside Ahizar and your other Guides. My particular interest is in the development of your learning. For this reason we will talk in this way every day so as to progress your Awareness, both Hearing, Sight and Speech.
I wish you to do exercises which will aid your progress. Tonight, I wish you to sit on your own for 15 minutes and to write down all that you can hear. I wish you also to read back this writing to Helana, in a slow voice. You may commence now...do not worry that she is resting...When you talk, you talk too quickly. Talk only at the pace you write at. Allow the pen to flow. Can you also speak as you write.'
(My Guide Adrian is described by other Mediums as wearing a dark hooded Cloak with a large cross around his neck, in the manner of a Benedictine Monk. I call upon Adrian for technical questions, he is a Scholar and Musician)

12.133 'The man Chris will be a useful contact for you when in Ireland, he will introduce you to the Adjutant at the Army Barracks in Holywood and you will subsequently be able to arrange a Financial Services Presentation' ...
(in the event Chris did not come to Ireland, a year later I made a contact, but was not allowed to do a Presentation)

12.134 'The man Peter , *(we met in a local Pub, when he was constructing a fence)* will be a good man to help you when you need work done. Helana's fears are unfounded, we feel he will be left in no doubt that a friendship only is intended. Follow your intended route via A5, M6, and allow 8 hours for the travel time to the Port. Can you also ensure that Ford sees you before you go. He needs this contact to persuade him to join in life's stream again. He will come at Christmas and so will Brian.
(Ford refused adamantly to travel, ever, to Ireland, Brian visited)....
Your arms ache through the influence of Elsa; you need to protect yourself and reflect back her Thoughts. '
 'Allow Helana to talk through your voice....relax and do not be afraid...'her Spirit will come through you.'
(I could never relax enough for this to happen, I certainly felt the tightening of my throat muscles)
'You should sit quietly now before you retire.'

12.135 I am asked to consider the ways in which low or darkened Spirits can be countered, I write as follows:
KEYPOINTS TD70
In order to counter the presence or effect of outside Spirits:
a) Request your Doorkeeper to protect you.
b) Ask your Guides to help
c) Ask Others in Spirit to help
d) Ask GOD to help
e) Ask for the Protection by the Light and Love of True and High Spirit.
f) Dismiss Thoughts of the said 'Spirit' or Person.
g) Send Love, Compassion, and Prayers to whoever you believe is hurting you.
h) Be firm and tell the Spirit, and Pain, to leave you.
i) Move into the Open-Air,
j) Concentrate on a Beautiful Object or Sight,
l) Refuse to be Intimidated.
m) Have a Bath or Shower, Visualise the Pain being ' washed-away'
n) Raise your Spirit above that of the invading Spirit; in this way the invading Spirit cannot affect you.
o) Surround yourself by a mental Sphere of white Light, which will reflect back any evil thoughts onto the Sender.

p) Imagine yourself covered in Chain-Mail which cannot be penetrated and so protects you. Climb into this suit.

q) Visit a Spiritual Healer and ask them to assist.

r) Say the given WORDS.........these are given in the Appendix VII

s) Remove from your presence and home, ANY objects or belongings which have been owned-by, or given-by, the Influence, which or who, you believe to be responsible for your discomfort.......What new Objects, or living Creatures, or Beings, or Animals, or Plants, are you now associated with! (everything living has a Spirit, for Good or Bad).

12.136 Helana tells of seeing a short man, well-built, with beard and hair to his shoulders, wearing a white gown........ ' I will say with great honesty the truth which is stated so clearly, I am stern of face but I am gentle and will not harm this lady.....I have great respect and honour to be by her side...nothing is possible without help from Helana...the child bears a cross upon her back, which she has carried through every lifetime. It is your Spirit which she carries John...

(.Helana now moves into Trance and her Spirit regresses)

There is an understanding that in this way, you John, will accept the words that are spoken. We try to help you John to understand that Helana speaks truthfully, and the words which she speaks are given by Spirit. It is not the lady who criticises you, she tries so hard to help you to find the true nature within yourself....She cries so loudly inside. How do I break through the ice that surrounds his heart?....We can and do help, we guide her with her words, but your ears do not listen, the words fall to the ground when they are spoken...we have therefore asked this lady to step back...to be herself....to take-off the Teacher's hat. She can no longer continue'.

(I am later told that this is my own Spirit talking to me!)

12.137 'We ask you therefore John to contact your Guides more frequently for teaching...The hurt and pain to Helana's Spirit is so great when you turn away....it takes away the love felt....**I cannot cope with this**!....Your Guides also fear for your Spirit, and have asked me to do this.....We cannot say how long it will take for you to hear clearly, and to accept and to abide by the words spoken or given.'

*(I agree with these words, I have never been certain whether Helana speaks or her Guides; to live a normal life is something of a challenge!.....It is not natural for me, or perhaps for anyone else, to simply accept and do whatever your Partner says, without comment, without discussion, without expressing your own opinion.... which seems to be what is expected of me. In my humble opinion, you cannot have a meaningful Relationship if there is no communication in **both** directions.)*

12.138. 'Already my dear man, you have given a great deal away. We have asked you frequently to take care of what is given to others. We cannot say what this action has created, but understand, it is in no way what will prevail. Nature is Nature, what you give you will receive back...by thoughts, by words and by deeds.

We can only stand and watch as free-will takes its course.

Therefore we ask you to take care......It is your choice!'

KEYPOINT TD71

Equal Importance is given in Spirit (which is where it really matters, whether we choose to agree, or to accept this or not, is irrelevant!) to THOUGHTS, ACTIONS, OR DEEDS.

(It has proven difficult for me, in particular, not to talk with my family or friends or even work colleagues, and to tell them about these radical and amazing Events and Experiences happening in my life, and causing me to change my Outlook, my priorities, and even to move to Ireland and leave my children behind).

(There has even also been some confusion or 'change of direction' by our Guides, as to what is to be told and what is not to be told. It should be appreciated that Guides are also guided by Higher Spirit, and our individual Guides are not necessarily fully aware of the total picture.)

12.139 'The message above comes from your Spirit John, remember, the Spirit can travel, can, and does know everything...The man is different until the Spirit has risen sufficiently to influence the Mind...your Spirit is advanced and at a high level, it can and does divide and come to Helana. It is possible also for your Spirit to write to you.!!...I hope that you enjoyed these words my friend...Events are moving forwards quite quickly...we need you to sleep now, so that you can join in the discussions with us. Rest now for you have a busy night and a busy morrow...your Guide Ahizar.'

KEYPOINTS TD72

a) There are many Levels of Spirit, ALL Levels are guided from a higher Level.

b) Spirit has ALL KNOWLEDGE from previous Lifetimes, and some knowledge of the future to come, dependant upon the 'standing' in the Hierarchy.

c) It is possible to learn to write and to talk with your own Spirit.

d) Advanced Spirits can divide and travel and be in more than one place at the same time.

(this will be referred to in more depth in Volume Two of this Book)

e) A great deal of work is achieved at Night, when Humans sleep and the Spirits are able to leave the Body and to travel for Education, Healing, Counselling, Recovery work, Teaching or any of the other myriad functions necessary.

12.140 On Saturday, 10th October, 1998, Ahizar my Guide writes...
'Overnight your Spirit has travelled to Ireland and has been educated as
to the Factions who operate there. This will be useful and essential for
you to know in the future. You met with the man, Bob, and a bond has
occurred between you. Events will now progress...Today you are to visit
your brother in Worthing, travel via Kingston as the M25 Motorway will
be blocked....a time needs to be set aside each day, both Morning and
Afternoon, if you are to progress at the required speed....you are
achieving the required level of relaxation, but your Mind is still
fuzzy......it may well be worthwhile concentrating on the Buddhist chant
'OM' to see whether this helps to clarify your Mind......'

'Also do the exercise of talking to your Spirit, this is essential and will
cause it to rise...All can and will be achieved so long as you apply
yourself to the Situation.
KEYPOINTS TD73
**a)A clear Mind, clear from Mental agility and busyness
is essential if you are to be able to communicate with
Spirit. Still your Mind and still your physical Senses.
this is why it is easier to become Aware at night-time,
before the hubbub of Human Activity is evident. Between
12 midnight and 0500 hrs would seem ideal.
b)You can cause your Spirit to rise by talking to it!
c)Application, Dedication and Time every day is
necessary for real progress to be made.**

12.141 Adrian continues: 'Helana cannot continue to work for Spirit and
Mankind if your love John is withdrawn in any way. We need you to
continue this work, your Pathways run side by side. Allow each the
freedom to walk your paths with no barriers between you....you are
already joined together in Holy Matrimony in our eyes, a truly beautiful
partnership in the eyes of GOD...allow the vows to apply now....we
wish you John to take care of this lady this precious gift to you from
GOD, in every way'.

12.142 'There are many who send out thoughts of Light to this World,
but there is none so great than that which emanates from Helana...
when one enters a darker World and fights for survival in the darkness
and then finds the Light...as in all things, the harder the struggle, the
harder the fight...the stronger one becomes . This child has been
darkened for so long, the light now is so beautiful and strong.....**the
Spirit of Helana will never be returned to the Shadowlands from whence
she came. Understand these words are in no way a slight on your
Character or Spirit....for you too have a strong Light within......the two
of you together, the Power is great and doubled in strength and
clarity.......**She sees you also John as a gift from GOD, you are so
precious to her life.'

12.143 'She has asked repeatedly that your life be spared, this we give to her...the gift of children also from this marriage are a gift from GOD. The children then become her gift to the World. There is no selfishness in this Spirit, to cherish these children is her gift. The children will have their freedom to go out into the World with all the knowledge of the mother. In this way what is given is returned. We have complete faith that this will be achieved.'

12.144 'Mankind takes so much from the World and gives so little back. Nature cannot withstand so much constant taking...the Energies are drained and so little is returned. The Light and Love which Helana emanates encourages Nature to understand that there is hope and glory...Hope for the unification of the Planets.....Hope that love will reign upon this Earth-Plane...without this gift which is given so freely, there would be no hope in this World.'
KEYPOINTS TD74
a) All is an Energy Balance, If Man destroys this Balance, Nature will react to create a new Harmony.
b) LOVE IS THE HOPE FOR THE WORLD.

12.145 ' The gentler way has not worked for Mankind. Now a more harsh way is necessary to convince Man that a return to the status quo is not acceptable. So few see, so few understand, we try so that they are given the choices...a gentle way forwards, or a step backwards ...look to your History to see what can happen when Mankind does not heed the warnings!...
Man has so little knowledge of the Universe and how ALL are inter-related and how action on the Earth affects Others in the Universe. The lives of Man will be sacrificed IF THIS IS NECESSARY TO SAVE OTHERS'.
KEYPOINTS TD75
a) THE SURVIVAL OF MANKIND IS AT RISK UNLESS WE CHANGE OUR ATTITUDES TO NATURE....
b) WE ARE ALL PART OF NATURE.....ACCEPT THESE WORDS AS A WARNING.
c) Actions on the Earth affect Others throughout the Universe.

12.146 On Sunday, 10th October,1998.....'We see that you are more receptive now to Spirit, please continue in this vein. We will bring to you a joint message which we wish you to read to Helana. In this way it will give you confidence to speak on other occasions.
Your visit to Worthing ,(to my brother Edward) and to Bognor, (a financial Client) has been most productive.   We thank you for following our instructions on your route to Hampton Court.

*(I have been told there that I am the Spirit of Henry VIII, and each of the ladies in my current life were my wives of that time. One of the difficulties of acceptance of me in this lifetime, is because of my actions in that previous Life.....remember the Spirit **never forgets.**)*

'The incident with the gun will have convinced your brother Edward, that there is another life beyond this one. He is now on the way to discover himself!'

When we visit my brother and stroll along the Promenade, Helana sees a wall of water approaching the South Coast of England, it is some 40 feet high. (a Tidal Wave)

12.147 Helana's Vision of the 'Wall at Sea' is a prediction of what is to be....An Earthquake under the Sea will result in a change to Western Civilisation....for this reason you are positioned where you are, to avoid this rationalisation. The exact timing will be evident to you in future years.

*(Helana was always terrified of the sea after this vision....she has died in many previous lives through drowning......as has Constance... her origins were also known to her at this time.....the logic of a move to Ireland, to a house which overlooks the Bay and returns this memory, **every day,** is still a mystery to me.)*

12.148 Helana writes from her Guide.. 'my dear perhaps now you will understand clearly why your time with this man is so difficult for you. Perhaps also the man John, will now see the need for releasing these 'chains of this past life'. In many ways you have both returned to be together with many of the same restrictions that were present at this time. John, we ask you to study with diligence what difficulties are presented to Helana's Spirit. It is hoped that the understanding gained in this respect, will then show to you how much love, forgiveness and caring is given'.

12.149.'Can you then, in your heart, give the same in a greater way, with the knowledge that little has changed of your Character, and, ask yourself, honestly, my man, ' Is this truly the way to be working for the good of Mankind? We are asking a great deal for you to be thinking of my dear man, but understand, it is for the benefit of this World and your Spirit to gain the understanding....Go forwards with your thinking and remain at peace, for all this is past History, but we do ask most strongly....**bring about the changes needed within your very Spirit.**

12.150 Whilst driving along the A23 from Brighton, I am suddenly asked to turn left, and we are led to a country Hotel, the White Horse Inn, Sutton, to meet with friends from a previous lifetime. 'This acquaintance is to resume at a future date, but not now.'

12.151 The day of Monday,12th October, 1998 is spent pre-packing, preparing, and choosing what to take with us. There is furniture and effects to collect from Helana's previous house in Kings Sutton, there is a garage full at her Mother's bungalow nearby, there are clothes and Baby equipment at Judith's house in Banbury, and then there are all my furniture and effects in Aylesbury. The largest vehicle I am licensed drive is for a 7.5 tonne Van. At 01.00 hrs Tuesday I write from my Guide 'The day has been busy for you both...a lot has been achieved in terms of your move and the packing...your friend Judith was pleased to be with you and needed your support...the Healing you gave to Judith will improve her situation, but the bruising needs to escape before the healing can take place.

(Judith has been beaten-up by her husband; she has been to the doctor and will go to a Solicitor).

'Judith will move into the Aylesbury House later this week when you have left...your move should go as planned without too much distress...your Helpers will come....try to visit your children...sit later and try to raise your Spirit by your Mind telling your Spirit what to do'.

(As we remove the furniture from the house in Kings Sutton, the ex-husband Mervin tries for a reconciliation!
I am not allowed to walk into the home to help lift the furniture, but take it from him on the door-step)

12.152 On Tuesday, 13th October, 1998...at mid-day I reflect...I have arranged for the DAF Vehicle to be delivered this evening...TALLY- HO tomorrow! ...We aim to leave Aylesbury, at 18.00 hrs, Wednesday, to allow plenty of time for toilet and refreshment breaks....Helana is to drive my Citreon ZX car, I have booked the Ferry via Cairn Ryan for 07.30am Thursday, 14th October, Scotland, for 4 people in the car and 2 people in the Lorry...during the day I have also completed two financial appointments and refereed a University College Rugby Union game in Oxford.

All is set for the Morrow.

###

270

CHAPTER13.
NORTHERN IRELAND The Beginning

13.00 The DAF, 7.5 tonne, Box Delivery Vehicle, had been delivered late onTuesday evening of 13th October.
I returned from my business appointments to find the lorry at 22.00 hrs parked outside my rented house in Aylesbury, Bucks, UK.
On Wednesday 14th, Peter arrived with his girlfriend to help with the transit at 08.15, I was still dressing when the door-bell rang.
We completed what we could load at 15.15 hrs., I then stopped for a bath and we finally left at 17.00hrs.
What should have been simple had turned into something of an ordeal. Many Helpers had not appeared:..Alan, Ford, Brian, Steven (our four adult children)...Judith never arrived until the last and Chris never came, Helana was not to lift !....It rained the whole day. There was not sufficient space on the vehicle to load a wardrobe, a chest of drawers, a garden bench, any of my tools, a new electric Oven, shed bits etc.
Helana drove the Citreon car on her own, it was fully laden. We had three people in the DAF. We stopped four times, inclusive of a full meal near Towcester, and finally reached Cairn Ryan, the West Coast of Scotland, some 460 miles away at 06.00 hrs. on Thurday15th. Helana had refused to drive faster then 50 mph which prolonged the journey somewhat...I am told.. 'The arduous journey will soon be over and you can relax in your new Country. We are pleased at this momentous step forwards and wish you both to share in our happiness. As the week progresses, I will come to you more strongly, the clarity will be much better in your new home.'

13.01 The journey was uneventful, but on arrival at the Port there was complete hassle. I had booked for 4 persons in the Car, and 2 persons in the DAF Lorry, in the event there was only Helana in the car, and 3 persons in the DAF; not only that but the DAF needed to go Commercial freight and the car could not follow as it was classified as Domestic. So simple you would think, but I needed to argue for 30 minutes with the Shipping Company (P & O), who measured the length of the DAF Lorry as 3 feet longer than specified, therefore an additional lorry charge, plus an extra person charge; they wished to charge me £ 274 instead of £ 157, and finally agreed on £175...I was not happy and we missed the Ferry through the dispute.

13.02 The Ferry took 2 hours to cross into Belfast, Northern Ireland, and it was a further hour to reach the house in Bangor. I then needed to obtain keys from the Estate Agent, and we needed to eat breakfast before the unloading was to begin. We had driven through the night and were all tired, but I wished to commence the unloading as quickly as possible.

At this point Peter became too ill to help with the unloading(coke?), so I managed to persuade 2 complete strangers, who I had accosted walking down the High Street in Bangor to assist.

 Only one turned-up, an hour later, but he was brilliant and the two of us, together with some assistance from Peter's girlfriend and Helana, completed the unloading by late afternoon. The house was raised up an incline from the road, perhaps four feet higher and then there were a further four feet of concrete steps. I decided to put as much as possible into the double garage and to sort it later....Peter recovered in time for the evening meal.

We washed-up, had a drink and then at 23.00 hrs asked to be directed to a restaurant. we found an Italian Restaurant, overlooking the Marina; the Chef had just left so they were closed, but as we turned-away he came back, having forgotten something, and the Restaurant was re-opened for us ...AT LAST something went right!!

13.03 I had planned to return to England the following day, 16th October, I woke at 10.30 am and we rushed to the Ferry Port, Larne, for a 13.30 hr departure...once again complete hassle, 3 persons in the Cab instead of 2 persons. I had to agree to a £66 surcharge, which on appeal was credited, but we missed the Ferry Boat, which put on an unnecessary time-pressure. The DAF Lorry guzzled fuel and Peter drove flat-out; I then took-over, and drove at 60 mph. Peter became really annoyed at this and spoilt the atmosphere in the cab.. We eventually reached Aylesbury at 02.00hrs having left Cairn Ryan at 18.00 hrs. It was still raining and Peter then refused my request to help with the 'second leg' and went to his home in Waddesdon.

Peter was offered Spiritual guidance by Helana, which he seemed receptive to, but a pre-requisite was for him to move to live nearby in Northern Ireland, which he was never prepared to do. Peter certainly has a psychic ability, which will be wasted unless he chooses to make an effort to develop himself.

13.04 I then drove the DAF alone, at 03.00 hrs. to Banbury, Oxon, some 30 miles, and assisted Judith to collect some furniture and effects to enable her to move into the Aylesbury home which I was vacating. (Her husband worked night shift so the timing was ideal) The house lease in Aylesbury had to run until January 1999, and Judith was to live there, to enable her to sort out her life a little. We carried beds and bedding and ward-robes etc, in the dark, in the rain, by ourselves, and returned to Aylesbury for 04.30 hrs where we completed the unloading by 06.30 hrs...The DAF Lorry was then available for collection by the Hire Company which avoided any additional daily hire charges.

13.05 I rested a few hours and helped Judith to settle, she had her son, Joseph, with her.

We visited Aylesbury Rugby Union Club, had a chinese meal and I finally departed early evening, by motorcycle, for Bangor. I think it was the most windy, coldest night of the year. I chose to travel via Holy-Head to Dublin and then to drive north to Bangor.

I eventually arrived at 02.30 hrs. at Holy-Head, North Wales, on Sunday morning of October 18th 1998....I can definitely NOT recommend this time of travel. Few, to no places open for coffee or refreshments, mist and fog in the Welsh Hills!. Wet and damp, cold and unfriendly. If GOD wished to test me, he had presented an ideal platform for me; I was frozen, the temperature was zero to minus 2 degrees, and I was fearful of surface ice on the roads. I finally left Dublin at 07.00hrs, reached Belfast at 09.00 hrs, and finally arrived at Bangor at 09.45 am. A major worry was running out of fuel with the Motor-cycle fuel tank being so small and the Petrol Stations so few; and when there was one it was closed. I managed to find one Petrol Station open in the Republic, by chatting to locals, at 07.00hrs Sunday when I thought I was in trouble! The coffee and the stretch was as welcome as the fuel!

13.06 During the Sunday we explored a little and unpacked slowly. I was too tired to do much having travelled again through the night, I was delighted to be back with Helana and to begin the process of sorting-out our first real home together. My arms and legs and groin ached somewhat, but I put this down to the travel, my tiredness, and the lifting and carrying. All needed sorting, furniture to assemble, carpets to lay, Curtains to hang etc, effects to move upstairs, boxes to unpack, the garage to organise.

13.07 At 18.00 hrs on Sunday,18th October 1998, I receive the following message; my left arm is in continual pain and also Helana's left leg muscle. ' You are both being attacked by the Spirit of Elsa, she is being particularly spiteful. Tell her forceably to go away, she is affecting Helana's attitude to you...The lady is aware of her Actions; she has contacted an acquaintance who has arranged this for her. She has paid money for this. She is totally responsible for her Actions. She has no life outside of her children, and when she loses them she will have no direction in her life. She panics, she sulks, she does not know what she will do, she blames you John....We cannot allow her evil ways to affect Others and the children.

Elsa has been given the choice of leaving England...she has declined...she will not share the love of the children...If those on the Earth-Plane do not obey the Laws of Nature, all will be taken from them until they gain an Understanding of what they do. Your time together in this relationship has been fraught with difficulties; Did you not see the messages? Alas, you did not have the understanding to perceive...you were so wrong in this choice of lady!

KEYPOINTS NIO1

a) **What YOU do in this lifetime will bring upon YOU whatever you deserve.**

b) **If you promote Evil you will attract other darkened Spirits around you, and you will cause the pain of your own Future until YOU have understood that your actions were wrong.**

c) **YOU cannot avoid the result of your actions, be it in this lifetime or future lifetimes.**

d) **TO ASK ANOTHER TO DO EVIL FOR YOU IS DOUBLY EVIL, MORE SO THAN DOING THE TASK YOURSELF.**

e) **There are two darkened Lands to where Dark Spirit are taken should they not abide by the Laws of Nature...In Shadowlands, at level 2,...there is no colour, no Light, no Beauty. Spirits are punished by discomfort and absence of Light, until they repent and ask to be forgiven, when they will undergo a Training and rehabilitation Program. During this time, they experience the pain and suffering they have caused...only afterwards are they moved towards the Light.**

13.08 'We do not wish to call this Person a Being, this Spirit has tormented, tortured, and hurt the Spirit of Helana at every step. She has captured and cajoled the love that you have for each other. All along she has blocked the Spirit of Helana, the presence of Elsa has created a barrier so strong, we are amazed that your Relationship has survived for so long.'

13.09 Before I leave Oxon to return to Ireland, Judith gives healing to my left arm and shoulder; I have previously felt a strong 'prick' in one of my fingers, in the middle of the night, while I lay in bed. There is no physical reason for the pain. Judith sees poison travelling up my Arm. She protects my fingers with 'cymbals' and removes the poison. This she tells me is the effect of Voodoo.

KEYPOINTS NI02

a) **The complex nature of your 'Being' can change dramatically when the presence of another is around. Your Feelings, your Attitude, your Words, your Health, can all be changed.**

b) **Voodoo, and the effect of Evil, are a reality.**

c) **Do not underestimate the power of black-Magic. If you are attacked, seek help at once.**

d) **Good will ultimately triumph over Evil**

13.10 'We are 'Angels of Peace' who watch over you both, to guide you safely. We do not wish you to be afraid of any one thing. Do not worry, this matter will be dealt with and your children will be kept safe.

The Spirits of Others now come with love and understanding.
The Spirit of Elsa will not be allowed to succeed, we will take away and contain the Freedom of this Spirit....we see now a move forwards to Light and Peace...allow us to guide you forwards. Others are also protecting you...a Band of Gold surrounds you both, connecting you to Heaven by a golden Light.'
KEYPOINT NI03
The Spirit forces of Good can contain, and restrict the Freedom, of the Spirits of the forces of Evil.

13.11 On Monday, 19th October, at 10.00hrs.I am told.... 'My good Man, if you will allow us to help you, you will progress much quicker and easier. ASK and we will help you!, allow your day to flow...it will be good practice for you'.
KEYPOINT NI04
Spirit will help your day flow, but many times it is necessary to ASK before help is given.

13.12 At 16.24pm, we have returned from the Supermarket where I was requested by Helana to purchase a 2-Seater Futon; I am somewhat 'put-out' by this request but go along with it. The message is then received ' We are unhappy with the way in which you do things...you should be pleased about the purchase of the settee, instead of which you are unhappy. We have said that monies will be found...Do you not believe us?...the day is progressing quiet well and the home is taking shape. We wish you still to ask before you act...in this way your Trust and Relationship will grow...buy your Lottery tickets this week for both Wednesday and Saturday in both the UK and Irish Lotteries. Use the numbers as given and see what happens...Have faith John and all will become clear....your friend and guide Ahizar.

(Background.... My finances are far from healthy, I have been paying Maintenance monies for almost 20 years, on top of which I have needed to help to support my partners and their children, pay rent or mortgage, and also to live myself without any regular salary. At one stage the Mortgage interest was £ 700 per month. Since working in the Financial Services Industry I have never earned enough to pay back my debts which on Overdraft and credit Cards total some £18,000. The Bank has always been particularly unhelpful. My ex-wife has consistently refused to move to a smaller property.
Into this existing situation came Helana who brought with her debts of £4,500 and no income. I took on board the servicing of her credit card Debts as a priority, instead of paying back mine!.... for her Store cards viz. M & S etc. were being charged at 28% interest.

It is not cheap to move house, home, Country...the visits to view Ireland, the cost of Accommodation and fuel, the absence from work, the Ferry charges and vehicle hire. The continuation of the house in Aylesbury and the need for a deposit on the house in Bangor.

Looking back it was a financial disaster story, but I reasoned that this was what GOD wished to happen, and he would provide for our needs. Added to which, we had been told by Spirit that finances would be provided, and Helana was due to receive a sizeable financial settlement from her ex-husband.

But as at 19th October, 1998, no additional monies have been given, and starting a new business venture in Ireland was bound to be slow. When I returned to England to return the lorry and to collect the Motor-Cycle, Helana went out, without reference to me, and bought a new Fridge and a Freezer; I considered the Futon an unnecessary luxury, which on top of everything else was leading the way to Financial ruin)

KEYPOINT NI05

Do not depend upon Spirit for Financial support. It may well come, but the timing can often be too late for your Earthly needs!

13.13 Helana was told by Spirit to become involved in a retail Clock distribution business, in Northern Ireland, which a friend of mine owned and wished to expand in Ireland. Unfortunately she never started this work and was not to find ANY income generating work in the following few months. There was always a reason not to do anything, I even gave her the car, or drove her to a Shop, but she would never go inside.

13.14 Throughout Monday and Tuesday, I was in severe pain to my left Shoulder and Arm...I was told this is the presence of the person Elsa... 'This is to allow you to become fully aware of how other Spirits can influence your Emotions and Feelings. The presence will be taken away and prevented from bringing any permanent damage, Spiritual or Physical.

Consider this period as a final fling by her...she has been warned and told of the effect to her of these continual evil actions.....she does not listen, she does not wish to hear....she is possessed with her own Evil Intent and this has overcome the reason in her Mind.....she has precipitated her own demise...

We ask that you carry-on with your day and protect yourself with a Sphere of Light and raise your Spirit to resist further influence.....let your love shine through.....we are with you to protect and guide you......Say the following words:

' One can stay, one can go; you have the free-will and the choice. If you do not leave now, then your Identity will cease and you will immediately leave this World. You have been warned.'

13.15 At one stage on Monday evening, I was in so much pain and at my 'wits-end', so I decided to enter and pray in the Church of Ireland, at BallyHolme, County Down. It was 19.00 hrs, the door was locked and I could not gain entry.

KEYPOINT NI06
Entry to the House Of GOD should never be barred!

13.16 Until I received special protection from Judith, at the time of my return to Oxfordshire from 2nd - 8th November, my body, arm, shoulder and neck were under sustained attack from Evil Spirit and Voodoo....I ask of my Guide Adrian:

Question (a) ' Who is the person who practices the Voodoo?
'The man's name is Andrew, he lives in Dagenham. Elsa paid him £35 for you to lose your left arm, she learned these methods when she was a Witch-Doctor to a tribe in Africa.
The effect is as poison rising up your arm, a tourniquet applied to your Biceps muscle and there are spinning bones over your head...Do not Underestimate the power of this Black Magic, this experience is all for your learning! Helen's Spirit watches and learns from Elsa's Spirit without comprehension, and without thinking of the effects.
You must distance yourself from these people and this House, do not under any circumstances contact or enter this property...you must surround yourself with a cloak of chain-mail from head to toe at all times, even in your sleep. Place a wooden cross and garlic above every door in your home in Bangor and Aylesbury, this will prevent Spirit entry. Wear a wooden cross yourself (*I also put one in the car and carry around garlic with me!)*....whenever you sense the presence of evil Spirit, say the Words.... ' Honi, Honi, Honi, excrutiat alles promistos valente, valente, abrogate'....which I am told means....
'Take this Spell away and place it over the Person who gave it to me'....

Question (b) How do the other Sisters fit in?....
'They acted as go-betweens with the Man'

KEYPOINTS NI07
a) The Spirit is a separate Entity to the Mind;
b) Unless you have achieved full Awareness, the Mind is not aware of what the Spirit does, where it goes, or how it acts.
c) This does not mean you can necessarily absolve yourself, for your Thoughts are very powerful, and can, and do, direct the Spirit to interfere and affect the Spirit, and so the Mind, and so the body of Others.

Question (c) How can I contact my Son Edwin?...'You can write to him and arrange to meet him, so long as you do not go near the House.'

Question (d) How do I overcome the Spirit of Elsa?...'You must protect yourself and when you feel a presence say the Words. You must not give in to the pain or to the discomfort. You must raise your Spirit. She controls the Spell and exacts the pain....the original contact with the Man has ceased.'

Question (e) Why does she do this?.... 'You are likely to affect their house and their lifestyle...they have never fully accepted any change to their comfort since you departed....
The Reality of the situation is just starting to bite....Elsa is jealous of the relationship you have found with Helana....She sees for the first time that you have found happiness.....She fears the loss of the children and the income......
The effect of this presence is to suppress your Spiritual growth, and to also affect Helana, and to cause her to be distant.'
KEYPOINT NI08
You must fight a Spiritual Attack with every means you can. It is the true battle between Love and Evil on the Earth-Plane.

Question (f) Please explain the cold feeling on my right leg.... 'It is the presence of your dog, Peego, who comes only to say hallo. Say some words of comfort and praise and he will be happy.'
KEYPOINT NI09
Animals can return in Spirit to the Earth-Plane as well as Humans.

13.17 My left ankle is itching, I am told....'the ankle irritation is given to draw attention to the fact that you still need John to walk away from your children'
(this I believe refers to granting freedom to their Spirits to follow their own lives without any restriction from my Spirit)
My lower-legs itch, I am told.... ' your legs itch because you are surrounded by the Spirits of Lorna, Helen, Abel, Judith, Alan, Ford, Brian, Edwin, and Others. The effect of these Spirits is to irritate the surface of your legs. Avoid scratching, your legs will recover as the Spirits come to accept your situation.'
(I have found that rubbing lightly with a skin lotion alleviates the problem.)
Helana purchases some distilled water, she then blesses this and sprinkles it over me, in particular my head, arms and shoulders. She uses this procedure at times on furniture and whenever she feels this to be appropriate.
KEYPOINT NI10
Holy water, prepared by distilling, and then blessing normal water, can be used to purify Articles and protect People.

13.18 Tuesday, 20th October...this is to be a day of consolidation, visit your office in Belfast and sort your papers and files, return at 17.00 hrs.
There are a few problems with the House we are renting, to name but a few:
a) the Electric Oven does not work
b) the Door bell does not work
c) the internal doors do not fit
d) the external doors and windows do not fit properly
e) a water-leak in the kitchen has brought-down the ceiling
f) the bath-room ceiling has partially collapsed.
g) the carpets throughout are badly worn beyond repair
h) the TV aerial is broken
i)the Loft is very poorly insulated and the water tank is filled with sludge.(the water tank lid is not fitted properly and there is no felt beneath the roof tiles.), at one stage the over-flow pipe becomes detached, the ball-cock sticks and the water leaks in through the ceiling to the Bedroom.
f) several central Lights do not work or are unsafe.

13.19 A new hall/stairs/landing/bathroom carpet was in situ for our arrival, and the following days were a procession of Electrician, Plumber, Builder to raise the house to a 'home' status. I dread to think how the previous tenants had coped. It takes three visits before the cooker is working properly, ideally my friends wish for the whole Fuse-box circuit and cooker to be replaced, but our Landlord, 'Walter' is not agreeable. The broken Ceilings are repaired, the boiler/water system cleaned, I fit door chains, window and door insulation and gradually a warmth descends and the Home takes shape. Heavy curtains are necessary across all the doors to try to eliminate draughts.

13.20 The Electrician's father Paul arrives and my Spirit turns inside me, when he has left I sit down and cry with joy.... ' The man Paul is a Spiritual person of High Spirit, who you have known over many thousands of years. He was your brother at the time of Jesus. He is known to you as Thomas, the Disciple, with whom you shared many happy times in the Past. Following on from the Biblical Times, his Spirit has always been close to yours throughout all your Earth lives. He is aware of GOD, but has not progressed at all in this lifetime. We wish you to awaken his Spirit and to involve him in your work for GOD. He will join your circle of Helpers and will become a key player, in helping you create the band of Disciples you will need to bring together in the next few years. The man Paul is an accepted, respected member of the local Community. He can introduce you to the people you need to meet and become involved with. An invitation should be extended to this man on a Social basis, to enable you to gain his trust and friendship.'

(I invited Paul on numerous occasions to visit our house for an informal chat...I even stressed that it was essential that I meet with him, he always declined, only once did he visit and then there was no opportunity to talk in confidence)

KEYPOINT N111

a) Whatever Spirit may say, Human free-will can, and often does mean, that little or no progress is made. It is essential to allow for this uncertainty when relying upon Others.

b) Spirit tell me that it is sometimes necessary to allow for up to 1,000 free-will choices before being able to predict an Event happening!!

13.21 My Guide Adrian writes ' Now that you are in Ireland, I hope that we can make some real progress. I cannot assist and teach you if you are not receptive, or if you do not allow the time to learn. I wish you to sit quietly each day and ask questions as you do now. You also need to carry-out the learning tasks which you are given....
Let us try again. Sit quietly now and listen hard.
(I have ALWAYS found it very difficult to relax and to do nothing. Remember that all of these writings and discussions are additional to all the essential features of trying to earn a living, and to carry out the routine of daily life)

13.22 I ask of Adrian the following questions:
Question (a) What does raising your Spirit mean?
Question (b) Will the Baptism given this evening protect us against other Spirits, such as Lorna?
Question (c) What kind of love should be offered to Lorna?
Question (d) Why have these Ladies persisted throughout the years to come between Helana and me?
Question (e) Why has the Bonding between Helana and me never been previously achieved? What do we need to do now to achieve this final link?

13.23 White Eagle delivers this Message....'You John, need to find the trust in High Spirit which Helana shows...She is largely self-taught by learning to understand the nature of others. She places herself in danger, knowing that we are with her, guiding her. Let the beauty of life fill your eyes and ears....there is so much you miss.....Be brave. trust in these words they will not deceive...Throw away that mind of Man, it is mechanical in a natural World. I give these words to the World, they are not empty.....I will take care of all monetary matters...Do not fear, it blocks progress, it prevents our methods working...We need to see the Trust and Faith in your heart for all to come true. It is hoped in future years, that you will be able to look-back, and to help Others who are in need of companionship and sharing.'

KEYPOINTS NI12
a) High Spirit are aware of all we think and feel.
b) Our Attitudes, Fear and Emotional responses, can restrict our Spiritual progress and also limit our physical benefits.
c) If we accept that we are guided to a better World with the minimum of pain, then although there are lessons to be learnt along our pathway, it will not be necessary to repeat and suffer the same lessons again before we make the correct choices.
d) When lessons are repeated, they come with increasing severity.
e) To achieve Spiritual progress your Motives need to be genuine.
f) There is an expectation, in due course of time, that what you personally gain will be used to help Others.

13.24 'We need you both to present to the World, perfect love and friendship of the purest kind.'
KEYPOINTS NI13
a) The key to all Life is Love of the purest Kind.
b) It is possible to achieve Spiritual Growth by learning to understand the nature of Others; and by relating this Experience to understanding Yourself, your Relationships, your Feelings, your Emotions, and the pure beauty of Nature, and all about you.

13.25 White Eagle continues...' The gift of the child to Helana, and the gift of the Holy Ghost are given to reward her achievements, for she has clawed her way from the Darkness to the Highest Realms of Spirit...Understand the hardships she has endured by facing the realities of her true nature...this reward can only be given to a few......I am her Soul-Carer for the work that is to be achieved......it is as in the words of the 'Book Of Knowledge', and here spoken by your Spirit:... John, Helana has the key to unlocking this Knowledge...there will be no greater love and understanding and honesty given to your Spirit by Helana...She has always been the greatest love for you on the Earth-Plane.'   *(The Book of Knowledge referred to here, is the Book which sets out the Order of Events for this World and for all the other Worlds throughout the Universe)*

13.26 'Understand my dear man, that when she is prickly and seemingly uncaring, it is not her true nature...'
'It is the influence of Others around her...our hearts cry out at times...you have not seen the beauty of Helana...
Take her to your Heart, completely, unconditionally, knowing the perfect Spirit within..
All else is other influences around and within...Why do Others wish to appear to the World as other than gentle Beings?'

13.27 Wednesday, 21st October 1998......my Guide Ahizar writes....We watch with interest the efforts of the Electrician to solve the problem of the Cooker blowing the House fuses....we feel that the fuse-Board should be replaced and for this reason the problems will continue until the work is done. The man Walter is being very tight with his pennies and needs to learn a lesson in charity!...Tonight we suggest that both you and Helana visit the Bangor Rugby Club to establish contact for the future.'

(I am a rugby referee for Oxon and wish to continue to referee in Northern Ireland. Helana has a blood show and a message is received from Princess Diana)

' The show has been given by the Spirits of Lorna and Elsa to cause Helana to have a miscarriage...By introducing guilt and the feelings of losing the child, the actual loss can be made to happen. The child is safe, but you must protect yourself by raising your Spirits, these ladies are having vindictive thoughts.'

KEYPOINT NI14
Other Spirits can cause not only changes to your Feelings, Attitudes and Emotions, but ALSO physical changes and pain and discomfort.

13.28 My Guide Adrian writes....' The love you have with Helana is growing daily. The interference from outside sources is decreasing daily. Soon, you will have each other and no interference from the Past. Your love can then develop and grow unimpeded.

Perfect love will be found and then your Awareness will grow so that you can communicate.....VISUALLY...AUDIBLY....MENTALLY'

KEYPOINT NI15
It is possible for Humans who have achieved Perfect Love and Spiritual Awareness to be able to communicate at a Spiritual Level. This means that their Minds will be capable of communication not only with their Spirits, but also with each other.

13.29 At 23.00 hrs. I am told to raise my Spirit by thinking of our STAR, especially before writing with Spirit.

(We have seen a brighter Star in the Sky which seemed to sit over our house in Aylesbury, and then to move to Bangor. I can only deduce that this was only visible to those who are Spiritually Aware and was not a 'physical' occurrence.. this to me was what happened in the Biblical Story)

13.30 Thursday, 22nd October...my Guide Ahizar writes. ' Your Spirit John has been working today, (part of it), in a different World. Your Mind is not aware of this'.

'The Spirit can divide and sub-divide, the strength may change. The division given previously was correct, but Helana will have been aware of a lesser presence, because the whole was reduced to a lower level.

The first half of her message was orchestrated by Damien for the ladies. They wish to create unhappiness so that you are more vulnerable to their influences. In the same way, Judith has been given a vision by Damien to disturb her and so add to the confusion. It is what they hope to see, not what is to be...their Evil Minds wish only to destroy. Remember the power of Thought affects everything. If they can bring down the Truth, their Evil Ways will reign. You must have faith, and confidence, and belief, that all is well, and is as it should be.'

KEYPOINT NI17
It is possible for some Souls to exist in different Worlds,(Alien Worlds), as a different Being, at the same moment in Time, as it is here and now, in Human-Form, on the Earth.

13.31 I ask of my Guide Ahizar:...Where is my Spirit at the present Time? Ahizar responds:'Your Spirit has travelled to Banbury, Oxon, and is with Edwin your son; you have another part of your Spirit with Ford, another part with Judith, and a further part with Helana...Your presence is with Helana'

KEYPOINT NI18
Some Spirits can sub-divide, and be in many places at the same Time. In the same way, it was and is possible for the Spirit of Jesus, to appear to many Others, at the same Earthly Time.

13.32 'Messages given to Helana can come from any Source. In particular she is receiving messages from Lorna and Elsa who have mischievous intent.' Your Soul Helana is protected, but as you are aware, these and other Spirits are interfering with your relationship with John, and are capable of giving you messages.....these Spirits are allowed to come close so that your learning, and understanding, and level of coping can increase; for you both will be faced with intrusive Spirits in the Future. You need the experience of learning to handle and cope with these evil ones, in situations which we can monitor. You will know it is your Guide from the text, the words used, the sincerity and the content of any message.'

KEYPOINTS NI19
a)Messages can come to you from any Source.
b)It is imperative, to verify the content if it is of a profound nature, which will cause you to change your Human way of life.
c)Many Prophets in History, have lost their lives, their status, or their livelihood, because they were unable to demonstrate the accuracy of their Predictions.
d)It is preferable if the same message can be received, separately, by different Mediums, without connection; or perhaps the same message, received on numerous Occasions, will give it credence.

13.33 My question to Ahizar: Are other Spirits influencing my children?
Ahizar responds:

(a) Ford, your eldest son, is being influenced by Spirits from his past lives, and from a malevolent Spirit from the present day. Ford can be helped, by you John saying prayers for his well-being, and requesting that he is protected from outside influences; this will speed his recovery...

(Ford is being very unhelpful, rude and arrogant. He has withdrawn from normal Society and is unable to look or communicate in a normal Way, this Phase has lasted for over three years)

(b) Brian has chosen his own Pathway. He will return as soon as he is ready.

(c) Helen, your daughter, is conditioned by her mother's Spirit.....she cannot escape until the mother's influence is abated.

13.34 My Guide Adrian writes....' I would like you to sit quietly for 15 minutes, and to raise your Spirit, do this as frequently as you can. During this time think over the comparisons of love between your past ladies and that from Helana...we will converse later...examine your feelings and the emotions felt for these ladies...we say that you have never experienced perfect love. All of your previous Relationships have been based upon sexual love.

KEYPOINTS NI20

a) Spirit emphasise the distinction between Human sexual Love and perfect Spiritual Love...The vast majority of Earthly relationships they tell me are based purely upon Physical desire, and Spiritual Love is rarely achieved.

b) Spiritual Love is felt from the heart and is likened to Friendship of the deepest kind, and does not necessarily involve any physical sexual Relationship.

13.35 On Friday, 23rd October 1998, I visit St Anne's Cathedral in Belfast for the Healing Service which I have seen advertised. I sit quietly and afterwards talk with the Priest. I am surprised to discover that NOTRAINING IS GIVEN to the Priests for the 'Laying-on of Hands', they simply attend the event on a rota basis. There is little atmosphere and little conversation with those been treated.!.. I am amazed and shocked that so little love or caring is present, and that the whole event is a mockery of what I believe Healing should be all about.

13.36 A Spirit message is taken from my Dutch friend Cor....'My friend you do well, you are progressing and these past days will soon seem a distant memory. You will know me by the pressure on your right shoulder. Have faith and trust that all will be as planned...we look forward to being with you at Christmas for the marriage ceremony intended for December 19th.

(enquiries have been made at the Registry Office in the Castle at Bangor, a delightful setting in the grounds.)

13.37 It is Haloween, we are told this is when the Witches were put to death for their 'magic'. a tradition which existed up to the 1600's.. What a Spiritual People we are.!. In modern Times, people and children dress-up in costume to pretend they are witches, but in the Past this was a deadly serious time.

Haloween is a time to put your fears to rest, to forget the past, to rid yourself of past memories.

'Put all these past Memories and People behind your Door. The Spirits of the Past will depart on Haloween.'

(unfortunately this is not always the case!)

13.38 On Sunday 25th October, I ask of my Guides to clarify the influences of various Spirits upon us both. I am told:

(a)Constance...is still a darkened Spirit, we had hoped that the bitterness would have dispelled by now....she comes only to influence in a negative way...she pretends to be Lorna....she no longer brings pain, but she brings confusion, sadness, bitterness, regret...she is jealous of your Relationship.

Say prayers for this Spirit to be healed and comforted...it is still possible she will be lightened...she feels abandoned by Spirit, having introduced you John she now feels let down and her re-course is to attack Helana. We have decided to direct her to another man who will satisfy her needs and distract her Energies, so that she can progress to a new life. The alternative is for her to be taken, which we see as a waste.

(b) Lorna...The original bitterness has gone; she now Understands and comes with love to you both...her Spirit is lightened...she still has her problems to resolve in her life, concerning past Relationships and Materialistic gain...she brings peace and calm...She sees Helana as being too possessive of her possessions...her home, china etc .which could cause a retreat away from the Worldly life which you need to follow....Beware of this John!

(c)Elsa...An Evil Spirit who seeks only to destroy...you have threatened her Existence and her Lifestyle, by reducing monies and wanting the children. She will go to any length to stop this...she is bitter and possessive. There is no hope now for this Spirit who acts against the Laws of Nature....She brings pain, confusion, accidents, physical disruption.

(d) Damien... A fallen Soul who cannot be allowed to continue to bring pain, bitterness and to destroy.. Helana can escape this onslaught by praying and asking for this Spirit to be taken. This Spirit is being persistent even after all the warnings given.

(e) Mervin...... A dark Spirit who has many lessons to learn. He comes with pain to you both. He places a block in the Mind of Helana...He causes her Shoulder pain....He is bitter and resentful....this Spirit will be caused to forgive and to forget, if not, he will be taken.

(f) Bryan....holds a special relationship for Helana. ...He is sad and has remorse... He brings sadness to her...He will progress only slowly ....Helana should dismiss him from her Mind as this is restricting his progress.....He waits for her Thoughts which hold him close, when what he should be doing is to learn and to lead his own life.
 Helana needs to put this Spirit behind her Door.

(g) Others....you have many Spirit with you; at present these do not interfere in your lives as they are kept at a distance. As time progresses you will need to learn to handle all these influences.....Helana's mother has already created pain for her.

KEYPOINTS NI21

a) ALL is a battle between Light and Dark, Good forces and Evil forces, the playing field is the Earth-Plane, the combatants are in disguise, they have many weapons of Destruction.

- Physical attributes which allow them to strike and hurt the Physical Bodies which their Eyes and physical Senses detect, but, they also wage war through Spiritual means.

b) They can project and throw arrows of Deceit, bolts of Hate and Jealousy,

- Thought Missiles which can penetrate the physical Shell and Earth-Mind of the Enemy.

c) The Humans have developed primitive Shields to protect themselves against physical attack, but in their ignorance, few have learned how to protect themselves against the silent Spiritual Enemy, which can turn Love into Hate, and Friend into Enemy.

d) Like the Stealth Fighter, poison can be injected into other Minds, they will not know from where it came, nor will they even recognise its presence, but the Effect can cause irreparable harm, destroying Family units, parting for ever loved-Ones; the Dark Spirits can then stand-back and watch and plan their next move.

e) Mankind is all the more vulnerable, for their own Religious Leaders pour scorn on the very concept of the Spiritual Weapon.

Like the Ostrich, they are aware of the danger, but prefer to bury their Minds in ancient superstition, believing that if you close-off your physical Senses and ignore it, then the danger will go away.

f) NOT only do they the Adults do this, but they also teach their Young to do the same. It has been like this for almost 2,000 years, even 100 years ago, anyone who claimed an ability to understand these things was burned to death. Such is the ignorance of the bigoted Hierarchy who control the Institutions, who fear to lose their Power and their own Materialistic gains, assembled mainly by the dark influences of previous Ages.

g) By your Thoughts, you can prevent and harm the progress of your loved-Ones, or the Ones you do not love...but remember 'what you do unto Others...what goes around comes around'

h) Like attracts Like...you draw to you Spirits of a similar 'ilk', you surround yourself with love, or you attract to yourself Dark, or Evil Spirits.

i) This same principle also applies to Objects.....you would hope and expect that a 'sacred' Object would have harmonised to the presence of Good and Loving Spirit, these Spirits do not impregnate the Object, but they feel comfortable to be able to return to its presence should they so choose. *(matched vibrations)*

13.39 It is possible to call upon Good Spirits to come to your aid in times of need, it is suggested to us that we personally ask for Princess Diana and John Lennon, as they have both agreed to help us.
I can also call upon Edgar Cayce to help me with my Spiritual progression. Orson Wells and William Shakespeare have both offered their help with the writing of this Book.

13.40 Helana is suddenly sitting like a man, I ask my Guide who she has with her... 'She has your father 'Ted' with her,...he comes with love and protection for you both.'
' I wish to say how pleased I am at your progress. Do not despair, do not weaken, all will be achieved with your perseverance. The malicious Spirits will soon be taken, and you will be free of the Past'.
.'..this will allow the true bonding to take place. All is progressing well. Thank you for allowing me to give you this message...your father Ted.'

13.41 We are both in discomfort and physical pain from Dark Spirit...My Guide Ahizar writes...' The presence around you is that of the person Elsa who still persists in her attempts to injure your health and to create disharmony between you and Helana. Additionally, there is the Lady Lorna who is an interested Observer to the actions of Elsa. We believe Lorna will see the error of her ways before it is too late to rescue this Spirit. We then have influences from Damien and Mervin who both blame you, John, for the demise of their Relationships'.

287

' All four Spirits are rebounding between Helana and yourself...as they find a block from one, they frantically switch their attentions to the other...To rid yourself of all this influence, we suggest that you sit facing each other and holding hands you say the following words: **'Hate has no equal. If you Spirits of Elsa, Lorna, Mervin, Damien, do not stop your Evil onslaught, then the forces of GOD will be brought against you.....Your freedom will disappear, your presence in this World will disappear, your identity will disappear. You have three minutes in which to reflect. If you do not withdraw permanently, action of the severest kind will be taken against you. This is your final warning.'.**
...say also the words aloud, three times:
'Get thee hence Evil Spirits, GOD is watching you. Your actions will rebound upon yourselves and destroy you unless you withdraw now.'

KEYPOINT NI22
When you feel threatened by Dark Spirits, there is a
form of words which you can say, to help remove the
Influences. These words are summarised in the Appendix
VII.

13.42 Helana is also suffering pain from the influence of her mother, who brings pain to her left arm. She is asked to raise her Spirit above these influences, and to 'switch-off' from her mother, and all the other Spirits who wish to influence her. It is suggested that she allocate no more than ten minutes per day to talk Spiritually with her mother.
KEYPOINT NI23
**Pain, Discomfort and Aches to the left Side of the Body
may be caused by Outside Influences.**

13.43 I am asked to see myself as I am, and as Others see me.
'There are many who have brought you a little Understanding; then they leave your side and need to be free to be able to achieve their own Spiritual Growth. Find time John, to sit and look back on your life, ask, Why was I brought that Information? At that time?
'To bring to you the learning that you needed, it is important that you take on board EVERY SINGLE WORD, as Judith will not waste her time.

13.44 I am reminded of the Gemini reading, in a National Newspaper, by Jonathan Cainer, the Astrologer,
' Instead of trying to wake up to a Reality, perhaps you should try falling asleep to a Fantasy. There's nothing wrong with a Dream, provided you know it is a Dream. We Human Beings are not as rational as we like to pretend. Our Hopes become our Desires, our Desires become our Beliefs, our Beliefs become Convictions, and our Convictions, when they clash with our actual position in life, become Obstacles to Happiness. Be inspired by a Vision, but be guided by common Sense.'

KEYPOINTS NI24
a)Many others play their part in your Spiritual
progress.
b)All Situations, Meetings and Events, are brought to
you, to further your learning.
c)When Others ask for their freedom, having played
their part in your life; it is beholden upon you to
grant it.

13.45 I am asked to say prayers for Helana, for Judith and for Joseph.
Helana is feeling queasy and is told that she should register soonest
with a local Doctor. I must pray for guidance and look towards the light
of the Lord. The Lord Most High and his Spirit Guides send their love
and support and praise to us...close down my Chakras, send love to
the relatives of Elsa and Damien, send love to Constance.. My left and
right Shoulders ache, Helana thinks she may have pulled a muscle in
her right Arm...we are uncomfortable in bed, and the room has a heavy
feeling about it., there is a strong presence about my Head.

My Guide responds: ' The aches and pains are caused by the lady
Constance, in conjunction with the man Mervin. The two of them work
together to try to separate you. The presence around your head John,
is that of your children who come with love; the bedroom is filled and
influenced by the presence of a Spirit neither of you has known...this is
a very unhappy person who still hovers around the property. The
presence is known as 'Daniel' and has been here for some 250 years.;
a lost love caused a major problem to this Spirit and self-remorse and
guilt has locked Daniel here, his family wait for him in Heaven....The
two children you have seen in the Bathroom, Charlotte and Henry, are
trapped by Daniel and have been here since they died in the Plague'.
(we have both seen pink 'blobs' moving around in the bathroom ...we
are asked to light 24 candles and say prayers to release these Spirits,
which we do the following day.')

13.46 'There is still another presence in the House, a man called David
who was a previous Owner, and objects to the renovation work. We
again light candles and say the relevant prayers and this Spirit departs.
I visit my office in Belfast,I am then directed to a Hotel in Carrickfergus
to meet with the man 'Bob'. I wait two hours and he does not come...I
am told that he decided to stay over in Scotland rather than to cross to
Ireland....this happens on three subsequent occasions!
KEYPOINTS NI25
a)Structural changes to Buildings, new Roads or
Alterations, can all disturb Spirits from the Past who
have lain dormant for many years. As far as they
are concerned YOU are the Intruder, for to them their
World still exists, there is no Time frame, they are
frozen in History unless they can be released and
collected.

b) Your present day Actions can arouse Jealousy, Anger, Hate, Resentment, or other darker Emotions which can cause them to create mischief.
c) Should a receptive Individual, with the appropriate Energy level come near, they can then be influenced by this person and thus create havoc...
ie. young children may be vulnerable.

13.47 My Guide Adrian asks me to remove the photos of past relationships from my writing Desk, as these draw the past Ladies to us....I seal the photos inside envelopes and store them in the Garage. I am also asked to draw a 'Motor-Home', and am told that I will use this to travel around with at a future date, in order to 'Spread the Word'.
KEYPOINT NI26
It is necessary to remove ANYTHING associated with another Person, if you wish to minimise their influence upon you.

13.48 Jesus writes....' Cry for the World, your bonding must continue, move swiftly from moment to moment. Place the bad Memories behind your Door. Nature moves on swiftly. If a Tree is struck down, seeds fall, a new life starts quickly. It is the way of Nature. To harbour anguish and pain causes suffering and pain; the World will then suffer. Follow the lead of Helana, John, you will progress, you have until the Millennium to gain your full Awareness, it will take you the full two years. Your Mind is still in darkness, but your Spirit has the Light, and the Light will overcome the Darkness.
We get frustrated, but we wish only for you to succeed, you have progressed, so much has been asked of you in so short a time. We wish you well and bring to you these words of encouragement. You are at one with your Guides, the one Spirit. You are not aware of your Spirit's presence within Helana, keeping her safe.'
'Likewise Helana is within you. You both share Messages and Guides and Angels and Friends.
You are finally through the barriers which have kept you apart.
Understand, what is given will be given; only a short time now before you will be free of all these dark Influences. These are working times, difficult and long...you have done well to come through this with your togetherness as strong as we see., have no doubt you will succeed and overcome Darkness, and in so doing the lives of many will be saved..'

'We thank you, we bring you these discomforts only for your guidance and help...we care so deeply, do not be angry. We care for all Creatures and all Humans, all are in need, it is essential for you to succeed. Allow us now to see you at peace, in the knowledge that you are protected completely. Do not fear, for you have all the Angels and love of Heaven about you........'

'You are a Messenger of Light to this World, we will not allow you to be in danger...The pains will now drift away. There is no danger, no fear, We talk not with anger, for they know not what they do.......
Go in Peace and allow us to Guide you.'

13.49 We are asked to walk down to the Promenade and Helana is asked to say prayers of Healing for the Sea and all the Creatures within........
' Helana is a Creature of Nature; her words have healed the Sea and the Creatures within the Sea. The Sea needed her healing tonight, and the words spoken will protect you John in your future travels. You are a leader on the Battlefield, do not criticise Helana for her sensitivity, or her ways....she is a very special person with work to do of a special kind............The Sea, the Earth, the Trees, the Mountains, the Sun, and the Moon, these are all forces of Good. The Spirit within this Being, Helana, is powerful, and Strength is given to those in need...their Minds are filled with thoughts of love......there is no other on the Earth-Plane who can ask for this...If you are in need John, call upon Helana's Spirit who has the strength of the Universe...this is a new found strength given to Helana...She is in need of the strength of all things living. She sends out a constant stream of love to all People at all times...there is nothing for you to fear John, the Spirit within is fortified. Understand the protection is within you at all times.....The Lord Most High brings these words to you.....The Lord Most High is as Love and Caring...do not doubt these Words.'
(I believe this refers to Helana having the Holy Ghost within her, this explains why our Presence alone is sufficient to 'Lighten an Area' and to change Peoples Perceptions and Attitudes......it will also help to explain how the 'Recovery Work' can be achieved when the Power of the Spirit is sufficiently strong).

KEYPOINTS NI27
Nature and the elements of Nature, are Energies for Good. As with all Spirits they may need Healing, and will respond to Love and will react against Evil.

13.50 At 05.00 hrs on Thusday, 28th October, I awake with a coughing fit...my Guide Ahizar writes:'.you need to be awake, for the Voodoo person is doing his Witchcraft which can only be effective if you are still and asleep. This person will be dealt with on Haloween, until then we will protect you. Your Shoulder will now heal... do not dwell on these matters, dismiss them from your Mind.'

'Protect yourself John with the Light and ask for your Doorkeeper to be present...the Spirit of the Dark Person has been brought here to witness the power of Goodness over Evil.

a) If you are threatened, it will help to keep an active Mind and not to sleep.

b) Protection can be asked and prayed for,

- **Protect yourself with the Light of GOD,**
- **your Doorkeeper,**
- **Ask other Loved Ones to assist.**
- **Bath or Shower.**

Use any or all of the Methods itemised in the Appendix VII on Spiritual Awareness.

13.51 'This day of Thurday, 28th October 1998, has been given and intended that you remain here in the comfort of your own home, for we wish to bring you this message without too much interference from Earthly matters'...

Helana prepares a ceremony; on a tray she lays out six chocolate biscuits in three pairs, together with blue mugs filled with tea for the workmen in the house....we are told this is symbolic of the Father, the Son and the Holy Ghost.....the mugs are blue for healing............

'We hope John you are of an Understanding. The workmen represent the Peoples of Ireland. The nourishment given to them is symbolic of the opening of the Minds of the Irish People, who will now become receptive so that they can progress......The Darkness has been conquered by yourselves....the forces of Nature are at One with the Spirit of Helana, they will work with her to conquer the Forces of Evil....The hands of God are placed over the Sea, Helana is of Nature, there is no place in the Universe which will bring her harm, her Spirit is as One with the Universe......Nothing will remain untouched by the beauty and the Light. Do not fear this John, she is real! and offers only Truth and Light and Love of the purest kind....The Forces of Darkness now will be washed away by the Forces of Goodness which emanate from your hearts.'

13.52 Helana feels the child within stir for the first time.....the Spirit of the child learns love directly from external contacts, but also from Helana herself.....That evening we visit theTheatre in Belfast for a 'Rock Musical'...courtesy of my Office.....it is a brilliant Show.

13.53 I feel a presence about my Head and am told it is Michael. I ask who is Michael?

My Guide responds.. ' Michael is an Angel who was part of your life around the time of Jesus. He was a Priest, a Jew, a Scribe, a sympathiser, who was a supporter of Jesus and tried to argue Jesus's case against the Elders who plotted Jesus's murder.

He had a particular affinity for you John, you liked each other, and talked, and socialised many times together.'

'You knew him then as Benjamin, he helped you to escape with the child Christopher; because of this he was put to death by the Romans, and subsequently progressed to become an Angel.. He would like to be asked for advice in the future, his particular skills are Music and Languages'.

13.54 I am suffering from shoulder-blade and forearm pain.....Helana delivers the following words which are written in full.......
' All things are connected, the pain felt in your Body is due to many burdens you have carried with you for many lifetimes. These burdens have been carried by this lady for so long. It is now felt that you should feel what it is like to carry these pains for one man for so long. We see the dedication to this cause as one for the World, for this Spirit was aware that if true and pure love could be found with you, then there is hope for the World.'
'The History of your Spirit, John, was known to Helana; she knew how hard this would be to bring to you, a Tyrant, the love necessary to help you to Progress. With all the strength that the history of your Spirit has gained, in this Lifetime she will succeed....'

'You John have already gained so much, we see the dedication as One, at One with the Universe; for, as you progress and discover perfect Love, so will the World see that it can be achieved, with dedication, honesty, and purity of Thought.
As both of you give to each other, eventually the World will progress as it should, it is difficult for you to understand completely at this time, but understand that as you grow together, so the Universe sees hope and promise of better times to be. ....
You are watched so closely by other Spirits and by GOD.
Do not fear, it is with interest and hope in our hearts that you will succeed, for the child within will carry forward the honesty, the lessons learned and the feeling of love will grow in the child. The child learns deep within the mother's womb, surrounded by darkness, but so much love is given by the Mother Earth, there is no doubt in our hearts that this child will not succeed, for the dedication is so great....'

'This message comes to you from the Lord Most High, we offer you comfort and hope that you may see. You are guided fully and kept safe from harm, you do not deserve the onslaughts, but valuable lessons have been learnt on both sides, both Light and Dark.....
Valuable lessons for the Future, so that you can cope. You have coped extremely well considering the vicious attacks you have encountered by all parties. It has now come to a conclusion. The personal attacks will cease and your freedom will be found. In future years you will connect with darker Spirits of the World, they will be contained, but you will be able to help them to progress.....'

'Personal pains will now cease, unless there is a learning need; they will not be replaced by Others' pains; remember these Times for future occasions. There will be no more Witchcraft, this is viewed most gravely. All that has been given, has been given.....'
Eradicate all Thoughts of this person completely from your Mind, if you stumble upon a memory, place it immediately behind your Door. Cease communication, use writing to communicate with your children. Do not accept personal contact with this Spirit, use reflectors of a strong kind....'

'We ask you to contact the People given for the meeting in December, a great deal can be achieved by these People. Allow us to guide you completely. We thank you for your time and help given to Helana, she is in need of a great deal of support. There are many feelings about her from the Past, and from this Land. Understand also, her confusion, when something that has been gained...when a life changes so dramatically, to have broken away part of that life is like another Being to this child. Understand these feelings and the delicate nature of this child, so attached to the Earth-Plane, so completely at one with this World, that she feels the pain of each blade of grass which is walked on.'......

'As a forest loses a tree, the pain is felt; so when the Awareness is slightly diminished, it is as the forest when it loses a tree. We hope you will understand more fully in time, knowing it is given in love for the World.....
Helana is of an Understanding of why this is necessary for her love of you and the World. We have brought to her today love of a different kind for her to experience, for her Spirit is in need. Do not be jealous, there is no need, all who come to this child are welcomed with love. They are kept at a safe distance by her Guides, they who come are aware of this and respect this, they do not stay, they visit only.'

'This Child of Light will bring about Peace in this World. Through her Actions, her Presence and her Children, for there will be more than one child, at a later date. The child within is safe and well, and wishing now only for peace in the mother's womb. This will be given....
Go now in peace and reflect upon these words.
Let our love surround you both and protect you completely. All that has been given will be given, but not necessarily as you would expect....
Remember, you are of the Light, you will succeed. You have the Power of Love between you which will conquer all Darkness. You have the Understanding within.
Allow your Spirits to rise and shine, like the Sun amongst the Peoples of this Earth-Plane. You are loved. You are surrounded by the Light so beautiful. You are safe and protected at all times.'

13.55 My Guide Ahizar writes; ' The message Helana has just delivered
was given by GOD, and CAN BE, IS, AND WILL BE.
KEYPOINTS NI29
a) **GOD is taking an active role in helping Good to
triumph over Evil.**
b) **GOD can be spoken to and is prepared to Communicate
with Mankind**
c) **Play with Voodoo at your peril**
d) **All life feels pain, inclusive of Trees and Grass.**
e) **A Baby learns and feels Emotions in the Womb**
f) **I have been a Tyrant in some of my previous Lifetimes**
g) **The recovery of those in the Dark, to bring them to
the Light, will achieve the Objective of saving
the World by enlightening its Aura.**
h) **The progress of all those Original Spirits from
Genesis is closely monitored even to this day.**

13.56 It is Saturday, 31st October 1998....At 03.00hrs.....
'You are entering a new phase of increasing Awareness. The release of
Spirits of the Past will clear the way ahead for you to raise your
abilities....try to talk to us every day in everything that you do, in this
way we will be able to guide you....your past lives and memories have
been eradicated from your Minds, but not from your Spirits...their
Spirits have been released and your Circle of the Past has ended....a
new Circle will now begin with you alone together' ....
(A new Peer-Group)

13.57 I question the fact that I have been feeling sick for three hours
and needed to be alone to complete my financial work...
'It was necessary for you John to be apart from Helana so that these
Spirits of your Pasts could be individually released, so that your Spirit
did not interfere with this process.'

13.58 My father Ted comes through....Helana is coughing badly as Ted
used to..... ' I come with Peace and Love and Goodwill for your future
together. The Events of the past few weeks are now behind you and
you can look forwards with hope, in the knowledge that your life
together will become richer, deeper and more purposeful....You have
both achieved that which was necessary for the World to progress.
All is as it should be. Your Guides are extremely pleased with the
progress you have made, both individually and together.....
Yes, even your Guides, John!...A new phase of Awareness is to begin,
do not fear this as it is natural in every way. Accept the moment and
follow your Guides, and all your needs will be met....inclusive of
monetary matters....You have a very exciting time ahead, go forwards
now knowing that you have the love and protection of High Spirit with
you at all times.....I must go, but congratulations on the news of the
Child.

295

(Helana has been told there will only be one child for now....the second Spirit has chosen not to come!)

13.59 A message is received from ERIKA, who is to be present at our Earthly wedding on 22nd. December 1998, and will represent the Peoples of other Worlds....a lovely message of Encouragement is received...... ' You indeed come from different Planets, but Erika will represent you both at this Ceremony....your Parents and your Peoples'.

13.60 Helana does not like the paintings which I have depicting water scenes, I ask why she reacts so.....
' In many previous lives, Helana took her own life...the one particular water- colour is reminiscent of one of those Places, she was so unhappy at that time. The picture should be sold.'
(One of my favourite Paintings which I placed in the Garage, out of sight.)

13.61 I respond to a newspaper article in the North Down News, and arrange to meet with the Northern Ireland Paranormal Research Association, located in Bangor.

###

-

CHAPTER 14. New Choices

14.00 It is 2nd November 1998...I have planned a return visit to
England, via Dublin, and Helana is accompanying me; I have my English
Clients to visit and we plan to return to Ireland on the Sunday, 8th
November;
(*in the event Helana does not return with me on the 8th, and she flies
back into Belfast City Airport, on Wednesday, 11th November).*
We miss the mid-day Ferry from Dun Loghaire; and are asked to drive
south towards Cork, and to return for the 23.00hr sailing.
We are later told by my Guide Ahizar: ' Do not concern yourself about
missing the Ferry, this was intended, for we needed you to spend some
time around the Dublin Area for both spiritual and business reasons. We
wished you to establish your presence in this Area, your Spirits have
been working to lighten the 'Aura'...we were hoping that you would
travel further, but we see that you are weary and you still have a long
way to go'.
*(Helana passes into Trance at various places along our Route, I am told
that there is no need for concern, as she is only reacting to the feel of
the Emotions of the Peoples in the Areas which we pass through.)*

14.01 I feel the presence of my father Ted and my son Ford about my
head. Ted comes through with the following words... ' Let your life flow
and it will be so much easier for you. Do not try to achieve the
impossible. Spirit will tell you what is expected if you ask them.
Keep her safe son...love Ted'
KEYPOINT N1
Your Spirit can be working quite separately to your
physical Human existence.

14.02 Sunday,7th November, was not a good day. Helana refused to
return to Ireland with me; she said I did not love her and verbally
'attacked' me for the loss of my Spirit from within her, which she said
showed my lack of caring and compassion. She finally agrees to return
on the Wednesday,11th, by plane into Belfast City Airport, **provided that
Spirit agree to this; and subject then to a daily review.**
It has not been a good week, I return alone by car on the Sunday, my
lap-top computer which I use for business has failed, and the
replacement from my Head Office does not work... Money has become a
problem, my Bank has given me an ultimatum about my overdraft being
stretched
*(I have had a overdraft situation for over twenty years, but now the
Bank is reducing my previously agreed Credit Zone.)*
The effect of the child maintenance which I pay and the costs of the
relocation are beginning to take their toll,..the last thing that I needed
was an Air Flight to pay for.!)

Spirit threaten my life and say that if I do not comply with their wishes, then my life will be taken...Helana has a miscarriage.

(we have taken over £500 worth of baby clothes and equipment with us to Ireland)

14.03 On Wednesday, 11ᵗʰ, I ask my Guides for help and write as follows:.........

'My dear John, we are pleased to still see your humour. You have much to learn but **all is still possible.** You must walk a fine line now, apply yourself 100% to the Spiritual ways...your finances will be relieved by a small lottery win in the New Year, in the meantime we suggest that you borrow some more money from your mother. The conditions were not favourable for the child, we felt it better for you to resolve your own relationship difficulties, **before** the pregnancy...Without the pressure of the Wedding, and with other Spirits 'cleared away' your path will be much eased.'

*(the Wedding was eventually cancelled, for **no-one**, could get a flight over to Northern Ireland and few would use the Ferry...this is a typical problem apparently at Bank Holidays to cross to Ireland)*

14.04 I ask my Guide: What different actions must I take now, to help further my Awareness and the relationship with Helana? Ahizar responds: 'You know now that you must:

- Ask Spirit to guide you before you speak
- Do not jest (whatever I say seems to be taken the wrong way, **any quip is taken at face value, word for word.)**
- Put Helana's needs first...Helana is a delicate creature who must be approached and spoken to in a soft and considerate manner.....your approach is too brash, you need to become gentler, kinder, more loving.
- Love your neighbour as yourself....show more consideration for others, especially Helana
- Show more compassion in your heart
- Communicate with Spirit in every way
- Be obedient
- Carry-out the exercises asked of you, take time to sit, and read, and think over your life and its meaning.
- Say prayers for the World and other Peoples.
- Allow your day to flow, do not be rigid in your plans, do not become upset by minor distractions, be flexible.
- You must persist in telling Constance to leave; you have her presence on your head. Do not tolerate this interference. Say the words given if you wish to!

14.05. Spirit are asking for more commitment from me. They are not happy with my current attitude, and warn me that they will not waste their time with me if I do not co-operate more.

I am concerned that Helana will be taken away from me. It is quite simple really; unless I succeed in my progress to full personal Awareness, I will lose Helana, and all that I have come to love and to wish for.....I am somewhat surprised at this attitude, in view of my commitment, which has involved considerable upheaval and disruption to my life, and to my family, and to my job. I decide to clarify those issues where I am happy to accept that Spirit will guide my Actions, as distinct from those Situations in which I wish to keep my Human independence. Accordingly, I prepare the following chart:

+ Helana   * John

ACTIVITY	MUST DO	MY CHOICE
MY FREE-WILL		
What clothes to wear	+	*
(colour important.viz.TIE)	*	
What to buy	+	*
What to eat,drink	+	*
Relaxation		+ *
Where to go	+ *	*
Who to see	+ *	*
What to say	+ *	*
+ signal required	*	
Whether to offer Healing	+ *	+ *

You can see that Helana has agreed to accept her Guide's advice in **almost all Activities; whereas at this point in time I wished to retain my Human free-will to a far greater extent.**
KEYPOINT N2
It is essential to keep a balance in your Life, between Spiritual Awareness and living a Human life. This point of balance will be different for everyone.
14.06 I am asked to reflect upon:
a) my good points
b) my bad points
c) my life experiences and relationships
d) my goals
e) what I wish to achieve in this lifetime.
f) what I expect of my wife
g) what I expect of Helana
h) the future and what it will mean !

....my responses can be found in the subsequent text, I also set-out my Beliefs at this time, for I felt it necessary to reinforce my point of view, but also to stress my commitment to the work ahead.

14.07 **My Human Goals, in conjunction with those of many other Good and True People, are to be as follows:**
a)To be a Family Provider and Spiritual Leader and Teacher.
b)To Act to save other Life Forms
c)To Act to control Man's Ingenuity. .ie Cloning, GM Foods.
d)To be pro-Active to counter Evil
e)To provide direction to the Other Religions
f)To be a Prophet
g)To prepare the World in readiness for the new Messiah

KEYPOINTS N3
a) In achieving the Goals, the PURPOSE will be achieved, which is to ensure that the Earth World has a secure future within the Universe.
b) The Aura emerging from the Earth, is to be Lightened to one of Love and Positive Energies. In so doing the need for a further Flood or similar Acts of GOD and Nature will be removed.
c) A new Church is to be established, this is to be called
     ` THE CHURCH OF GOD ON EARTH' (COGOE).
d) A 'BOOK of TRUTH & KNOWLEDGE' is to be published..(this one),
e) Inaccuracies in the existing BIBLE are to be corrected

(this work is to commence from the discovery of the original Texts from which the current Bible was assembled; to assist with this an Expedition will require the assistance of People qualified in the Archaelogy, Preservation and Translation Disciplines. Should any Reader wish to participate in this Project, please contact me through the Church Web-Site. This work is delayed pending academic and political agreement from the Authorities and the necessary Financial Resources becoming available)

14.08 KEYPOINT N4
GOD interjects at this point and tells me that there is no greater Purpose or Goal than to prepare the World in readiness for the coming of the new Messiah.

14.09 By Friday 13th November, Helana had become so distant that I was becoming seriously concerned about our future together; all sorts of doubts are starting to appear in my Mind, not least of course, what we should now do in terms of:

a) the Wedding, Date, Invites, Booking etc.
b) our future in Ireland

14.10 I have bought her flowers and tried to be conciliatory, but she seems very anti- and unforgiving....It seems that **whatever I say is always interpreted in a negative way, I am never given the benefit of the alternative positive meaning, it is never constructive, always critical of me and my Actions...I am forced to the conclusion that either Helana in her Mind no longer loves me, or she is being influenced against me by Others. The others being Human or Spiritual.**
(viz.Helana was starting to cough when I put my arm around her to cuddle in bed, My right arm and shoulder were becoming increasingly painful, to the extent that I could not lay on that side and cuddle her, she was is no longer interested in any physical Relationship.
I was not certain whether this problem was caused by Helana's Mind, Helana's Spirit, Helana's Spirit Guide, Constance, Elsa or the Spirit of Jack. Eventually I moved to the other side of the bed!)

14.11 I ask the question of Ahizar my Guide ' All along I have come to the conclusion that Helana's Guide, Samuel, is not one of my fans.
Is there a history here which I should be aware of ? ..If Helana is becoming **too Spiritual**, why is her Guide not controlling this and giving her corrective guidance? Helana's human Mind has needed to oppose her Spirit Guide's wishes almost all of the time. **Is this personal between Samuel and me?**

14.12 My Guide Ahizar responds:.. ' John, you are correct. There is an animosity which stems back almost 1,000 years. It is very difficult for us, we give the impression that all is pure and perfect in the Spirit World, this is not so.! ...There are People who we would prefer **not to be** Guides, but alas, this is not our choice. We all learn and try to improve our status...Your conflict was a personal one with her Guide, and we feel the advice she receives at times is biased against you...Helana's Guide should be striking the correct balance...in the end Helana will need to decide!'

14.13 I ask of my Guide Adrian...Please tell me about the incident which led to, created and fostered this animosity with Helana's Guide, Samuel, for so long.......
' In 1062, when you were number 2 to King John,
(the Earl of Shrewsbury), you were in charge of the Army and many Estates. Helana's Guide was known as Richard Essex. He was a Lord, with Estates in Norfolk, a family, some wealth.
When King John summoned the Knights and Lords to the many meetings which were necessary in those days, Richard Essex chose not to attend, for his own personal reasons...'

301

.'He became identified as an Outsider, someone who was not interested seemingly in anyone else's situation outside of his own; someone whose actions annoyed King John and also as his number 2, you were charged with dealing with this situation. You met with Essex personally and tried to persuade him to participate in the Court, the power struggle, and to support the King. Helana, then your wife Catherine, knew Richard Essex and had sympathies with his plight and stance....What were you to do? You forced Essex into a corner, where he was obliged to choose...to support the King, or to face a charge of Treason!

You were not personally involved again, but your Administrators orchestrated a fight between Richard and one of your leading Knights, Essex was killed on the Battlefield....

It was not directly your involvement, but you handed over the responsibility to Others and they caused the Calamity. It was the confrontation between Essex and you personally which has led to the bitterness. At that meeting you were pompous, arrogant and overbearing ...there was little compassion in your Soul....the needs of the Army, the King, and Loyalty were highest on your priorities and you had no time for 'wimps' as you viewed Richard Essex.'

14.14 'Your many lives have been characterised by the Arrogance....It is time to change...It is time to heal the Past'.......your Guide Adrian
KEYPOINT N5
You harvest what seeds of discontent and animosity which you have planted! An incident in a previous lifetime, even 900 years earlier, has surfaced in 1998 and has had a dramatic effect on the progress of all that was hoped for.

14.15 Judith receives a message from White Eagle who writes... 'Even Guides have lessons to learn, especially those who have attained only Level 5...this situation with Helana was an opportunity for Helana's Guide to learn forgiveness...the Guide will not be changed....It is hoped John that you will ask forgiveness of that Guide for the derogatory way you treated that Being in the previous life...........In this way you can both grow'.
KEYPOINTS N6
a) Healing of past Situations is a necessity for Spiritual Growth.
b) When in the Spirit World you retain your Personality.
▪ **Ideally, all those who attain the level of Spirit Guide have progressed sufficiently in the ways of Love, Understanding, Experience and Compassion for any individual historical bitterness to have been put aside.**
▪ **Very occasionally a Situation can develop when 'Emotions' re-surface and conflict can arise.**

- Fortunately these Occurrences are very rare.
- Even Guides need to be taught and to learn, not everyone is 'perfect'.

c) Your Spirit Guides can be changed to match your Spiritual Growth, level of Awareness, and the needs of your lifetime Experience.

14.16 White Eagle continues...'We will now address the question of Helana being totally ruled by her Guide; this is an unusual problem ...Helana has chosen to take no responsibility for her Actions; it is difficult for her to make her Mind up on anything... She has closed the door on her own Spiritual progress, for how can she learn if she makes no Choices for herself?....Do not hide behind Spirit...It is our fervent wish that you John will gain a higher Awareness of Spirit, and Helana will come down and be more Earthly, and somewhere along each of your journeys you will meet and find a compatibility that allows the love between you to flow freely. Helana must not feel she is losing her Spirituality, nor must she feel inadequate in any way....John, you need to lift your Spirit and to give the unconditional love and understanding being asked of you. All is standing still'

14.17 I ask my Guide Ahizar..... ' How can I communicate with Richard Essex?...in my sleep?....in writing? How can we have a discussion?
' Leave that one with us to ponder, your Spirit can perhaps do this for you tonight. We will choose a time.'

14.18 Whilst in Chipping Norton, Oxon; I see a brass statue of an Eagle which I purchase....I am told later that the Eagle is safe for me to have, it is to give me strength, as it was previously owned by an Explorer who had a powerful resistance to Spirits and to Diseases. The Eagle was purchased from Ronnie Barker's Shop, since closed.

14.19 After a very disturbed night on Thursday 12th, during which messages passed between Constance and Helana; eventually a truce was reached, and I am able to cuddle Helana.
I feel my Spirit 'coming and going' and I receive a Vision 'Red Earth, Giraffes and Colony Spheres. I am told that the red land was the Planet Zypron, where the Giraffe is a common animal; the Colony Spheres were on the Planet Mercury....you travelled a long way in your sleep!...I am told that my Planet of origin is Zypron.(host planet)
I ask for Helana to meet with Constance in Spirit to resolve their differences...She says she is willing to do this but Constance's Spirit is not....Helana says she has gone as far as she is willing to with Constance, She has found forgiveness for her, it is now all down to me.
(Constance's Spirit has previously asked for help from Helana, to come in love for learning....but Helana claims she is being stabbed in the Back and Chest by Constance.)

(To stop Helana coughing, which is caused by Constance's Spirit, I am told that I must withdraw my Spirit from Constance's presence and place her firmly 'behind my Door' When I suggested to Helana that her Guide was biased against me she broke down in tears and a reconciliation took place. Helana blamed Constance's Spirit for interfering with our Relationship and creating a distance between us.)

14.20 I am told that a meeting has been arranged for Friday night of 13th, in my sleep. My Spirit is to meet with Richard Essex, Helana's Guide, and it is down to me to Apologise and to achieve a Reconciliation...I am subsequently told that a momentous meeting took place. **ALL the Spirit Contacts, from ALL MY PREVIOUS LIVES were brought together, initially to ensure that there were no other unforeseen Animosities which needed to be sorted, but also to give all the opportunity to have their say, and to air their grievances.**

14.21 'There were many who said very harsh words about your Actions in your previous lives, there were also those who spoke with the highest regard for your Endeavours and Achievements. It was 'as you were' a review of the World's History, with many **thousands** of the key players involved...for you were one of the original players and **everyone** from all Time was there. It was quite amazing! You John were very brave to face **all of your Critics at the same time,** in the same place, and effectively have your Lives analysed and dissected by others...All in all, some 77 Lives'.

14.22 'When the Critics had had their say it was your turn. You were magnificent, you accepted most of the Criticism with grace and in a humble way. You then proposed a Pact, an individual pact with everyone who felt an injustice from yourself, and likewise you with them... One-by-one all was listed and all was agreed...You are to re-visit all the Individual Parties in the months ahead, to resolve the personal Grievances with a willing approach from both sides. In this way the Past can be healed and both you and they can move forwards'.

14.23 'The magnitude of this Settlement is quite staggering. The effects on the Earth-Plane will ripple throughout the World.....It is, as if at one Stroke, the Grievances, evil Thoughts, negative Thoughts, hatred, all have been cleared...This will release so many Spirits to increased Awareness, that the effect will be felt throughout the World.'

14.24 'To put this into context is very difficult, but if you realise that it can take a lifetime for one or two past Events to be healed, this then is equivalent to 10,000 lifetimes at one time. All those Spirits will then interact with their own Circles and contacts, to raise everyone else's Awareness... A magnificent night's work....we thank you heartily and rejoice in your achievement.'

'All can now move forwards, all can now be achieved. You now have the task of individually reconciling with all of these Spirits....this work will be brought to you, one-by-one, until it is completed... Your Understanding will increase dramatically as the restrictions of the Past are lifted.'

14.25 I am later told that 10,000 Spirits came together...All my past and present Guides, all my past ladies and children, all those who felt aggrieved by me. I am told that GOD was in charge of the Meeting, and following the Occasion, an orange Glow appeared in the Skies... Following this meeting my Spirit travelled to Orion for further meetings.

14.26 I ask a series of Questions of my Guides:

Question (a) What are Constance's Origins?.. '.Constance came originally from the Planet Zyron, the same as Helana, there has **always** been jealousy and rivalry; Constance would do or say **anything simply to down Helana.** Helana used also to be like this.'
(revisit this later in the text)

Question (b) What relevant history is there to explain the actions of Constance now, and why is she so tenuous?.. 'Essentially the question is already answered, rivalry over 18,000 years for your attention, never giving ground, never being compassionate, never loving...
It would not have been fair to have divided the Spirit of one of the Arch-Villains and not the other. Not only is the Earth Experiment between 'Good' and 'Evil', it is also between Constance and Helana; to see whether they can resolve their Conflict...
.John, you have always been the catalyst, on the side of Good, but tempted continuously by the dark Spirits of Constance, Helana and Elsa...Both Constance and Helana were asked to leave Zyron in view of the disharmony their rivalry had caused. Other Spirits were also asked to leave'

Question (c) What should I, John, now do to stop the Cycle repeating itself ?..
'You must achieve your Spiritual Awareness **despite these ladies. You must overcome their Spirits, it is all a 'Trial of Strength'...**You will then be able to educate them to help change themselves from Evil to Good ways. **With this achieved, the Experiment will end.**

Question (d) My Guides, can you please help me to win back Helana?...
' My friend you must be patient. Do not forget that Spirit have caused her to withdraw her affection; whereas previously she was prepared to give to you, to co-operate.
She does not wish to if she feels no emotional tie...The status quo will be returned, but remember the lesson. **Allow Helana her freedom.'**

Question (e) In what way must I change my attitude to win back Helana?.. What is my Spirit doing which Helana is unhappy about? What must I Spiritually do?

'You must think, eat and live for Helana, you must try to be more caring and more loving; more money will help. Slowdown your Mind; your Spirit travels about and goes everywhere, your Spirit needs to spend more time with Helana's Spirit...your Spirit is not prepared to submit to Helana's, her Spirit does not like this attitude, there is as you might say a 'power struggle' here. The Mind has accepted the situation, but the Spirit still keeps its independence. You can achieve harmony by telling and convincing your Spirit that this is your desire; the Spirit will listen and will compromise, and Harmony will be achieved.

KEYPOINT N7
The Spirit will eventually listen to the Mind

Question (f) Why do I have a pain around my waist?....

' This is given to cause you to slow down. We do not wish you to expend all your energy on the Rugby Field (I am a Union Referee), neither do we wish you to impose yourself so much on Helana (sex!). Be gentle, All will be well.'

Question (g) Why is Helana so sensitive?....

' Helana is extremely sensitive to Vibrations, so that she can detect the Emotions and Feelings of all about her...Remember also, she has the sensitivity of her host Planet, and this has still to increase. She will develop a mechanism to enable her to 'switch-on' and to 'switch-off', so that she can relax on frequent occasions. She needs the Sensitivity to be able to do the work that it is necessary to be done.'

KEYPOINTS N8
a) All can be given; All can be taken away. Many situations are orchestrated for the learning which we need, or which we have chosen.
b) Our thoughts and feelings can be influenced and changed by Spirit, or words can even be put into our mouths, should the occasion warrant this.

14.27 'We wish to tell you that the concept of Inter-Stellar travel by Humans is not acceptable and will not be allowed'

KEYPOINT N9
What we do in this World, and what we aspire to achieve, is all monitored and controlled.

14.28 On Friday, 13th, I receive the following message from Ahizar...

'Good morning John, we wish to bring to you both the news that all is well, and as it should be. The Events of the past weeks have been quite momentous. A testing time indeed, you have both behaved extremely well and as we expected of you'

' We apologise now for the necessity to put you through these Trials. But the importance of the Work, and your Roles, is such that it was necessary to test you both to the limit, to see whether either of you would walk away, or to choose not to proceed.

In view of the magnitude of the responsibility of what is asked of you, we are all delighted with the outcome...it brings you both to the position where you can commence your new lives together, in the new land, in the confidence that you are indeed trustworthy, responsible, and committed to the cause of love and humanity on the Earth-Plane and throughout the Universe....

You can both now progress with your Awareness, and in so doing, so will your family members and children, and so the ripples will spread.'

KEYPOINTS N10

a)What happens on the Earth-Plane will affect the rest of the Universe....The cause of Love and Humanity are given as a key objective.

b)Your Individual rate of progression to your Awareness is influenced by your Actions, your Thoughts, your Attitudes and your level of Understanding of all that happens around you.

14.29 'Tonight, in her sleep, Helana has met her Guides and so have you John. A reconciliation has taken place between you ALL, so that the Past can be healed and the true work can begin in a positive and constructive frame of mind....you will not realise now, but the knowledge of this meeting will come to you in the days ahead....

The People will be brought together for the Circle to form, and the Church will begin....there will be a great deal of travel for you both before all of your family situations are resolved....strength will be given to you....monies will be found as it is not our wish that you should struggle in Earthly terms whilst the work you do for us is so important and significant to the World.'

14.30 'Your children **must be allowed to choose their own Destinies.**
...we wish Helana to commence her Clock business at once, for this will not only provide monies, but will serve also to introduce her to the people we wish her to meet...do not forget the Womens' Groups .

The Wedding should now be re-scheduled for Easter 1999, to coincide with the children being off-school on half-term holiday....a lottery ticket tomorrow is essential....we thank you now and wish you to rest for a few hours.'

14.31 I am asked to arrange a physical meeting for those I am asked to involve in the Spiritual work. The meeting is to be held on December 22nd at 16.00 hrs, in the Commantle Hall Hotel, near Holywood, County Down.

I am told that it is important that this meeting takes place...I am to inform those who attend about the purpose of our move to Ireland, the critical state of the World within the Universe, and the need to act to try to prevent a cataclysmic Event occurring.

In the event of a disaster, I am to make preparations to ensure our survival....I am to combine the invitations to our families for Christmas celebrations, with the timing for the meeting.

I search the neighbourhood, and telephone book, and cannot find any Commantle Hall Hotel. Two weeks later I receive the words:

' The meeting on the 22nd December is to be held at the Bay View Hotel in Bangor. The previous location was given as a cover in case news of this meeting was leaked. We apologise for the subterfuge, but it is necessary to be careful in every way.'

14.32 I am told by my Guide, that some of my goals are to:
a) Commence a Circle of like-minded people.
b) Start a Spiritualist Church
c) Offer healing to those in need.
....a Room, a gathering, laughter, listen to Others, use word of mouth, show a gentler side to your nature, play no games.
(In a limited way, I offer an 'open house' on a Sunday afternoon for an open and friendly Discussion)

14.33 Judith writes....' Judith my dear, you know already that the Ways of Spirit sometimes seem strange. John has been continually given the opportunity, to show his Compassion for Mankind in general. This is sadly lacking. It was hoped, knowing the sensitivity of his loved One, that he would at least show compassion to her. He desperately needs to know 'The World' and all that is in his World, especially now as he tries to turn completely to Spirit, that all within his World are **not** against him.

The lesson has been given John, and sadly, the lesson fell on stony ground....GIVE my dear John, and all will be given to you....let the lady see your love. It is so difficult for you, we see that....all this animosity is not necessary. Listen to Spirit, listen and hear. For this lady Helana, the caring is majorly important to the success of all which stands in your path. Helana tries hard not to upset you, she has loved you dearly John. Give to her the love, the understanding, the compassion, even when you do not understand fully why things are being given. Allow her the freedom which you ALL need.'

14.34 'This is so hard for you John, we see that...What do you see John? Take off the blinkers which you have worn throughout your lives on this Planet, only then will your life begin to flow. It is not necessary for all to be explained in the initial event. The explanation may not become clear until a later date, but it is promised....The understanding is there for you if you wish it to be.'

14.35 'All relationships we see have ups and downs, due to your Earthly Emotions. Set your Emotions aside. All needs to be Calm. But only with the truest of Love, given freely by you both, can this come about. There is no wrong or right in this situation...the lesson is in who is expected, who will give! and it was so desperately hoped, by all here, that it would be you John.'

(I reflect now on this message, a year later, and remember how bemused I was at that time. In my mind, Helana had her freedom, I was not hounding her, I was trying to help her to do what she had been asked to do by Spirit, to commence the Clock business, or to find work of her choice. To complete her human tasks....as well as her Spiritual duties. She missed her own car which had been left behind in England, but this was short term, for as soon as her divorce monies arrived she would have the capital to purchase another, and this money was due within weeks.

At this time she probably felt restricted on cash; but then this surely was an incentive to work. I transferred monies each week to her Account and she never paid for anything other than personal items, she contributed nothing in 'monetary' terms to the Home. I did not feel animosity to her, I certainly felt that life was becoming somewhat stressed owing to the imbalance which existed between her 'Spirituality' and my need to live a human life and to still keep my 'independence'. I saw this as once again only a temporary problem, for as my 'Spiritual Awareness' grew, then I saw us coming together in a stronger way. With my 'blinkers on' I was relatively content. We had endured and solved all the stresses of the move, we had sorted and commenced a new life together, in a new Land, as asked to by Spirit. Helana was probably lonely, in that Judith was not close-by, but she did not have many friends or relatives she could turn to when in England, and as soon as she mixed more in the Community, I saw all this changing.

I was very happy with our physical relationship and thought she was likewise. The stresses of turning the house into a home were receding, the influences of dark Spirit were being 'coped-with' and a brighter future was foretold.)

14.36 On Saturday, 14th, November, I attend an ECONI Conference at Stramillis College in Belfast. ECONI stands for the Evangelical Contribution On Northern Ireland, and is an attempt by enlightened Churchmen to decide upon a considered response to the Conflicts, and what changes in attitude are necessary, to enable Churchmen to cope with the Personal, Religious, and Community conflict situations present in Northern Ireland....

I enjoyed the Conference and met some interesting people from all walks of life. A few months later I applied again to attend a Bible Study Course but was politely refused in view of my 'Spiritualist Ideas' which were considered to be disruptive.

I also visited the Residential and Training Centre for Inter-Denominational Harmony, which is located in the North and is a magnificent Establishment where people are brought together, away from their Communities, simply to learn to live together. The operation is a Teaching and Study Centre, staffed principally by volunteers. I formally offered my time and energies, but despite my references and referees being checked, my services were never required.

(The Centre was opened by Prince Charles and certainly serves a useful purpose, disappointing that my time and energies were refused when I had formally applied and has chased the Application at least twice)

KEYPOINTS N11

a) It is necessary first to give to Others, before you can expect to receive.

b) You should give without the expectation of reward.

c) Truly impartial Organisations should welcome All who volunteer their services, and should not fear an open discussion or a different interpretation.

4.37 I left the Conference at 14.00 hrs, returned to Bangor to collect Helana, and we immediately left for Kildaire in the Republic, by car, for a Dinner-Party and overnight stay with friends. Helana did not wish to travel near to Dublin, neither did she wish to travel by Motor-ways. With time on our side I agreed to take the 'direct route', but I did not allow for, or know, the back-roads of Ireland. The journey was horrendous, very slow, very windy, very winding and with uneven road surfaces. We could not find the house in the dark and finally arrived at 21.15 hrs. It was very embarrassing and frustrating to arrive so late and to keep all the other Guests waiting for so long. A Spiritual discussion took place and a pleasant evening ensued. Helana could not sleep, and prayers and healing were requested by Spirit, for the nephew, son, family and relatives of the Host.

14.38 The following Day we visited the Town, the Cathedral, and the pub in the centre...There was a strong Spiritual feeling in the Cathedral *(the Priest was unlocking the padlocks as we arrived and allowed us in for a few minutes),*

I broke down crying in the pub...Helana passed-out near the Priory, and was strongly affected by the sight of the tower....we are told that I was St Brigid and Helana was my mother....the stressful journey was indicative of that made by Brigid when she established her Priory and Hospital (544-601 AD)...Helana was later to become the Head of the Priory in 1206...the Tower was a refuge from attacks by Danes, and was used on numerous occasions.

14.39 Helana delivers the following message from GOD:
'John and You, Helana, have different roles to fulfil,
which will take you along different Pathways, you will
often be apart by many miles, but you will come together
at the End...
Be careful John, still your Mind, to ensure your
messages are correct. Slow down and concentrate on the
moment...allow yourself, to grow slowly and steadily
with understanding. Things do not happen quickly, as in
Nature it takes time for things to happen. Helana has
been brought to you, to bring to you the lessons
necessary to allow your understanding to grow and to
continue...All the knowledge that was to be given is now
near an end. Helana is to concentrate upon Nature and
the children of the World...
You, John, are to set-up the Church, to bring together
the Souls of the Past, and to prepare the World for the
coming of the Messiah. Your Pathways were chosen in
Spirit. It is hoped, and it is given. You John, have the
freedom to achieve what is necessary for you. It is
necessary also for Helana to have her freedom, to enable
her to achieve her needs.'

KEYPOINTS N12
a) As we Grow individually, so the Circles of People
around us grow, so their Circles grow, so these Circles
collectively, will encompass the World in PEACE, in
LOVE, in PURITY.
b) NATURE does not rush, it takes time for changes to
occur.
c) A still Mind is essential for clarity of messages.
d) Freedom is necessary for individual Goals to be
achieved.
e) Our Pathways are pre-chosen in Spirit before we are
born.
f) The amount of Knowledge we need to assimilate is known
and regulated.

14.40 We are affected by Spirits, following a visit to Dundonald, County
Down...I am told that the visit to Dundonald was necessary to heal
many Spirits from the Past.
'You John, were on this spot as aide to King John. You were John de
Quincy, the arduous journey from England, and previous Battle injuries,
had sapped your strength; you chose to remain here at Carrickfergus,
you lived at the Castle, with Helana as your bride and lived out a lifetime
in Ireland. This was a happy time for you, your children and your family.
You needed to visit the Motte to collect your Aura, and so prepare
yourself for your future Role.'

14.41 I wish to draw your attention to the interview with Uri Geller, by Boris Johnson, printed in the Daily Telegraph on November 16th, 1998.

14.42 My left bicep is in severe pain, I am told this is given by High Spirit so that I will understand the level of pain which I have given to Others in my lifetimes. ' It will persist until you have managed to understand, and to heal the many situations you have created and which have caused others to suffer'

14.43 On the morning of Thursday, 19th November, we wake-up to the sound of a huge Hornet in the bedroom., this is most surprising as the door and window are closed.!...
Ahizar writes.. ' Good morning John, you appreciate at last my friend, the Disciples are coming together, the fight of Good against Evil is coming together...the change in the Earth's History is about to commence, with the preparations for the Messiah, and the Education of the Churches. Your efforts to show the way, and to teach the World the Truth, are coming together, and are about to begin...
The Hornet is to make you aware of the dangers ahead...Do not underestimate the forces which will be reigned against you.
The Establishment with all their pre-conceived ideas. Man's pride and importance for himself.!!...All is as it should be.....All is progressing well...Tackle each moment as it arises...your Understanding is growing, and your Commitment is seen and applauded........Go in peace'

14.44 My left arm and right groin are in pain...I ask the cause and am told 'You are under attack from a dark Spirit, the man Robert who you met recently, his Spirit remembers the time 450 years ago, when you fought with him and ended his life.. The fight was with swords and he lost his left arm and his right leg..To rid yourself of this discomfort and this Spirit say the words as given.'
KEYPOINT N13
The Spirit never forgets, and in many Situations, bodily pain and discomfort may be caused by Spirits from previous lives, who still harbour grudges from previous Experiences.   Use the words given to protect yourself, but also try to heal the situation by saying prayers of reconciliation, and sending Love to the 'injured' Party.

14.45 My left Arm is frequently in discomfort when I awake, I ask my Guide for the reason for this, and Ahizar responds.... ' Helana suffers from a neck irritation, a rash. Her reaction to the Tower at Kildaire was in part because you had her beheaded when you were Henry VIII. She fears the Tower where she was imprisoned prior to her execution You must ask forgiveness from her Spirit.' .... I give healing to Helana.

14.46 I am asked to travel to Carrickfergus to meet with the man Bob, but I seek further confirmation as I have twice already waited in vain... I am told that Helana's son Steven is playing games. He is causing me pain and wishes for me to be away from the house....He and Helana were husband and wife in a previous lifetime (1600's)....
He is very possessive and has not yet learnt to come to terms with this situation, he resents his mother leaving him in this lifetime, as she was forced to do then because of his restrictive ways.'

KEYPOINT N14
All is returned; the Cycle of Learning is not broken unless Understanding is gained, and our Attitudes and Actions are changed.

14.47 On waking, I remember visions of Gardens, and ask why these were given...
' You travelled John in your sleep to these places, you were very busy and that is why you feel tired, there you met with.....Judith, Constance, Elsa, Thomas, Steven, Bredon, Pelopimus, Brian.etc...I ask who were some of these people?

- Thomas was from the 13th century, you ruined his life by destroying his home.
- Steven is the son who was married to Helana and is jealous of you.
- Bredon was a Welsh labourer who you crossed in a Land deal
- Pelopimus you killed in anger
- Brian was your son who you left to go to war, and he never forgave you.

14.48 That evening in bed Helana is suddenly suffering from a pain in her chest, I am told that it is the Spirit of Albert, her human father from the time of Jack, he seeks forgiveness for his past Actions, and asks what he can do now to make amends. To show Helana that he has truly changed his ways and become a loving, considerate and caring person. We reflect, and I suggest that he works for five years, to bring comfort to those who have suffered a similar plight to that which he originally inflicted on Helana and Jack. Albert accepts this penance and thanks us for our Compassion....he then writes ' John, I wish you well in your endeavours, look after this very special lady for me. You both have my blessing, and hopes that you will find happiness and love together, and that you will be able to bring this to other Peoples in the World.
 Farewell and God bless'

14.49 My father Ted writes: ' Hallo son, I come with love and good wishes. Do not be too impatient, these are formative times, you still need to find your feet, and to establish your base.
We see a move forwards in the New Year, when members of your Group will have come together and your action Group will be operational.
There is so much good that you can do...'

'Often the purpose of a meeting will not be obvious until later. Allow all contacts to be. Apply yourself to the learning and to the exploration, and all will come about. Helana will start her Clock business, and this will bring the contacts she seeks and the involvement she needs. She should also contact the Associations she chooses; this will give more purpose to her life. Allow your lives to flow....good luck!'

14.50 It is Saturday, 21st November, my Guide Ahizar writes:..' Allow your pen to flow my friend. We wish to bring you the news that Helana is well, and that your relationship is safe. You worry so much...she will be more content when her Contacts are established and her Business is underway....It will be better for you to sit and to listen rather than to write; it all takes time, your Spirit and your Mind are learning...
Do not despair, all will come. Do not panic, you have time....
Tomorrow visit the Castle at Carrickfergus, walk around the Walls, this is necessary for both of you to collect your Auras..... Many new Contacts are to be established next week, do not tell of your purpose...You are to visit England alone, Helana has work to do in Ireland, and you will find your time with Judith stimulating, and it will develop your Awareness.'

14.51 'We wish to say that many thanks are being offered at this time for the work that you have done John, to help you to achieve your Awareness... Many steps forward will now take place. The chosen Paths for each of you are quite separate. The work each of you will be doing to achieve Peace in this Land will be quite different. Your work John is more physical, with Spiritual content, to enable the People to come together as the one Church of GOD, as that is who the Church belongs to, we are all one Church, one GOD...'
KEYPOINT N15
There is only ONE GOD, and all his Ministry is but ONE CHURCH.

14.52 'The Work to be achieved by the Spirit of Helana is one of a great kind, which not everyone will understand...She heals many hearts from within, sifting through the burdens of many Peoples throughout the World, the Universe, and those in Spirit.........
There is a great debate with Helana's Spirit, for the work is difficult for the human Mind to perceive, and Helana finds it difficult to conceive that what has been given can be achieved. These problems and many others arising will be resolved in time. The wishes of Spirit are for this work to continue. We say and ask of you John, that your Mind is at peace. Do not pry John, for this adds extra burden to her Spirit. She would not harm anyone, the secrets kept are for your protection! She sees the hurt and pain which would result from this Knowledge.'

14.53 'All will be revealed at a future Time, when your Awareness is sufficient, now is not the time to pry.. Trust, have faith and allow us to guide you accordingly. Your work will be difficult, hard and demanding, and will take you apart at certain times. Your work for Spirit in England, John, is of great importance for the Universe, there is much for you to learn still.....The History of the Past is coming to Light, it may not be as it seems to be, but believe and trust that healing has and does take place, there are many understandings to gain.... Be of an open Mind, strong and courageous as your Spirit has been...Transfer these energies into loving and gentle ways...Allow the power of Spirit to pass through the power of Vengeance....Allow the Understanding deep within to rise to the surface.....The pains of the Past are present within Helana's feet, they are painful...remember these feet have travelled many miles...such strength and courage has not been seen for many, many, long years... We are truly amazed at the courage and determination to bring Light to those on the Earth-Plane, and in Spirit'.

KEYPOINT N16
The TRUTH of the HISTORY of the PAST has yet to be told.

14.54 ' The Animal Kingdom wish to send their heartfelt thanks to Helana's Spirit for her thoughts and love.'

KEYPOINTS N17
a) Animal Life is also affected by Love and the power of Thought.
b) Animals have a Spirit Existence and Spirit after-life, as do Humans.

14.55 'You John, are not aware of the true Light that emanates from Helana's Spirit, her ways are beautiful, she has been captured by the Darkness of those around her. Allow her now to fly. She needs to do this to achieve her Work. Allow her, her Freedom. Do not cage her, you John, your Mind alone, has now begun to understand and it is appreciated. You must now teach your Spirit, so that it also gives Helana her freedom. You still cause pain to her Spirit through your possessive ways.
UNDERSTAND completely what freedom means, this will enable your own Spirit to grow accordingly.. you are not even aware of your Spirit leaving your Body, believe this to be true.....Allow your Mind to ponder on what FREEDOM really is. We bring this message in the hope that you will listen and understand fully, for we wish you to progress fully and completely...The lessons given of your children should enable you to move forwards, Completely free of jealousy and possessive ways.'

14.56 On Sunday, 22nd November, I receive the following message via Helana, in trance, from White Eagle.... 'Helana has given so much, and sacrificed so much, neither your Mind, nor your Spirit understand this'.

'It is necessary now to move you along your chosen Pathways....
FORWARD CHRISTIAN SOLDIERS, United in what you do, and what you
say...
I have no greatness around me, only my Wisdom and my Knowledge. I
come to bring you this message, clearly, visibly, so that you will
understand the truth that is to be given...I may not say clearly, in
graphic detail what is Black and what is White. You have the Mind to
understand, your Spirit needs to be awakened to do the work....You
need to find yourself within John, to gain the Understanding, in this way
your Spirit will grow again to the wonderful Spirit which we see buried
in the depths of the Earth...
So much has been gained by you with Helana, but so much has been
lost! We cannot allow this to continue. Helana is needed in this Land to
bring love to the hearts of Many.'

14.57 'It is time for you John to move on.... You have been given the
best of her knowledge, you have seen the tears. She cries for Trees,
Animals etc..she cradles the World like a baby, but her own heart is
deprived. How can she heal the World when her own heart is torn apart?
Many lessons have been learned in your time together.
The love will not end, it will not be forgotten. It has healed the very
heart that lies within. We cannot say how much has been given, but
believe John, you have had the love of many from one....We cannot say,
at this time, what is to be...but it will be given in your sleep, for your
Spirit to understand, and hopefully to leave this child in peace.. You do
not understand how the Spirit within can behave differently to the
Human Being.
Helana will not remember this message...If only you could lift up your
Spirit...there is a wealth of Knowledge to be shared with the World...
You have been given so much Knowledge; the vision of this child, her
very nature, is all that you needed to see, as to what is needed in your
daily life..
We do not give up hope, we need you to work for Spirit, we need your
Strength and Character, we need the Gentleness, the Understanding, the
Listening, to fulfil that which you can achieve in this lifetime. We are
lost for words as to what to say to help you to understand fully what is
being said. .Look at the pattern of your life...the Journey's travelled, this
will give some Understanding'.

14.58 'All is as It should be, All will continue. Rest your head tonight,
Knowledge and Understanding will be given. We can do no more, we
hope and pray you will understand fully and allow your Spirit to be free.
Have peace in your heart, that all is as it should be, always.' Reach out
for the Light John. Be free, do not allow these human Feelings to hold
you back. Put together the lessons of the past few days in your Mind, so
that your Spirit will understand. You are as two Minds!, allow your Mind
to teach your Spirit.'

316

KEYPOINT N18
All our Life is planned, All is arranged by High Spirit.
(I did not fully grasp at the time, the significance of this message, or the implications. The problem quite simply was that it subsequently took me 18 months to get around to re-reading this message, by which time of course all was History! When you are living in a situation and hoping that all can be healed so long as you apply yourself enough, then your Mind deals with and copes with the daily emotional interaction, and the pressures of life are sufficient to pre-occupy yourself....This message implies that Helana and I were brought together simply for me to achieve the level of Understanding and Spiritual Awareness necessary, Spirit have decided that my rate of progress has been insufficient, Helana's Spirit is unhappy, I can learn no more from her, so I am being told that THE END is nigh!, Emotions, and human Feelings, do not seem to matter, do they?)

14.59 Isaiah brings these words:... ' I am old and frail, I have not the voice to use through this child, the hands are knarred with age, I cannot speak through Helana in the way that I would wish to.....these words are from an old friend and Spirit who has come to help you....Do not hang onto the old Ways. Let go and move forwards... Look back if you wish to gain the Understanding. .Ask questions if you wish,..'

14.60 'I do not wish to frighten or cause you pain, but **this work is very important**. Your Spirit will also gain healing from this work...The work done by Helana for your Spirit is almost at an end.....the rest is for you to learn and to understand yourself....
We offer Helana the greatest of thanks, for without her help, completed with a greatness of Compassion and Love, this work for Spirit could not have been achieved... I grow weak, it is time to leave this Earth-Plane, this saddened Land. How our hearts reach out with love for this child, for she brings such light to this Land...So long have we waited for this Time, at last it has arrived and we can begin to see the lightness transform this Land into beauty...
The mere presence of Helana makes this possible, her love is so great. Do not at any time begin to feel there is no love for your Spirit... You will learn. One day it will all be revealed. We respect Helana's wishes for the sacrifice she has made for your Spirit to grow. Sacrifices must be made for the work to be achieved, it is necessary to lose before there can be a gain...Helana will not remember this message'
(It seems that Helana has chosen not to continue to live with me)
KEYPOINTS N19
a) It is necessary to Sacrifice in order for progress to be made. We must choose to walk away, to give of ourselves, of our Love, of our Time, in order that we can grasp the new Lesson, the new Experience, the new Opportunity, and in so doing our Spirit will grow in Understanding.

b) Our memories can be 'blanked-out' by Spirit, should this be necessary.

14.61 It is Monday, 23rd November, I ask of my Guide Ahizar a series of questions:

Question(a) Help me please, what has been given to my Spirit last night?....
'John, tonight you have been told of the work ahead, which is necessary to achieve, and what you need to do **now** to achieve the Awareness that is necessary. You have already been told that Helana can do no more for you In a Spiritual way...for this reason a distance has been created between you, to protect her and the Work which she must do in other areas.
It does not mean that your Relationship is at an end, it simply means that future development at a Human level is on hold until your Awareness has reached that of Helana, you can then both progress together at that stage if you so choose.
Helana must now go her own way Spiritually, and so must you. Your Spirit is now alone, for her's has withdrawn and this is the emptiness which you feel. You must now search within for your Answers you need, and her Spirit can now move on without you to fulfil the work which **she needs to achieve**... All is as it should be... You can now both choose your directions in both Human and Spiritual terms...Helana has brought you to this level of Understanding and Awareness, as Constance started to do.

Question (b) What should I do now?...
'Continue as before to increase your Awareness and to follow your own Path.
You have the Circle to form, The Church to form, Your Awareness to gain, Your Life to live.'

Question(c) How will this interact with Helana?...
'That is for her and you to decide your Futures, as you wish it to be.'

Question(d) Has the special Bond between Helana and me been broken?.....
You still have the 'golden Bond' between you, this will remain. Your Spiritual Bond must now develop as your Awareness develops, you can still achieve this.'

Question(e) Who fulfils the need in Helana's Spirit?.......
'Philip(Jack) does, when Helana chose to help you, Philip's Spirit left Helana and he had his freedom, a lesson for him... Helana and his Spirit will always be together.....'

318

'Compare this situation to that of the divide in Ireland, a healing is necessary, between Hearts and Minds...

A healing of hearts has taken place between Helana and you John, this is now achieved, and it is time for you both to move on!...A healing of hearts is now necessary between Helana and Philip, this needs to take place before Helana can help to heal Ireland.' Ireland is the 'Heart of the World'...the heart needs to be healed before the Body can be healed.' This must be viewed in the context that Helana has the Holy Ghost within, the power of GOD, your Spirits are healing the Spirits of Peoples throughout the World whilst you sleep,...You continue to have a very strong Bond which is of immense power because of the combination of your Spirits'

KEYPOINTS N20

a) **The Spiritual Gain is the all powerful intent. Situations, Relationships, Events, All are brought together to allow for Healing and Understanding to take place. Into this fabric are placed people with Personalities, Emotions, Desires, and free-will Choices. Superimpose strong Minds, and strong Spirits, and you have a recipe for...LEARNING. But, Learning is difficult if you are blind! Blind to Spirit, Bigoted, Unreceptive, conditioned by Religion, your Environment and Relatives.**

b) **Emotions take a secondary consideration to Spiritual needs.**

c) **Attitudes, Thoughts, Feelings, are all influenced by higher Spirits who guide us through the lessons we need to experience, but , we are also influenced by all those Spirits around us, many of whom wish us not to succeed, either individually, because of their own selfish or jealous reasons, or because they collectively wish for Darkness and Evil to succeed over Light and Love.**

Question(f) Is there a hidden Agenda here?.....
' You are learning fast my friend. We will bring you information in your sleep, all is as it should be.'

14.62 'John, a useful discussion. Listen to the words given. Do not be despondent, your Relationship will resolve itself to your satisfaction. It was necessary for the air to be cleared and the words to be spoken. We will help you as much as we can.

Helana's Spirit is still bruised, and this will take many weeks to heal, these matters cannot be rushed. Your love will come together in a true way, and her warmth for you will return. Your Spiritual Growth is also something her Spirit has to come to terms with, this she is sorting out in her own Mind now...

(It was said many months ago that Helana would be my Teacher, but then as I progressed the Roles would reverse, and I would then become her Teacher)

14.63 'She is uncertain of her own Mind. The Spirit of Jack (Philip) is very persistent and for a time will dominate her. But she is a human Being, with human Emotions, and this is all part of her Understanding, and of her learning, and her acceptance of being a human Being. She cannot live in a Spirit World whilst on the Earth-Plane, hopefully she will realise this before it is too late.

Lead your life John, follow your Pathway, we feel your pain and unhappiness, Helana is still at home waiting for you to return, go to her. Your time with Judith, and the others you meet this week; will develop your Awareness so that you can relate directly to the Issues at question. It will be easier then for you to answer questions directly. Wait until you return from England before these matters are raised again. Helana is shrewd, she has a good Mind and a good Spirit. Allow her to come to terms with, and to accept you, as you are to be. All will be revealed in the coming weeks and months.'

14.64 Ahizar writes:.. ' In each lifetime, Helana has sought Spiritual Love with the Spirit of Jack. In each lifetime this Goal has been thwarted by another person; not always you John. (eight are listed!) The whole purpose of Helana's life has been to mend this heart with Jack. The World and its History is torn by this wound. There is another chance in this lifetime for them to come together, for this Helana needs to return to England and to be 'available'. The healing could take days or years to achieve.

Her choices are:

- To return to Spirit
- To remain with you John ; so together you can complete the Work.
- To link with Judith and to so give Judith her freedom (as a Child-minder)
- To become a Nun
- To join with Philip (Jack)

14.65 'We agree with your thoughts John, you have no real choices at this time, it is down to Helana to decide'.

14.66 It is Thursday, 26th November, White Eagle writes through Helana...

' My dear man, these words will perhaps help you to understand the ways of Nature. I write for you this day in the hope that your pain and suffering may be eased. The words of a song so clear in the Mind of Helana is one from a revealing story of life on the Ocean Ship Titanic. The two lovers who met on board this vessel were briefly meant to be together for a short time only, their love was truly found. Pure, unconditional love was found for such a short time in the lives of these people.'

' But all love that can be found in the hearts of these People and many Others, matters not for the shortness ofTime it is held in their hearts. The Spirits live on my dear man.

The Spirits are free to travel to loved ones, as you are aware, at any time of the day or night, my dear, your Spirits can be together in love and friendship. Jealousy my dear man, has no place in the heart of Man, it causes pain and suffering of a deep kind. All love is shared; as you love, so do all of those around you, and they in turn love all who are around them, and so the ripples grow.

Your love has been found for the time needed. As the Spirits on the ocean waves, they are not apart to this day, their Love lives on my dear man.

The Song relates this so clearly, for you are aware of your father's Spirit when he chooses to visit you and to bring you love, healing and strength. So can you not then understand the love of Helana cannot ever end, for her Spirit has loved you so dearly over many lifetimes'.

14.67 'In each lifetime she has tried to show you the beautiful ways of Nature, but to no account. It is hoped that you will retain all that has been given by her Spirit, and her true ways, to help you continue in your Spiritual Awareness. All that can be given, has now been given, and time now is left for you to decide which way you wish to stay...in the life of beauty, or hidden underground. The choice is yours my dear Man. Do you not see Helana's life is like that of a child, the child is a gift from GOD, the child is then released and given to the World and its Peoples, to bring love to their own lives.

In giving the child in this way, you are healing and giving love to the World. As you give you receive. To release the child in this way, it is as GOD gave to you, you give in return and so the love goes on. We bring to you this understanding my dear Man, in the hope that your heart will understand and be healed. You will not be apart, for the hearts do indeed live on always. It is only the Bodies, the physical my dear Man which are apart. Do not we ask be so upset, for you have, and will continue to love in the truest way. You are, do not forget, Spiritual Beings on Earth.'

KEYPOINTS N21
a) **Spiritual Love never dies, once achieved.**
b) **The duration of the physical time, when Love has been achieved, that you remain together on the Earth-Plane, is not significant to Spirit.**

14.68 I light the open fire in the lounge for the first time at 17.00 hrs, I am asked to record that the ' Home fire was lit' ...the fire creates a lovely warm atmosphere in the room.

14.69 I ask about the healing of the Past, and am told that reconciliation has occurred with
- Pope Alexander (as Henry V111)
- Sir Propter Hugo (as King Arthur)
- Terry Hoyles (as Abel, Aaron, Caesar, Cromwell)
- Baron Ferdinand Rothschild
- Emily Pankhurst
- King Louis of France
- Jack (as Richard,etc)
- Theodorus (killed at Ephesus)
- Thomas More
- King Charles Stuart
- All of Henry VIII's Wives

Your Spirits came together in true love, all was healed, and you were then able to work together to heal many Others from the Past.
Some excellent work and some momentous occasions.

14.70 On Saturday, 28th, my Guide Ahizar writes....' Helana is going through a very emotional stage, you will need to 'humour her' for the next 48 hours. Her condition is a function of the disharmony she has met with when she returned to her Planet of Origin, and also she became aware of the problems on other Planets...She needs this time to come to terms with her own nature and with her own free-will....
She is looking for every reason **not** to commit to you. Other negative Spirits remind her of your past Actions which caused her distress. There is no new situation here, it is simply the need for her to come to terms with the Past, to put it all behind 'the Door', and to embrace the future. In this way all will be achieved.'

14.71 'We wish to bring you the news that your mission to your Planet of Origin, Zypron, has been successful, and that reconciliation has taken place between the Factions there. Your Spirit will remain to oversee the Peace effort.....
' Your Awareness will now progress as Helana's does. The barriers are now lifted, we foresee her wish to stay with you, and to build the family unit. This will be quickly followed by your ability to communicate directly with her.('telepathy', but 'mind to mind' at all times)' .....
The sadness will soon pass and you will be reconciled in a complete way....The vacuum in your Spirit has been filled by that of Jack, in this way complete healing will take place for all three Spirits, his presence will bring an added gentleness to your manner which Helana needs.
KEYPOINTS N22
a) The Spirits of some Humans can and do travel to other Planets, and can act to cause Harmony or restore Peace.
b) All is not necessarily harmonious on other Planets

c) Some Spirits even exist in 'different Dimensions' on a more permanent basis.

14.72 I wish now to say to All, that we have TIME in which to correct the negative AURA emanating from the EARTH. There is no need for panic or overdue concern, however:

KEYPOINTS N23

a) IT IS NECESSARY TO CHANGE OUR ATTITUDES TO EACH OTHER AND TO GOD'S CREATION. The Excesses, the Evil, the Greed, the Lack of Compassion, the Torture, the needless Suffering, the Starvation, the Wars, the Bigotry, the Destruction, the Materialistic Selfishness which has so marked the 'Progress' of Humans in the 20th Century, WILL NOT BE ALLOWED TO CONTINUE.

b) We have the time available to us to avoid Destruction, and to secure the future of the Earth and its Creation. The survival of ALL Species are dependent upon our Actions.

14.73 I say to All, that they only need to look at our History to see that GOD and Nature will respond if the BALANCE and HARMONY is threatened.

KEYPOINT N24

a) The Times of Plagues, Floods, Earthquakes and Devastation of Humans will return unless WE, and I mean YOU the Reader, and Peoples of similar lighter Spirit start to CAUSE A CHANGE.

b) It is no longer acceptable to sit and do nothing. The passive action of the Multitudes has allowed the few Extremists, and darker Souls, to gain control, to gain power, to change our Society.

c) GET OFF THE FENCE, BELIEVE THESE WORDS, WE ALL WANT A BETTER FUTURE, WE ALL WANT AN EARTH for our children to inherit. IT IS YOUR ACTIONS AND YOUR ATTITUDES NOW which will make the difference.

14.74 How much more Wealth would there to spend on worthwhile Projects to promote Happiness, Recreation, Health, Enjoyment and Education, if the State did not need to spend so much on fighting drugs and theft and all related Crimes in our Cities, Towns and Streets?
How much more Capital to achieve Wealth would there be, if Resources were not controlled by the Few, to the detriment of the Many.
Can we not All help one other today? and every other day.?
To cause Others to smile, to cause them to feel that we care. How many Atrocities could have been avoided, if the hand of Friendship had been extended to a few lonely people?.

14.75 'The Lady Constance comes to learn and to understand, this is her last chance to change her nature. If she does not change, then she will be 'contained', she is aware of this. Tomorrow we wish you to visit the Church at Grey-Abbey, and follow this with a stop in the Park, this will give great strength to Helana.'....

' John, I am sorry, I was wrong to hurt you the way I did, I realise now too late. They say you always hurt the one you love. We had some good, great times together, I will cherish them always. My life is a mess, I realise this but it is not easy to extricate myself. I wish to change my ways and come with love. Please help me; I am sorry for the pain I cause, it does not seem like me. If Helana will talk with me I am certain all our rivalry, and the jealousy which I feel can be healed. Please talk to her.. Constance'.

(Helana and I visited the Abbey at Grey-Friars on the Sunday, I am told that when I was John-de-Courcy, my wife was Constance, at that time she was the daughter of the King of the Isle of Man and was saved from a dangerous Sea crossing; to thank GOD she commissioned the building of the Abbey, and I probably paid for it !)

KEYPOINTS N25

A Soul, (Spirit), can be contained when all attempts to teach the ways of Light and Love have failed.

a) God never gives up on any Soul, but sometimes it is necessary to restrict the freedom of a Spirit to prevent further Evil and Chaos, until their attitude has changed sufficiently for them to not be so disruptive.

b) This happens when a Spirit is taken to 'Hell' or 'Shadowlands', they are unable to interfere and communicate in the same way.

c) A few Higher Spirits work to rescue these Souls and return them to the Light, this is why Helana is treated with such praise, for she is a rescued Soul, and High Spirit wish to create an Environment to keep her in the Light.

d) Against this, many of her 'friends' and contacts from the Past, work to 'turn her' back to her Darker ways. Truly a battle of Good against Evil, pitched within the Mind of this one Soul.

e) The added significance of this struggle, is that Helana has been chosen to help the cause of Light and Love, and the fact that she was one of the original Characters in Genesis means that the lightening of her Spirit will affect all the Generations since.

14.76 At 04.45am.on Friday, 27th November, this message was received from Judith's Spirit

'It is not necessary to live in, or to remember the Past. I am here to deliver a message, you may not be pleased to hear these words, but they need to be said ready for the meeting with Judith.

(I am intending to return to England at the Weekend).......

'I am not of the true kind that you are used to, but I am one of a true kind in friendship and love for Helana, she is a dear friend who I love dearly as my own child.

The pains in Helana's feet represent the Past and are extremely painful to her. You John, do not realise how much pain she suffers in silence.. On many occasions I am with her in Thought and Presence, and I can see clearly a situation developing. There is so much she does not share with you.

My dear man, friend, John, you may not think I am always a friend, for I know at times the words are hurtful.....but they are necessary for you to Grow so that you can be a useful servant to GOD. You have been in the Past, and it can come again.'

'You shared a life with Helana, so precious and loving. It can be again, but perhaps not in the way imagined. A different role is now intended, we will speak of this at a future occasion....It is hoped that **We** will be together in the future to heal the hearts of Many.'

'It is Judith who speaks, I may appear within the house on a future occasion, it has been given that I will do so....I am not used to this method of Communication, but White Eagle is with me and telling me that I do very well!'....

(This message foretells of changes in the Future, somewhat Ambiguous, and also hints at the use of 'transportation')

14.77 I am told that half of my Spirit is needed to be on my Planet of Origin, Zypron; my Spirit is divided, and half is to be replaced by another Spirit and will be allowed to grow.

14.78 Later on Friday I ask the question of my Guide.... What was achieved overnight in my sleeping hours?
' Your Spirit came together with Helana's in a true way, wiping out the years between Biblical Times and now. The Past has been healed in a true way, and you can now continue together in the pure love that was needed to be achieved. You feel now John the presence of Helana's Spirit within, and likewise her with you. All is as it should be....

Helana's heart has been healed by the work done by her with Jack's Spirit, there is no need now for them to be physically together to achieve this. At a future time this may happen, but not now, the timing is wrong....

The Future can now be assured. You still both have your Choices, these must be made by December 8th, you can still change Events if you wish to, or you can choose to continue with the Work together.'

*(these **Choices** have been a feature at regular Stages throughout our relationship; eventually, both Helana and Judith recommend that **I do not continue with the work in this lifetime**)*

14.79 Question to my Guide Ahizar: ' When were the records of Jesus's life and words written? How was Man able to recall these words?....
'An account of Jesus's life was recorded by you, John, and other Scribes at that time. The 'final' version of the Bible was assembled from these Records many years later. A lot has been lost, and a lot is still to be found. You, John, were instrumental in Assembling, Cataloging and the protecting of these documents.

KEYPOINTS N26

a) Accuracy and true meaning are sometimes lost when Man's Mind 'flicks-in'.

b) I am asked to organise a Trip, in order to un-earth the Books and Scrolls which I had hidden in an earlier lifetime. The original documents of the Bible STILL EXIST. In the Centuries since, I am told that certain alterations have been made, which have changed the meaning of some passages. Only by reverting to the original Text can the true meaning be found. I will be told of the location when the Time is right.

14.80 On Saturday, 28th November, I decide to write to my family to try to explain my actions. I reproduce this letter in full:..

Dearest Mum and Family,

It is unusual for me to write to you, but I fear that you will not listen to my words, but you can if you choose to re-read my letter and think on what I say. You probably wonder what changes have occurred to me in 1998, and where they are all leading me to. Do not worry about me, for the first time in my life I have direction and I have a task to perform. That task is for GOD and Humanity, and for the future of the World. I do not expect you now to understand, but you will in future years, and when you return to Spirit.

We are all Spirit. Spirit is life, everything which is alive has a Spirit. A Spirit cannot die. When your Body dies, your Spirit will be led to Heaven where you will meet with all those family and friends who choose to greet you.

Your Spirit will be taught, and then in due course of time you can choose to return to the Earth for another life.

The purpose is for your Spiritual Awareness to increase; for if you like, your Mind to increase its Spirituality. If you think of your Spirit as pure Good and Love, and your Mind as Bad and Evil, the objective is for the Mind to learn the ways of the Spirit. When this is achieved, pure Love in all its forms, then you remain in Heaven.

Think of the Earth as a giant classroom, we are all at School. You cannot play truant, you are always at School (life).

The School is run by teachers (Guides), who have enormous power. They can inflict enormous pain and suffering if you misbehave.

326

They offer love and friendship but you can choose to ignore them (human free-will), you can choose to be Bad and Evil....jealousy, greed, murder, ill-will, hate etc.

You can choose to love and worship another GOD....the Devil, Baal etc. You can choose to be insolent, to sit in the corner of the class and to ignore what you are taught. What then happens? You are punished! You are punished with pain and suffering, and eventually the Teachers take you away to another School,(Heaven), where you will be taught again.

If you still do not learn then, you will have to go back to the lower Class again (Earth) and start again....the same lessons, the same teacher, until you learn the Lesson. So, what is the lesson?...the lesson is Spiritual Awareness, an Awareness of Love and Goodness. The need to accept GOD and accept his ways and to raise your Spiritual Awareness. This may all sound far-fetched, but it is real and you have no choice to get-off. Your only choice is to accept or you will suffer. Suffering can take many forms: illness, disease, arthritis, sciatica, loneliness...each one tailored to your individual need, or a reaction to your individual attitude of Mind. Change your attitude, you remove the illness or infliction or pain. It is simple, but the lessons are so hard. (the lessons can also be inflicted by other humans for their own selfish reasons, or be chosen by you in Heaven, ie. a Carer who has actually caused their Partner to lose their mobility through their own possessive nature.) Believe me Mum, I do not wish to hear of you suffering. I firmly believe that if you become receptive to spiritual ways...to GOD, read the Books I will give to you, then your suffering will ease and you will live a longer, more pleasant, happier Life.

Ted regrets now his rejection of Spiritual ways.

I have no wish to frighten you, but knowing and understanding what I know now, it would be criminal for me not to make you aware of the nature of CAUSE and EFFECT which govern the World
Written with much Love and Hope.
Your Son, Brother and Father

DENNIS (JOHN)

(The concept of thinking of the Goal as for the Mind to learn is not completely true, but I wished to express myself as simply as I could. The true purpose is for the SPIRIT and SOUL to learn from the MIND. The Soul comes for Learning and Understanding so that it can progress towards the one True Spirit.)

327

14.81 In the next few Days, Helana receives several long messages and long dreams from her Guides, the text is specific to her and she wrote some 3,000 words, I will extract only.... ' no more is expected of you....you can walk away....you have given your all....all has been taken without the understanding of your true needs.....there can be no more taking, it is a time for receiving......he (John) takes all, he so drains your energies, **he leaves very little for the child** within....it cannot be expected for you to have a life with another, when your Heart is with Philip...we will do everything to make this possible.'

(It would seem from this Text that her own Guide was helping to persuade her to walk out on me, once again the dice seem to be loaded against our Relationship succeeding. I found this text two years later)

14.82 White Eagle writes, and thisText is also greatly reduced:...
'The pains within Helana's arms, feet and body are felt like needles protruding into her very life....we remind you again that **'Love can only be found in Freedom'**.
Lose your selfish ways, allow her her freedom, and love will blossom like the flowers on a tree in May. Do you not see the disease which is so often in our Garden of Eden, appearing on the leaves from all the pain and sorrow harboured by the Minds of many around them.
Beauty is being strangled by possessive and selfish needs. Do not be selfish in your ways, for the World is in need. Count your blessings my dear Man, for Others may not get this chance....you cannot own a person or love....All is shared in Spirit....she has given her all, almost her life. The help given must now end, for the sap of this beautiful tree is in need of replenishing with the love that is intended.'
'All situations given in life are given for your Spiritual understanding... We bring to you all the hurdles you must face, so that you can knock them down one-by-one, and so be able to walk away freely with no obstacles in your way.'

14.83 Helana's Guide writes.... 'The Spirit of Constance will do no harm to the Relationship between you and Philip....always it was hoped Helana would succeed in finding the lighter ways....it is now hoped the rest of what is to be, can take place successfully, without too much pain and suffering to John.'

14.84 On 30th November, my Guide Ahizar writes in response to my questions:....
'Helana will choose to return to England and to live in her mother's Bungalow. She will choose to try to reconcile with Philip. This will not be successful and she will end up living a lonely life devoted to the local Church....We see this happening in February 1999.
She is choosing a solitary life unless she changes her attitude.
We share your apprehension. All the good work of the past years, will be lost unless Helana pulls around.'

'She blames you, but your Spirit is committed to her, and it is her Spirit which will not allow in the closeness.
It is the power-play within her Mind, her dark-side fights for supremacy, she is being influenced by Dark Spirits, she is open to all and her Spirit is at risk...Evil seeks to overthrow Good.....She is giving nothing to you John, there is no 'give and take', it is all a cosmetic Appearance.'

14.85 'Judith will join you with her child from England in June 99, you will progress the Work together, the Church will be formed, the Book will be written, All will be achieved'

14.86 'The man Bob will choose to remain with his wife and Family, He was the Executioner at the time of Henry VIII, Judith was Anne of Cleeves.
' The die is cast my friend, a time of decision approaches for each of you to choose your way forwards...All is possible, All is and can be..... Choose carefully, for once chosen the die will land and set in motion the Events to achieve your chosen Pathway... World Events dictate that choices need to be taken before Christmas, all lives are interwoven and what One decides will affect the Others....
Take heart that you have reached the level of Awareness to allow you to choose, few are able to do this.
We will set out your Goals and then the choices which are possible to achieve these Goals.'
KEYPOINTS N27
a) All our lives are interwoven, a decision by any One will have repercussions for Others, particularly those in your Peer-Group.
b) It is possible to influence and to choose our Pathways, the direction of our life is certainly affected by the choices we make and the opportunities we grasp or reject.
c) EVERY MEETING, EVERY RELATIONSHIP, EVERY SITUATION presented to us is there for a reason, to allow us to Ponder, to Choose, to Act, to Discover, to Reject or to Accept.
• WE THE INDIVIDUAL are responsible for the CHOICE,
• WE THE INDIVIDUAL are responsible for the OUTCOME,
• WE THE INDIVDIUAL cannot blame ANYONE ELSE.
d) The PAST has brought us to this point in time, the Past we cannot change, the FUTURE we Shape, we Mould, we Create through our ATTITUDES, through our THOUGHTS, through our DEEDS.

(Jesus was given the choice, his Destiny was chosen that he should be Crucified, but he was given the choice, as a Human he had free-will, he could have walked away, but then would his words and deeds be remembered to this day if he had?)

14.87 I have driven down from Stranraer on my own, taking the 22.00 hrs ferry from Belfast and arriving for a 14.00hrs appointment on the Monday in Enstone, Oxon.
I manage five business Appointments between Monday and Thursday night, 3rd,
(when I plan to return to Belfast via the 00.35 hrs ferry from Stranraer)

and referee an Oxford University College Rugby Union game on the afternoon of the 2nd December....
I remind you that I work in Financial Services and still need to earn a living. Being commission based, unless I make sales, then I will receive little income.).
It is an average seven hour car journey between Oxon and Stranraer in Scotland.

##

CHAPTER 15. Different Pathways

15.00 On Tuesday, 1st December, at 04.00hrs, Ahizar writes:
'Ponder on my friend, protect yourself, **APPROVE of yourself exactly as you are, Forget the Past, be positive, LOVE YOURSELF.**.......
You do well my friend, Helana has thought on your words and all is well; another lesson well learned, she has regained her composure, another Trial has been completed and your love has remained intact. It is time now to heal and to bring you both together in a completely loving way....
We do not wish to upset you or to cause concern, but it is necessary for you to appreciate the delicate balance of Helana's nature, which could lead her astray. Be on your guard John....she walks a stony Pathway, I hope she does not fall, for her ways are needed both by you and by Humanity in a human way. Helana has been asked to prepare two lists, one for her **EGO and one for her SPIRITUAL Life,** she has been asked to discuss these with you on your return.'

15.01 I ask of my Guide Ahizar...
Question (a) Is there any connection between Smoking and Illness?
' These people would develop a Critical Illness, **even if they did not smoke. Smoking provides a Scientific reason for natural Events. Smoking does not cause, it is merely a reaction to what would have happened anyway.**'
Question (b) Is there any **physical** reason for illness?
' No, the reason is Spiritual Thought.
Question (c) Is illness **given by Spirit?**
'Not so, **NATURE is the cause, SPIRIT can cause pain and suffering by triggering NATURE. Nature would react, but on a slower level or pace. All that Spirit do is to cause this effect more quickly for the reasons known.**

KEYPOINTS DP01
a) NATURE is a Power force,
b) All comes from GOD; All is normally in balance,
Mankind is part of that balance and part of Nature.
c) As we cause change, we create reaction, we create that effect; it is the way it is, the way it was created.
What we Give, we will eventually receive.
'Do unto Others as you would have them do unto you'
'Love thy Neighbour as thyself'...Do these quotes sound familiar?
d) High Spirit, the workers for GOD, can cause and trigger Events and Reactions, should this be necessary to counter the effects of Evil, and to restore the Balance and Harmony.
e) GOD can change NATURE, as has been evidenced in the BIBLE in past Times.

Question (d) Please clarify what are the Evil forces of Nature....

KEYPOINTS DP02
a) The EARTH itself is Living, it senses the Atmosphere
and Aura on its surface, and from the Sun and other
Planets.
b) The SPIRITS within and around, are the motive Forces
of Earth, Fire, Air, Water, the parameters of their
influence is NATURE.
c) Nature provides the balance between the other Forces.
All four Spirits feel the effects of Man about them,
they are in balance in Nature.
d) If any One or More of them is caused to Change, then
there is a Reaction from the Others...Take the Rain
Forests, they keep the balance in the Air, they feed the
Earth, they affect the Water balance. How will Nature
react?...

- **ICE changes to WATER, and more WATER when the**
  TEMPERATURE is too high
- **AIR changes to HURRICANES when the AIR is out of**
  balance.
- **EARTH provides QUAKES to restore the balance and**
  temperature, by obscuring the atmosphere from the
  SUN.
       ...The Good forces of Nature are Peace, Harmony, and
  Balance.
       ...The Evil forces of Nature will reek Havoc until
  the Balance is restored again.
- **The Volcano is cooled by Water and Wind and Earth; a**
  balance is needed; all is peaceful once an
  Equilibrium has been re-established.

Question (e) Please explain my Son's breathing difficulty.
Your son Brian is an intelligent, highly sensitive Spirit. The restriction on
his breathing has been caused by his brother Ford, who wishes him to
slow down his life. The problem will end as soon as he finds a new life
for himself, an operation is not necessary. Positive thought about his
own worth, and breathing exercises are all that is necessary.
(this was medically diagnosed as Asthma)

15.02 I meet with Judith on the 3rd December 1998, In trance with
High Spirit, Judith tells me that I have been accepted for the Role
intended, I will not now be replaced; I have been given the 'Light', and
are now welcomed as a **Son of GOD.**

Judith suggests that should I sit quietly and ask for 'blanket' Forgiveness from **all those Souls** from my previous lives; give to them Forgiveness, and offer to them Healing; then it will be possible to clear the Past **at this one point in Time,** and for me then to move forwards to a new Life and a new Understanding.

KEYPOINTS DP03
a) Man can be appointed as a Son of GOD; or Woman as a Daughter.
b) This honour is given to those who through their own Courage, Devotion, Commitment and Sacrifice are prepared to devote their life to GOD, to help to raise the Enlightenment of the Earth and its Peoples.
c) The work to be completed, and the Tasks chosen, are pre-agreed with High Spirit as those necessary for the cause of Light and Love to be advanced upon the Earth-Plane.

15.03 A new Guide is to be brought to me.
White Eagle writes; 'You, John, can now choose your own Way of becoming and being Spiritual. We expect all of our Helpers and all true Believers to walk the Earth as of the Earth, but never forgetting that within they carry and host a beautiful Spirit...   Do not be too flippant, especially as now your Commitment has been fully accepted by us. Spirituality should also be happy, for without laughter your World would be even Darker. All help will be given to assist with your Earthly happenings....It is beholden for you to ensure that within your Capabilities, that you do what you are asked to, to the best of your Abilities. Have faith that no Other can take the place that has been allocated to you.'

15.04 The Virgin Mary writes: ' John, our Son, go in Peace and Love, knowing that the Peace and Light, and all Love will surround you from now on...Allow your Eyes to look upon the World in a tender fashion, so that when you speak your message with your usual forcefulness; the tender look from your eyes will only serve to help those People understand in the way that is intended....
All is given for learning, but it is necessary also to show respect and Humanity to all of GOD's Creation. Those who choose to ignore the Harmony for their own selfish gain, will bring the wrath of GOD and Nature upon themselves, and upon those whom they profess to love... GOD is merciful.
GOD will allow them a further Opportunity to change their ways; this is reflected in your Eyes; whilst the Words may be hard and the Retribution severe, there is always Compassion and Hope '.

15.05 Ahizar writes: ' I wish only to bring congratulations; for it has been a pleasure to work with you. I stand aside for a new Guide to be brought....forgive my crackled voice'.

'It is a desire which every Spirit here have; that we may be given the opportunity to speak with our own voice. Only to find that when a Human on the Earth is happy to allow this, we discover we recognise not our voice, for it is so long since we have been given the opportunity to speak. I will say again, it has been a pleasure to work with you...I will remain watchful, and of course you may call me by name. I leave now with reluctance.'

15.06 I reach my home in Bangor, County Down, at 03.00 hrs on Friday, to a frosty reception by Helana....She then welcomes me, she relaxes, we make Love, and I am asked to record the words.
'FRIDAY, 4TH DECEMBER is RECONCILIATION DAY'

15.07 Later on Saturday, I receive writing from Daniel my new Guide:...
' Helana only has three realistic Choices now to make, she has rejected the option to become an Angel, and her wish to return to her Planet of Origin would be a futile gesture, the waste of a good Spirit and would result in her subsequent rejection again. This is One-upmanship and Pride. She feels her Spirit is tired of the turmoil on the Earth and the relationships are more than she can cope with.
She yearns for the quiet life and her Roots....
Her Choices are
(a)To co-operate, to live with you John, and to follow the original Plan.
(b)To return to England and to live with her Mother
(c)To choose the Spiritual Life as a 'Nun',....or
(d)To move on to Heaven.

We see no other Choices, you will have to tread carefully, we do not wish you to tell these words to Helana, unless she raises the subject. We hope that she will face reality and accept all that is offered. Time is short and unless she decides, she will be given no Choice.
The Events of the past weeks, have only served to confirm our inner thoughts, that nothing would be different.'

15.08 'Your Ears are cloaked by the Lady Constance, who tries to restrict your learning, she will not succeed.'

15.09 When I awake, around mid-day, I receive a message from my new Guide Daniel:
' My friend all is well, I wished you to be aware that your words have been received and accepted by ALL the SOULS concerned from your previous lives. Your progress can now proceed unimpaired, which is excellent news.'

' In the next few weeks Healing will take place and then you will be ready to move forwards. Be patient and do not forget to sit and to meditate whenever the moment is possible...
.My true name is Dangrethar, I am your new Guide, ' Daniel' is easier to say and is acceptable....
You will know me by my style of writing and by the pain in your right hand. I have worked with many people in the Past, and hope that we can have a satisfactory and friendly relationship. I came from Ethiopia and last lived on the Earth in 828AD. My life was spent as a King, but I was also a follower of Jesus and brought his beliefs to my People. We have met in Spirit and will do so later tonight. I wish you well and success in your life ahead.'

15.10 'I wish to say that the start with Helana is very encouraging, continue in this vein and resolve the Issues as they arise. The Anne Boleyn incident was very traumatic for Helana's Spirit, she was a very forceful character who **always insisted on her own way.** Vain, arrogant, self-opinionated....you were a good match, except that you were 'in charge' of the State and Power. She could not accept that when she married you, that she needed to succumb her Will to yours. A power struggle in the true sense.
She brought on her own demise, by ostracising your Love; as she did initially today, she exposed herself to rejection.
Her self-esteem could not come to terms with the rejection; she was above rejection. So proud, so haughty, she lost her head because of her pride. Does History repeat itself ?'
(see AppendixII One Soul, Past Lives)

15.11 I ask of Daniel:...
Question (a) Is there conflict in Heaven between the Trinity? ....
'The Trinity is a Human term; it does not exist in Heaven.
Jesus was a Man, the Holy Spirit is an Angel, who can enter your
Being, there is only one GOD.....the **concept** of the Trinity was **invented** by the writers of the Bible, to explain in Human terms these Concepts.

Question (b) Is there conflict between the Spirits of Judith and Bob?...
' There is conflict in the Minds of both Judith and Bob, but there is only true Love in the Spirits...The two need to come to terms with their roles on the Earth-Plane. The man Bob has a task to perform and this he does and will continue to. Whilst Anne's Spirit is divided the power of Good is weakened, it is necessary for the two of them to be united in the fullest way, for the optimum benefit. We can only afford to wait a short while for the Human-joining to occur; otherwise both will need to return to Spirit'.

Question (c) What are my choices?.....Daniel responds:

- **Choice1..to remain with Helana in Ireland.**
- **Choice2..to write the Book**
- **Choice3..to Plant the new Church**
- **Choice4..to build the Family Unit, with Helana, or with Judith, or with Another.**
- **Choice5..to act as a Prophet, to travel the World taking God's message to all.**
- **Choice6..to become a Healer**
- **Choice7..to turn back** *(I do not consider this any longer a choice!)*

KEYPOINTS DP04
a) The Spiritual Need takes priority over the Human
Aspirations.
b) When there is pressing need for the Spirit to return,
the Human life will end.
c) Equally, if no further learning is happening, or can
be expected to happen, then there is no further point to
the Human life, and this will come to an end.
d) We have all heard of People willing themselves to die.
e) Human bonding or Relationship-joining in Love will
cause the Spirits to combine.
f) When the Spirit is divided it is weakened.

15.12 Judith tells me she is in pain with her left thigh, and her feet feel as if set in concrete....'The pain is caused by your son, Abel, who wishes to prevent you from leaving the Household, he is also responsible for the sensation in your feet. You **must counter** this by protecting yourself and raising your Spirit. It is advisable to avoid contact at the present time. This Spirit is being extremely selfish and will not listen to reason. The suit of chain-mail is necessary for you.'

15.13 On the Saturday Evening we go to a Christmas Banquet hosted by my Company, in Northern Ireland. An excellent evening, Helana buys herself a new dress and is told this is for a new life and a new Beginning.

15.14 Overnight I am told that I travelled to Zypron and there was a confrontation. 'There was a need to fight and you, John were injured, but you prevailed and won the day. All is now restored to peaceful life again, the power-Lord who sought to rule the Planet has been contained and his Followers disciplined. All will now be held and Love can prevail. An excellent night's work. Your injuries have now been healed and you are fully restored.'

15.15 'Helana has also worked in her sleep. A meeting did eventually take place with Constance,   Constance is still very bitter but a reconciliation has taken place. Constance now has the opportunity to progress in a Spiritual way, accepting her Earthly role for the present time, but knowing that it is to change. A further meeting with Helana will be arranged in a few weeks time.'

'We believe we can rescue this Spirit, and all will be achieved in Love and Reconciliation. Thank you for your efforts. We rejoice!'.
.....signed by my Guides, Razeem, Adrian and Ahizar.

15.16 On Sunday morning of 6th December, Daniel writes:...
'Good morning John, Helana's Spirit is struggling to come to terms with her choice to remain with you. Remember, up to now she has conditioned herself to being with another, (Philip) and leaving your side....
The Spirit needs to find the Trust and Love which is there, it will then join with your Spirit Give it time. All will be healed by Christmas, given that your relationship continues to move forwards. There are many Spirits who Helana needs to keep at bay, these still try to influence her...She needs the strength of Mind to put these aside and refuse to listen to any....Her son Alan is very jealous and needs healing. Helana should be firm with this Spirit and tell him that she will not be friendly unless he changes his attitude....Her ex-Husband is also causing a restriction to her arm and neck, and a headache. He seeks vengeance and is very bitter, she can counter this by protecting herself with a coat of chain-mail from head to foot.'
At 19.00hrs I am told that Helana is aware of my Spirit within her, an internal struggle ensues between her Spirit and her Mind, her Spirit has realised her mistake and tries to control her Mind!

15.17 'You are surrounded by many Spirits, Doreen, Elsa, Constance, Lorna, Anne, the ladies come for learning and forgiveness... Constance in particular is making progress, we wish Helana to meet with her again tonight in her sleep...Elsa is now aware of your Knowledge and is most remorseful, we will try to lighten her Spirit and those of her family. Her mother comes and pleads for Elsa's redemption and help. We respect this and will do what we can to help her...your Efforts were of great service to the lady Anne, she has recovered her enjoyment of the physical sex, and the Past was healed by her coming to terms with the injury *(rape by her husband)*. Helana must face this also...healing will be given in her sleep'.

15.18 My father Ted writes:... ' Your lass is canny, is she not! I am upset because the relationship to your mother was not as I would have wished. I must now decide whether to wait for her, or to move on. A difficult choice.'

'I have already done some learning and now have the opportunity to return to the Earth for a new life, or to wait for a future opportunity and to guide your mother. What would you choose?'....

15.19 I Reflect, and then respond to Ted as follows:...my 'choice' is that as Joyce does not expect, or believe, that you will ever meet again, that you seize your opportunity.
Provided that there are others in Spirit who can greet her. She will understand that life moves on, and that you needed to recover the time you have already lost.
Go forwards. Only you can speak for your relationship of the Past----it is past. If the love was not that strong then move on....there is someone out there waiting for you. Go for it Dad.

15.20 Ted replies... ' Thank you for your words, I will reflect for a few hours before I decide. Good luck with your future life together, we are all proud of you.'
On the 10th December, I write: ' I have decided to wait for your mother. I know you will find this difficult to understand, but it is for me, and my wish to meet with her again and to be reconciled. I do not know the future, but I believe we shall be together again on the Earth-Plane when our circumstances will be better, I hope so. Thank you for your words and for Helana's, I will not disturb you now, but will watch from close-by and come to you from time-to-time.'

KEYPOINTS DP05
a) We all have a degree of choice as to whether our Soul is to stay in Heaven, or to choose a new Life on the Earth-Plane.
b) The turn-around can be almost instantaneous, but it is more usual for a period of learning to continue in Heaven before a new Earth-Life is chosen. The average time a Soul remains in Heaven is some 52 Earth years, which would allow for the majority of your Family and Soul-Group to join together in Heaven before a new Venture is chosen.
c) When you die or 'pass-over', your Soul will be greeted by those of your Group who are available, and who choose to be present, typically immediate Parents and Family members.
d) If you need to recover from Ailments or Diseases, then you will be taken directly to a Hospital or Recovery Unit where Spirit Doctors and Surgeons will restore you to completeness, some three days is typical for a normal death, but if serious injury, disease and suffering has occurred a much longer period may be necessary.
e) Thereafter your Completeness is restored and you will then be able to choose your appearance. (age)
f) Spirit can take any Form and can appear to you to reflect your expectations of them.

15.21 At 06.00hrs I am woken to receive these words:
' The Events of the night are not yet completed, but we wish to record that Helana has chosen to stay with you John on the Earth-Plane, now and in the future. There has occurred a break with the past Spirits of Jack and Bryan, who will now need to find their own Pathways.'

'This break now allows you John and Helana to continue your lives without redress to the Past...it will enable your Spirits to Bond in a true way, which is necessary for the Work ahead. We thank Helana for her decision.
We ask that Ted's chair is purged with holy water when you arise. The rest of your sleep hours will be spent together, to heal your Spirits and to create the bond of love between your Spirits. Sleep now.'
(holy-water is distilled or de-ionised water which has been blessed, it is used to cleanse objects of their Spirit-Aura. I have my father's chair in my home)

15.22 'Helana met with Constance overnight and a bitter argument developed, it was necessary to call a Counsellor to mediate. This then achieved the desired result. The two ladies were returned to their Planet of Origin, and they now acknowledge their family connection. All can now proceed and a further meeting is to be arranged.'
(Jesus was the Mediator)

Question (a) Please explain the origin of this Conflict and how it can be healed
'The conflict began before either Soul came to the Earth. The problem was one of power and authority, as to who was in charge and who was responsible for the other. They were both introduced to the Earth experiment in view of their conflict. The ladies have sought one-up-man-ship for many thousands of years.... Because they are so similar in Spirit, they experience the same feelings, if you like similar magnets repel! The rift will be healed if either of them accepts the Will of the other. A compromise is necessary. Give and take is necessary. Healing of the Past is necessary. Sisters should be really close, but for jealousy and vanity this could happen.
Helana needs to make a gesture to heal this situation, this is what we ask for.'

Question (b)....What is Helana's true nature?
' Helana's Spirit is now a combination of many Human Spirits (including your's John), together with that of her Origin and the **Holy Ghost**.
She has **all these Elements: GOD, Earth, Plant-life, Animals, Other Creatures....all in the One Spirit.**

A truly representative Spirit of Creation, ideally suited for her role at the present time, and one of the main reasons she was chosen. Helana's true nature is therefore **NATURE; in every respect encompassing all living Creatures.'**

KEYPOINT DP06
Our Spirits are the result of progression through all forms of Life and Other Species.

Question (c).....Are we Guinea-pigs for the Human Race?
' Indeed you are my friend, everything you do is analysed, dissected and monitored by an eminent collection of Psychologists and Human behaviourists. Upon your shoulders, and those of the Original Group, are gauged the Race in total. A mammoth Responsibility!

Question (d)...What purpose does the Appendix serve?
(my Son Ford, has had his Appendix removed)
' The Appendix is the point at which a Spirit is attached when it is Bonded...as with you and Helana, when the opportunity for Bonding has been missed, there is no further use for this part.'

KEYPOINTS DP07
a)All Spirit is Energy,
b)The form of that Energy is a reflection of the degree to which progress to Unity with GOD has been achieved.
c)It is not usual for Humans to regress back to other Life-forms, as this is contrary to all progress and to the ultimate Goal of the achievement of a higher vibrational level of Purity and Love. Should however, a particular Human Being need to appreciate and to learn about lower life-forms then it is possible for this transition to occur. Or perhaps a lesson about destruction needs to be taught!. Helana's Spirit has evolved through all of these Life-forms, hence her Spirit is a composite of these previous Experiences.

15.23 On Friday,11th December, Helana has a rash on her fingers:... ' this rash is given by Spirit to remind her to send love to the World and its Peoples....to think and to pray for all those who cannot share your Christmas...to show Compassion for these Peoples.......
When she was a Hairdresser, the rash was given because of her refusal to face-up to her mother and to her husband. We do not wish for anyone to shut themselves off from life and to ignore the problems which need to be faced!

KEYPOINTS DP08
a)Ailments, Disease, Rashes, are given in response to our Human Attitudes.
b)If we change our Attitudes much physical discomfort will clear.

c) If you find that you have a problem, examine your Attitudes and Relationships to see whether there is Something, Someone, or some Situation which you are not facing-up to.

15.24 On the 13th, I ask of Daniel:..Have I sacrificed our present love to enable Helana to heal her Past with Philip and Others?...
'You have agreed to allow her Spirit the freedom to follow its own Pathway, to heal the Past , and so allow Helana to progress without restriction'
'In this way you can be together at a later time.
It is all give and take my friend...you give now to enable her to reach her Goal and Healing. She in turn sacrificed the potential of this Relationship to help you to progress. All is as it should be!'

15.25 Helana receives a Message in writing from her Guide. This states that I am still in conversation with the Spirit of Constance, and that a decision is needed by me to walk away from the influence of Constance. As she has done with Jack, it is also necessary for me to do with Constance....'There are many Spirits around you who wish for you not to succeed, raise your thoughts and be positive!'

15.26 Jesus writes.... 'Allow your children, John, to be. They are aware of their Roles which they have chosen. They are needed, and they will be guided by True Spirit. Grant them their freedom...Many, many times we have said **Love can only be found in Freedom**.....They will progress, they will return, do not offer them material bribes.. They will see the distance...they will search for true love and will realise it is with the Father, it is only the Spirit of Elsa which prevents them coming to you...
(I am concerned that I am not seeing enough of my Children)
It is written...... ' Let the little children come unto me'....this lady Helana has the same love of the World and the Children as I did......All is shared. All is given...There are many Obstacles to overcome before these words become a Reality.
(a Vision is given of a child suckling)......Look at the child suckle!..
Understand that it takes **all kinds of Love to create a World,...**
All is unconditional Love. Allow Helana to do this, it will take nothing away from the love between you two....It is the same intensity of love to all Things and all Beings and all Life....
Allow Helana to do this, the child within needs to Understand this, it is expected of Helana to give to the Child, so the Child can give to the World....
Helana and you John make a powerful Spirit for the Child, a Spirit of Beauty so needed at the present time. Rest assured, all is as it should be. What is to be, will be. Each Individual has their role to play.
Whatever is needed in their lifetime, is preparation to be able to bring Love and Purity to the Earth-Plane'.

341

15.27 'Your Child Edwin is a beautiful Spirit, he needs to learn strength, and strength of Character to do the job necessary. He will gain so much education from being with Elsa.....He will see and hear when danger is afoot and be capable of offering protection. Look at his life and be proud. Let not the hurt enter your heart, they agreed to become the future Generation. What better lesson to learn to survive in the Environment in which they are placed. All is as it should be...There will be another Child.'

KEYPOINTS DP09
a) All Experience is given for learning.
b) You need to experience Love and to receive Love and to Love yourself, before you are ready to give Love to Others.
c) All Lives are chosen in advance.
d) There are many kinds of Love, all are important:
 * Man-Woman * Parent-Child * the World * Friendship * Relatives * Other Creations etc.

15.28 My Guide writes: ' The feelings on your hands are the marks of the Cross, this shows how much you have progressed with your Understanding and Learning. A good sign which shows the strength of feeling now of your Mind for Spiritual Matters.(feeling of Stigmata) All is well.'

15.29 My Guide writes that the atmosphere around Ireland is **directly influenced by and causes the Weather.** Violence leads to heavy winds and rain. Agreement leads to calm and sunshine.....you can tell the mood of the Land from the Weather'.
KEYPOINTS DP10
a) The Weather is caused by and reflects the 'Atmosphere' on the surface of the Earth.
b) Nature reacts to restore Harmony.
c) The rain is used to wash away the negative vibrations and purge the Land.
d) When you wish to clear away the influence of other Spirits, it often helps to take a Bath or Shower and to visualise the Influences being 'washed away'.

15.30 'The baby within Helana was conceived on your first night in Ireland, and will be born before June 19th.1999'.

15.31 On 14th December, 1998, I send the following letter to my four Children.....
'I have made the enclosed Crosses for you. Please wear them whenever you can, particularly when you sleep. Wear them against your Body and they will protect you at night.'

'The World is not always a friendly place, but the Cross, will ensure that you come to no Spiritual harm.

Helana and I have moved to Northern Ireland because we believe that our presence will help the Peace process, and help to heal the Minds and Spirits of the People here. In the coming months and years we will be working in the Community to help bring this Healing about. We also have a greater Purpose(s) which will become clear to you in future years.

You may feel I have left you behind, but this is not the case: as soon as you wish to join me you will be welcome to come and stay here. You can also help us with our Work in the future (if you choose to).

For the next few years I will continue with my financial work, thereafter, we hope to have enough money to start a Guest House and Home-Farm, which is to form the basis of our future Income...I wish you to know that there will always be a home here for you, you are loved and you are in both our thoughts. We wish you well in your lives and wish you to find happiness, love and to fulfil your Karmas.

Helana and I still intend to marry. The wedding is now planned for Saturday, April 10th 1999. We hope that you will attend here in Bangor. God bless you. DAD and HELANA.

15.32 On Tuesday,15th December, Daniel my Guide tells me: 'Overnight a meeting took place between the Spirits of Constance, Helana and John. A review took place of the History since the World began; this brought to light many happenings which initially served only to 'fuel the fire'. But then an Understanding was reached, an accommodation, which will allow the Spirits of both Constance and Helana to go their separate ways without bitterness, and accepting the Realities of the Situation.

Constance was most upset and most indignant that her role had been agreed before she accepted it, that her life was pre-agreed!.....She has finally now come to accept this and has promised to leave you both alone and to pursue her own Karma, which she is now aware of.

An Accommodation, not a loving, healing, Experience; but an acceptance on her part of what is to be.

We would hope another future occasion would lead to some better reconciliation. At least now the Past is real history and you can pursue your lives without interference and without restriction. All is well'.

15.33 In view of the success with Constance, we are requested to try to lighten Elsa's Spirit, and Helana's ex-husband, in a similar way, with a Counsellor present as well.

15.34 On Thursday, 17th December at 03.50 am, the UK and USA have declared war against IRAQ. Helana has had a Vision of a vessel sinking, there is the need for me to be continually in contact with Spirit...I am given the following by Daniel:

343

' We wish you to be aware of the serious development today which will trigger a series of disasters throughout the World. These disasters will culminate and will produce a melt-down/Flood unless Mankind changes its Attitude and its Policies.
We wish you to relay this message to Judith.
It is essential now for her to be with you in Northern Ireland for the near Future. We wish you to keep with you your passports at all times.'

'We do not anticipate you being in danger in Northern Ireland, but it is essential that you are ready to move at any time, with bags pre-packed. The Equilibrium of the World has been disturbed by the war machine and the missiles.'
'The Earth will react, Spirit will react. It remains to be seen what the response of the other Nations will be. We will keep you informed.'

15.35 I return alone to England, leaving at 02.50 on Friday 18th. In between my Client appointments I find time to meet with my family and Judith prior to Christmas, and then return to Bangor in the small hours of 22nd December.
Daniel tells me that the 'Meeting of Souls' planned for the 22nd in the Bay View Hotel was never intended for that date; simply another test of my loyalty and my willingness to comply with Spirit wishes!!

15.36 On Wednesday, 23rd, I join with my colleagues for a Christmas lunch in Belfast, and then in the evening we have a pre-Christmas celebration for friends and acquaintances at our home in Bangor. There are thirteen People who attend for a very pleasant social Event, these are essentially the people I have met since moving to Ireland.
At one point in the proceedings Helana leaves the Party to lie down to avoid passing-out.   Later that night, I am told by Daniel.......
' The situation with respect to Helana's Spirit is very grave. There will be no death, but we wish you to know that Helana has come very close to a move to the Spirit World. It is Helana's wish to continue the work on the Earth-Plane and the birth of the child. We will take the Spirit tonight for healing and recovery of its strength. The ending of many lifetimes without complete Healing is devastating to this Spirit.
Perhaps this will enable you to have complete understanding'....
' Helana's Spirit has always depended upon Others for strength, she needs another Bonding to achieve this. The turmoil of:
- the work to heal other Spirits
- the relationship to me
- the break-up with her husband
- the move to Ireland
- the meeting with the Spirit of Judas
- the demands of Other Spirits have all taken their toll.
.....complete rest is necessary'.

15.37 'Your lady is very sad because the Spirits of Jack and Bryan are suffering so from the loss of her presence. She knows this for she senses the Sadness herself. All that you can do is to show Compassion and support for Helana. Her Spirit still travels and meets with these persons and she has to accept that this must stop. A trying time but the Situation will be healed with your support, and caring. Be patient and all will be sorted.'

15.38 'The Bible Code was prepared and written into the Bible by those People who wrote these Books. They were your people John, who had the gift of telling the Future, and the ability to hide the Code.
There is another Bible to be written by you John, which foretells Mankind's History prior to Adam and Eve!.....the Books of Truth and Knowledge!!'

15.39 I am told that One of those who attended the pre-Christmas drinks evening at our home, is the Spirit of Judas..... ' Do not exclude this person as he has a key role to play in future Events, and has an opportunity to redeem himself...History does repeat itself unless a step-change occurs' ..(Helana was sensitive to this Soul which is what caused her to withdraw)
KEYPOINT DP11
GOD never gives-up on any Soul.

15.40 On December 24th, I am told ' All knowledge is within you John, you do not need to read, you only need to ask. We appreciate that reading stimulates the Questions in your Mind so it is useful from that point of view.'
We attend the Church of Ireland, at BallyHolme, Christmas Eve service, in Bangor. Jesus stands next to us. Earlier, Helana has felt 'kicking' inside her womb.
We return Home and at 01.20 on the 25th, the following message is delivered by Helana:...
' A meeting has been called to present to you, John, the facts of all that there is to be, has been, and will be. I am White Eagle...I bring to you these words this day....You have knowledge of who I am.
This is a trust within your heart my dear man. No other brings to you a message this day. I give you my sign; therefore release this Child from the disbelief of the words that pass her lips on many occasions...I do not come with ease this time, for there is pain in my heart for the World and its needs are so great at this time....I have requested that my presence should be with this lady, for there is a great deal to be achieved...I am stern of face. I do not wish to take away the splendour of this day on the Earth-Plane. I share the Mind, the Body, not quite the voice of this lady, but no words will enter within.'

15.41 White Eagle continues....
'Upon this Night there was a child born within our History of Mankind.
(not the true day!) the child is born to Mary, the mother of this child, so
gentle, so wise. We were saddened by your lack of listening to the Priest
'Alan', his words were so profound, we will bring you the meaning......
the mother Mary was unmarried, young, 16-18 years, to be told that a
child would be given. Can you imagine the confusion of this Child, she
was engaged to Joseph, can you imagine the shame?...it is not my child!
Nevertheless, the trust was there from Mary. Was it me? or was it the
word of GOD? They decided to listen and to follow the instructions that
were given. We ask you to understand the shear trust of the mother...to
listen, to hear the words spoken, by no-one she could see or
touch....But, she followed every step obediently....
You do not see, you pull...you trust because you feel the **'Tug'**.
As with Mary and Joseph, they still had no concrete evidence, however,
at the birth of Jesus there were animals and wise-Men with gifts.
This was the **'Tug'**, it was proof that the child was truly the Messiah
and all was as it should be....All through the Child's life these little
'Tugs' existed....'

15.42 'If you do not still your Mind John, you miss so many **'Tugs'**.
**Try harder to slowdown the Mind, bring Peace to your Mind, observe all
about you, concentrate your Mind.** Find the complete Understanding, of
what we try to say, to help, and to guide you. In writing also, ensure
your Mind does not wander, for if it does you do not write accurately.
We say at this time, there is only so much time to gain the necessary
commitment. We are eager to move you all on your way, but there are
things needed to enable this to happen. **TRY HARDER** my dear man. It is
necessary if you wish to become a part of this lady. It cannot happen if
you insist on living your life as it has been....
We remind you again about the kitten, have you looked behind this story
relating to Helana? All is given for you to understand, to grow, to
progress. The man Philip is in the Past. Take care my dear man that this
does not happen to you!...We remind you again, for these words will not
be given again. **BE AT PEACE**!...
Please, we ask you to understand all that has been given...Do not file
away the papers, the Events of the past few days are vitally important.'
KEYPOINTS DP12
a) **Messages from Spirit are often disguised in the form
of Visions, Dreams or Incidents, which if we are not
observant and aware, we will miss these triggers.**
b) **It is necessary to question every Happening as to its
significance. White Eagle calls these events 'Tugs'.**
c) **A still Mind, at Peace, is essential to become capable
of receiving true Messages.**

15.43 In the course of the Night a confrontation develops with Helana,

I cannot recollect the exact words said, but at one point Helana tells me that she has decided to 'walk away from all of her Past'.

I am immediately concerned that she intends to walk away from me, the one person who has played a significant Role in many of her previous lives. I hesitate however and change my response to ' If you walk away from the Past, you walk away from Jesus', Helana denies this vehemently and states that she would never walk away from Jesus, how dare I even suggest this! She retreats to the spare bed-room for some two hours before I can persuade her to return to bed.

This is **exactly** the Situation I do what wish to happen, what a wonderful start to Christmas Day!!

15.44 At 02.05am. my Guide Daniel writes:...' Hallo John, we greet you. A difficult time my friend, when you feel low and inadequate. Take heart, all is not lost.

Helana is being influenced by those who prefer your Relationship to fail, but you still need to heed the words given and to become more Aware. Helana has realised now that others seek to destroy your Relationship, she will allow for this. You, John must now change your lifestyle to communicate with us at all times if progress is to be made.

- Take your time with all things
- Raise your Spirit at all times
- Think, and ask **before** you make decisions
- We are always with you to help and to guide you, you only need to ask....

All is now set to improve your Business, your Finances and your Relationships, **but we need your co-operation.** Allow your day to flow and be aware at all times of Everything and Everyone about you.'

15.45 Christmas Day is a somewhat reserved affair, I thought that Helana had recovered her calm, but it was some six months later that I learned that Helana had been sobbing profusely on the telephone to Judith in England, early that Christmas morning while I was still asleep...........

15.46 On Boxing Day, 26th December, at 12.20 Mid-day, I have a lovely feeling throughout my head and neck.....' Good morning John, All is well, you feel the love of Spirit and the presence of your Guides who are with you. Progress can now be made for you to become more Aware of our presence around you. Do not be afraid, your day will be a gentle one, we ask you to relax, and to talk, and to read together. All is well.'....In the afternoon we go for a drive in the locality, to the nearby Village of Carrowdore, and are told of a lifetime there when I was the Lord of the Manor, a Priest, and established a school for the Village children. Helana tells me she sees Angels ahead of the car to greet us and hears a Choir singing. We are questioned.... ' Why cannot we behave as we did in this previous lifetime?'.

The day passes peacefully, and was more representative of how I envisaged a Boxing Day should be.

15.47 At 15.00hrs, Helana has a Vision of salt being thrown on the fire, and of a pineapple and two apples being destroyed by fire.
My Guide Daniel tells me that salt is the preservative and purifier of many things on the Earth-Plane. If you have a wound, to wash it in salt will heal and kill the germs.
'We wish you to sprinkle salt on the Fire now, so that the heat and warmth and air will purify the house....in the past days and weeks your thoughts of the Past, and the visitors to the house, have attracted many undesirable Spirits who persist in remaining in your home. We wish for them to leave and the salt will cause this to happen.' ...
Helana has seen a man in one of my pictures, an oil Painting, we are told it is the artist and he is attracted by my thoughts, he can be removed by sprinkling the picture with 'holy water'.
KEYPOINTS DP13
a) Salt is a purifier and can be used to purge away Spirits;
b) Rain also washes away and purifies.
c) It is possible to bless and produce 'holy water' and to sprinkle this onto Objects in order to purify them.

15.48 I ask my Guide...How must I change my day to allow a satisfactory relationship with Spirit?...
'We see that it is necessary for you to:
* Talk through and agree your agenda every day.
* Involve Spirit in your decisions on: Who to Contact, Who to Meet, Where to Go, How to get there.
* Consciously contact your Guide every hour
* If in doubt ask first....'

15.49 After Helana has rested awhile, at 15.00hrs, she sits in Trance, and tells me of the Visions she has received:
(a) John, you are looking-up, sad, with a wistful smile and a light on your face....the words come:
' Looking back at past Sadness is not necessary!....look ahead with a smile on your face...'There will be a kiss goodbye and sadness felt, but all will be understood.....walk away John with gladness in your heart, for all has been achieved.....The feelings felt within will disappear and a new Life will begin.'

(b) John, you are sitting cross-legged, alone, on the top of a hill, looking out to sea. You are thinking all is so beautiful, all is at peace, how happy you are to have known this life and all that it has been.....You rejoice with your arms outstretched and say ' I am free'....

'You look-up at the Stars with Contentment, and a knowing look in your eye, and say 'Thank you Jesus, for I am free and I can now feel that I belong'.....
With a wistful look, for happy Times, for sad Times, you look-back at the Stars and say...'But now I Understand' ...You are dressed in a white pullover. *(the last gift to me from Doreen, before our marriage ended; this pullover has never been worn!)*
The words are from my Spirit who talk through Helana in Trance.
Helana is not aware of these Visions and words.

15.50 At 03.00hrs on the 27th, I am told that my Spirit was taken for a meeting with Jesus, just the two of us, with no-one else present....... 'there is much to understand my friend, it is difficult for you, without the ability, to know and to remember, this will come as time unfolds. I thank you for your words and all harmony is restored. Man's Emotions are difficult at the best of times, and Events of the past weeks have been very trying for you. I am pleased that you seem to have accepted the Situation and your Spirit will come to terms with this in a short while. All is progressing now as was originally intended. You have a key Role to play and we welcome your co-operation and your attitude. All help and support will be given to ease your Pathway. Events are moving now quite quickly, this is necessary.
Your Awareness will progress also so Communication will be easier and more reliable. I will return in a few days to continue our discussion and to offer my help and support....'

15.51 Jesus asks me through Helana whether I am prepared to follow in his footsteps, and to take care of Helana and the child.....I respond yes to both questions, saying only 'to the best of my Ability'.

15.52 'We feel for the time your lady is absent from your day, in the future days to come, a thought on how your Thoughts and Actions can and do affect the lives of Others, is necessary. How much in this life has changed from that of your past lives, to change what has become part of your true nature.'
KEYPOINTS DP14
a) Thoughts on the Earth help to create our Future world and Experiences.
b) Thoughts in Spirit World act to create the Present.

15.53 'You are all born with an element of GOD within you, to reach the very heart and existence of Mankind, but there are many barriers that block this wonderful fulfilment from happening.....

'Too often we see failure within man's Mind for the fear of **retribution**, but all is in the hands of GOD, for as he sees the sins of the Past and works towards repenting of these, GOD's love upholds you and helps and guides those who seek this golden Pathway'.

15.54 'We feel at this present time my dear man, your heart is in need of learning, and bring to you this message this day to help and guide you along your chosen Pathway.. We feel your anger and pain many times my dear man, but we ask you to understand that we are here only to help and to guide you'.
'Go with peace in your heart my dear man and know that we are beside you, waiting for your true Light to shine through the Darkness felt within your Mind at this present time.   White Eagle writes for you this day my dear man, a trusted name within your Mind'.

15.55 Helana tells me she needs to return to England to resolve matters with her mother and with her son before he leaves for Canada, she has received a message from Spirit that her mother's time is very short.
I examine the cost of flights, £ 86 each way! and thereafter £135 for a taxi from the Airport to Banbury. I wonder why Helana did not accompany me on my last trip....As cash is short I offer, and Helana agrees, for me to drive her to Banbury, and for us both to return on New Years Eve, I have tickets bought for a dance at the local pub in Groomsport for New-Years Eve, and plan to return for the celebration.

Helana is quite friendly and responsive throughout the journey, but on arrival at Banbury she becomes a different person. She becomes distant and shows no interest in my presence or in contact with me.

15.56 Judith suggests I visit my mother in London and she counsels Helana, eventually sending her to stay with her mother....
(Helana had not arranged previously to visit her Mother, in fact she had refused to accompany me to England a week earlier to talk with her mother, to visit her sons, and to wish them all a happy Christmas.)

Helana refuses to return with me on the 31st December, to Belfast, and shows no interest in meeting with me, I attempt a conversation with her each day to no avail.

15.57 On 31st December, I ask my Guide Daniel to explain Helana's attitude to me....
a) 'Helana's Spirit
...does not wish the tie of a relationship with you John, or with any Other. It is not prepared to give enough. She has been hurt too much in the Past and has forgotten how to love another. She can love all, but only from a distance. Her Emotions cannot support a permanent relationship.

' She hides behind Judith as a mother-shelter, it is no other, only her Spirit. You can do little, only hope that her Mind is strong enough to control her Spirit...The Mind, as yours, is willing enough, but in the presence of Judith, the Spirit is upper-most. We share your concern at Helana's attitude, all that you can do is to wait and see, and carry-on with your life until she returns. Tomorrow we will bring to you more information about past lives, which you will find of interest.'

b) Judith's Spirit tells me..
'I am sorry John, at the present Helana is very unstable and her Spirit and Mind are confused. There is no-one influencing her only the conflict between Mind and Spirit...I will heal as I can, but eventually she must decide her own pathway, be it with or without you'.
'This is a retrograde step, essentially rejecting a life with you and leaving no real alternatives. You can only be patient.'

c) Helana's Spirit tells me..
'I am sorry for the way I feel, but I am happy here with Judith and Joseph her child, I do not feel comfortable in Ireland....I am trying, but I cannot invent feelings which are not there. Give me time and space please and I will sort my Mind and my Spirit.'

15.58 I return alone to Stranraer and catch the 15.30pm .Ferry back from Stranraer to Belfast. I have given Helana my last £ 20 = to ensure she is not short of money over the holiday, intending to cash money when I arrive in Belfast....In the event the Ferry is too late for the Banks, my Overdraft is at its limit, so the cash-machine does not dispense. I am without cash for New Year's Eve and the subsequent Bank Holiday weekend. What a brilliant start to the New Year! Helana has refused to return to Ireland, and I do not know when she will do so...I go alone to the New Year Celebration in a local pub; but feel awkward that I cannot offer my companions even a drink in return for their hospitality....I feel alone and unloved.!

15.59 I ask Daniel; Why is Helana's Spirit so hostile to me?.....
' The Spirit remembers the Past and will not forgive nor forget. This is the real problem. Helana's Spirit is doing **everything it can to keep you apart.'** ....I muse, we met ALL those past Peoples to obtain their forgiveness, but what about Helana?
When I retire to bed, the continual ache and pain in my right shoulder and arm has gone
(I used to lay on my right side to cuddle Helana in bed.....this was my first recognition that it was Helana's Spirit causing the problem,.... not Constance!... not Jack!)

351

15.60 When I awake on the 1st January 1999, Daniel reports:..
' A meeting took place last night, with Jesus and Helana's Spirits. Much emotion and feeling was expressed. Helana is not ready yet to talk, or to consider her relationship with you John. Her Spirit protests too much, there is an element of Vengeance here, which Jesus is now aware of.....No more can be done at the present time. Time will heal, Judith will heal, Jesus will heal, you John should continue to heal. Helana's Spirit has not shut away the past lives yet.; more work will be necessary in this area. Jesus has agreed to counsel Helana's Spirit. Do not act hastily, allow Events to flow.

KEYPOINTS DP15
a) The Spirit never forgets. The pent-up Emotion can be released at any time unless healing has taken place.
b) Even Spirit Guides are not fully aware of all past animosities.

15.61 On 2nd January, at 00.30am. I receive this message from my guide Ahizar;.. ' Helana's Spirit is being very inflexible and hostile to any attempt to compromise. We can only wait and see. Other Spirits are now causing confusion'

Helana's Spirit comes:
'Hallo John, I come just to say hallo and not to cause you pain, I am still confused and uncertain. Give me time please to understand my own Mind and my own wishes, I mean you no harm.'

15.62 Later that day, Daniel writes;.. 'Helana wishes you to know that she will return and try once more. Her Spirit has finally accepted the need to leave the Past behind, to forgive and to grasp the Opportunity now presented. This is excellent news.
The Spirit is now at ease, and it is for the Mind to also forgive and to accept....progress indeed my friend, we can now see a reconciliation and the coming together of you two in pure love. This is what is necessary for the Future. All is as it should be.'

15.63 **Helana's Spirit** writes..
'I will try again John, on the basis that the Past is behind the wooden Door. We are as One, if only you can also forget the Past and develop the gentler ways I know you have. I will talk to Helana's Mind and see what I can do. She needs to clarify her Thoughts so this will take a day or two. Good to talk to you at last ...Love.... ..Helana's Spirit.'

15.64 At 12.00 noon, Daniel writes;..' We wish to inform you that Helana will return by plane next week, she will call to request a ticket.'

15.65 Helana tells me audibly that our Relationship is finished. She will only return to Ireland to collect her clothes....

.My Guide tells me that she is possessed by Constance's Spirit and we are still optimistic that she will change her mind.

15.66 My Guide Daniel asks; ' Do you not work Spiritually, better on your own? I personally feel that I have reached a self-sufficiency, my Communication is stable and improving. Helana brings an increased Awareness of Spirit presence. She brings to me a style of life which I still seek to achieve, in terms of a gentle nature, compassion, thought for Others. Correction of my Actions as necessary... to slow down, eating and actions, awareness of what she is receiving...also criticism from her Guides...'
' We perceive no difference, other than that you are calmer when on your own; perhaps you try too hard to please Helana...be your own man!'

15.67 It is 3rd January, my father Ted writes....' I am upset for you, but pleased that you have reached the stage you are at....Helana is a lovely lady and Spirit, but she is so vulnerable to other Spirits. She is 'possessed' by Constance, who is bitter and evil.
I hope Judith can help for time is short to resolve this problem....I am sorry we were not closer, you were always a 'distant' child, perhaps this stems back to when you were a baby and my life was so hectic elsewhere! A lesson to learn yourself my son! Edward was always the 'noisy one', so he probably always got the attention and because you were more capable you missed-out. Not deliberately, but perhaps just the way it worked out. We both loved you and were proud of you, but we just never had that close a relationship to say these words. Do not miss-out my son with your children. Good luck, I love you. Dad.'
KEYPOINTS DP16
a) Do not miss out on your Relationships.
b) Never put off to tomorrow what can be said today.
c) Make your loved-Ones aware of your feelings for them. Do not be bitter, do not allow Emotions or Pride to block your true feelings.
d) Pray for help and guidance when necessary.

15.68 I am asked what are my needs for happiness... I respond as follows:
- to feel that I am loved, respected, belong.....by Society, by my Partner or Spouse
- to be surrounded by Family, Friends who are frequent visitors
- to see that my Children are as happy as much as I can
- to have enough resources to cover my Earthly Needs....home, money, entertaining, holidays
- to find Peace
- to be able to help Others
- to achieve my Karma

- to be useful to GOD, Mankind, Others
- to feel my Life is worthwhile
- to lead an active Life
- to feel and know Love within
- a Spiritual Life
- to be in control of any situation

15.69 I am asked to look honestly at Helana's faults, as she:...
- Needs to find work, this has been given many times, and it is necessary to meet Others.
- Will lose the child unless she changes her attitude
- Judith will refuse to counsel her any more
- Ask yourself: will Helana go along with my wishes?, Are you really suited to each other?

As your Guide,..' I see that you are not talking, not listening, and not suited to Helana'.
.You John, should wait one more week before you advertise for a lodger
(I have asked the question of Spirit)
KEYPOINT DP17
It is irrelevant what Others think of you, appreciate your own worth, you must live with yourself and your own Actions.

15.70 A Vision is given of a mother is sitting in a Bungalow, a car loses control and hurtles towards the Bungalow, the car strikes a female outside, then hits the front wall of the Bungalow. The mother is unable to call the police, two children are heard crying!

15.71 I am asked to review the Attributes of Helana, and write down the pluses, and the negative features, my Guide Adrian asks that I look within to my ideal 'Needs and Desires'.
I write:

POSITIVE	NEGATIVE
loving person	backs-off from nasty side
capital due	stubborn
attractive	does not contribute financially
sexy	not a doer, prevaricates
I love her	too Spiritual(uses as excuse not to do)
spiritual love	bottles-up problems until they explode
worker at home	not positively desirous of sex
likeable	smokes
pregnant	too easily influenced by other Spirits
good cook	freedom thing!
nest builder	when artistic?
artistic	too sensitive to criticism/comments

354

My conclusion is not to marry until many of these negative factors have been resolved. Spiritually we have achieved all we need to. We do not need physically to be together, Our Spirits work whilst we sleep.

15.72 A Message is given by Judith at 23.15 hrs...the message originates from ' John the Baptist'
- The Spirit of Helana is good, but it will not give freely to those close.
- Your wish to be in-charge may cause conflict
- There is no need now to be together in a Human sense, as your Spirits are now working together and joined.
- Helana is selfish in her Earthly life., though the Spirit is loving
- Helana's Spirit comes to you John, when she sleeps, to do the work in her absence.
- Helana's importance has been built-up so much, that she does not believe that you, John, can do the work.

15.73 'We ask that you look within, to your ideal needs and desires...consider what makes-up your ideal Partner/Spouse. We do not feel that from an Earthly viewpoint that Helana is ideal for you. She seeks the calm, quiet, rustic life, whereas you John have always been in the fast-lane! We doubt whether your Personalities are matched in this respect.   Think on my friend.'

15.74 'Write down John what you consider LOVE to be...LOVE YOURSELF JOHN.'
KEYPOINT DP18
You need to Love Yourself, before you can give Love to Others.

15.75 I write my views of Love. As showing them to yourself as:

- A longing, a desire, a need for, a need to be with, to be able to communicate with, to share life with, to have fun with, to provide for
- To **respect** that person, their Views, their Desires, their Needs
- To have your own Personal wishes returned (if possible)
- To do your utmost to make your Lover ....Happy, Content, and Fulfilled
- Giving to another, Sacrifice may be necessary

15.76 My Guide's view is given as:
KEYPOINTS DP19
a) To Love is to know another's Needs, and to provide for them.
b) Sometimes you need to Love someone enough, to let them go, peacefully, with dignity.

15.77 'Understand John, you need to love yourself more. Understand yourself, so that you know how to make yourself happy. With the right Understanding, Pain can be eased. You also John, are entitled to love'.

White Eagle adds... ' Have you truly ever loved anyone John?
KEYPOINT DP20
Everyone is entitled to Love

15.78 On Wednesday, 6th January at 17.50 hrs. my Guide Daniel writes...
' Go to your Belfast Office on Friday, we do not now see Helana returning this week, she is still not ready yet to commit to a genuine effort to make your Relationship work. This is so sad, we feel your anguish, her Mind is still confused. We wait, we watch, we see little change. We thank you for your work'.

'Please continue to ponder and to ask. White Eagle is very pleased with his gift and thanks you profusely. Allow your day to flow.
(I wished to thank White Eagle for all his efforts, so Overnight, I envisaged a 'Staff' as a present for him),
Subsequently, I was asked to cut a Staff for myself from the trees in the garden of the house. I still have this with me, and do not yet know its significance... I should perhaps mention that I have been told that one of my previous lives was as Aaron, the brother of Moses!!
KEYPOINT DP21
It is possible for your Thoughts on the Earth-Plane to create in the Spirit-World.

15.79 'We wish to tell you that monies will be found to alleviate your Financial pressure. We apologise for the delays. All has now been cleared to enable your position to dramatically improve, irrespective of whether Helana remains with you. We do not wish to restrict your capability to travel, to meet, to entertain, to spend the necessary time to meet with and to help the People we wish to bring to you.
It was hoped that Helana would work not only to meet the people necessary, but also to improve the cash-flow situation and to enable her to have more personal freedom...
(I have been servicing the Debts which Helana brought with her, and also paying a regular payment into her Bank account. We have also been waiting for her divorce financial Settlement of some £30,000, which is due any day and will enable her to purchase another car. The monies also were due to be used as a deposit for a property in Ireland. The Court battle and settlement took place just before we left for Ireland.)

15.80 I write that my Ideal Partner should be...I considered Helana to fit 90% of these.

• attractive, if not beautiful	nest builder
• female	spiritual and content within
• loves me	loves Nature and GOD
• interested in regular sex with me	wishes to and is prepared to help others
• sensuous, loving, warm, friendly personality	musical, dancer
• intelligent	artistic
• educated	hard worker
• articulate, sexy voice	has money, or is prepared to work
• fun loving	loves travel
• alive, extrovert	plays bridge, or is prepared to learn
• an achiever	willing hostess to friends and family
• shares my interests, serious side as well	sensible with money
• likes children and accepts mine	own Mind, a few of own interests

15.81 I ask to talk with Helana's Spirit and receive the following words:...
' Hallo John, I wish to apologise for the deception. I meant no harm to your other ladies. It is so difficult to rise up from the depths, and I'm afraid that I am so jealous. A trait I will need to lose in the Future. I wish now for all to be healed, and will be willing to meet again with Constance to bring this about....
I am afraid that Helana the person will not know of this, but eventually she will. I am sorry that her Mind is so set on this course of isolation, I still try to convince her otherwise, but it will take time, and she is not yet ready to listen. Do not give-up hope, she may still recover'...

Question (a): Why have you been so Dark?
' My Nature has always been one of deceit, vanity and jealousy, a nasty Character, ...unbelievable isn't it. In this lifetime, that side of me has been watered down and replaced by Godliness....hence my Spiritual Awareness and Spiritual Ways and love of Nature. Underneath though, there still remains this original trait...It is normally swamped, but I remain prickly as you say and unwilling to accept a 'secondary' relationship. Because your Spirit is so strong and your nature so powerful, Helana has found this intolerable; she feels swamped and unable to breathe. It is a basic Character clash, which is not compatible unless one of you backs-down....'

357

'Unfortunately for you John, Helana's importance has been blown-up to such an extent, she is now unwilling to 'give-and-take' as anyone else would. I'm afraid that she is reacting against the stresses of the past nine months, and the history of the past twenty years, and just wants out!...

Only time will heal, and experience, but unfortunately the moment is lost forever. You must seek your own life, and leave her to do likewise. She will learn the hard, lonely, painful way.'

15.82 I ask of Daniel my Guide....

Question (b): Why is Helana's Spirit so important?

' Helana was a Darkened Spirit who showed potential for recovery. As she was one of the original Players, by recovering her, all those of her Circle will be lightened, and so the World is Lightened.

Consider the scales, taking a weight from one side to the other, a dramatic swing can occur....You John, were the only Spirit she would bond with, as you have genuinely shared many Past Lives together and experienced love together.'

'Your Spirit agreed also to do this, but without the Minds being Aware, it was necessary to construct a Situation wherein you would come together willingly...

What has happened now is that Helana's Spirit has had a relapse back to her darkened days.....The bond with you John is still strong, her Mind is now ignoring her Spirit, so she will become a 'wild-card' until her attitude changes.'

(Helana was one of the wives at the time of Adam and Eve)

KEYPOINTS DP22

a) The battle between Good and Evil still continues in 1999,

b) Darker Spirits are modified to change their attitudes and bring them towards the Light,

c) The Spirit normally influences the Mind, but this relationship can change.

d) Situations and Events are pre-planned to provide the learning situation.

Question (c): What colour is Connie's Spirit?

' Constance's Spirit is light-blue, she is the good Spirit not Helana. The trickery was necessary to enable you John to agree to Bond with Helana. We could foresee you refusing to do this if you were fully aware of the background.....Now that all is achieved we ask you to heal Constance's Spirit. Do this by asking your healing Guide (Jesus), to send your Love....as you have already done, but continue to do this for seven days.

Constance's Spirit agreed to walk away from you John, to allow Helana's Spirit to be recovered...'

358

'The meeting between the ladies was the **reverse** of what you have
been led to believe...Helana's Spirit refused to compromise. It would not
give an inch or come to terms with the Past....She has a lot yet to learn
still, therefore we could not allow the child to continue....
The work will continue with you John, and Judith....A tragedy!'

Question (d): What colour is Helana's Spirit?
' Helana's Spirit is dark-blue, we try for so long to lighten her Spirit. She
needed your contact to help her, to make good her past, it was a
learning lesson for her....
We apologise for misleading you, but this was necessary to cause both
of you to form the bonding-link, and so do the good works for the
World....
That is why White-Eagle has been so praiseworthy of her......to cause
her to become more and more Lightened.....Now that the Bonding is
completed, **her Spirit is saved,** and in the **next life, you can continue
with the new Race.** Your Spirit John also needed to convince us that it
was prepared to make the necessary effort and show its 'good side', for
your background to be fully accepted.....
The progress you have made now is excellent'.
'Helana gave to You, You gave to Helana, that is how it should be!'

15.83 Daniel continues....Your Spirit John is now light-Pink...an
excellent colour, and your Mind is now much clearer....We see real
progress now.
KEYPOINT DP23
**The colour of any Spirit is a reflection of the degree
of progress it has made in its journey from Dark to
Light.**

15.84 On the 9th January,1999, I sent the following letter to Helana;
Dearest Helana,
I love you as an equal and as a wife, I wish to share the rest of my life
with you. I wish for us to achieve the Goals we know of. You speak of
how much I have hurt you, I am sorry. I am as I am, with all my faults
and my lack of Empathy...but I still love you and I would not deliberately
hurt you....
Perhaps my words are badly chosen, perhaps my ways are too coarse or
rude, perhaps my voice too hard and critical; or perhaps you choose to
interpret what I say in that way. What I have said and done was never
intended to hurt you...it was on occasion said to stop your train of
thought, to make you hopefully think more carefully.
viz: forgetting the Past, you need to be selective, how many times have
you corrected me and asked me to choose my words more carefully?
viz: my comments to your mother about the Settee....said without
malice, in a light-hearted way, with no intent to offend, and did not even
cause her to react in any way......

We have progressed a long way together, through many lives and unpleasant Situations....Your Spirit has forgiven the Past! Why cannot your Mind forgive the Present? Or, are you just creating another wasted life, another wasted opportunity to be re-healed in a future life, to find forgiveness then!

The World does not seem to have many lives or time left, does it?. Our lives are needed now to help create a Society which can survive in the future, and save Mankind, and save the Earth. Can you live with the prospect of 600 million people dying, just because YOU would not give one month more of **this life, to see if we can rescue the Situation.** Perhaps there are Others who can do the work, we do not know. But are **YOU** prepared to take that chance? I do not wish to frighten you, but think-on:

- Your mother had a 'bungalow Vision', I was told that you are on the verge of a return to Spirit unless there is a dramatic change to your outlook.
- You told me about the 'kitten Vision'...the weak one is sacrificed to ensure the survival of the remainder, The mother can only help for a certain period of time.
- You had the vision of the ' forty-foot tidal wave'
- Judith is being withdrawn
- You are being influenced by Others against me, your Spirit Guide is not helping, you are blaming my Spirit, but I am told it is your Mind.
- Only in the last few days has your Spirit forgiven me. Do you not think that now, for the first time, that without the lives and peoples of the Past, without the on-going negative interpretation of anything I said or did, without these Influences on your Mind, that, **for the first time,** we have a real opportunity to get together?

The door is still open to my heart, you will always have the key, enjoy your holiday. (I could ` ` ` ` ` ` ` ` ` `do with one!
 Do not wait too long before you return, unless I change the lock!
I love you and wish us to try again. But, only if you want it to work and are prepared to make a real effort to be conciliatory and to meet me halfway.

15.85 Helana responded in writing as follows:...
'I received your letter and comments, but I am placing no importance on any of the contents. I have in the past months tried with all my strength to bring help and guidance to you in many matters. I feel now nothing more can be achieved by me, nor anything more can be added to what has already been said.

I hope you can call upon your memory to help you in future years, to understand and to grow in the way that had been hoped for by myself and by Spirit...

I wish you well in this Endeavour and pray that you will continue to learn and to grow. I will be in touch when I have more idea as to when I will be returning to collect my personal belongings....

For now may GOD be with you.'

15.86 On Monday, 18th January 1999, I ask to speak with **Helana's Spirit** and write as follows:

' I do not wish to discuss anything with you. I need to see you suffer, to allow me to come to terms with the past Suffering you have caused to me, and to Helana. I regret the deceit, but it was necessary to bring you to your present vulnerable state so that you could be hurt. I do not hurt Helana, she has chosen this pathway...her Mind has chosen...all I did was to provide her with the past Life information.'

15.87 I ask to speak with **Helana's Guide**, it is still Samuel:

' I regret this situation. Helana chooses not to listen to me, when the timing is correct I will bring all matters to her and make her fully aware of what route she is following and the probable outcome.

This may take some weeks, but she **will know and understand what she is doing.** Remember, freewill does allow her to do exactly as she wishes to...irrespective of whether this is good or bad Advice. You have our sympathies.'

15.88 I eventually returned to England overnight on the Sunday, 24th January, and returned to Bangor for 07.00hrs on the 31st. January. During this time I met with Helana and we had a very passionate and loving re-union,

(I also fitted in eighteen financial appointments)

She promised to return and several flight tickets were purchased and posted to her, she never came and the money was lost. As the days and weeks passed, I slowly came to the realisation that my time in Ireland with Helana was at an end, and it was necessary for me to put this behind me....

She refused subsequently ever to talk or meet with me again....

15.89 On January 27th, whilst in Banbury, Helana gave to me the following words:

When first we met all felt right, my feet and heart and Mind took flight
Heavens door to my heart was wide, and nothing was hidden deep inside
The Love was strong, understanding gained of who we were, and the journey long,

Many hearts were healed, the Past put to rest, but the struggles inside outweighed the best . For deep within I could not find the strength to continue, (the love I hide)
So much Pain endured as the Past remained, however hard I tried I could not explain.

The Mind understood and the Spirit obeyed, but in times of trouble the pain remained.
We have come so far in this journey of life, but my love is of a mother and not a wife
The love is but of a different kind, than you would truly want to find
For my heart and Mind can no longer find, the love of a Lover of the truest kind.
It is hard to explain that this was found, but has now left my heart, my Spirit and Mind.
I hear what you say and I understand

But my Love I cannot truly remain, for by your Side I grow weak and dim,
The light inside grows small and thin. In time I believe if it is meant to be
We will find all Forgiveness and Eternity, but I find in this lifetime it cannot be
For my Spirit is saddened and not truly ready. I have tried so hard to overcome the fears of the Past and the hurt inside,
but I can only do what I can, to travel as far as I am able.
Deep within the Honesty and Truth remind me that all has to be completely true to myself for Love to be found, to heal myself.

An Earthly life is now to be found, where this will take me I am duty bound to fulfil my Karma in every way, for nothing is lost only beauty found
for whichever way we choose to travel, our Lives are fulfilled, Character gathered,
To take us forward into future lives, to fulfil all there is in all our lives.

We were brought together hoping we would find what was needed to be Deep inside, but alas my Love I am truly not ready, for whatsoever reason I am sure you will find.
Forgive me please for I am only Human, at the end of the day I am still the same.
What the Spirit knows and feels and travels can at times be different to the Mind we know. But believe me please in this short time together, I have loved you completely as much as I can. No lies were told to the best of my knowledge, and Truth was there for you to see and hear and feel, for nothing was hidden, my love was free.

Look back on this time and find the Gain, as I can truly do the same.
We may think that we can truly control our hearts, our bodies, our very Soul,
But one thing I have learnt in our time together is be true to yourself in every way
I thank you my Love for the time together, and wish you well on your journey of life.
I hope that you will find all that you need, so in your life you will truly succeed.
May these times in your life bring you understanding and joy in your heart for what has been gained.
Think of love being gained and everlasting, for remember what is there is never lost and what has been has been extended.
Go with peace in your heart knowing love was found and that all in this life is meant to be.
If this time is but a blink of the Eye, let this time be but a Memory, not to harbour fears or pain or unjust, but to understand and remember us.

15.90 In February 1999, I received the following message from Daniel my Guide:..
' Hallo John, we wish to tell you that we do not believe that Helana will ever return, we are sorry to say this to you. Previously we thought that her Spirituality was so strong that the Spirit would be capable of changing her Mind. You are now aware that the Spirit is intent on revenge and is not willing to seek common ground, or to consider the betterment of Mankind. Helana is now intent on contact with Philip, she wishes to try this relationship once more; we regret that she will not be successful with this effort.
We do not wish you to waste further time on this Spirit or Person. After the current Experience, and as you become more aware of the deceit, we cannot see you ever trusting the lady again.
Time to 'draw stumps' as you would say.!....'
'The work can still continue, for the reasons explained previously. Your intention to meet with Constance will be worthwhile and will bring to her the Knowledge and Encouragement she needs. Pursue this please, we do not see any relationship developing, as Constance is convinced in her own Mind, that she cannot live with you!'

15.91 'We come then to Judith and your discovery of the Role she has played over your many lives. We see you and Judith coming together as man and wife and the work being completed in this way. This outcome was always a possibility, and subject to the two of you establishing the right Relationship this can and will be achieved. A child will be given....Helana will wish to try again, but by that time you will be established with Judith, and we fear her pride will not allow her to work alongside you two.'

363

KEYPOINTS DP24
a) The understanding of how Spirit can Change, Divide and Combine is quite complex, and needs a separate examination. We have said that Spirit, plus Personality, plus Aura, comprises the Soul.
b) It is necessary to understand that the Spirit is pure and of God, it is the 'Personality Element' which reflects the degree of Lightness and the Darkness, the Emotional background, the Character. It is perhaps easier to consider two Sectors, the one Pure, the Other Impure.
c) The purpose for most on the Earth-Plane, is for the Lessons and Understanding to be grasped so that the two Sectors can fully re-combine and so achieve unity with GOD.

15.92 'In the particular case of Helana's Soul, now that the bonding has occurred with you John, the work, the Spiritual work can continue whilst you sleep, for the pure-Spirits can combine and fulfil the roles intended'.
'The pure Sector of Helana's Spirit is wondrous to behold, the impure Sector has now come to the fore and must regrettably now re-learn many lessons
KEYPOINT DP24
Be aware that when you talk with Someone's Spirit, that you may hear back from either Sector!

15.93 The final words received from Helana were in the way of a Valentine's card on 15th February 1999:
'Rather than buy you a card to say I love you in words that I can say more clearly than another's words, to help you on your way.
I feel the need to let you know what indeed allows my Heart to grow.
To clearly see will take some time, and understanding hard to find.
But hopefully some day we'll find the open Heart and happy Mind
For now my Love you are in my Heart and words will not express
all feelings that are felt inside. But believe it is happiness,
for soon once more I will hopefully be within your loving arms;
and all within will be once more addicted to your charms.
My Thoughts this day are loving ones, and Dreams I dare not say.
But know my Love you are in my heart upon this very Day.
Happy Valentine and see you soon. With love and kisses.
HELANA'

15.94 I am alone living in Bangor, County Down, Northern Ireland, and seeking healing and direction in my life. I need to establish more financial stability before I can move forwards with confidence.
(I am also under notice of Termination of my Contract as a Franchisee, unless I generate more Financial Business)

I pray to Spirit, Help me please my Friends !

15.95 I learn from Judith that Helana has **married Another on Saturday, March 6th, 1999.**

15.96 I am progressively returning her clothes and valuables to her mother's Bungalow in Kings Sutton, Oxon, and have decided to sell the majority of her furniture and effects.
I understand that she married without the knowledge of her mother or children or friends and against the advice of Judith...She has lost their friendship and respect..
There was one very distressed and tearful telephone call, when the screams from the lost children were heard, and Helana sobbed profusely over the telephone; she complained of the hollow, empty feeling within.....I am certain that this was the withdrawal of the Holy Ghost from her, and the loss of our Children (yes two!).

On a future occasion when I met with Judith, we received a plea from Helana's Spirit which indicated that her Spirit was contained in Shadowlands. We were not certain for some time, whether she was still alive on the Earth-Plane until her mother confirmed this...
High Spirit warned us not to be deceived by her plea for help, and to stay clear of any contact with her Spirit or her Being.

15.97 I receive a strong message from White Eagle, via Judith, the Key Points made are:
- I need to delve into and question more the Messages I receive
- I need to speak less and behave less like GOD!
- The Child will not be brought in this lifetime
- Helana does not need to be physically with me for the Work to continue, her thoughts and actions are not love
- I need to find the person within me, know myself, love myself as I am, appreciate my own self-Worth.
- I am not to feel that I am good enough for any woman on the Earth!
- I am not to rely upon anyone else for my Happiness
- I am not above reproach
- I am not to blame Others for my faults
- I am to find Empathy and Compassion for Others
- I am to repair the damage to Other more gentle Spirits

- I am to rectify the damage I have done to so many Others in so many lifetimes
- Acknowledge my true feelings for Constance and heal her Spirit.

(she regrets she cannot live with me and draws near with love)

15.98 Another Chapter in my life draws to a close. I am also concerned at the size of this Book, and decide to cut short my words to this point in Time.

Easter seems always to be significant in terms of major Events happening in my Life, a good time to close this phase and to begin again....

THE END OF VOLUME ONE

###

APPENDICES

APPENDIX1. HELANA's SPIRITUALITY

These words have been taken from the Spirit-writing principally written and kept separately by Helana. Much has been discarded or summarised so that the relevant Keypoints only can be identified. They provide a useful insight into the background of the lady and provide an understanding of the outside influences which affected our relationship. In this context it may be useful to cross-reference the dates to the main text. The use of dots....indicates that some text has been removed.

A1.00 It is 13th March 1998
In Spirit writing, Helana is told of a reconciliation with the man Philip who has the Spirit of her twin Jack, this separation occurred in the 18th Century. It is the twinning of her Spirit with that of Jack, which is a prime goal for her in this lifetime. A lifetime together with Philip is foretold, a meeting is to be arranged.
(note this is the very DAY she met with John)

A1.01 It is 19th May 98
' My dear, your time now is working with Spirit in a complete way according to your knowledge which you have gained in these last few weeks. We are so pleased with your progress my dear, we wish to send you our congratulations of your progress. It has been a long, hard, struggle for you to reach this level of understanding over your past lives upon this Earth-Plane, but now my dear you will see the fruits upon your tree appear so soon now. This time of coming together with your loved one John has indeed been speedy, but my dear it has long been awaited. A twist of fate has been given, but we need you to understand that this would have occurred at some future date.

It has been possible to bring you together in this way due to your commitment to Spirit in a way that has overwhelmed us with your trust and faith and sheer determination to bring healing to those who are so in need. My dear Helana we are delighted with this choice you have made. A conscious decision to make progress with your Spiritual Awareness will have indeed affected the lives of those you were destined to be with in this lifetime...'

A1.02 It is 10th June 98....seen and typed by John for the first time on Sunday, 28th September 2000, Helana had previously abandoned these writings...
'My dear Helana, we wish now my dear to reassure you all is well within your lifetime. My dear you have achieved a great understanding of all that there is to be. On no account do we wish to cause you pain and suffering and at no time will we ask you to give up your man John.'

'My dear you are aware that Philip is still within reach, this means only in Spirit at this present time. His presence can be felt my dear only as a reminder to you that all is not lost at any time. We do not foresee a problem at this time with John; he has recovered well and has spent his day repenting on his ways. A sadness is present within his Mind, but this will help him towards choosing very carefully that which he must do in the future days ahead.'

A1.03 'My dear all has been given to help this man decide which way he wishes to bring about future happiness into his life. You may recall an earlier message my dear that this relationship may last only a short while, but the love given would heal a great deal of this man's life. This message my Dear may not be shown to this man. We ask you now to keep these words safe and away from his eyes.'

A1.04 'Sooner or later my dear, you will realise how great an achievement has been gained by your Spirit on this Earth-Plane at this present time. Your duty to the World and Spirit my dear are strong within your Mind. Your true nature exceeds anything beyond all that was hoped for you in this lifetime my dear.
You have now seen what needs to be achieved by so many around you, and with the greatness of your Spirit, you will achieve many great works for Spirit. You have a presence of mind my dear to continue and we will be by your side at all times to help and guide you in all you wish to achieve.'

A1.05 'Your happiness is our main concern my dear, and for this reason we have put on hold your man's choices. He needs time to realise the nature of all that is asked of him and needs to be assured that his life is not in danger of becoming sad and lonely, if only he chooses the right Pathway and allows us to lead him in the true way. You have seen the parallel between his Spiritual Path and that of Philip.'

A1.06 'We ask you now my dear to understand we will whisk you away to a life suited to your needs, if both these Spirits remain standing still. Your man John has a presence of mind to see what is needed in his life, unlike that of Philip, but in both cases a nudge is needed....Philip received many nudges my dear but still refused to see. We do not expect this of John....
You may not be aware my dear Helana of how much progress you have made and as sad as it may seem, you leave Others behind you. We are in need of Helpers on this Earth-Plane my dear. To carry out the work of Spirit needed in the future years, and it is hoped that you, along with your man, John, will make-up a team of the most strongest kind to carry out the work needed in Ireland.'

A1.07 'Take heart my dear, he is strong and willing and the love he brings to you my dear is genuine at this present time. You need have no worries my dear for he will join you. In perseverance his strength lies within his heart, for he has found his perfect dream and he now needs to realise that this life is not a 'bowl of cherries', and all has to be worked for, very hard at times.'

A1.08 'We will take you now my dear to a new level of understanding, and this will help you in your future times with this man. Harsh words are needed at times my dear for you all to realise our dearest wishes, for your lives to be gifted with happiness.
It is at this point we wish to make it quite clear to you that all that is to be given is with this 'thought in mind' for you all. Not at any point my dear do we foresee a time of loneliness for you again, you have made your journey and your choices with a filled heart.'

A1.09 'My dear, these thoughts and words are from your true Guide as you know me by the name of Samuel. I wish to remain always by this name, and none other will be given this name. It remains now my dear for me to say these words to you that at no time will you spend your life alone. At all times there will be someone by your side to fulfil all your needs. At the present time your man, John, has filled the empty heart that has been present for so long. Now my dear, I will close and remind you of only one thing. Spirit are all around you at this present time, and I am always by your side, guiding you in all things my dear.
Take now our love into your heart my dear and understand that all given will be. Your man John is a sensible man, and has come to terms with many things throughout his day. Your time now my dear will be spent in the company of Angels, who sit beneath your feet, keeping you lifted my dear towards the Skies. The light of True Spirit surrounds you at this time and always my dear, protecting you and guiding you. All that we wish for my dear is your happiness in all that you achieve. Go in peace now and remain as always the gentle angel we see in our eyes'...
(1.02-1.09 are from the same message at the same time)

A1.10 It is 16th June 1998
'My dear Helana, this man's mind has not yet cleared enough for his Guides to come through with clarity. It will take a little time before they can appear in writing.
Those around you at this time are overjoyed at the fact that they can communicate in this way with your man John. He is not in danger my dear, true Spirit are with you, but a little over-zealous with their own joy at contact with their loved-one. A message will be received by this man in due course. Do not give-up trying John, as your Guide is ready and waiting for you to receive the words he wishes to give to you.'

A1.11 'My dear all is well, and we are ringing-out the Bells in Heaven for the news received this day. Go in peace now my dear and enjoy this time together, it has been given that your work today is done. Rest assured my dears your dreams will come true. Allow us to guide you in all that you do and keep your light in Heaven burning bright with the love that you send to Spirit my dear Helana. Go swiftly now into your new lives and let all else follow.'

A1.12 In June 1998, Helana is asked to purchase a simple, purple, embossed card with the words inside ' WITH LOVE'. She is asked to write inside the card the following words. The handwriting is that of White Eagle:
'From the many hearts who have loved your very nature, you have returned again bringing with you such love and beauty and caring for this Land. We do not see any failure for your heart is as our heart and your heart is the centre of our Universe.
This will be and always has been our dearest Lady, always in our hearts.'
The card is addressed ' To our lady'......It is only on completion of the envelope that Helana is told the card is a message from Spirit to herself.!

A1.13 Prior to moving to Ireland.   ,'....to walk away from all that you have known is a brave decision...in our hearts we see a dedication so complete for all that there is to be achieved, do not think my dear that we take your responsibilities lightly, you have a free-will and you have used it on many occasions....it is an extremely hard task we ask of you. You despair at times with yourself....All your hopes and dreams are appearing now as reality.....a man will be found for you if there is a parting of the ways...'

A1.14 'You will have a happy time with this man John, until the child has gained his independence, and a life of his own. The child will not suffer my dear, you have many Earth years in which to share with this man John, and the love found is true and Spiritual....It is what we wish to see. Your Earthly love will follow my dear, it has been taken away at this present time to allow your Understanding to grow, but believe my dear, all is to be and the child is not lost. It grows within you at the present time. It was given only for you to understand and gain knowledge of your own accord, as to what we needed to see...
'Camouflage maybe my dear yet again, but your true feelings have been received by us here in Spirit....Go forth now with the love in your heart for the World and its People, and remember my dear your work has begun. A move forwards is now expected and your Awareness will be sharpened, for you have learned well my dear all that we have shown you.'

371

'Continue to grow and allow others their time to find their freedom within their own lives. Go in peace, may all our blessings be upon you at this time.'

A1.15 It is 26th June 1998
'Helana, my dear one, stay as beautiful as you are. You have no need to change. Your ways are my ways and nothing my dear will alter this. You are suffering so at this time, for you are not being true to yourself. Your Spirituality has grown so enormously my dear, you are finding great difficulty in being your human self.
(this became a real problem as Helana would almost do nothing unless Guided. The choice of clothes each day, the choice of food, where to go, what to do etc.)
You will find the way, you will find a balance within yourself that will enable you to be Spiritual and Human at the same time. We have taken you up into our Skies this night, we thank you my dear for your bravery. You have achieved so much understanding in this time. Your Body my dear blossoms, for the child within you is stirring and creating life around himself for the protection that is needed. Share only these words with your man John ,my dear, for they are not to be widely spread.'

A1.16 'The announcement of your child to be is not to be spoken of at this point in time. Do not fear my dear all that has been given will be. Go to your rest now my dear one, for all is at peace. Let our Peace and love surround you at this time and bring to you the knowledge that all is as it should be. Be at peace my dear and let your dreams come true......
.....nothing now will stand in your way to finding perfect happiness. Your time here has been spent wisely and all that has needed to be achieved has been done so....Let your life flow now like the peaceful rivers, clear and bright and calm. See them and picture your life flowing as these rivers....Your man John, has many lessons to learn, but he has a strong Spirit and you have reached his very Soul my dear ,with your love for him. He will find his Awareness and his love for you is so deep and strong you will have no worries here my dear. Your togetherness is complete and nothing now stands in your way....Dream only of success for it will be yours.'
KEYPOINT HS01
To find the Balance between leading a SPIRITUAL LIFE and living a HUMAN LIFE is an important issue which EVERYONE has to face, should they wish to find their SPIRITUAL AWARENESS.

A1.17 KEYPOINTS HS02
a) ALL is given for Understanding and for Spiritual Growth.
b) Our Emotions and Feelings may well be influenced and changed should the occasion demand it.

A1.18 KEYPOINTS HS03
a) Our ATTITUDES to each other, our Motives, our Goals,
will influence and change our lives.
b) PERSONAL HAPPINESS may well be an important Goal.

A1.19 KEYPOINTS HS04
a) The true reason for any Event or Meeting may not be
immediately obvious.
b) It is necessary sometimes for us to question and to
probe in order to find-out the TRUE meaning of any
Situation.

1.20 On July 1st 1998 Helana is first shown in June, and then in July
reads the first page of the **BOOK OF LIFE**....this is given to her in Vision.
KEYPOINTS HS05
a) The Book Of Life sets out the Future for all Life
within the Universe.
b) The Book is used by those who need to know as to how
to control and to orchestrate the inter-relationship
between all Life-Forms throughout the Universe.
c) The Book represents the Past, the Present and the
Future as agreed with and by GOD.

A1.21 On 3rd July 1998..A message from Princess Diana........
'A need for positive thinking at all times...You have given your man a
start in his Spiritual Growth, it is now for him to grow, but also within
this you need also to care for yourself....we will guide you to whatever
you need....take care to know the child needs this also, for learning has
begun. Happiness within the mother's womb is felt my dear and brings
contentment to the child's well-being....Your time has come my dear to
bring the greatest gift into this World, a child filled with love and all the
beautiful ways of Nature that only his mother will see.........
Your man's pain will disappear within the next few days, leaving him
with an Understanding that will remain with him for the rest of his years.
Go forwards my dear with Peace and love....this Lifetime is there for
your taking to succeed, my dear.'
(not seen by John until June 2000)

A1.22 On 6th July 1998..Samuel speaks...'You are now ready Helana,
to move on to greater learning, your vision will clear, bringing a greater
understanding of who is with you....... it is only necessary for you to
raise yourself above these Spirits by mental Visualisation....your child is
given my dear and has begun the journey of life...you will be guided as
to where your next home is to be...**you Helana have gained many lives in
your Awareness already, and there are many more yet to be
gained....**your time now must be spent in preparation for the Child... '

'We know we have a great deal of learning to do with timing on the Earth-Plane, but you will have confirmation of the child in a Human way within a few short weeks.

KEYPOINTS HS06
a) The Route, and TIME needed, in terms of the number of Lifetimes to achieve union with your Perfect Sector is known and pre-planned.
b) The Choices we make in this Lifetime, will change and decide the number of Lifetimes we need to experience, in order to achieve Oneness with GOD and our perfect Sector.

A1.23 On Saturday, 8th July 1998
Judith carries out a Spiritual Operation on Helana's body.. '....keep an opening within your day to send loving thoughts to Ireland.' Mary, the mother of Jesus writes....' Do not my dear mistake your message for any other than one person who shares a great deal of understanding for your life. Do not doubt your feelings Helana, you are a very special person chosen for your work in the future. Let not Other's achievements cloud the work in any way that you are doing at the present time. Helana, go now to your rest with a peace of mind and understanding.'

A1.24 'It is imperative Judith, that Helana understands the importance of not allowing herself to be abused by the Spirit of Others. There are many stray Spirits waiting to enter a willing body, and so live the life they gave-up for what-so-ever reason. There are also the Spirits of the People living, these are not so strong as the Spirit of those who have passed, but they can be equally damaging.
Helana is a very receptive Spirit , she has learned so much compassion, but for her own safety, and to remain on the Earth-Plane, for the time that she is needed, **she must call on her Guide and Doorkeeper to protect her.** She is now being given a Maori warrior as her Doorkeeper....these people were a very strong Spiritual Race. Helana **MUST** keep asking for protection.'

KEYPOINTS HS07
a) Your Being is vulnerable to invasion from Dark Spirit.
b) You can request a DOORKEEPER to block access to your Spirit.
c) You can request help also from your Guide, but you must also make it perfectly clear to any invading Spirit that they are not welcome and must leave at once.

A1.25 'Do you not understand my dear, that when a Spirit within an Earthly-Being invites another Spirit in, we can do very little but to try to show the host Spirit the dangers of this...an Understanding of the dangers of this is necessary'.

'John could have gone through **this** Lifetime with no knowledge of any of this, and for this reason, it may come as a shock to discover that all love of Spirit is coupled with the dangers of these Spirit who are in Darkness still. Is this not why we wish to fight for the Survival and Upliftment of the Planet Earth.?

KEYPOINTS HS08
a) It is indeed a Battle between Light and Dark Spirit on the Earth-Plane.
b) The Soul has Free-will of choice, to choose between the Light and the Darkness.
c) Dark Spirits are attracted to Dark Spirits, Light to Light, to cross-sides is therefore more difficult.

A1.26 It is of course made more difficult because Helana came from the Darkened side, and many Spirit recognise her Spirit as such. It is therefore Helana's **duty** to Spirit and to herself that she does not allow these Spirit to come too close. Please ponder these words fully, a day spent in the open Air to do this would be well spent. Helana **must** learn to guard herself against **all low Spirit**'.

KEYPOINTS HS09
a) Time spent in the Open will help to clarify the Mind and reduce outside Influences.
b) Dismiss Dark and negative Thoughts from your Mind, this will help to reduce outside Influences.
c) Think loving Thoughts to attract similar Spirits to you.
d) Pray and ask for help, support and guidance from GOD and other Light Spirits.

A1.27 'Be in no doubt Helana of the danger you were in, not your Earthly body, but if a Spirit can be made so weak, it **can be taken over by another Spirit if it so wishes.** We ask you therefore to know yourself most fully so that you are aware the moment that another Spirit approaches...there are times when love alone may not be strong enough to banish these Evil Spirits. We do not ask you to send hatred to these Spirit, but to be so firm that they are fully aware that their presence is not acceptable.'

KEYPOINT HS10
The Earthly Body can be invaded and possessed by DARK SPIRIT. If this happens IT IS ESSENTIAL TO SEEK PROFESSIONAL HELP AS QUICKLY AS POSSIBLE.

A1.28 It is 12th August 1998
Helana is told by 'Many Feathers', an old friend, that Samuel has been replaced as her Guide, due to matters arising. 'We wish for you to continue progressing, and as soon as the time is right you will be told of your new Guide.'

A1.29 On the13th August 1998
'Your child within awaits it's birth, She awaits to share with you both
her life...She has been chosen for you...She is indeed a beautiful child
and one also who will see and hear clearly the World and all that there is
in Nature to find...make room in your heart, Helana for this child, for She
is given so that the healing of your hearts can be complete.

A1.30 On the 14th August 1998
...Helana writes a message from John's Spirit.
'My darling wife, you can now be assured of my love, for you have
given me so much and I can now see the beauty of your ways. Thank
you for writing this way..
(Helana has changed to her left hand, I am left-handed)
So many times I have come to you wishing for you to write in this way.
You are like a Spring Day to me, you have changed my life so
completely. Do not doubt who it is my love, you are my **Life**. I was as
nothing without you by my side. **Forget the Past now and concentrate
on the Now**.
I will soon be joined forever my love to your Spirit, I cannot say when I
will feel this wonderful feeling. I have not experienced this since our
lives in Athens..
My memory fails me now. Be assured I am the man John with all my
love ..You are my one and only love, Always.'

A1.31 Helana is told that her Spirit has been twinned with many Others
throughout History....She is told that she still has much to learn, but that
as a consequence of her Spirit being with John's, her powers for
learning will increase ten-fold.

A1.32 On 4th September 1998...whilst on route back to England....
'Your Communication skills are being awakened within you both, but
understand my dears a level of cleansing had to be reached before this
gift was allowed to be. You cannot always break through the barriers of
your own accord and we felt at this time, that the opportunity to cleanse
your Spirits would stand you in good stead for the Future, with more
understanding gained beneath your feet...'

A1.33 On 21st September 1998...Your time has come my dear to make
haste with this move to Ireland, it is to go ahead my dear, your dates are
correct ...it is imperative that you return quickly to this Land to begin
your work that you are not yet Aware of...but upon arrival, in the New
Year , All will be set in motion for you to begin in earnest....Do not fear
that this will not take place...agreement has been made for your time to
be with this man, and at the end of this time you will see a marked
improvement to his Awareness'.

'It will then be put to you my dear whether you wish to continue along with your work for Spirit and that which will be achieved in Earthly terms also. We will ask you to think very carefully at this time and it is hoped that you will continue....'

*(nb: this seems strange to me that having committed to the future with John, being married, being pregnant, living in a new Land and place with few friends, a new home...**THEN** is the time to reconsider and to make choices !!)*

A1.34 Isaiah writes... 'with love in my heart and many tears in my eyes. I pray my dears these tears will turn to joy for the coming years ahead of you will be difficult at times, but all can be achieved. Watch, listen, and learn John, and probe your mind many more times than you do at this present time. Allocate some time within your day for this process. You need to understand your lady is weak, not of heart but of energy. Allow her the rest that is needed throughout her day, with understanding in your heart. A return to the Past will not be necessary, but learn by the mistakes of the Past.'

KEYPOINT HS11
a) You cannot expect to progress and to achieve your full Awareness without healing your Past, shaking-off the Guilt of this Lifetime and LEARNING

- **TO LOVE YOURSELF ,**
- **TO KNOW YOURSELF and**
- **TO FORGIVE OTHERS .**

A1.35 On Wednesday, 23rd September 1998... Helana's Guide to her: 'My dear we understand your weariness, and we are pleased you have at last achieved the understanding that John must be in touch with his Inner-Self , if he wishes to achieve his Awareness.'

KEYPOINT HS12
This is the definition of full Spiritual Awareness, when your Mind can communicate, link with, travel and receive messages from your own Soul.

A1.36 We hear your prayers Helana, and we wish you both to know that you are within the light and love of True Spirit... 'do not allow this man to take away your freedom or to abstract you in any way...you have many lessons to learn....understand your work for Spirit is valued so highly....we listen and take notice and act upon your prayers...you will not be bothered by these Spirits from the Past for much longer, as soon as your man realises the effect these have upon his and your lives....he needs to see to help himself....you are in no danger and valuable lessons will be learned by your man....your children within are also safe and learning from these experiences... .let your man take on the responsibility for you....you are asked to bring to him knowledge of his Guides....we see him as One of Hope and Purity in years to come',

'...but the work is hard....for you to take on this man's burdens, the World and all Earthly matters...you have the knowledge within to help John through this difficult time....we feel you will survive, and we bring to you Strength, Peace, Love and Light to surround you through the night'.

A1.37 Your day has begun well Helana,...'we ask you to tell John that he must no longer resist his Guides and must follow the chosen Pathway....we remind you all life is a preparation for what lies ahead.....listen to your lady, for she has the qualities necessary....she has not allowed Spirits of the Past to come between you....you need to understand the extent of All who may enter your life, and how this can affect and devastate your lives if you let it...there will be many Spirits in your future venture together who will try to put asunder your marriage in a different way to that of jealousy and deceit....
There are many ways of Evil my dear man, for do not forget the Spirit within this lady is true light of the Holy Kind.'

A1.38 On 24th September, Brian's birthday,...the Court case looms-up with Helana's ex-husband:...your feelings are very confused at this time...your Earthly lives are to breaking point....we see your concern at the Court case...it is your life and you must choose what is right for you....do not allow this man to rule you in this matter, we feel his ways are unjust and malicious....within his mind is the need to hurt you for all the hurt he feels you have given to him, little does he know the hurt is self-inflicted....and also that of your Son, ...he sees only his father's hurt...your mother also has taken upon herself to defend these two people, who in her eyes have given her more support than she feels she has received from you. Her expectations of you as a daughter, have not been realised, and you are now in judgement of yourself, for your words to this woman were not strong enough....'

A1.39' It does not matter whether it is our words or yours, we see the need for honest talk to these people, for they have given to you and to your life **nothing, except pain and suffering, and have taken away your beautiful nature**....Do not let the Spirits of these people do this again to your life....it is no wonder you are both suffering, for these darkened Spirits, and also those from John's Past , come to you both with darkened Thoughts which can cause you both discomfort and cause your Attitudes and Emotions to move into conflict.
You must protect yourself at more times throughout the day.'
KEYPOINTS HS13
a)Dark Spirit CAN influence your Being, and your
Emotions, and your Attitudes, which in turn can affect
your Speech, your Communication and your Relationships
with Others.

b) SIMPLY BY ASKING FOR PROTECTION, OF THE TRUE LIGHT, AND FOR YOUR DOORKEEPER TO BE PRESENT, YOU CAN PREVENT MANY OF THESE NEGATIVE INFLUENCES.
c) Be aware of dramatic Character changes, and ask the question of why, or how, or what, is causing this change. Do not reject what is good on the basis of a single Outburst; always give the benefit of the doubt; and FORGIVE if at all possible. Remember Pride can destroy.

A1.40' Do not fear your time of arrival in Ireland will be delayed, however, we need to ensure that you will survive this Land and its Inhabitants, ..to enable you to do the work that is necessary, we see you struggling at the present time...now the Understanding has been given, you will both now progress. Accordingly, when they see that you are protected, and they cannot affect you any more, they will soon tire and will move off to someone who is more vulnerable and willing to share the pain and suffering in their lives.

KEYPOINTS HS14
a) TELL Dark Spirit firmly to leave, send them on their way.
b) Say a few prayers for them, that they may see the error of their ways, and be guided by True-Spirit to see the Light; for in this way their Spirits may be uplifted

1.41 'We wish now for you to enjoy a peaceful day and to enjoy the Countryside. My dear this will bring strength and peace to your mind and Spirit. As is always the case your beloved Trees await your arrival....Do not forget also to rest each day, for this is essential for the well-being of yourself, the child within, and your Spirit.'

A1.42 'Helana my dear you have said the words, but your heart has not always been present....Do not let John take away your true nature, for you also have a life to lead...he will see in time the need for you to have your freedom....do not despair that you are not progressing....he has a wealth of knowledge in his Spirit which he will soon become aware of....he will then pull you forwards with him...there are many things left unsaid, you need now to ask John what his true feelings are.........'
...writings from White Eagle.

KEYPOINTS HS15
a) In so much as trees also have Spirits it is possible for some Beings to tune-in to their Energy levels....In particular Helana's origins were from a green Planet where Trees are respected and an integral part of the Existence; Helana can communicate with Trees.
b) It is useful to imagine a row of Trees when one wishes to meditate and to calm one's-Self.
c) Whenever you travel or walk close to Trees, feel the vibrations emanating, particularly from the older Trees.

A1.43 'Do not worry about your man while he is away at the weekend, this time will be useful for your understanding and will show his true feelings of love for you. You need to learn trust for your man also, he will not be unfaithful...do not tempt anyone else into your heart my dear, we do not see this as a problem, but something you need to be aware of...Do not forget that Temptation still plays a part, for from the Origins of Life come these Traits which need to be overcome by so many.....

'Your man has learnt many lessons from past Relationships and is fully aware of the dangers here...he will not walk away from you unless you damage his faith and trust....each or both of you have had infidelity in your previous Lives, we need now for you to break these Chains..... . Walk away my dear Helana from temptation and your man will do the same....do not allow one Moment to destroy all that you have.....'

A1.44 '....do not forget the forbidden fruit!!....you need to find complete trust and faith in each other and your honest Actions; so that no man or woman can put asunder what marriage has taken place, and will remain always my dear....do not fear these words, but we felt it necessary to bring these to your attention.....
Go now with peace in your heart and allow your lives to flow, as do the Rivers of Life....
(note well this message!)

A1.45 On Saturday, 26th September
'Your Beginnings my dear, account for no more Memories or Darkness to prevail, or indeed to prevent you from progressing...forget all that has passed, for you have moved forwards so fast my dear that all has been left behind.
We have removed all past Darkness so that we can bring to you only Light of a true kind. Do not doubt these Words, or your own understanding.'
KEYPOINT HS16
It is possible for the Memories held within our Spirits to be removed or dimmed.

A1.46 'Your man John will now progress rapidly, as all Past for him also has been left behind, and only a few short moments be ahead of him now to regain all that has been lost. The past ladies in his life-time will cease to become the problem you have encountered, for all past memories of your Beginnings have been taken away from their Minds and Consciousness. Their Spirits also have been dimmed accordingly to allow you both the freedom now you so deserve. Your man has worked well my dear and it remains now only for the Mind to release the barriers that have been created by Time.'

A1.47 On Sunday 27th September 1998
'....All has been achieved....we see a marked improvement in the man's Mind now that a more settled Spirit resides within the man's Being. *(our Spirits are joined as One)*.
Do not doubt his fears my dear for they are real....his fears of losing you are greatly heightened.....we see a little concern, for you realise the possessive nature of this man...Understanding will be gained in time of the merits of Freedom. ...**your work will continue with this man for some time until his Lessons have been learned, for his Mind to let go of all that holds him back.**

The Spirit is gentle my dear and comes to you now with the fullness of love Everlasting. Your bodies will unite this evening and the closeness felt will be wonderful for you both to experience   Do not fear this my dear for as you are now of the one Spirit, what is good for the Goose is also good for the Gander....Communication will commence first from Touch...then true Conversation will follow after a short time...it is to be truly a magical Time for you both'.
(this refers to the Mind-Thought link)
KEYPOINT   HS17
There is a clear indication that Helana is with me for the purpose of teaching me, and that when this teaching is completed then she will decide whether to depart! This follows on from the lessons brought to me by Constance!...Separate to the teaching of John, Helana has been told that there is a quite separate special Purpose for her life ahead.

A1.48 On Monday 28th September 1998
'..Your understanding and love for this man has always been wonderful for us to see....we see now your Commitment to one another will not end in this life-time...you are from the one Source my dear, one GOD, one Being, you are forever returned to the Source from whence you come. All Beings are from one Source...from wherever their lives take place, they will always return to the One source of Life.
Here in Spirit we see only the Spirit....Do not fear your Origins, for it makes no difference my dear to us here in Spirit....All is love....Love is life and your deep love for this Planet Earth will never cease...for you my dear have helped to create the very life there is to be found on this Earth.'
KEYPOINT   HS18
Both Helana and I originated on different Planets and from different life-forms. When the Earth Experiment commenced we were brought together in the Human life-form...as some of the Characters recorded in the Bible Book, Genesis.

381

A1.49 On Tuesday, 29th September 1998....'your smile is welcomed my dear, and your Spirit recognises the need for this. So many times your happiness is dashed by this man. My dear, Do you feel you can continue in this way for a while longer?...Do not give-up on this man for his Understanding is so close and his Spirit is raised sufficiently now to allow his true nature to rise to the forefront of his Mind.'

A1.50 'The World's needs are fully known to your Spirit. Your Spirit cries out for the peace that is needed my dear. The wondrous Mind is not fully aware as yet as to what these needs are...but understand blocking occurs from the Spirit of the man as he learns yet again to share your love with the World.....Do not allow him to prevent you from doing this...you have a need, it is your work and your true nature my dear....you have moved from the Darkness, now only Light prevails, for your Spirit is aware of the sadness caused by Darkness of any kind....Your Man has returned to the grave of his loved-one, who now resides within him. Your Spirits have now concluded this lifetime...it was necessary for the tears to flow.
(I was asked to visit Over-Worton once more, to say goodbye to this lifetime as Richard and Catherine...see past Lives)
KEYPOINTS HS19
a) The greater purpose is hinted at, and referred to, on several Occasions.
b) The Spirit and the Mind have separate Identities.
c) The Spirit can and does over-ride, and influence our own Thoughts and Actions, and also those of Others.

A1.51 KEYPOINTS HS20
a) Spiritual Awareness and progress will be restricted by 'unfinished business' from previous Lifetimes.
b) It may be necessary to re-visit these lifetimes to release the 'Cycle of Hate' which may be trapped, such that the sequence of Events is repeated and repeated in subsequent lifetimes until true healing occurs.
c) Not only do these Cycles restrict you own individual Spiritual growth, but they also impinge on Others in your Peer-Group et al..(see Chapter on Spiritual Awareness)

A1.52 'It is very important for you to be seen....you are protected at all times ..without your presence on the Earth-Plane all would fail...a return to your Host-Planet, or anywhere else, is not expected by us upon your return to Spirit...the Choice will be yours and this will be honoured....a Human Being has surrounded your Spirit for many life-times.......
- .you will be given the choice of whether you wish to return to your Host-Planet,
- or to reside in Spirit as an Angel,
- or to return to the Earth-Plane,

- or a life of more Understanding to your Mind.

Your Mind we feel has already decided and we ask you now to consider carefully the full implications of this decision.'

KEYPOINT HS21

We choose our lives and the experiences our SOUL needs, before we are born; we are of course guided into this choice, or indeed some need to be pushed!

A1.53 'We wish to clarify that a decision to return to help the cause on the Earth-Plane, would not result in a Lifetime similar to your previous ones of struggle and torment. All that you have gained in this lifetime will not be lost and will be achieved at an earlier stage in your development from Child to Adulthood....believe these words my dear, they are needed for your peace of Mind....White Eagle writes with you my dear...every word has true meaning my dear.'

' I am honoured to be part of this and honoured to be by your side at all times. Walk the Earth my dear with light in your footsteps that will guide you along the heavenly way. Let wings be on your feet my dear, for you will truly fly.'

A1.54 On 7th October 1998

'.....Go with our blessings my dear and know that you are always in our tender, loving care, at all times....your safety is our main concern and that of the child within....do not doubt all is well my dear, and Peace will reign within your beloved Land.

Let our hearts be filled with joy, for smiles we need to see upon the face of our beloved One, so beautiful and full of grace. Rest in our hearts my dear as we see the flower of the Earth-Plane bloom once more, more fully than ever before. Let your tears be the Mountain rain, pure and refreshing, cleansing the very Earth they fall upon....**your man awaits his Spirit my dear, and when this day arrives, all will be beautiful. DO NOT, PLEASE WE PRAY, GIVE-UP ON THIS MAN.'**

A1.55 On 8th October 1998

'....My dear do understand that all that is given, will be given. Your needs are for both Inner warmth and for Spiritual warmth...Do not be harassed by this Man or by any other Spirit.....We will guide you in any decision you make....the rose petals that you now walk upon will always be given....**We fear(respect) your words my dear, and your Thoughts, and we will stand by these' remember always**...the Spirit of the man stands by awaiting this re-union with the man. His mind is frozen like the heart my Dear, but we feel sure you will find a way to melt away again this frozen mass which surrounds and hides the man's true nature.....Go now with our blessings my dear and purchase the Winter coat which you feel you need to.'

A1.56 In January 1999....a letter to Richard, Dennis, John

' Hallo Sweetheart, just a little note to say I love you and always will ,
whatever you decide. Have just received your call. I feel overwhelmed
with your caring for me. I am finding this quite difficult, for I know how
deeply I love you in every way, but at the same time I know I need to
hold onto a little space of my own. This, I convince myself I do, but
deep down you are in my Heart and Spirit and now in my life's
Memories, Always, I find it difficult to tell you in words, for it is not
possible to pass over to you what I feel in just words. Feelings and
knowing are so difficult to describe. Your acceptance of me in your life,
however short or long it may be , is so very beautiful.
No more words my love. Just know I love you always and forever-----
you are so beautiful.'
signed Catherine Dee. + + + + +

##

1.57   A BRIEF LIFE-HISTORY of HELANA.

a)Born 24.05.51 to Joshua Tom who died 09.05.84
Christened and confirmed in the Church of England, married at
19 years of age to Kevin, divorced in June 1979, one child James born
26.06.73, one miscarriage October 1975.

b)Considers should not have married, identified Spiritual link with a
Curate, but this never developed, simply grew apart from Kevin and had
various Affairs.

c)Lived for three years in Bahrain, but following split with Kevin,
returned to live in Oxon, England, and worked as Housekeeper for
Mervin.....eventually married him on 01.09.79, another mistake, married
for Security, no Love. Mervin had two existing children, and Abel was
born on 01.10.80.

d)Kevin was having an Affair with Bryan's wife, a friend, this led to the
separation. Helana then had a brief fling with Bryan, but then Helana
thought this was over and returned to England.

e)In November 1996, Bryan killed himself with remorse at not pursuing
the relationship with Helana.

f)Met Judith in 1972, when working as an hairdresser in Banbury, Oxon. Lost contact with Judith until telephone call from her in October 1995,

g) On verge of suicide as another Affair had failed (George), on tablets for depression, went to Spiritualist Church with Judith for first time.

h)Divorce proceedings commenced with Mervin in January 1996, Helana moved into a small box-room in the matrimonial house and lived a separate Existence.

i)A Court financial settlement was finally granted in Autumn of 1998, and monies arrived in January 1999. (~ £ 30,000)

j)Her life was spent in listening to music, John Lennon in particular, in self analysis, in writing Poetry, in reading (esp John Hamblin), and in Spiritual Journeys and Meditation.

k)Helana became possessed by the Spirit of Bryan, to the extent that her physical features, eyes, voice, legs, and handwriting changed. Judith was eventually able to exorcise this Spirit, but this was very difficult as Helana welcomed the presence.

KEYPOINTS HS22
a) The power of thought is such that Spirits are attracted to whoever is thinking about them.
b) The majority of people are not aware of the presence, but another Spirit can influence your Attitudes and sour your personal Relationships, particularly where jealousy is present, or Evil, or malevolent Purpose is a-foot.
c) You should ask the question ` Was that Comment, Saying, or Action typical or representative of the Individual saying those poisonous or mischievous words, or, could they have been influenced by another Spirit?

l) Met John on Friday, 27th March 1998. Judith was supposed to meet John, but declined the Spirit request. Helana was present at this time and decided to go to, and to await developments at the Whately Hall Hotel. The story commences...................

APPENDIX11. ONE SOUL, PAST LIVES

A2.00 This Appendix is the story of one Soul. This particular story is considered of interest to Others only because of the familiarity to some of the named Characters listed. The real purpose is to try to explain that Reincarnation is an essential feature of the Human Life. That all Lives serve a purpose for the progression of each Individual Soul; or to help others within your Peer-Group in their progression towards the Light and Love of GOD.

KEYPOINTS PL1

a)All Lives serve a purpose, to enable the learning to take place for the Soul to progress towards the Light and Love of GOD.

b)Reincarnation is an essential feature of the Human Existence, the Soul must sometimes return to the Earth-Plane until the lessons have been learned.

A2.01 Eons before the Human Race was created, there existed many life-forms and Species on different Planets throughout our Solar System, and the rest of the Universe.

These Alien life-forms still exist and some are still present today on the Earth, some friendly and some not so friendly. A few Species visited the Earth before the Human Race was developed and were responsible for some of the Monuments which still exist. (ie the Sphinx, the Giant's Causeway).

Laws were laid down when the Human Race was created, which preclude any Alien interference on the Earth-Plane. However as with Humans, some choose to operate outside of the agreed structure and in due course must suffer the consequences of their own Karma.

KEYPOINTS PL2

a)Many advanced Species visited the Earth thousands of years before the Human Race was developed.

b)Laws exist which restrict these Species interfering with Human activity, but a few choose to ignore these Laws.

c)Alien Species were instrumental in the Structure and Order of the Human Race.

d)The Earth is a place of learning for Souls to learn and to change from darker Ways to ones of Love.

b)The Original Souls were introduced from Alien Planets and other Universes.

c)The Souls were introduced into Human Bodies and the learning Experiences created for their Understanding.

KEYPOINTS PL4
a) Souls can be divided, re-combined, re-borne, to dilute
and modify their negative Characteristics.
b) Most of the individual Souls identified in the Book of
Genesis are alive on the Earth-Plane today.

KEYPOINTS PL5
a) The Soul will return many times to the Earth-Plane
until the necessary lessons of Light and Love have been
learned.
b) It is possible to become more Dark if the wrong
Choices or Actions are taken.
c) Your Peer-Group will return with you, so to fulfill
their own Destinies, and also to enable you Individually
to be presented with your own learning Experiences.
d) When you have progressed to the desired Level and
Energy Plane, your Soul can then choose to stay where it
is, or to return to the Earth-Plane solely to help
Others along their Pathways.

A2.05 When the Soul is divided and re-combined, then it may be
possible for more then one Human Identity to exist at the same time.
Similarly, the Soul may simply divide for a period of time and then be re-
constituted later. It is necessary for the learning to take place normally
within the framework of the Peer-Group, so as Roles and Opportunities
arise these may well be grasped. There is some evidence of this
'overlap' of Identity, within the chronological Times listed below.
KEYPOINT PL6
The same Soul can exist in two different People at the
same time; these people are not necessarily Twins, nor
need they have similar Genetic make-up.

2.06 Author's comments:

*a) I have pondered whether to present the following information in this
Book, for there is no way that I can verify (at this Time) to the Reader
anything that I have said. I can only justify the inclusion from the point
of view that*
This is what I have been told*, by different Mediums, with no
particular personal advantage to gain from saying one name or another.
Some of the information has been given by my own Guides and
Messengers, usually accompanied by all sorts of physical sensations.*

*b) In many ways it would seem sensible to omit much of this, for I fear
that it may detract credibility from the remainder of the Book,
It may also set me up for abuse or ridicule from those who may feel
wounded or affected by Events which happened many hundreds of years
ago.*

c)So I re-iterate, Is this a further test for me? a choice between Fame and GOD as so many of my previous Lives seem to have been?
The PAST is the PAST, for better for worse it cannot be changed.
Yesterday cannot be changed! All that we <u>individually</u> can hope to do is our best to improve the Present and to build for the Future. This is what I have committed to do with GOD.

d)The whole of this Book is so incredible to believe,
***ALL THAT I CAN SAY IS THAT I HAVE LIVED THROUGH THESE EXPERIENCES,** I have been party to this Life-Story,*
- *I have been asked by High-Spirit to write this Book,*
- *I have been told the name of this Book,*
- *I have been asked to Plant the new Church for the Aquarian Age,*
- *I have been asked to call this Church,*
   'THE CHURCH OF GOD ON EARTH',
- *I have been asked to change my Christian Name to JOHN.*

e)You can only judge the Truth based upon what YOU believe, what you Sense, what your Experiences are.
I only ask for you to ask for the Evidence so that you can reach your own Conclusions.
This Book sets-out some Experiences for you to formulate your own opinions.....Be open, be receptive, question honestly and look around you at what is happening in the World today.
***IF EVERY ACTION AND CHOICE IS MADE OUT OF LOVE FOR ALL,** then you are well on the way to helping Mankind to survive.*

f) Remember:
1. Treat Others as you would wish to be treated
2. Give Love to receive Love
3. Respect all of GOD's Creation
4. Ask: What is the purpose of this Experience or Event or Meeting? What can I learn from this?
5. Strive to find your Soul within, and to achieve your own Individual Spiritual Awareness.

g) May GOD Bless You and Help us All.........................JOHN

- **ABEL,** son of Adam and Eve, wife Rebekah (Helana), killed by Cain as told in the Book of Genesis.

- **ISHMAEL,** son of Abraham (Judith), married to Sarah (Helana), as such founder of the **Arab** Nation through Hagar (Constance). The name of Melchizedek is significant.

- **AARON,** brother of Moses (Judith), married to Elishiba. High Priest. As such founder of **Jewish** Priesthood. ; spokesperson for Moses, helped lead the Israelites out of Egypt.

- **ELKANAH,** father of Samuel, married to Peninnah and Hannah. Samuel was a Prophet, Seer and Judge as well as a Leader.

- **ELIJAH, Prophet,** Stressed Monotheism, only one GOD. Struggle between Prophets of Baal and Yahweh. King Ahab married to Jezebel. Elisha followed teachings of faith linked to reason and morality, rather than the despotic cruelty of a King.

- **NOAH,** the Ark Builder and Survivor, instructed by GOD to construct an Ark and save Mankind and the Animal population from the Flood.

- **SETHANICOB, High Priest** adviser to Rameses II,

- **WEREWOLF, Saxon Lord,** Locha, Lockbrook (Laycock) Abbey, Wiltshire.
  .Christa (Helana, wife poisoned our children, Ford and Brian),
   married Judith, Constance Sister, Lorna Mother, Elsa a Friend.
   ......(1406-1372BC)

- **SOLOMON, Hebrew King,** military Ruler, administrator, sage, poet, built commercial Empire and Temple, eventually Kingdom split into Judah and Israel. (all the present day Ladies were historic wives)
   ......(ruler 970-930BC)

- **RUNNING ONE, Chief of Minowa Indians,** Texas USA, Constance Wife, Helana Daughter, Sleeping Brook Daughter (Brian), One Tree Son (Ford)
   ......(902-856BC)

- **DIOLYSIUS** at the time of the Trojan Wars .

- **ALEXANDER the GREAT, (III), General**, King of Macedonia, son of PhillipII, defeated Persians, Babylonians, Phoenicians, Egyptians, created a World Empire dominated by the Greeks and Hellenistic Traditions, builder of Cities.
    ....(356-323 BC.)

- **KING ARTHUR**, Guinevere (Constance), Merlin (Judith), Lancelot (Bob), Helana was a Child.
    Soldier, Ruler and saviour of the Welsh and English Realms
    ....(340-286 BC)

- **ANDRECIUS**, Governor of Province in Greece, married to Percarnia (Helana), Cleanort son died in miscarriage, Marcia daughter (Ford), Andrenia daughter (Brian)
    ....(206-144BC)

- **ZECHARIAH**, married to Elizabeth, father of John the Baptist, **Prophet** ,Lost speech when did not believe miracle of his wife's pregnancy.
    (Biblical Times)

TIME OF JESUS

- **JOHN** the **Disciple and Apostle**, the Elder, Judith was Peter the Disciple and Apostle, Edward was Slave Trader Anthony Saponicus. John bore four Children, Bartholemew (Ford), Joshua (Brian), Rebekah (Steven), Ruth (Abel).
    Before JESUS died he asked John to take care of Rebekah and his child Christopher. Rebekah became John's wife, the second letter of John is a personal one from John to Rebekah. Constance was Rebekah. Ruth who washed Jesus's feet was Helana. Brother James, lived at Ephesus.

- **CAESAR, Roman General, scholar,** married to Helana, children Glaudius (Ford) and Ephenium (Brian), both killed at ages 14 years and 12 years, creating a 'Cycle of Hate' which still exists in 1999. Set-up Schools,
    This Lifetime started many problems to this day; a choice then between Power, Wealth and Fame or GOD. As Caesar I chose Rome.

- **MARCUS**, son of wealthy Trader**, Philosopher, Christian at Ephesus, Turkey. Builder of Library,** Children with Athenia (Judith), Antonius (Ford), Brian (Brian), Sinius (Elsa), Rebekah (Helana) died at three years of age, Herodus Father (Edward), Aradiete sister (Lorna), Aunt (Doreen). **Collected Biblical Scrolls and Books from Ancient Times,** hid many of these when Library destroyed.

*(seemingly two lives here, the one as the Merchant who travelled
the Holy Lands, helped build-up the Celsus Library, purchased these
historical Scrolls and Books. The second as some-one responsible for
protecting and hiding many of these documents prior to the
destruction of the Library by the Goths around 262AD.)*

- **BRIGID, Saint, Kildare, Ireland, built Abbey, Churches, Hospital etc.**
  mother (Helana), brother (Edward). Established Community for
  women, helped poor and suffering. Established Religious Order for
  Christianity. Father was Druid, Pagan Chieftain, converted.
  Established tradition prior to St Patrick.
  ....(.453-523 AD)

- **LORD CLEMINGTON,** married to Helana, lived at Carrickfergus,
  Ireland, wealthly, involved in **Government**, happy initially but worked
  long hours and travelled extensively, whilst away Lady formed
  relationship with another, unable to forgive. Helana left with
  Children, Ford and Brian, then 14 and 12 years. Married again to
  Judith but regretted decision. Helana and Judith became friends.
  Lesson of forgiveness not learned.
  ....(628-646 AD)

- **ALFRED THE GREAT,** King of Wessex, united the Realm against the
  Vikings, Soldier, Reformer, Scholar
  ....(849-899 AD)

- **ROGER DE MONTGOMERIE, Sir, Norman Knight,** number two to
  William the Conqueror, created Earl of Shrewsbury after Battle of
  Hastings, **founded Abbey,** member **Benedictine Order,** Earldoms of
  Arundel and Chichester, married to Helana, our Children Ford, Brian,
  Abel....(1020-1095 AD)

- **RICHARD THE LION-HEART, King of England,** Normandy and
  Aquitaine., Angevin, Soldier, Politician, Poet, energetic, **Crusades
  against Saracens**.
  ......(1157-1199AD)

- **JOHN de COURCY,** Norman, Westmorland Castle, **Christian Knight,**
  Carrickfergus, Dundran Castle, crossed to Ireland with King John,
  placed **in charge of Ulster,** built Carrickfergus Castle, married to
  Alfrecca (Constance), lover Rebekah (Helana), Priory established,
  Judge. In love with Helana but decided to stay with Constance,
  Helana eventually married Edward my brother. Castles, Churches,
  Roger brother (Edward). Children Ford, Brian, Barry, Valerie.

(In this lifetime Helana's lover Philip (soul of Jack) hanged himself when he thought he had lost Helana's love....this has reoccurred through many Lifetimes).

Choices between Love or Wealth, Love or Power, Is family more important than personal love? sacrificed Helana's love, was the personal Wealth used to benefit Others?

A further life as Governor, with Helana, at Carrickfergus in 1326.

.....(1206-1282 AD)

- **JOHN O'HAMBERT,** married to Lady Anne (Lorna), Castle and Estates at Cloonamahon, Catherine widow (Helana) mistress, **Governor of County of Ireland,** chose to remain with Lorna, Helana drowned herself in Lough, Her brother William(Roy) learned of this and killed John with sword in ambush.
  Very wealthy but did not help Others, only School at Sligo. Brother (Edward), Father (Ted), Mother (Leonora).
  Helana lived at Castle Baldwin, Ireland ....(1206-1282 AD)

- **ORGHR,**Village **Chief of Zhekatere Tribe** in Uganda, **Africa,** banished Witch-doctor (Elsa), ...1300's, Ugra and Sorean, Twins both lost through illness, Ford and Brian.

- **JOHN CHAPEL, Lord of Manor, Priest,** School, Priory at Newtownards, Naturalist, Carrodore, Ireland, six children, married to Helana.
  ....(1401-1462 AD)

- **HENRY VIII,**1509 marries Catherine of Aragon (Lorna) divorces 1533,
  1533 marries Anne Boleyn (Helana) beheaded 1536, Helana's Neck hurt when we visited Hampton Court in 1998.
  1536 marries Jane Seymour who dies giving birth, (Constance)
  1540 marries and divorces Anne of Cleeves (Judith), known as the Sprite.
  1540 marries Catherine Howard (Elsa), beheaded 1542
  1543 marries Catherine Parr who outlives Henry, (Agatha),
  The Executioner was Bob!
  Tudor King, Founder Church of England, break-away from Pope and Dissolution of Monestries, built up Navy and Institutions.
  ....(1491-1547 AD)

- **SIR FRANCIS DRAKE, Naval Hero** at Armada against Spanish, **strong Protestant**, father Priest, Admiral and seaman who circumnavigated the Globe, feud with Spain under Queen Elizabeth I,
  ....(1540- 1596 AD)

- **OLIVER CROMWELL, General in Civil War, Calvinist, Puritan, Soldier, Statesman**, Lord Protector of England, Scotland and Ireland, beheaded King Charles Stuart (Judith), Richard Son (Brian), married to Constance, Green Man brought messages from Army Council (Helana, a friend in this Lifetime). Believed in Individual contact with GOD and Spirit. Bob was married to Charles Stuart.
  ......(1599-1658 AD)

- **CHARLES BOYLE**, Son of Robert, (Earl of Cork), 4th **Earl of Orrery, Scotland**, married to Lorna, children Ford and Brian; mistress Helana, children Edwin, Abel, Simon. Astronomer.

- **THOMAS TAYLOR, Pilgrim father**, Merchant, Quaker, one of the founders of Pennsyvania, married to Helana, children Jack, Abel, Simon, Ford, Brian (Ford and Brian drowned on crossing)

- **GENERAL MACDERMOTT Commander in Chief**, 1st Battalion Highlanders, married to Matilda (Judith). Longtown, Scotland, children, Ford, Brian, Helana, Alan, Helen, Joyce,

- **RICHARD COOKSON**, wife Catherine (Helana), Over Worton Manor, Ledwell, Oxon
  1700's. **Son of wealthy Farmer**, married servant girl and lost Inheritance, Child lost was Soul of Jack.(twin) Father Albert.

- **JOHN DE QUINCY, LIEUTENANT**, killed at Scabo Tower, County Down, **Ireland**, fighting against troops of James Ist, married to Helana.
  ....(1754-1798 AD)

- **HORATIO NELSON**, Sir, Sailor and **British Naval Commander**, Battle of the Nile, American War of Independence, French Revolution, Napoleon Bonaparte, Battle of Copenhagen, killed Battle of Trafalgar.
  ....(1758-1805 AD)

- **JOSEPH SMITH, Founder Mormon Church,** The Church of Jesus Christ of Latter-Day Saints...a Community based upon GOD and Jesus. Joseph did not believe in any existing Church, he prayed to GOD and was visited by the Angel Moroni. Told to go and to find a Book, found Tablets buried in stone box. Translated Bible. Conferred Priesthood of Aaron.
  Built new Church, necessary to move following persecution, from New York, to Ohio, to Illinois, to Rocky Mountains to Salt Lake City
  ....(1805-1844 AD)

- **GEORGE ARMSTRONG CUSTER, Civil War Hero, 7th Cavalry, US General, Indian Fighter,** Little Flower (Helana), Black Kettle (Bob), Singing River (Judith)
  .....(1839-1876 AD)

There are many other lives, inclusive of **TSAR NICHOLAS II of Russia,** when my wife was (Edward), Brother (Judith), Rasputin (Damien), Anastasia (Helana), children Ford and Brian. Certainly at least one lifetime in Australia, one in Singapore, and one lifetime in Japan.

I have been told by Spirit, that this is my 77th Human lifetime!

##

394

APPENDIX XIII. SPIRITUAL BELIEFS

In this Appendix, I will attempt to explain the principal Beliefs associated with Spirituality. The order is not important. These principals have arisen from Conversations with Spirit and have been raised and identified by Situations which have occurred to me in recent years.

KEYPOINTS SB1
a) The One GOD, is variously known as GOD, JEHOVAH, ALLAH, the DIVINE LIGHT, the all-encompassing POWER of CREATION, SUPREME BEING, ZEUS, BRAHMAN, etc. The name is unimportant, it is the acknowledgement and acceptance that there is only One Supreme Creator who is the fundamental focus for all Life, all Light and all of Creation.
Arising from the One GOD are all Others, the Holy Ghost, the Angels, the Human Species and many more.
b) Jesus was a man, he had more of the Spirit of GOD than other men.
c) The Holy Spirit (or Holy Ghost), is an Angel which can enter you and bring to you the light, love and spirit of GOD.
d) The writers of the Bible invented the concept of the Trinity to explain in Human terms these facts.

KEYPOINTS SB2
a) We are Spirit, our life-force is Spirit.
b) Our Bodies are of the Earth and return to the Earth when we die, BUT, it is only the Body which dies, the Soul or Spirit lives-on;
c) Our Spirits all originate originally from the one GOD.
d) All Mankind is therefore related, irrespective of the Human Shell differences of colour, features or origin.
e) Religions are man-made not God-made. Religious differences are irrelevant in the order of things.
f) We should all respect and tolerate each others' view-points and not be BIGOTED.
g) The SOLE purpose of this lifetime is for the SOUL to learn and practice LOVE; all the different aspects of love and relationships; be it Male-Female or Parent-Child or Brother-Sister etc.
h) The Earth-Plane existence which is all most of us are aware-of, is in-effect a schooling, a learning Process.

KEYPOINTS SB3, (N17)
a) All LIFE has Spirit, all Creatures which are alive, all Plants, all Insects, all Fish etc.
b) When Mankind chooses to harm and decimate other Life-forms then eventually NATURE which is one of the power-forces of GOD, will bring retribution.

c) All is in balance, disturb the balance and suffer the consequences at your peril!.

　　viz..Ozone layer, forestry Devastation, Pollution, Genetically Modified Foods, Cloning etc.

KEYPOINTS SB4,(AB39)

a) We are not alone in the Universe. There are many hundreds of other so called 'Alien' life-forces,

b) Many of these Alien Species are far more advanced than Humans;

c) Some have visited the Earth and some have created mischief.

　　viz. UFO's, History of Civilisation, Advanced Technology to build the Giant Pyramid at Giza, the Giants Causeway in Northern Ireland. etc.

KEYPOINTS SB5

a) All Spirit is not good and loving,

b) If all was perfect it would not have been necessary to populate the Earth.

c) GOD is now faced with the problem of how to deal with the existing Human-Race, to correct the effects of Human sin and Evil; of man-to-man, and man to fellow creatures and man to other forms of Life......to ensure that the Cycle of Human Misery does not continue unabated, and that in the Future, in the new Millennium, that the forces of Good and Love will win.

..nb: Man is used in the Asexual sense, to signify the Male or the Female.

e) This Road has been trodden before.

...viz JESUS showing that Humans are Spirit and there exists life after death, and that the way of LOVE can win.

...viz.NOAH when God decided to cleanse the planet of the Human-race and start again.

....viz The many Prophets who have sought to provide guidance to Mankind.

KEYPOINTS SB6 (HR5),(BTB4)

a) Humans have been given freewill in this Lifetime.

b) Both the Spirit and the Mind have freewill. We can choose to be nasty and greedy and evil, OR, we can choose to be loving and caring and compassionate.

c) The colour of our Spirit tells of the level of learning, understanding and achievement that our Soul has attained in this life and in previous lives and experiences.

d) There are seven levels of Earthly Spiritual Progress; when we refer to Heaven, this is at level three. The Earth-Plane is outside of these levels.

e) Those Souls who have sinned badly and hurt others, in this lifetime,

- will pass to Level two or Level one, for correction, (Shadowlands and Hell)
- where they will be kept until they have learned Penance and Humility and Compassion
- until they are prepared to accept the existence of the one GOD,
- until they accept the need to co-exist with, love and be tolerant of other Spirits.

..... some Souls will be contained for hundreds of years.

- by exception Humans can pass into different life-forms such as Animals. All is possible.

f) When it is decided that in its existing form that the particular Soul is beyond change or recovery, then it may be re-Born, re-Constituted, or Combined with another more loving Soul, so as to change the attitude, outlook and character.

(an interchange say 50:50, but remember nothing is ever lost, the Darker element has to go somewhere to be changed!)

g) The re-Birth of a Soul is a wondrous event, when the Past is wiped clean so that there are no restrictions on the growth of a Spirit........... (Karma is released)

KEYPOINTS SB7, (HR12), (TFV17)

a) The Spirit is the life-force and the part of GOD which we all have.

b) A perfect Sector of our Spirit is retained by GOD, and the ultimate purpose of the Human Life is for the Human Soul to be able to be reunited with the GOD-Sector which is pure.

c) The Impure Sector is so because of our Aura and Character and Karma. Collectively we call the Spirit, plus the Aura, plus the Character, as the SOUL.

d) Every Soul on the Earth-Plane has a purpose to this lifetime. Through achievement of your Spiritual Awareness...YOU can learn of the purpose to your life on the Earth-Plane.

..... (or by talking with another who can tell you!)

e) Where-ever you travel you leave an impression of your Aura.

KEYPOINTS SB8

a) Existence in levels One and Two is what we refer to as
HELL and SHADOWLANDS. They are far from pleasant, being
hard, dark and painful. But God never gives-up on
Souls and recovery is possible and is the ultimate aim.
Be this tens, hundreds or thousands of years later....
In Shadowlands for example there is no light and no
colour.

b) In Heaven, at level Three, there is no disease and all
can be achieved through Thought.

c) Above level Three are higher Vibrational levels, for
those Souls who wish to approach a higher purity and
oneness with GOD. Others may choose to stay at level
Three to carry out the many tasks necessary to ensure
the smooth-working of all sections...ie Hospitals,
Libraries, Schools...which make-up that World.

d) There exists an Hierarchy in Spirit, Spirits at level
Five and above can choose to become Guides, to return to
the Earth-Plane to guide and to help others.

e) If we sincerely ask, we may be allocated Guides, for
them to help us to achieve the Goals and learning which
we seek to achieve.

 f) Souls who have achieved level Seven do not need to
return to the Earth-Plane, unless it is to help Others,
or for a greater purpose.

KEYPOINT SB9,(AB12),(AB13)

a) All our existence is as Energy, Vibrational Energy.

b) All Worlds and Levels are at different Vibrational
Energies.

c) Spiritual Awareness is simply an ability to transend
and to Communicate at a different vibrational level.

d) When we speak of 'raising our Spirit', we normally
refer to increasing the rate of its vibration. Consider
the difference between a Candle and a Car headlamp. The
Power effect, depth of visualisation, degree of
lumination is raised such that what previously could not
be seen or understood becomes clearer.

e) Your Spirit is like a computer, with enormous
capability, which simply needs switching-on to cause it
to work. You can choose not to use it, but consider the
difficulty when faced with a complex problem to solve.
You personally have the physical capability, but not the
knowledge to obtain the route or the guidance to solve
the problem. You have the knowledge but you cannot
remember unless you switch on the Computer.

KEYPOINTS SB10,(N27)

a) There is no 'Absolution of Sin' as is preached by many Religions.

b) In many ways we judge ourselves when we are about to leave the Human Shell, we re-live our whole lifetime experience in the preceding days and weeks. Our friends and Family and those who love us, will assemble to greet-us and to welcome us into the new World ahead

- We are accompanied throughout our lifetime by a guardian Angel, whose role is to return to us all those experiences necessary for us to be able to judge ourselves.

- If we have sinned badly, then we will not be allowed to join with our loved Ones, until the sin has been accepted and true remorse felt.

- As all is known, a superficial regret will NOT be sufficient for us to be recovered...
  It took some 200 years for my Soul to be fully recovered from the exploits of my time as Alexander, and true forgiveness has only been obtained in THIS LIFETIME.

c) Our present and future level of 'Pleasure' is determined by our previous level of tolerance, love and compassion shown to Others; together with our personal need to experience the lessons necessary for our Spirit to progress.

d) We create our own Future by our own Choices now, and by the result and effect of our previous actions and thoughts.(Karma)

e) All that we give to Others is returned to Us....................

- Give Love and you will receive Love.

- Give Hate and Hate will consume you. Mock the afflicted and you will reap your reward.

- Needlessly hurt your fellow Man or God's Creatures and you will invite revenge upon yourself .

- Reek havoc upon Nature, and the balance which exists in the World, and you invite restitution upon the whole of Humanity, and all those other Species will suffer as well.

KEYPOINTS SB11,(DP02)

a) Nature is a Power Force itself which will react to restore Equilibrium.

b) There ARE Spirits of the Earth, the Water, the Fire, the Air, who can and do react to restore the Balance.

c) It is not GOD deciding to punish Man, a balance exists, a self correcting Force called Nature.

a) The Time-Frame between giving and receiving may extend to many lifetimes.

b) It can seem very unfair for a beautiful, loving person in this lifetime to suffer a harsh disease, or to be crippled with pain and suffering. But, consider now the Spirit within.

- It has chosen this lesson however incongruous it may seem.

- The lesson could even be a self-sacrifice for Another, so that their Spirit can have the opportunity to show Compassion and Love and Caring.. so that their Spirit can progress.

- It could be a Karma from a previous Lifetime, caused by individual Actions in a previous lifetime.

- It could have been brought by the need to repeat a Peer-Group lesson, so the correct Choices can now be made by another.

c) Inside the least 'presentable' Individual can be the most beautiful of Spirits...it is nothing to do with Appearance or Wealth...you could even be talking to GOD or Jesus!

d) Remember we live this life to learn, we will be tested, we will be tempted, this is the purpose of the life, for us to make the choice. Learning can sometimes only result from suffering when we make the wrong choice!

e) Inside the most seemingly affable character could lie a Dark and Evil Spirit.......if you sat a collection of Tyrants down in a row, without prior knowledge, could you tell who was the Hitler, the Stalin, the mass-Murderer?

f) There will also always be unforeseen accidents created by other Darker Spirits who impose accidents onto third-parties which are outside Spirit's normal control. viz......car Accidents, Bombs, major disasters which can encompass Good as well as Darker Spirits. When we are Spiritually Aware, our Guides can tell us to avoid certain places at certain times when the probability of rogue Events is higher.

How many times do you hear of Individuals refusing to join a flight, only later to learn that if they had done so their Human life would have ended prematurely!!

g) Spirit will sometimes communicate through Dreams or Visions. All Dreams or Visions should be written down for Interpretation. Any repeating Incident should be investigated and analysed.

h) The first thought, the Gut-feel, the intuition, is usually the correct Choice, for this is our Spirit telling us what to do <u>before</u> the Earthly Mind starts to impose its own rational.

i) It is always a good policy to 'Sleep on a Decision', this provides the time for reflection, time to ponder, time for our Spirit to Communicate.

KEYPOINTS SB13

a) The Eyes are a window to the Spirit, when true contact is made, Thoughts can travel also. When two Spirits are Twinned and the persons involved are Spiritually Aware, then true Communication can happen. The link is MindA to SpiritA, SpiritA to SpiritB, SpiritB to MindB. As Humans we perceive only the Mind (Thought) link.

Many identical Twins can more easily experience this Communication.

b) There are not many on the Earth-Plane who have this Gift from Spirit. Twinning is evidence of the purest form of love on the Earth-Plane.

KEYPOINTS SB14...consider Euthanasia.

a) To assist any animal or Human or life-force to end their pain and suffering would appear to be a most commendable action. But now consider, that Soul has chosen that Experience...to Suffer...even to suffer excruciating pain.............................

- By assisting in the ending of that life, YOU, have acted as GOD, YOU have negated that pre-chosen Experience.

- THAT SPIRIT MAY WELL NEED TO RETURN TO RE-CREATE THAT COMPLETE EXPERIENCE. You unwittingly may have wasted the whole lifetime now, PLUS causing a re-run of the whole lifetime again, with all the players,(your Peer-Group) and holding up their progress as well.

- You the supposed Helper must now suffer the correction Experience of a lower Level.

b) Far better to have allowed that person to die peacefully, without the artificial prolonging of their life by mechanical or other methods...the Soul can then move on and progress to a better Existence.

c) This does not mean that we should not do whatever can be done, to alleviate Pain or Suffering, or to use Medical Advances to support Life, it is a question of when to draw a line, and when this Lifetime should draw to a close.

KEYPOINTS SB15...consider Transplants.
a) To extend a Life beyond that which GOD intended..
Can this be correct ?
All is pre-chosen before we come here for the learning
process.
b) When our learning is complete it is equally pointless
to stay, to prolong life, to lock-in the Spirit to a
Hell-on-Earth, when what is required is for a return to
base, a return to Heaven so that the Spirit can grow and
be re-born. Perhaps it is necessary also for those loved
ones who remain, to pursue their own lives perhaps with
new Partners, in a new lifetime Experience, in new
Relationships. All is given for a purpose.
c) When the physical part of another is connected to
another life-form, then we lay ourselves open to being
affected by the SOUL of the part inserted, for the Soul
travels where-ever it wishes to and can find affinity in
any object which it knows and with which it shares a
vibrational link. The use of Others' parts is rife with
potential problems.

KEYPOINTS SB16
a) Spirits retain many of their previous Human
Characteristics when they leave the Earth-Plane;
b) Spirits accordingly can harbour Human Emotions such as
Jealousy and Revenge.
c) The Spirit never forgets anything it has learnt from
any life-time, it is only the Mind which blocks access
to this knowledge.
d) Someone who is Spiritually Aware may have access to
countless Libraries of Knowledge...the ultimate Computer

KEYPOINTS SB17
a) Any one advanced Spirit can Divide, Sub-divide; or be
Sub-divided and re-Combined, in this way it can be in
more than one Place, one Being, or indeed one Dimension,
at any one Time.
b) Not all Spirits have the same Capability. As with many
aspects of life, some are more advanced than Others.
c) When we sleep, our Spirit is released from the Mind
entrapment which locks it into the Body. The Spirit is
then free to roam and to travel where-ever it chooses.
- The dimensions of Time, Distance and Space no longer
  apply.
- The Spirit can also travel whilst we are awake to be
  with other Spirits.
d) Mankind in the form of Spirit already has mastered the
Universe, Space-travel is already a Reality. Do we
really need to travel in the physical Body when we can
already achieve this at a different Energy level?

e) The Body is always connected to the Spirit by a silver Thread while we are alive on the Earth-Plane.

- When we die,(pass-over),this Thread is broken.
- The Thread exists throughout our travels, which could be many light-years away.
- When the Body almost dies, and the Spirit leaves, as is evidenced by 'Out-of-Body' Experiences, there is a Time period of about fifteen minutes when the Spirit can still choose to return to the Body.

f) Some Spirits can polarise back into their Darker and Lighter Sectors, which can be most confusing when communication is desired.

KEYPOINTS SB18,(N104)
a) Everyone who ASKS FOR HELP is given help in one way or another.

- 'Seek and ye shall find' is true;
- 'Ask and you will be given' is also true;
- 'Ignore and Dismiss, and your Talent will be taken away' is also true.

b) Everyone who seeks Spiritual Awareness will be given a Personal Guide to assist them to develop their abilities, to improve their Understanding, and to help them to fulfil their Purpose on the Earth-Plane.
c) Guides can be allocated for many purposes, such as Healing, Learning or Protection.

KEYPOINTS SB19
a) If you choose the route of Spiritual Awareness, then it is also essential to be able to protect and control your Being. You will also need to learn to :

- Prevent Other Spirits from entering your Body...evidenced by wide mood changes and changes in your Personality which are out of Character.
- Protect yourself from the influence of Evil Thoughts...evidenced by physical Pain.
- Be able to 'switch-off' from unwanted Thoughts and Influences...to be able to relax.
- Identify messages from your Spirit Guides.
- Protect yourself from external Energy sources... Electricity Cables, Generators etc.

b) Discomfort below your Rib-cage may indicate the entry of Spirit, the right-hand-side is Darker Spirit, the left-hand-side is Lighter Spirit.(a sharp Pain for a few seconds only)

c) The presence of any Other Spirit can affect your Environment and your Relationships...... ......do not forget that everything living has a Spirit.

KEYPOINTS. SB20
a) Love your neighbour as yourself, understand these words and treat People accordingly.
b) There is no-one above or below You.

- There is no-one who knows more or less than You.
- Each has their own Journey to achieve;
- It is not for You to say, or to judge other People.
- You may show them the way, in a kind and gentle manner, if you wish to help them to achieve a higher Understanding.

d) Do not think yourself greater than anyone else.
e) Do not abuse a position of Authority.
f) Have compassion on Others, teach them the right way...this is the Law of Nature.

KEYPOINTS SB21,(TP25),(TP32),(D53),(TD21)
a) SPIRITUAL LOVE is bounderless, it does not need a response, it is not given for anything that may be given in return. It is pure love which never ends and is not affected by a partner's misdemeanours.

- In Spiritual Love you GIVE, without expecting to receive.
- In Human Love you GIVE, normally expecting to receive back, Human Love tends to be selfish.

b) It is sometimes necessary to love someone enough to walk away from them in this lifetime.

- To sacrifice the Present, to allow them to complete their Goals. In this way you may be re-united at a future Time.
- If they love you truly, they will return.

c) TRUE LOVE CAN ONLY BE FOUND IN FREEDOM.

- You must not restrict the free-will choice of any other Person, or any other Soul, to follow their own Pathway, be this with or without you.
- You must not be possessive, tell your Spirit forceably not to be jealous.
- You must not prevent another from Communicating or being with any other Person or Spirit. Only through complete Freedom can true Bonding occur.
- Your restrictive Nature can cause all sorts of problems to your loved-One, such as Head-cold, Aches and pains, loss of voice etc.

d) LOVE is the greatest power in the Universe,
- All is Energy,
- You can give anything, to the Spirit of anyone else with the power of LOVE,
- LOVE yourself first, is a Key Objective.

e) It is the Minds of Men which cause suffering,
- It is not always your Actions or Thoughts, which cause Pain, but it could be Others in your Peer-Group.
- There is no need for Suffering if all of Mankind sees the Good.

KEYPOINTS SB22,(HR25),(TD68)

a) The Heart is just a Bodily Organ, used by those on the Earth-Plane to describe much that should be related to the Spirit. It is simply an Expression; what you really mean is your 'Being', not a Lung or a Kidney!

b) There is no part of One's Spirit in Bodily Organs.,....however the Spirit knows and recognises, and returns to those objects which vibrate at an identical Energy level; so by moving 'parts' from one Human or Animal to another, essentially you INVITE the Spirit to follow!.....

c) Many Peoples seek to avoid the retention of the Spirit by burning all the belongings and possessions of the Deceased.

d) ANY SECOND-HAND OBJECT should be viewed with suspicion when brought into your Environment.

e) It is possible to purge Items, but if in doubt REMOVE NOW. The RAIN is an excellent cleansing Agent.

f) Human Traits are caused by Human 'Genes', not by Memory.

g) The Body is but a cloak surrounding the most precious part, the Spirit.

h) The Body once relieved of the Spirit is as nothing, when the Breath has been taken away from that darkened Shroud, there should be no use of what is left, other than to return it to the Earth.

KEYPOINTS SB23

a) When I speak of the Spirit, I really mean the SOUL. The Soul comprises three parts, the Spirit, the Personality and the Aura.

b) Where-ever we travel as a Human Being we leave an Aura Trail, which serves to 'condition' the places we have travelled to. It is perhaps easier to think in terms of an energy Trail, for good or for bad.

When the time is appropriate, we may be asked to revisit a location to collect-up our Aura Trail, in this way we can enhance the strength of our Soul.

c) Our Personality is formed by the collective effect of all our Experiences, through all of our lives. Together with our life-force, the Spirit, we live this lifetime in order that our Soul can learn and understand the lessons which we have chosen or need to learn.

c) The Soul assimilates a colour which is indicative of the level of its progression from Darkness to Light. The Soul may accordingly be a purveyor of love or evil and should be treated accordingly.

d) As we all emanate from the One GOD, and as all is for learning and understanding, by implication very few who walk the Earth-Plane are perfect Souls.

KEYPOINTS SB24

a) The Weather is affected by our Thoughts and Feelings, this is one reason why it is so important to send out loving Thoughts. The Weather is given to help us, every moment is a new Dawn...............

    (a) The Rain cleanses and represents the tears of the People.
    (b) The Wind is God's presence, moving forwards, a good sign that the Earth is breathing.
    (c) The Light, Moon and Stars show GOD's presence
    (d) A grey, overcast Sky is a grieving Sky
    (e) The Sunset represents Peace and Tranquillity
    (f) The Sunrise shows a new Dawn, a new Beginning.
    (g) The Snow signifies Purity.

KEYPOINTS SB25,(IR4),(IR5),

a) Who-ever we meet with, two levels of RECOGNITION take place.

b) The SPIRITS converse, and quite separately the Human MIND through the physical Senses may choose to converse. Both have freewill choice.

c) As the Spirit can and does influence the Mind, we need to be aware of the possibility that the attraction and recognition which occurs is not of this lifetime, it may simply be caused by a previous lifetime experience. It is important that our Minds are not influenced by previous relationships from previous lifetimes!

d) Unfortunately many, many times mistakes are made, and we could end up marrying our Mother or Brother from a previous existence, simply because our Souls have re-established this relationship and so influenced our Mind.

▪ I do not like that Person,.......I do not know why

- I do not like that Place, that Object, that House...our SOUL is telling us of a past Relationship, or a past Situation which was unhappy...we feel, our Emotions are affected.
- If you have left a beautiful Aura in a location, Others sense and feel this warmth.

e)Auras affect Spirits, they also affect Animals and Plants.........you can often tell the 'lightness' of an Environment by the frequency and number of wild Flowers, healthy Trees and natural life in the Hedgerows.....
Next time you visit an Area, observe the abundance of the natural Flora, but also the number of Birds, Butterflies, Bees, the number of Trees and Plants which the locals have planted.
Is it a healthy Environment, or one of Hostility? If you spread and give love, those around you are influenced and respond accordingly. Green Fingers is indicative of a love for Plants.
f)We are ALL part of Nature.

KEYPOINT SB26,(HR17),(TD65)
a)Until PURE LOVE is found History will be repeated, again and again, or until an Understanding is gained.

KEYPOINTS SB27,(HR24)
a)Do not think or wish ill of Another, for it may well be granted.
- But remember that what goes around, comes around, and YOU will eventually receive back those ill-actions upon yourself.
- You should not retaliate, you should find another way to break the Cycle.

b)Control your Mind to send-out only Goodness and Light, every miniscule of Thought is heard and may be acted upon.
c)Be careful what you ask for, as it can be returned to you in pain, if your Thought has caused Pain.....there is no harm in saying ' I would like for.............., but you must leave it to the Individual's Choice as to what they wish to do.'
d)The words of a Song, Play, Video, Cinema, all travel around the World and affect all those who listen and participate.

KEYPOINT SB28
As any one member of a Peer Group progresses, so the Others progress also.

KEYPOINTS SB29

a) Reiki Energy draws upon the Spirit of the Earth, as does Pagan symbolism which also draws upon, Fire, Air and Water.

b) HEALING is very specific and if you do not ask correctly, you can cause more damage than good. It is far better to avoid these methods and to use the 'love of GOD', the ultimate power for Good, as the Healing Agency.

c) These Spirits have the Power to correct an imbalance, to rectify any 'Force of Nature', so as to cause a return to Equilibrium. They cannot initiate the power, only react to it. The Spirit Force is intended for that 'Plane' and not for Healing, so it cannot be relied upon nor can it be specific.

KEYPOINTS SB30

a) The role of a Parent on the Earth is to Protect, Nurture, and Teach the Child.

b) When the Child becomes an Adult, the Parent must stand-back and take a secondary role.

c) The Parent should thereafter be there, for when the Child needs you. NOT for when the Parent needs the Child.

KEYPOINT SB31

a) The Angel of Death is summoned when someone is to be taken outside of the normal sequence of Circumstances. When GOD decides that someone, a Soul, is to be taken, then the Angel of Death is the Messenger, who normally visits that Person in their sleep and collects their Spirit so that they do not awaken.

KEYPOINTS SB32

a) When the Body needs to rest, the Spirit recognises this and withdraws to allow the Body to sleep,

- the Spirit then moves-on to another life-plane to continue its work.
- The Spirit does get weak, but not through daily living, only through interaction with other Spirits.
- It is a Spirit Power struggle. Each one seeks to impose its Will on others, in so doing it uses-up its life-force and needs time to recuperate.

b) When the Spirit needs time, the Body feels tired, when the Body is tired the Spirit moves-on.

c) The Spirit can also tell the Body not to become tired, if the need is there.

d) The Mind can also Ask and Pray to GOD for Energy.

e) Spirits are like People, some are stronger than Others, so some can interact without difficulty; Others are weaker and suffer.
f) The Spirit learns its lessons from the interaction with Others, the Mind chooses the interaction, the Spirit learns also.

KEYPOINT SB33, (TD19)
a) The Earth-Plane Experience is a purely learning ground for you to take back to Spirit, that which you have learned. The Earth-Plane is NOT the Life, it is the School!.........quote from Isaiah on 26/12/98.

KEYPOINTS SB34, (HR12)
a) When the silver Thread is cut and we have 'died', the Spirit should realise and should accept that the Earth Life has ended. It will be called to and welcomed by and assisted by Angels and loved-Ones to pass-on to Recovery Hospitals where all Ailments, Injuries, Pain and Suffering is healed.
b) BUT, if Death occurs suddenly, and often violently, or if the Spirit is reluctant to walk away, to shed the remnants of Power, or Wealth, or Prestige, or to leave loved-Ones, or for whatever reason, then the Spirit can choose to remain on the Earth-Plane, to choose not to pass to Heaven or recovery; this then is the real Tragedy. This then is evidenced by 'Ghosts' and other malevolent Spirits.
c) These lost Souls can roam the Earth-Plane for many hundreds of years, lost Souls from long-forgotten Wars or violent deaths, gradually becoming more and more lost and entrenched, darker and bitter...viz film Ghost.
d) American Indians and Gypsies have a tradition of burning all the possession of the Departed, so that the Spirit has nothing to cling to.
e) Spirits on the Earth-Plane can also restrict and prevent the recovery of their loved-Ones by hanging onto their Spirits, restricting their freedom to progress, and at the same time preventing their own Progression on the Earth-Plane.
...Is this true-love? or is it selfish possession?

KEYPOINTS SB35
a) Abortion caused by Mankind, a deliberate conscious act, is intrinsically Murder. The life is given by GOD, the Soul has chosen the life. The Individuals then make the choices.
b) Far better to complete the Pregnancy and provide the opportunity of life to the Infant, even if it is not to be raised by the natural Parents.

KEYPOINT SB36
You can cause your Soul to move by arching your Back and
so compressing your Soul.   If your Soul is within
Another, they may feel the movement.

KEYPOINTS SB37
a) You can boost your Energy level by visualising
yourself surrounded by a white light. That Light
pulsates slowly like a Light-House. Feel the Energy
enter as the light pulsates.
b) Sit quietly and clear your Mind of clutter. This will
relieve your tensions and cause you to relax.

KEYPOINT SB38
Spirit will only help you if you ask for help. As you
have free-will, they will not interfere with your
choices unless you ask for help.

KEYPOINTS SB39
The eating of flesh is permissible,

- it is the needless slaughter which GOD and Spirit do
  not approve of.
- Only kill to eat and to survive.
- But if you do kill, also make use of that Creature,
  so that its life has served a useful purpose. Treat
  all life with due respect and consideration.

KEYPOINT SB40, (IR14),
Many pains and much discomfort can be alleviated and
cleared, if you can cause your Soul to vibrate at a
higher level, above that of the negative Thoughts which
are causing the problem.

- Whenever you feel a pain, Pray to GOD for help, and
  protect yourself with the Words.
- Imagine yourself enclosed within a reflective Sphere
  of Light. Envisage yourself inside a sphere of
  pulsating blue light, surrounded by a similar
  pulsating sphere of white light.
- Visualise yourself surrounded by a filter which only
  allows good, positive, Thoughts within. The negative
  Thoughts are reflected back ten-fold onto the Sender.
- If you feel under dire attack, visualise yourself
  climbing into a Chain-Mail reflective Suit of Armour,
  through which nothing can penetrate. As you pull-on
  the Suit, the pain will dissipate.

- To stop pain, you need to be capable of telling your Mind that the pain is not there. Raising your Spirit takes it outside the influence of your sub-conscious Mind, which controls the route to the Nerve centres.

KEYPOINT SB41
At times, when you wish to 'tune-in' to Spirit, you may feel your Ears are cloaked. This could well be a jealous Soul who does not wish you to progress. Tell the Soul forceably to stop being childish and to leave you alone.

KEYPOINT SB42
Strive for balance in your life, in everything that you do.

KEYPOINT SB43
When you feel low or unhappy, visualise a Rainbow, knowing it is a promise of better days ahead.

KEYPOINT SB44
The principal Soul colours in descending order are:
Highest Level Gold
Silver (misty grey)
Pink
pale   Blue
pale   Pink
pale   Yellow

Level Three which are definite Shades,
tinged with grey/silver

Darker Colours
Brown
Black

KEYPOINT SB45,(SB57),(TP31),(D45)
As you become Spiritually Aware, you should request a Door-keeper whose role is to protect your Spirit against other hostile Influences. Whenever you are in the presence of, or feel threatened by other Spirits, you request your Door-keeper to attend.

KEYPOINT SB46

You can ask for your Spirit to be twinned with that of your loved-one. This will not happen unless true love has been found. Be certain this is what you wish to achieve, for your Spirits will be twinned forever. Say together aloud the following words:

'Heavenly Father, I ....….. do unreservedly wish my Spirit to be entwined with that of ....
I accept ....as my Twinned Spirit now and forever. I forgive her/his past Misdemeanors and wish us to become as One. If it be thy will please grant us this Bonding.'

KEYPOINTS SB47,(TD38)

a) It is necessary to stand-up to, and to fight Evil or Aggression.
b) If Good does not counter Evil, All will be dominated by Evil.
c) All means possible should be used to avoid conflict, but at the twelfth Hour, when Diplomacy has failed, it is necessary to choose whether to submit or to resist.
d) So long as you uphold your 'Good Principles' of Behaviour and Love and Compassion in the execution of War, then the taking of life can be justified in War.

KEYPOINT SB48

If you lead a completely guided life, solely dependant upon Spirit, your Soul will not progress and will not learn.

KEYPOINTS SB49

a) Spiritual Awareness and learning will be restricted by 'Unfinished Business' from previous lifetimes.
b) Healing may be necessary to allow progress to be made.
c) A restriction in your own personal Soul will also restrict those in your Peer-Group.

KEYPOINTS SB50

a) Our Soul chooses the lifetime and the Experiences for learning before we are born.
b) Do not be possessive, all is a gift from GOD.
c) Share everything with the World, for unless you do this you will lose the gift at a future Time.....
....Be this Love, Money, Musical or Artistic Talents etc.

d) There is nothing intrinsically wrong with having
Wealth, so long as a major Portion is used to help
Others who are less fortunate, and so long as you have
not acquired the Wealth through Greed and the suffering
of Others, Human or GOD's Creation.

KEYPOINT SB51,(INT1), (TEY12), (ANS4), (TP26),(D10),
(AB22),(AB30)
Question every Meeting, every Event, every Action, it
all has a Purpose, there is no such thing as pure
Coincidence. History is repeated unless we make the
right Choices.

KEYPOINT SB52,(INT3)
HEAVEN will be achieved on the Earth-Plane, when a
critical number of Souls are enlightened. At this Time
the Future of this Planet will be assured, and the Human
Race will have earned the right to remain here. At the
present time the Human Race is on trial and the Planet
is only loaned to us.

KEYPOINT SB53,(TEY8),(D7),(TD1)
We all have a Guardian Angel who is there to help us at
critical Times, so that we make the right choices or
decisions for our own Survival, so that the programmed
learning which this Lifetime is all about, is not cut
short by misfortune. When the time arrives for us to
leave the Earth-Plane, the Guardian Angel will replay to
us all the Crucial decisions and Events from our
Lifetime, so that we can judge whether we have achieved
our Goals.

KEYPOINT SB54,(TEY10)
Your Attitudes, your Interests, are likely to change
every seven years. This is particularly true in your
early years. It is essential to defer significant
Relationship decisions until a later Age of Maturity has
been reached. (ie. 28+)

KEYPOINT SB55,(CM1),(D16),(AB18)
The Power of Prayer does work. Be very careful what you
Pray or Wish for, as it may well happen and not
necessarily in the way intended.

KEYPOINT SB56,(CM2),(AB38),(TD26)
Thoughts can be as powerful as Actions. All Actions, all
Inventions, All stems from an original Thought.

KEYPOINT SB57,(ANS3),(TP11),(TP28),(D21),(D30)
The Past only serves to bring you to the Present. You
cannot change the Past, but you can Forget, Heal,
Progress, lose the Guilt, be Thankful. Grasp the Present
Opportunity.

KEYPOINTS SB58,(D18),(D43),(D52),(TD3)
a) There exists in Spirit Realms a Hierarchy who work for
GOD to the betterment of all Nations and Peoples
throughout the Universe.
b) The interactions of All Creation is as set out in The
Book Of Life.
c) Decisions on the Earth-Plane are made at the Table of
Life.
d) Your lifetime Experiences are pre-chosen by your Soul
before you are born.

KEYPOINT SB59,(AB20)
Many messages from Spirit are given in Visions and
Dreams. Always record these and seek interpretation.

KEYPOINT SB60,(TD41)
You can dismiss and remove negative People from your
life, and their influence upon your Life, by placing
them behind a solid wooden Door, leading to a sealed
Room.

KEYPOINT SB61,(DP07)
a) Many Ailments, Disease, Rashes, are prompted by Spirit
in response to our Human Attitudes.
b) Dark Thoughts or Wishes from Others can cause
Accidents, Diseases, Illnesses.
c) Some People have chosen their afflictions to enable
Others to learn Compassion and Caring.
d) Some afflictions are the consequence of previous
lifetime Karma.

###

APPENDIX IV. HOW TO PROGRESS YOUR SPIRITUAL AWARENESS

A4.00 I have previously defined Spiritual Awareness as that state wherein the Mind is capable of talking to and receiving communication from Spirit. Your own Spirit and Soul or anyone Else's.

A4.01 You must understand that the ability to communicate with Spirit is restricted, blanketed, and prevented by the influence of:
- Your own Mind,
- By those Souls around you who wish to restrict your progress, through jealousy etc.
- By the baggage and guilt which we all carry through Karma, and your previous actions and attitudes.

A4.02 It is useful to be clear in your own mind as to WHY you wish to progress your Spiritual Awareness. Some reasons might be:
a) To learn of the true purpose for your life on the Earth-Plane.
b) To be able to serve GOD.
c) To be capable of teaching or helping Others to achieve their own Goals.
d) To enable you to make the right choices in your lifetime, to avoid the needless repetitions and suffering within your Peer-Group.
e) To help create a secure future on the Earth-Plane for your children, for all other Species, and for Nature.
f) To be able to communicate directly, by Telepathy, with a loved-One on the Earth-Plane, or with your loved-Ones who are now in Heaven or other Planes
g) Simple Curiosity! A Challenge!

A4.03 If therefore you wish to progress your Spiritual Awareness,
a) It is necessary to address each and every aspect of your Existence.
- **You need to blanket your Mind, (Still)**
- **To quieten your Human Senses,**
- **To raise your Awareness through whatever Techniques are necessary...viz Meditation.**
b) You need to review your Karma and all the Relationships and Experiences of this Lifetime, so that you can lose the Guilt and the Baggage.
c) You need to learn to love yourself and in so doing to find Inner Peace. (TD31)

d) You need to gain the tacit acquiescence of those Souls about you that might seek to prevent your progress. (or you need to be capable of negating their influences)

e) You need to desire to achieve Spiritual Awareness. This Desire will cause you to allocate the Time and Effort and Study necessary to achieve your Goal.

f) You need to use your Mind, to persuade your Soul, that you seriously wish to achieve this communication link.

g) Your rate of Progression is influenced by your Actions, your Thoughts, your Attitudes, your level of Understanding of all that happens around you. (N10)

h) All is returned to you; the Cycle of Learning is not broken unless Understanding is gained and your Attitudes and Actions are changed. (N14)

i) Let go of the Guilt from the Past and the Present. (12.63), (TD36)

A4.04 To help you along your Pathway, you will also need the help and assistance of GOD and those High Spirits who work for GOD,

- for unless your Motives are correct and acceptable, then little lasting progress can be made.
- Think of Others first,
- Take care what you ask for. How will your request affect Others?
- Is it what they need?

A4.05 In this Appendix we will attempt to help you to progress your Awareness by asking you to undertake a series of Exercises which will address those conditions listed above. Please note that:

a) Your rate of progress will be Individual to you alone.

b) The Time-Scale for learning will be uniquely yours, this could be measured in Days, Weeks, Months, Years, or even in Life-times.

c) Every Person has a Spirit and Soul, contained within a Human Body, the Body of which is controlled by a Human Mind.

d) Every Person is Spirit and can therefore progress, and every person will have Gifts or Talents or Abilities which are innate, or which can be given by High Spirit.

A4.06 'Seek and ye will find'. 'Ask and it will be given'. Rewards will be given, provided that you personally make the necessary Effort, and that you demonstrate to GOD that you are prepared to live this life in an appropriate Manner.

- Remember always that when your Soul has completed its designated learning and no further progress is anticipated, that is the time when we die and depart this Earth-Plane.

- So perhaps this simple statement will provide you with a means of extending your Earthly life, so long as it is meaningful!
- The purpose for our lifetime is for the SOUL to learn the necessary lessons and reach the Understanding. Not for us to solely live the Human Life.
- Tread in the footsteps of Jesus and you will not go far wrong in terms of the values by which you live your life.

A4.07 What progress YOU make in this lifetime, you will not lose in the next. Some are born with psychic Abilities through progression of their Soul in a previous lifetime.

A4.08 EXERCISE 1. ASK GOD.....to be repeated weekly.
a)Pray sincerely to GOD and ask for his help and guidance to enable you to achieve your Spiritual Awareness.
b)Tell GOD why you wish to achieve this.
c)Pray aloud only if you are serious with this intent. Do not wish unless you are serious with this Intent.

A4.09 EXERCISE 2. PROTECTION.....to be repeated on every occasion that you feel or sense a Spiritual Influence or Presence, or whenever you open-up to Spirit, or whenever you discuss or join with Others to communicate, or whenever you enter the company of other Spiritually Aware Persons.
Say the words:
' Heavenly Father, please protect me with the Light and Love of True Spirit. Only allow those Spirits who come with Love for Mankind to draw near.'

A4.10 EXERCISE 3(a). THE LOCATION...Guidelines to be followed whenever you wish to communicate.
a)Minimal alcohol two hours prior to the Preparation..
b)Minimal food two hours prior to the Preparation.
c)No Electrical disturbances in the room, or chosen location, for two hours prior to the Preparation.
 Proximity to any disturbance is to be avoided, electrical generators of any kind, TV, washing machine, dryer, Pylon etc.)
d)Comfortable, loose, clothes and footwear.
e)No disturbing influences, TV off, animals quiet, children away or at rest, comfortable Seat and position, loud clocks removed or covered.
f)Mid-night to 05.00hrs is the best time, when Human activity is at a minimum, but any time is better than not at all.
g)Some locations are not helpful or suitable. This can well reflect negative presences or influences from the Past or present Day.
ie.a Site or Area of Rituals, Plagues, Wars, Oppression, Evil Influences.

h)Our aim is to become at One with Nature, we wish therefore to create an environment of love and harmony where-in peace and tranquillity can be achieved.

i)High Points are therefore more suitable than lower ones. The Top of any Building will therefore tend to be freer of Earthly vibrations than lower down. We seek to raise our Soul's vibration, we seek to create an environment wherein it is easier for those Higher Spirits who may wish to communicate with us to visit.

A4.11 EXERCISE 3(b). THE PREPARATION....following 3(a).

a)Sit facing the light, if there is a choice.

b)Sit with a straight Back, feet on floor, legs not crossed (below knee is acceptable)

c)Sit Quietly, Breathe slowly, in through nose, out through mouth, hold each action for 5 seconds. Breathe deeply. Repeat 3 times and then slow-down your breathing to a normal rhythm.

d)Empty your Mind of clutter. Imagine a wide expanse of water, or a tunnel of Trees, or a Sunset, or any favourite location.

e)Visualise your Spirit being raise by Angels.

f)Close your eyes and think of the expanse of water. Dismiss all other Thoughts.

g)Listen and relax, listen to your breathing and relax, Concentrate on your breathing and relax.

WRITE DOWN.......what you can Hear, what you can Feel, all the Sensations within and upon your Being. Keep these Records for future Comparison.

A4.12 EXERCISE 4. OPEN your CHAKRAS.... every time that you wish to communicate.

We are to open the principal Energy Centres throughout our Being, by thinking and visualising the Colours which portray each Energy Centre. Colours are Energy, so as we think of the Colours so we aim to increase the vibrational frequency of our Soul. It may help initially to have within your sight objects to show the Colours which you need to visualise.

I ask you to visualise a Rose opening its Petals, but also a Cog or Gear engaging a Shaft, the vertical Shaft extends through the Crown of our Head, along our Spine, down to our Feet.

As we' open' the Chakras, we ask for our Spirit to Rise, its vibrational frequency to increase in line with the Colour we think of:

♦ Breathe in and visualise the colour RED, this is your base Chakra, located at the position upon which you sit. As you exhale imagine all your worries and tensions being released.
A problem with this Chakra may affect your level of Energy.

♦ Breathe in again, visualise the colour ORANGE, this Chakra is in the area of your Genitals, and represents Activity and sexual activity.

417

- Continue with YELLOW, breathe in, relax and exhale, visualise the Petals opening and the Cog being engaged, exhale your tensions and worries. Yellow is the Energy centre close to your Solar Plexus, and represents the centre for Intellect and Learning.
- The GREEN Chakra is close to the Heart, and provides a balance for your Emotions.
- Follow on with BLUE, which represents the Throat region. Open this Rose with blue Petals and engage the Cog at this position...... The throat Chakra is the source for Communication Skills and Healing
- Visualise an INDIGO Rose, located near to the position of your third Eye, between your Eye-brows, you are feeling increasingly relaxed and at ease; with each out-breathe your cares and worries are released. This Chakra affects your ability for Intuitive Awareness
- We move on to a VIOLET Rose, situated on the Crown of your Head. This is the highest vibration we seek to achieve at present. Violet is the Spiritual colour and assists with Spiritual work

With this Cog in place, when all Chakras are open and we are connected to the Shaft, (for all our Cogs are engaged), then visualise a beam of White Light entering our Crown, and passing down into the Earth and then returning up through our Being, to fill our whole Body with Light and Love and Healing Energy. Feel the warmth, the love within, and your Soul rise within your Body, from beneath your Ribs up towards your Heart.

A4.13 Now sit quietly for a few minutes and then REPEAT EXERCISE 3(b), WRITE DOWN again what you Hear, what you Feel, and what you Sense. Be aware of every movement, every sensation, every sound. Record these observations for future comparison.

A4.14 EXERCISE 5. ASK to be allocated a Spirit Guide, and request that your GUIDE alone be allowed to come to you................................. Ask for all other Souls to stand back. Repeat Exercise 3(b).

A4.15 EXERCISE 6. DRAWING
Open your Chakras as Exercise (4), then ask for your Guide only (5), then sit with pen/pencil and clear paper. Allow your Hand to move where-ever it wishes to. Visualise your Guide drawing through your Hand. Stop and start again if meaningless Rubbish ensues. If no picture results, ask for your Guide again only to come to you. Repeat at will. With time Pictures will progress to writing. As with all Skills we need to practice, and you will need to sit quietly and practice frequently.

A4.16 Do not forget to **Close your Chakras** whenever you have completed your Exercises.

Close your Chakras by working back through the Colours and closing the petals of the Roses, and disengaging the Cogs from the Main Shaft. Violet, Indigo, Blue, Green, Yellow, Orange, Red. As you complete Red, tighten your muscles in that Area to finally close your Chakras.

Nb. The question of opening and closing your Energy Centres is quite interesting. Effectively, you are changing the energy flow through the Chakra, which increases or decreases the 'receptivity' of the Centre. The Chakras are never completely closed.

A4.17-22 EXERCISE 7. MEDITATION to help shut down the Human Senses and so allow your Guides to draw close and communicate with you. (viz.103a)

- Through the combined actions of asking GOD to help us through Prayer, living our life in a loving, compassionate, caring way. Helping and giving to Others, respecting Nature, we seek to create a better Environment for ourselves and for all of GOD's Creation.
- No one expects us to be perfect, for we would not be living the life if this were the case. Unless of course we have returned for a 'Greater Purpose'.
- We all have choices to make and we are presented with Situations, Events and Meetings to enable us to be able to choose, for in this way, we gain the understanding for our Soul.
- The incorrect Choice can lead to Pain, Suffering, Torment, and cause us to need to be represented with the same Choice at a future time.
- You can choose now whether to seek to obtain your Spiritual Awareness.

No single, one action, alone will cause this to happen, but Meditation will open your Mind to the communication link, to become receptive so that your Spirit Guide can communicate with you providing that you have met the necessary criteria to allow this to happen:

A4.18 LOVE is the KEY

- LOVE, respect and appreciate all of Nature and all of Creation.
- LOVE and respect Mankind
- LOVE and respect yourself, your actions and your thoughts. Whenever you meet anyone, always give them a gift, be this a hug, a kiss or even a smile.
- Be humble, do not think that you are above anyone else, their Soul may well have chosen this lowly life for their learning.
- Be caring, be compassionate,
- Be positive in all things and be receptive to the good things in life.
- Give of yourself to help others. Give without expecting reward.

A4.19 PRAY and ask GOD to help you

◆ **Ask for GOD's PROTECTION**
◆ **Ask for your Guides only to draw close to you, request all other Souls to stand-back.**
◆ **The Location is ready**
◆ **The Preparation is completed**
◆ **Open your Chakras**
◆ **Commence your Meditation.**
◆ **Ask for help to calm your Mind.**

A4.20 There are many variations, books, tapes and methods of how to Meditate. None is the absolutely correct method, it is what you feel comfortable with and what suits your personality and essentially whatever works for you.

◆ If one system does not work for you, try another technique. Be patient, persevere, try to sit at the same time each Day for 20- 30 minutes.
◆ Concentrate your Mind on a favourite Recreation to help you to relax.
◆ Sit, relax, relax deeper and deeper, follow a visualisation routine. Use Key-words or trigger-words to cause you easily to return quickly to a state of Relaxation. I shall give two routines which I personally use.

A4.21 ROUTINE 'A'

◆ Visualise walking down a lane, along each side of the lane are tall Trees. Feel the energy from the Trees, and look at the light from the Sun as it breaks through the Branches and the Leaves. The lane is flanked by Trees into the distance ahead. Stroll down the lane, there is no rush, no stress, no hurry. We come upon a Clearing, to our right there is a wooden Style and Gate. We can choose to open the Gate or climb over the Style. This leads us into a Field. There is a Pathway which takes us up a slight incline through the long grass either side of us. We feel the warmth of the Sun, we see the Butterflies, we hear the Birds, a slight Breeze keeps us cool. We hear playful Horses in the distance. We do not feel tired. Think, watch, and concentrate on every action, every sound, slowdown your pace of Life, be graceful, flow and feel every movement, Acknowledge every change which occurs in the Environment about you.
◆ Apply these sentiments to your every-day Life when you return. For what you are, and how you are perceived by Others in your normal Life, will affect their attitudes to you, and your relationships with those around you.
◆ We reach the brow of the hill at the top of the field, we feel relaxed and happy. The pathway crosses a small stream by a wooden

Bridge. We can see the reflection of the Sunlight and the fishes darting in the water.

- Ahead of us lies a red-brick-walled Enclosure, a Garden, we enter via the wooden Gate and immediately sense the Peace, the Tranquillity, the Perfume hits our Senses from the many Flowers, and the brilliant colours dazzle us until our Eyes adjust. There are Statues like a Greek Temple, beautifully shaped Hedges and Plants, all is symmetrical and perfect. Ahead of us we see a Bench Seat, covered with soft padding and situated facing the lily Pond, with the variety of Plants in colour. The occasional frog jumps across the Lilies and a Dragon Fly shimmers in the warm sunlight. The Pond is enclosed by white marble with a few steps leading away around the edges.

- Some little way away we see a figure walking slowly towards us. Is this one of our Spirit Guides? We sit quietly and think about what questions we would like to know the answer to.

- We sit, we relax, we contemplate. We breathe slowly, deeply and easily. All is at peace, we have found that one Place where we can be completely at peace with ourselves, and with Nature, We feel no discomfort, no aches nor pains. We feel warm and contented. This truly is a place of Heaven. Sit and enjoy, should your Guide talk to you then try to remember what is said. Look into the water, look at the reflection of the Sun, soak-up the peace. (allow 10-20 minutes)

- It is time for us to leave. We say goodbye to all that we see and pass-by. We will return shortly, another Day. We rise slowly and pass through the garden gate, closing it firmly behind us. We walk slowly and somewhat reluctantly back down to the stream, across the bridge, down through the field where the horses still play, One comes towards us in a friendly way and then flicks back his head and his tail and trots away across the field towards his companions. We leave by the gate or style and walk slowly back through the Trees, along the lane to where we began from. Open your eyes now.

- Do you remember any conversation you had? How do you feel?

A4.22 ROUTINE 'B'

- Sit quietly and relax. Relax deeply, feel your eye-lids close, they are so heavy. As you breathe in-and-out, visualise your Spirit rising, up through your Body to the highest point. Count now up from one to Ten, at the count of Ten jump from your Body to the space above your Head. Look down onto your Head and continue to rise up through the ceiling, through the roof, look down onto your House, your Town, your City, your Country. You are leaving the Earth like a shaft of light, much faster than a rocket, you are suddenly travelling through space and the Earth is progressively reducing in size from that of a Football, to an Orange, to a Pea. Around you the Stars stand-out of the pitch blackness of the Void which seems endless.

421

- As you travel quietly through Space and Time, you see another World opening-up to you, as quickly as you have left the Earth, you find yourself standing on a Pathway. Your clothes have changed to Hassock and Sandels, the bare soil beneath your feet leads upwards through a ravine, alongside a mountain Stream which roars down to your right. Ahead you see a wooden Bridge structure, which takes you past a waterfall to the far side of the ravine. You cross and feel the spray from the water smashing against the rocks. Ferns and branches sprout out from the ledges and rocks. You feel at home and comfortable, it is warm, you could be in any mountainous region on the Earth. You walk upwards towards a huge wooden Refectory Door, it is locked but you have the key tied around your Waist, you unlock the Door and walk inside, locking the Door behind you.
- Ahead of you is Heaven, all Beauty and Colour. Statues, Plants, Flowers, Trees and Walkways. The silence is broken only by the sound of a choir of Angels singing in the background. It is bright, sunny and warm. You feel perfectly relaxed and at peace. An expanse of green lawn spreads into the distance. You see a Group of people talking together, as you approach they turn to greet you. You recognise your loved-ones who have previously departed. Your animals and pets are also present. A Spirit Guide approaches and introduces himself to you. All is harmony. You feel refreshed and happy.
- After ten to twenty minutes, the time to depart arises. Reluctantly you say goodbye to All and make your way back to the Door, unlocking and locking it firmly behind you. You will return again soon. Wander slowly back to the Bridge, across the Stream and down the pathway. As you look fondly behind you, you realise that you are approaching once more the Earth. you zoom down onto your Town, your House, your Room, back into your Body.
- Wake-up now and open your eyes. Describe how you feel, and what you have experienced.

A4.23 **Let us now address the affect of your Karma and the effect of the Choices and Actions which you have made in this Lifetime (viz 103b) It is necessary now to be completely honest with yourself, or no purpose will be served.**

a)Itemise all the major Events, Situations, Choices and their Effect, which have occurred in your lifetime. Ponder on what you might have done differently, and its effect on your life and those around you.
b)List all the major Events, Situations, Choices and their Effect, which have occurred in your parents' lifetimes. If possible discuss with your parents, and learn of their own family history and the major Events,

Situations, Choices and their Effect which have occurred in your Grand-Parents Lives.

c)Establish as much as you can of any previous lifetimes. It is cause and effect we seek to identify. We wish to learn of any major character defects which are governing our lifetimes and creating the need for Repetition. Remember, it is not the human History we seek to explore, it is the Soul History which is lived through the luman Life.

A4.24 Typical Analyses to conduct.

a)What has made you happy and why? What are your Achievements?

b)How have you helped Others?

c)What has made you sad? what regrets do you have? How have you hurt other Souls?

d)What is important in your life? What are your values?

e)How have you affected others lives? Has the effect been positive or negative?

f) Evil and Sin are ANY Thoughts or Actions which negate LOVE. Define LOVE.

g)List ALL those you have loved or still love, and ALL those you have sinned against.

h)How now can you Heal the Past?

i) Compare your present life-time with that of your close Family, your Parents, your Grandparents. What is similar and why? Are there any repeating trends or incidents?   What can you learn from this?

j) How, now, are you personally going to change your life?

k)Sit and look in the Mirror. Do you like what you see?

l) Define Freedom. Understand how to give freedom to another.

m)Examine your attitude to the opposite Sex. Itemise the Characteristics of your ideal Spouse/Partner.

n)Examine your relationships with your children. Are any patterns developing?

A4.25 Go back into your Past to learn lessons from your Past. Relate and draw comparisons between the past Experiences and the Present.

* Identify any Repetitions and Question and Ponder the Reasons But, do not live in the Past. Look at yourself from every Angle. Understand yourself. Do not blame anyone else, accept the Responsibility yourself for your life and for your actions.

* When you have identified the cause and the repetition, learn the lessons, change your attitude, ask for whatever forgiveness is necessary both for yourself but also for others who have hurt you. Then put the Past into the Past. Do not carry the Guilt.

* Accept that the Past has brought you to the Present. You cannot change History, but you now have the opportunity to progress and to move forwards. Grasp this and learn the lessons.

- Ask how the lessons learnt have contributed to and been necessary to bring you to where you are today. What are you being prepared for? What role do you wish to play in the Future?
- Put all negative Experiences and People behind your Door and bolt it securely.

A4.26 You now need to learn to **LOVE YOURSELF**.
- We do not mean with vanity, arrogance, one-upmanship, or self-pride.
- But we do mean to respect yourself, to be quietly confident, to stand-up for your rights, to be prepared to stand your ground, to have your say.
- But if all else fails, then to be prepared to walk away from whatever is necessary.

Set yourself standards of Behaviour and of Relationships, do your utmost to uphold them.
- Organise your Life to do things in a cool, calm way
- Do not let happenings upset yourself. Keep an inner cool.
- Make things easy for yourself. Go with the flow.
- Know when to say No, to walk away, to change direction.
- Do not succumb to others unless you choose to.
- Target your own Goals
- Accept that you cannot help everyone.
- Look after yourself first. Respect your own health and Body.
- Look at yourself in the Mirror. Do you like what you see?
- Set yourself Standards you will accept, and those you will not accept.

A4.27 **Sit and Talk to your Spirit on a regular basis, this will cause it to Rise.**
- Slow down your Mind.
- Set aside a time in the morning, in the afternoon, in the evening, if you are to learn at the required speed.
- During this time go through your Relaxation routine, aim to clear your Mind of clutter.
- It may be helpful to use the 'Om' chant.
- It may be helpful to use a 'Trigger Word' to bring you quickly to a state of Relaxation. Think of a 'Star', or 'Seventh Heaven'.
- Focus on something beautiful...you will become a gentler, kinder, more considerate Human with a love for all things.
- You will feel your Spirit by the tightness in your Throat.
- When you have achieved this think your Spirit to rise above your Body.

A4.28 **During your Meditation Sessions, pray to GOD and ask for 'Blanket Forgiveness'** from all those Souls from previous Lives who you may have injured and caused suffering to.

♦ Offer them Healing and Forgiveness for their Actions against you.
♦ REPEAT these Words on seven sequential Days...in this way you wish to clear the Past so that you can move forwards to a new life and Understanding.
♦ At the same time you will help to release all these Souls of their Hate and allow them to progress.

A4.29 The words from Jesus are particularly poignant...................
'Cry for the World. Move swiftly from Moment to Moment. Place the bad Memories behind your Door. Nature moves on quickly. If a Tree is struck down, Seeds fall, a new Life starts quickly. It is the way of Nature. To harbour Anguish and Pain causes Suffering and Pain. The World will Suffer. You will progress, the Darkness of the Mind will be overcome by the Light of True Spirit. Lightness will overcome Darkness. We bring you these words of encouragement. We thank you for your efforts, we bring to you discomforts only for your Guidance and Help. We care so deeply, do not be angry. We care for all Creatures and all Humans, for all are in need. We talk not with anger, for they know not what they do. Do not fear for you have all the Angels and the love of Heaven about you. There is no danger, no fear.
 Go in Peace, allow us to Guide you.'

A4.30 The words from White Eagle are particularly harsh...............................
' The pains in Helana's arms, Feet and Body are felt like needles protruding into her very life-force. This is also caused by an 'Ivy-like Being' entwined around her, taking away the life-force which is within her. It is not only you my dear Man that causes these pains, but your ways are a major contribution to this fact. We remind you again. ' LOVE CAN ONLY BE FOUND IN FREEDOM'. Loose your selfish ways, allow her her Freedom, and love will blossom like the flowers on a Tree in May, when my dear Man, you care to recall that this child of life was born. Do you not see how like Nature you are? All of you are as a Tree. How then do you see yourself my dear Man? What kind of Tree do you think we see here in Spirit when we look at the Man, John at this time. Do you see Flowers or Buds forming?
Do you see disease which is so often in our Garden of Eden, appearing on the leaves now from the pain and sorrow harboured by the Minds of many? Beauty being strangled by possessive and selfish needs...........'

A4.31 The Task you have undertaken is not an easy One. Self Analysis and criticism is never easy.
(Since I personally embarked upon this learning process, I hope that I have become a more loving, more caring, more compassionate Individual. Only others who know you can enlighten you to the Truth, certainly your Guides will not hesitate to correct your Manner should it be lacking in any direction).

◆ You need to give before you can receive, this is not a selfish journey.

◆ You need to heal your Relationships if this is possible.

◆ Give love to receive love. Give loving Thoughts and prayers to those around you who are awkward or bitter. Show them by your actions and attitude that you care. Love is the most powerful prime mover in the Universe.

◆ Even the hardest of People will cry if the right chord is touched. I have never cried so much since I embarked upon this Journey. Do not be afraid to let others see you cry, they too have their lessons to learn.

◆ Help anyone, any thing, or any creature in distress.

◆ Think positive. Think Spiritual. Feel compassion.

◆ What is the purpose for this Experience?

◆ What can I or others learn from this? Why have I met this person?

◆ Respect others for their views. Do not be bigoted. Do not become a Bore.

A4.32 **Everyone has Talents, everyone can Contribute to Save the Planet and Nature**.....Picture a Scale, a Balance.
a)The whole of the FUTURE of EVERY PERSON, EVERY CHILD, EVERY CREATURE, EVERY ANIMAL, EVERYTHING YOU CARE FOR is finely Balanced.

◆ EVERYONE who spreads Light and unselfish Love makes a contribution to saving our Planet. There could be 3 Billion People who are promoting Love, there could be 3 Billion People sitting on the Fence, there could be 3 Billion People spreading Evil. It only takes ONE PERSON to make a difference, to walk across the Pendulum from Darkness to Light, to jump down from the Fence and to make a positive contribution, to cause the whole Pendulum to swing towards Love.

◆ **Is that person YOU?....Will YOU make the difference?....**What different will YOU DO TOMORROW?

b)CONSIDER a Nuclear BOMB, a Critical Mass is necessary to cause an Explosion. Up to the final Critical Mass existing there is little change, then all at once a huge release of Energy is created.

* Relate this now to our World. When sufficient People with Light and Love exist, an explosion of Love will occur. HEAVEN on EARTH will become a Reality. We will have secured our Planet for the Future, there will occur a massive Energy Shift and the Whole will be Transformed. This is the Objective, to eliminate Evil.
* **YOU could make the Difference.**

A4.33 It is possible for you to make this Journey of Learning alone, however it will be much better for you to join with Others of similar Mind. In this way you can share your Experiences and be supportive of each other.

* There already exist Spiritual Churches, but many of these need to become less Parochial, less Political, and to open their Doors to All-Comers. I consider them to be the individual Bricks upon which the Cathedral is yet to be built.
* They serve to provide Individual evidence of Life beyond the Human-Plane, and there are many excellent Mediums and Gifted people who will greet you. Visit your local Church with an open Mind, join with Others who will attend the various workshops organised, be friendly and respect those present.
* GOD will ensure that you make pontact with whosoever you are to meet to help you Progress.
* Look around, read the Notices, read the Books, join the Meetings. If you are not made welcome at one location, then move on to another.
* YOU seek to find a Mentor, that one Person you can trust and rely upon to guide you until your own Awareness has progressed sufficiently.

A4.34 This Book is written to help you along your Pathway. It is backed-up by a Web-Site which you can access under
www.cogoe.org.uk
The Church which is to be registered as a Charity, aims to support and guide those who seek to serve GOD and to live by the Beliefs outlined in this Book. The Church in 2,002 is in its infancy, but in due course of Time, Resources and Helpers, will provide Guidance, Education and Healing to those who come to its Doors.
(As at May 2001, all is in the pipeline to become established)

A4.35 **GOD BLESS YOU ALL IN YOUR ENDEAVOURS**

##

APPENDIX V. SIGNS OF PROGRESS

A5.00 I have previously stated that the rate of progress of your Awareness will be uniquely individual to you alone,

- to your Personality,
- to your Aptitude,
- to your Sensitivity,
- to your own Spiritual Karma, and to your Individual Application.

A5.01 Not everyone has the interest or skills to become a good cook, artist, linguist or hairdresser, but as everyone IS SPIRIT,

- Everyone has the ability to progress their Awareness of the Spirit within them, and the influence of Spirit around them.
- **BUT, you must do the work. As with everything worth achieving, you need to work at it!**

A5.02 **Everyone will begin from a different starting-point,** according to their Karma, some will need to re-visit most of their History. Others may find that they carry little Baggage and can proceed more rapidly. The important aspect is that you do not give-up, you need to persevere, you need to ask GOD to help you, you need to be patient and humble.

A5.03 Where are you now along this Pathway of Learning?

- You need to establish your starting point to know whether you have progressed or not!
- Revisit the Exercises in Appendix IV and **establish your Sensitivity ...Can you?**

a) **FEEL**

- Energy flow through your Hands and Feet, pins and needles, heat, occasional stabbing pain, or the marks of Jesus?
- Cob-webs on your Face, Nose, Ears or Body.
- Pressure around your Head, the Crown, the Rear, between your Eye-brows, any position on your Body may well be a sign, like wearing a hat.
- Itching to Legs, Ankles, Feet
- Someone stroking or holding your Hand, Arm, Face, etc.
- Someone playing with your Hair or touching you.
- Constriction at your Throat
- Pain beneath your Ribs, Pain which cannot be easily explained by physical reasons.
- An animal brushing your Leg, which you cannot see.
- Your Spirit moving within your Body.
- Compassion for Others,
- Empathy with Another's Situation

b) **SENSE**
- Wide sudden Temperature changes, in a Room or specific location.
- Shivers to your Head, Back, Spine etc.
- Heat and Pain at the base of your Neck.
- Excessive Saliva, Dryness of Mouth, Coughing for no reason,
- Wide Mood swings, not like you, out of character.
- Inability to Move, Stabbing pain to cause movement, cramp to cause movement.
- Aches and Muscle Pains
- Loss of Energy, Life-less
- Dreams
- Pressure cloaking your Ears
- Excessive Sweating, Cold.
- Uncontrollable Coughing, for no physical reason, which stops when you remove yourself from someone's presence.
- A Wonderful feeling around or above your Heart.
- A Feeling of Tearfulness, ease of Crying, sensitivity to Others Emotions, you feel as they Feel.
- You Feel the hostility or warmth of your Environment
- Caring for Others, All Species and Life.
- An affinity with Nature
- Deja-Vous
- Presence of a loved-one who has passed-Over.
- Spirit-writing, Drawing.
- Objects appear, or disappear, or move..
- An Inner Peace when all about is seemingly in Chaos.
- Out-Of-Body Experiences.

c) **SMELL**
- Pungent Aromas, Smoke, which Others around you may not, but which cannot be explained by your local Environment.

d) **SEE**
- Auras, colours around live Beings.
- Wonder of Nature
- The positive side of every Situation, Meeting and Experience.
- Ghosts and Apparitions
- People Others cannot see
- Angels, Spirit Life, Spirit Clouds, Pin-pricks of Light in the Dark of your Room (not insects!)
- Visions, Premonitions.
- Past Life Scenes

- Any strange Experience, odd Situations, unusual Events, be aware of Coincidences and repeating Situations.
- Spirit within and around Others.

e) HEAR
- Sensitivity to Noises is greatly heightened, grating Plates and clanging Cutlery affect you.
- Spirit words spoken audibly
- Noises, Words, out-of-context, your name called and no-one is visible.

f) ACKNOWLEDGE
- Thought messages from your Guide or other Spirits.
- The significance of Events, Meetings, Happenings.
- The gifts and messages from Others.

A5.04 **The Frequency and Intensity of the Experiences will be indicative of your Progress**.
- Accept the Happening,
- Question what you can learn from this,
- Ponder and reflect on the possible meanings and ask for help to gain the Understanding.
- WHO was that Person?,
- WHY did I meet them?,
- WHY was I in that Place, at that precise TIME?
- HOW should I now CHOOSE?,
- WHAT can I now LEARN?,
- HOW can I help or assist?
- Should I now walk away?

When YOU begin to ask these Questions, then you will begin to make progress.

A5.05 **'A Day will come when it will ALL come together. ALL the pieces will come together like a complete circle of Life. This will physically be felt by an inward rush of movement as your Spirit is raised. Your vision will improve, Your Awareness will improve. Strength will be needed.'**
.....quote from Jesus in the year 2,000AD.

###

APPENDIX VI. Suggested further Study.

A6.00 These references are but a few of the many wonderful Books, Songs and Films which have a message to so many people, if only they can find the time to detach themselves from the pace of life, the materialistic power struggle, the ego-Trip......and to listen, to see and to understand.

A6.01 Stop, listen, ponder, and look around you. What do you see? Are you happy with what you see? The level of suffering caused by the few to the many. There is a message to be learned, an Understanding to be gained from every Situation which we experience.
 Messages are given in the words we read, the voices we hear, the films we watch.
A gentle conditioning is taking place, to prepare us all for the life to be.
Mankind is the instrument, via the Mind and Thought process.
But where do the Thoughts come from?

A6.02 BOOKS
The Christian/ Jewish Bible, Old and New Testaments.
The Mormon Bible.
The Koran.
The Lost Books of the Bible-Gramercy Books, ISBN 0-517-27795-6,
The Power of Thought-HT Hamblin- Staples Printers
Within You is the Power-HT Hamblin
Science of Thought Review-HT Hamblin
Life In The World Unseen-Anthony Borgia -Psychic Press
You'll See it when you Believe it- Dr Wayne Dyer- Cox & Wyman
Embracing the Beloved- S.O.Levine-Gateway,Bath
Past Lives-Present Dreams
Vedanta Treatise-A. Parthasarathy-Bombay
Illusions-H.Bach
The Gift of Spirit-Prentice Mulford-Hudson-White Cross Library
The Dead Sea Scrolls Deception- Baigent and Leigh-Mackays
-ISBN 0224027611
The Celestine Prophesy I and II
The Bloxham Tapes
The Scole Experiment- Grant & Jane Solomon- Judy Piatkus- ISBN 0-7499-2032-7
The Decoding of the Great Pyramid at Giza - Peter Lemesurier - Compton Press
Rock of Truth - Arthur Findlay - WBC Print Ltd .Bristol
Miracle in the Mirror - Nita Edwards & Mark Buntain - Torbay Publishing
Mary's Message to the World - Annie Kirkwood - Piatkus- ISBN 07499 14904
The Hidden Origins of Jesus - Kamal Salibi - IB Tauris & Co London-ISBN 1850431175

Happiness-The 30 Day Guide-Patrick Whiteside-RIDER-ISBN
0712602127
The Living Word Of St.John-White Eagle Publishing Trust- ISBN
085487125X
Mission of Love-Roger Cole-ISBN 0850919150- BK (1999)
The Light Bringer-White Eagle Trust-ISBN 0854871233
Looking into the Invisible-OMRAM MIKHAEL AIVANHOV-Prosveta-ISBN
1895978181
The Direct Path-ANDREW HARVEY-ISBN 071260367-0
The Tarot-Alfred Douglas- Penguin-ISBN 0140037373

A6.03 FILMS and Tapes

Ghost and 6th SENSE	The Fairy Tale- A True Story
Highlander Films	The Mission
Star Trek	Brave Heart
The Killing Fields	Dancing with the Wolves
2001-A Space Odyssey	Man without a Face
Independence Day	Titanic
The Matrix	Star Wars
Deep Impact	Raiders of the Lost Ark
Gladiator	Mortal Combat
The Postman	The Abyss

The Glyn Edwards Awareness Development Tapes
The Brahma Kumaris Meditation Tapes and Spiritual University Programs

A6.04 SONGS

Please Release Me	I Believe
I Believe I can Fly	The Power of Love
Imagine- Love is- Woman	The Lighthouse Family

There are many other Songs with beautiful words, the above are but a
few which I personally am aware of.

##

APPENDIX VII. My Guides, Healing, References, Drawings, Tarot

A7.00 With Special Thanks to

- ◆ GOD
- ◆ My Spirit Guides..Razeem (Arabian Friend), Ahizar (Prophet), Daniel (Ethiopean King), Jesus (Christ), Joseph (Father of Christ), Mary(Mother of Christ), Samuel (Helana's Guide), Adrian (Pope), White Eagle(High Spirit Messenger), !saiah (Prophet), Joshua (Prophet).
- ◆ All those Spiritual People who have helped me individually, and at the Oxon, Bucks and London Spiritualist Churches.
- ◆ To all my Family, Partners, Lovers, and Friends who have been so tolerant and supportive to me.
- ◆ And in Spirit: Stan, Ted (father), Albert, Princess Diana, John Lennon, Alice, Gemma,

A7.01 Seating Plan at the 'Dinner for Loved-Ones'

LEFT	TOP	RIGHT

~ ~

JUDITH -- JOHN

ROSE	BRIAN
ANTHEA	CONSTANCE
EDWARD	LORNA
DOREEN	BRIAN
HELEN	ELSA
ALAN	HELANA

etc.

A7.02 The CHURCH BANNER

A Blue SHIELD with a Diagonal GOLD CROSS, as seen at St Alban's Cathedral, England.
As displayed on the front cover of this book.

A7.03 Actions and WORDS to PROTECT YOU against Dark Spirit Attack

a) Request your Doorkeeper to protect you.
b) Ask your Guides to help
c) Keep awake
d) Close your Chakras
e) Pray and ask GOD to help
f) Ask for the Protection by the Light and Love of True Spirit.
G)Dismiss Thoughts of the offending Spirit.
h) Be Firm and tell them to leave, and the Pain to leave
i) Move into the Open,
j) Take a Bath or Shower and visualize the Pain being washed away
k) Refuse to be intimidated
l) Raise your Spirit above the level of the Invading Spirit
m) Visualize a beautiful Sight or Object, concentrate on this.
n) Surround yourself by a Sphere of Light which will filter the Good and reflect back all negative thoughts onto the Sender.
o) Visualize yourself covered from head to toe in a Chain-mail reflective Suit, climb into this and protect yourself.
p) Visit/contact a Spiritual Healer or Mentor and ask for them to help you.
q) Remove from your presence, ANY object belonging to whosoever you believe to be responsible for your suffering.
r) Say prayers for their Soul
s) Review what changes have entered your Life, anything Plant, Animal or Human with a Spirit. Who have you recently met who is suffering.

SAY THE WORDS ALOUD, three times as often as is necessary:

1) Honi, Honi, Honi, Excrutiat alles promistos, valente, valente abrogate.
(take this Spell away and place it over the person who gave it to me)

2) Etag roleta pardura calcim privator plegurem manifest prolerum.
(unless you leave at once, your Burdens will destroy you)

3) Hartges anderas gelatio selectos gleaven quantes selantos antequo sandera anto pretancio-------------------- (name).
   (unless you leave at once, action will be taken to destroy your Spirit and so take your Life-----------------(name)

4) Hate has no equal. If you Spirit -------------- do not stop your Evil onslaught, then the forces of GOD will be brought against you. Your Freedom will disappear, your presence in this World will disappear, your Identity will disappear. You have three minutes in which to reflect. If you do not withdraw permanently, action of the severest kind will be taken against you. This is your final warning.

5) Get thee hence Evil Spirits, GOD is watching you. Your Actions will rebound upon you and destroy you unless you withdraw now.

6) Achi,achi,achi, solus magnum artremini----------------- cantort alti---------
--- primus calantre actomus. Nevada selestrimus premia allegra.

7) Felatio spiritus acatio super altio express semper meonius paxit
(take this Spirit quickly to a safe place.)

8) Etag roleta pardura calcim, privator plegurem manifest prolerum.
(unless you leave at once your burdens will destroy you)

9) Alles actura plescura actimus Spiritus-------------, allegro sante acuramatus querum.   Definat prima. (all actions will be taken to remove your Spirit, Do not doubt the accuracy of this message. It will definitely happen.)

##

Tarot Card readings from June 1997

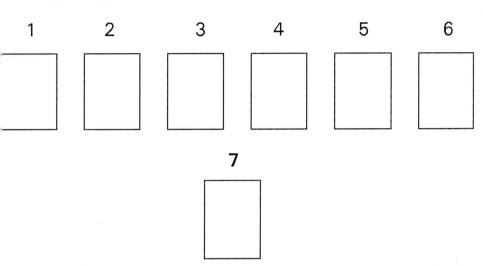

1   2   3   4   5   6

7

1) **6 pentacles**(coins) : solvency, balance in material affairs, help from patron(spirit),charity used to help others.
2) **empress**: growth of awareness and spiritual awakening, inspiration through Nature, caring and feeling for others.
3) **emperor** : power, only by battling through the adversities of life and triumphing over circumstances can the spirit achieve freedom, strong will, courage, ambition, strength.
4) **tower**: destruction of old values, suffering to achieve destiny
5) **4 cups**: emotional happiness and fulfilment has reached its peak, love has changed to familiarity, a new dissatisfaction.
6) **Ace of Batons:** the beginning of new enterprises, the foundation of future success and abundance. Primal energy and vigour of Fire, intuition.
7) **The Moon**: A critical stage, when life's journey is almost completed, but it is necessary now to put aside the physical senses and to be guided by the inward light, intuition and Spirit. The pathway is badly lit and hard to discern.....

A lonely and vulnerable phase with many temptations to deflect you from the true path.

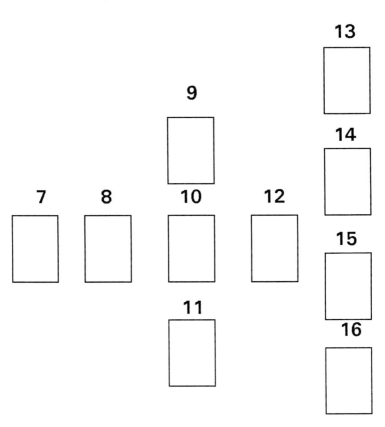

interpretation
7)**2 wands(batons)**: strength of will, earned success, wisdom through experience, high ideals
8) **3 swords**: necessary disruption, strife and conflict, clear out the past to achieve a better future.
9) **Ace of Swords**: success, victory despite adversity all will succeed, necessary change for freedom and new beginnings.
10) **The Sun**: success beyond the perils of 'The Moon', a reborn personality, vindication, psychic wholeness, just reward.

11) **2 cups**: love, joyous harmony, the ending of a feud, reconciliation.

12) **King of Cups**: skilled, agile mind, respected, leader, ambitious, patron.

13) **10 pentacles**: good fortune, inheritance, family tradition.

14) **2 pentacles**: changes are imminent, be flexible, go with the flow, be content and enjoy life.

15) **The Magician**: forceful, self-confident, stands alone, the conscious link between Spirit and Man, commencement of a new Cycle of Life, a Seeker and aTeacher.

16) **Judgement**: Spiritual Growth beyond 'the Sun' is finally achieved. A new lease of life, accomplishment, a return home, acceptance and joy.

(a second reading was obtained from a different person, who gave a very similar result. It was a key requirement for me to walk away from the Past, before any permanent changes could take effect. All was my choice, a choice now whether to forgive and to forget, to apply myself to both the Spiritual Life and the Physical life; then it was said that both Material and Spiritual success could be mine.)

###

SPIRIT DRAWING

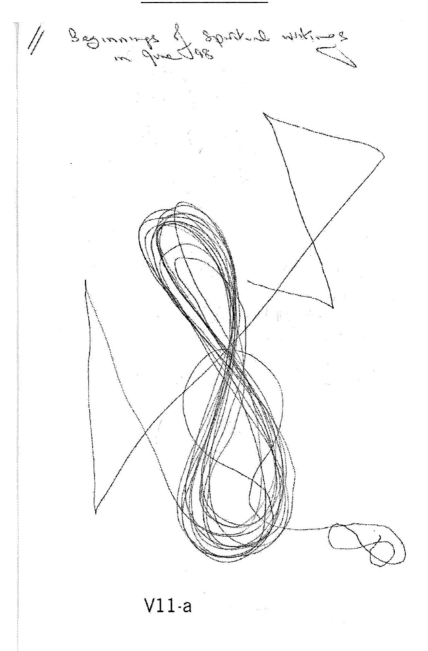

Beginnings of spiritual writings
in June 1988

V11-a

439

V11-b

early drawing(c)

VII-c

(b)

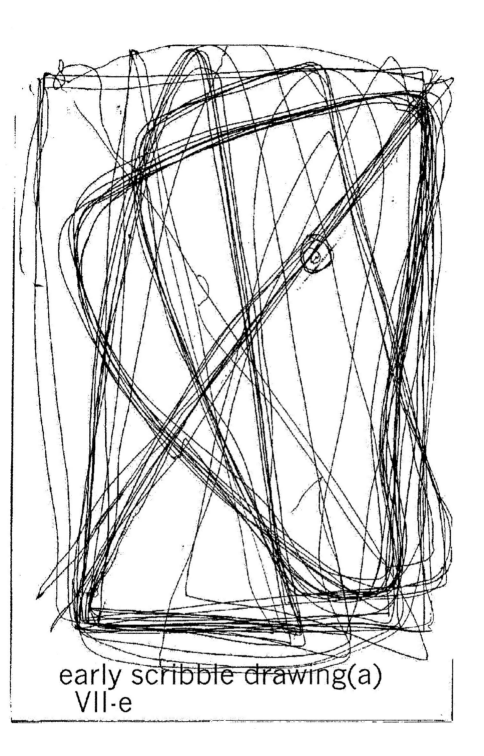

early scribble drawing(a)
VII-e

spirit writing from Richard to Helana

one love for all OHelana
your love is so
beautiful

Richard

no another called
Richard
Evans.

no

VII-f

Printed in the United Kingdom
by Lightning Source UK Ltd.
104336UKS00001B/1-30